Geoffrey Miles is Senior Lecturer in the School of English, Film, Theatre, and Media Studies at Victoria University of Wellington, where his primary interest is the reception of the classics in English literature. He is the author of *Shakespeare and the Constant Romans*, and editor of *Classical Mythology in English Literature.*

John Davidson retired as Professor of Classics at Victoria University of Wellington in 2009 and as Head of the School of Art History, Classics and Religious Studies in 2010. He has had a long-standing research interest in the work of James K. Baxter, alongside his extensive publications on Greek tragedy, mythology, and Homer.

Paul Millar is an Associate Professor at the University of Canterbury where he coordinates the English Literature programme and directs the Humanities Computing Unit. He has published extensively on Baxter's early years and has edited a number of selections of Baxter's poetry. His most recent book is the literary biography *No Fretful Sleeper: A Life of Bill Pearson.*

THE SNAKE-HAIRED MUSE

JAMES K. BAXTER
AND CLASSICAL MYTH

GEOFFREY MILES
JOHN DAVIDSON
PAUL MILLAR

VICTORIA UNIVERSITY PRESS

VICTORIA UNIVERSITY PRESS
Victoria University of Wellington
PO Box 600 Wellington
victoria.ac.nz/vup

First published 2011
Reprinted 2011

National Library of New Zealand Cataloguing-in-Publication Data

Miles, Geoffrey.
The snake-haired muse : James K. Baxter and classical myth /
Geoffrey Miles, John Davidson, Paul Millar.
Includes bibliographical references and index.
ISBN 978-0-86473-658-1
1.Baxter, James K.—Knowledge—Mythology, Classical. 2. Baxter,
James K.—Criticism and interpretation. I. Davidson, John. II. Millar,
Paul. III. Title.
NZ821.2—dc 22

Set in Bembo, 11/13pt
Printed by PrintStop Ltd, Wellington

CONTENTS

ILLUSTRATIONS BY MARIAN MAGUIRE

Reproduced by kind permission of the artist and PaperGraphica.

PREFACE

This book had its earliest origins in John Davidson's pioneering work in the 1970s on James K. Baxter's use of aspects of Greek and Roman antiquity. However, it was almost thirty years later that he approached Paul Millar, who by that time had established himself as a Baxter scholar, and suggested that they collaborate on a book-length study of Baxter's use of classical mythology. Paul in turn recruited a third member for the team, Geoff Miles, a specialist in the classical tradition and the uses of mythology in English literature, who became the lynchpin of the project and writer of the largest share of the chapters.

The original plan was modest: a short monograph on Baxter's mythic allusions, of interest to specialists and perhaps a useful reference work for classically-baffled students. It grew inexorably under our hands as we gradually came to appreciate the vast amount of material, not only in Baxter's published poems and prose but in his voluminous unpublished notebooks, and its crucial importance in his poetic work. After several years of delayed gestation *The Snake-Haired Muse* has emerged as what we think and hope is a significant contribution to the study of New Zealand's most iconic poet.

Of the debts we have incurred in the course of the project, the most fundamental is to the Baxter Estate, to John Baxter and to the late Jacquie Baxter, for generous support and permission to quote freely from unpublished Baxter material.

Stefanie Head played a crucial role as research assistant at the start of the project, reading through all Baxter's published and unpublished writings to compile a 'Myth Master Index' that covered 75 closely-spaced pages from Absyrtus to Zodiac. Stef was our Ariadne, without whose thread we would have been lost close to the entrance to Baxter's mythological Labyrinth. Near the end of the project, Greg Martin took time out from his own

PhD research on Baxter's 'gaps' to cast a scrupulous eye over our references and quotations.

We gratefully acknowledge support from Victoria University of Wellington's Faculty of Humanities and School of English, Film, Theatre, and Media Studies, and from the University of Canterbury's College of Arts and School of Humanities, including two grants of a full year's research and study leave (for Paul and Geoff), and for grants towards travel and research assistance. We are grateful to librarians at Victoria University (especially the enormously helpful Nicola Frean of the Beaglehole Room) and at the Hocken Library of the University of Otago. We owe a great deal to the support of our colleagues in the English and Classics programmes at Victoria, and in Canterbury's School of Humanities; for particular acts of encouragement, advice and assistance we are deeply grateful to Patrick Evans, Howard McNaughton, David Norton, Vincent O'Sullivan, Art Pomeroy, Harry Ricketts, Kathryn Walls and Peter Whiteford.

We are grateful to Jeny Curnow and the executors of the estate of Allen Curnow for permission to quote a Curnow poem, to Catherine Kelway and Jane Finnimore for the unpublished letter quoted in chapter 9, and to Lawrence Jones for assistance in tracking down a key review article.

From early in the project we thought of Marian Maguire as the ideal cover artist; her visual explorations of Greek myth in a New Zealand environment were the perfect complement to Baxter's poetic explorations of the same theme. We are enormously grateful to Marian for supplying not only a cover image but a whole series of original illustrations for the book.

Finally, we would like to thank Victoria University Press, our eagle-eyed editor Gillian Tewsley, and Fergus Barrowman for his enthuasistic support and and handsome production of the book.

The basic plan of the book, and the primary authorship of individual chapters, is as follows. The introduction (*Miles*) explores how and why Baxter's use of classical myth has been neglected and undervalued by critics, and broadly surveys his idea of myth and the patterns of his lifelong engagement with the figures of

Greek and Roman mythology. Chapter 2 (*Millar*) looks at his first encounters with myth in childhood and adolescence, and his first uses of classical characters as 'figures of self'. After that, given the vast range of available material, we have chosen in the next six chapters to focus on case studies of a few mythic figures and stories which seem particularly significant in Baxter's work. Chapters 3 and 4 (*Davidson*) deal with his female figures—a notoriously problematic area of his work but, as our title suggests, crucially important to his poetic inspiration; we trace a continuum from the love-goddess Venus/Aphrodite to such monsters as the Furies and the Gorgon. Chapters 5 and 6 (*Miles*) look at his treatment of three heroes: Hercules and Theseus, opposed figures of Edenic innocence and worldly experience, and Odysseus, the lonely voyager and quester for freedom who is his favourite mythic character. Chapter 7 (*Davidson*) deals with Bacchus/Dionysus, god of alcohol, inspiration, and madness, a liberating and imprisoning figure ambivalently close to his heart. Chapter 8 (*Miles*) explores his treatment of Hades, the underworld, both as a literal image of death and (more importantly) as a metaphor for human life and the human psyche. A concluding chapter (*Millar*) looks at the implications of the book for Baxter's place in New Zealand literature, and scouts some avenues for further study in relating his classical myth to his uses of Maori and Christian imagery. Last but by no means least—indeed the longest section of the book—comes a 'Mythological Who's Who in Baxter' (*Miles*), an encyclopedic alphabetical guide which attempts to catalogue and briefly discuss all his references to classical figures, major and marginal.

Although we have thus divided the primary responsibility for the chapters, we have all contributed to one another's chapters and collectively reviewed and revised all of them, so that *The Snake-Haired Muse* is a truly collaborative project. We hope that readers will find it as stimulating to read as we have found it to work on.

Geoffrey Miles
John Davidson
Paul Millar
Wellington, March 2011

ABBREVIATIONS

Aspects	*Aspects of Poetry in New Zealand*
AT	*Autumn Testament*, ed. Paul Millar
'Conversation'	'Conversation with an Ancestor' (in *MH*, 11–35)
'Criticism'	'The Criticism of Poetry' (in *FA*, 13–34)
CP	*Collected Poems,* ed. J. E. Weir
CPlays	*Collected Plays*, ed. Howard McNaughton
CS	*Cold Spring*
CW	C.G. Jung, *Collected Works*
'Education'	'Notes on the Education of a New Zealand Poet' (in *MH*, 121–55)
FA	*The Fire and the Anvil*
FC	*The Flowering Cross*
FM	Baxter papers in the Frank McKay collection, Beaglehole Room, Victoria University of Wellington Library. References are by box, folder/envelope (where applicable), and item number: e.g. FM 27/1/11 = box 27, folder 1, item 11.
JD	*Jerusalem Daybook*
'Man'	'The Man on the Horse' (in *MH*, 91–120)
'Mask'	'The Creative Mask' (in *FA*, 35–55)
MH	*The Man on the Horse*
N	Baxter's manuscript notebooks, Hocken Library MS 704/1 to 704/28. References are by notebook and poem number, e.g. N4.183 = poem 183 in notebook 4. From N1 to N14 Baxter numbered the poems sequentially, 1 to 1025; from N15 onwards he abandoned this practice, and for these later notebooks we have simply numbered the poems in each individual book.
NSP	*New Selected Poems*, ed. Paul Millar (2001)
RW	*The Runaway Wife* (unpublished play)

SP	*Selected Poems*, ed. Paul Millar (2010)
Spark	*Spark to a Waiting Fuse*, by Paul Millar
'Symbolism'	'Symbolism in New Zealand Poetry' (in *FA*, 56–78)
Trends	*Recent Trends in New Zealand Poetry*
'Virgin'	'The Virgin and the Temptress' (in *MH*, 65–90)

For ease of reference in the text each poem is tagged with its date (sometimes approximate) and its single most easily accessible location—either in *CP*, or in other published books or periodicals (with preference given to sources still in print), or, for as yet unpublished poems, its location in Baxter's manuscript notebooks.

Poems and prose pieces published in periodicals are given shorthand references in the text (e.g. '*Listener* 1959'), with full details in the Bibliography. Unpublished pieces are referred to simply by title; details of their manuscript sources can be found in the Bibliography. *Landfall* references use the continuous numbering of issues.

CHAPTER 1

BAXTER'S CLASSICAL BAGGAGE

Baxter, myth and the critics

In 1960 the literary quarterly *Landfall* circulated a questionnaire to a number of New Zealand writers. It asked about their economic circumstances: how much do you earn by writing, what outside work do you do, what kinds of state assistance would help you? Most of the respondents reported back in the same matter-of-fact terms. James K. Baxter's response came from a different universe of discourse. The problems raised by the questionnaire, he suggested,

> are chips off a single granite block, possibly from that remarkable boulder which Sisyphus, streaming with sweat, shoves uphill every day and night in the not-so-imaginary Greek underworld. [. . .] The real problem raised concerns the weight, size, shape, geological or theological formation of this boulder, and what handholds (if any) can be found on its surface.

After describing his own hardscrabble literary existence, in which the time and energy for writing must be found by 'robbery' from his employers and his family, he concluded that this way of life was nevertheless the necessary condition of his writing:

> If my economic or social or domestic condition were alleviated in such a way that I had more leisure to write, and possibly more stimulus to write, I would be a Sisyphus divided from his boulder. The gritty touch of its huge surfaces, the grinding weight, the black shadow which it casts, are the strongest intimations of reality which I possess, and the source of whatever strength exists in my sporadic literary productions. ('Writers in New Zealand: A Questionnaire' 41–42)

In the following year, writing to his friend Bill Oliver (21 Feb 1961; FM 27/1/11) about Bohemia and respectability, Baxter returned to the image of Sisyphus. 'I think I agree fundamentally with the kind of thing the Boulder is likely to say to Sisyphus,' he declared, and improvised a Goonish dialogue between them. 'You bloody great heap of the fossilized dung of a dinosaur!' curses Sisyphus. 'Ssh! Ssh!' responds the boulder primly. 'You mustn't swear.' The dinosaur which excreted Sisyphus's stone is presumably the same beast which appears in Baxter's famous description of New Zealand morality: 'the Calvinist ethos which underlies our determinedly secular culture like the bones of a dinosaur buried in a suburban garden plot' ('Notes on the Education of a New Zealand Poet', *MH* 125). What Sisyphus is pushing uphill is the Calvinist work ethic, a system of values Baxter loathes but knows he must remain in touch with—shoulder to the rock—if his writing is to remain relevant to the lives of his fellow New Zealanders.

Yet for many of those fellow New Zealanders it is precisely this habit of mythological reference that is one of Baxter's most alienating qualities. Critics and fellow poets have seen his use of classical myth as an irritating and distracting barrier for the ordinary reader; they have judged it self-conscious, artificial, pretentious, a kind of stage trapping. For the poetic sponsors of his early and middle years, it was a symptom of a fundamental falsity or tendency to self-dramatisation, which culminated in his theatrical pose as the guru of Jerusalem.

This mythophobia is a strong and lasting strain in the critical tradition. Even sympathetic contemporary reviewers dismissed the classical imagery of 'Henley Pub' as 'mere paraphernalia' (Brasch 22) or criticised the 'incompatible images' of 'Guy Fawkes Night'—'Poseidon is surely out of place' (Leeming 10); and in 1997 Robert Sullivan, reviewing the posthumously published *Cold Spring*, still saw the mythological symbolism of these early poems as 'a mask, a blindfold, muffling the clear Baxter that emerged from *Jerusalem Sonnets* onward' (51). Hal Smith criticised the reliance of Baxter's plays 'on alien, time-smothered, and now cryptic myth, or on mutated Christian ritual', arguing that 'Today's theatre audience, by and large, finds the very word "myth" so pseudo, so antiquarian, and academically tainted as to guarantee a sparse house in any but the most committed university or literary circles' (Smith 12). Iain Sharp, who in 1988 told the Australian poet Les Murray that it seemed to be the majority opinion that 'Baxter was a bit of a phoney' (Murray interview 154), located Baxter's classical pretensions at the core of his phoniness: 'He was determined to prove to the literary world at large that he was not just a hick from the sticks, by parading his classical learning at every opportunity.' Sharp responded to the resonant lines about Troy and Carthage in 'Wild Bees' with, 'Aw, for Gawd's sake, get off your high horse, Jimmy' ('My Grudge Against Baxter' 13). Howard McNaughton attributes Baxter's use of mythology to 'the strong ghost of academia', a conflicted desire to stand well with the academics and intellectuals he despised—a ghost which he finally exorcises in the course of the 1966–67 Burns Fellowship years, discarding the need for 'the classical referential spread as a yardstick for personal experience' ('Baxter's Strong Ghost' 64). John Goulter, whose 1980 MA thesis is the most comprehensive and useful survey of the topic so far, nevertheless follows a similar line, suggesting that Baxter jettisons classical myth in his later poetry when he finds a more satisfying imaginative matrix in Christianity:

> There is a sense in which Baxter, through myth, was attempting a sonority that ill-fitted his undeniable talents, which lay in another direction. And he moved in that other direction in the Jerusalem poems. There is, perhaps, something a little anachronistic if not disingenuous about a New Zealand poet of the middle twentieth century carrying about such a heavy baggage of Classics, ready to drop it into his poetry at any opportunity. It is an ironically scholarly aspect of an otherwise iconoclastic poet. (124)

Other critics deal with Baxter's 'baggage of Classics' by ignoring it. While Elizabeth Caffin in *The Oxford History of New Zealand Literature* celebrates Baxter's 'distinctive mythopoeic talent' (476), her discussion never mentions classical myth. Even critics sympathetic to Baxter's mythmaking seem to find his Christian and Polynesian symbolism easier to take than his classical symbolism.[1]

It is not the purpose of this book to argue that Baxter's mythological poetry is consistently successful. In a corpus so enormous and diverse, some poems are inevitably trite, or obscure, or clotted; we would not seriously quarrel, for instance, with Brasch's strictures on 'Henley Pub' or Leeming's on 'Guy Fawkes Night'. What we set out to argue is more basic: that Baxter's use of classical myth needs to be taken seriously; that, far from being dispensable baggage, it lies close to the heart of his poetic project; and that the criticisms made of it often rest on assumptions about poetry in New Zealand—what it is and what it should be—that are positively unhelpful in dealing with the kind of poetry that Baxter was trying to write.

The first assumption is that the literary use of classical myth is an artificial and elitist practice, and (hence) Baxter's use of it was a self-conscious attempt to inflate his literary credentials. McNaughton is right to argue that Baxter was conflicted in his view of 'the academic crew / Whom [he] despised for undue cerebration' ('Letter to Noel Ginn II', *CP* 70–72); but he is surely wrong to see Baxter's classical allusions as stemming from a desire to impress them. As the example of Sisyphus suggests, Baxter alludes to myth not only in his published poems but in questionnaires and newspaper interviews, private letters to friends, notebook jottings and scraps of bawdy verse which he can hardly have intended for publication.[2] Myth is not a trapping which he assumes for public effect, but a fundamental part of how his mind works. Baxter's essential mode of thought was mythic and symbolic: as his sister-in-law remarked, 'Other people talked and thought in prose and had to switch to "poetic mode" when they began to write: with [Jim] it was the other way round' (Lenore Baxter to Frank McKay, FM 10/7/32). And certain classical myths, encountered

1 Although Baxter's use of Christian symbolism and Maori myth lies outside the scope of our study, we have no intention of denying or downplaying their importance in his work. We will discuss these issues in our Conclusion.

2 For a particularly striking example see the Who's Who under Antaeus: a couplet on copulation which Baxter apparently feels is so discreditable that he spells it backwards in his notebook to conceal it from casual eyes—which nevertheless turns on a quite arcane mythological allusion.

in his childhood and adolescence, assumed 'a powerful private significance' for him (*CS* xxi). He draws repeatedly and almost obsessively on these myths, just as he draws on the Brighton and Central Otago landscapes of his formative years. Both the myths and the landscapes are 'an integral part of the poet's mental equipment' ('Symbolism in New Zealand Poetry', *FA* 62). For Baxter it would make no more sense to call the images of Venus or Dionysus hackneyed or second-hand than to make the same accusation about images of the sea or the mountains.

The charge of elitism has a little more plausibility. Undeniably, classical mythology in English literature has been a 'code' associated with the educated elite, and with the decline of classical education in the twentieth and twenty-first centuries it is a code which is accessible to a shrinking minority of readers. For Baxter, however, myth belonged not to the public school classroom or the literary salon, but rather—in the spirit of twentieth-century students of myth such as Frazer and Jung—to the realm of the 'primitive', the natural, and the instinctive. He associates it with the tribal societies which he valued—the Maori, or his own Scottish Highland ancestors—and sees it as a direct route to the collective unconscious, a way of 'rediscovering [one's] own buried natural self' ('Conversation with an Ancestor', *MH* 22). Repeatedly he privileges an unsophisticated response to myth and poetry over an educated one. Rejecting the suggestion that 'you need a civilised educated audience for what you write', he cites the barman who gave him the word 'omnivorous' for 'The Sirens'—'I doubt if a university lecturer would have had the answer' ('Conversation about Writing'; cf *CPlays* 335). Similarly he comments on a 'Prayer to Hekate', by an Australian woman poet, that educated readers may not understand the poem, but 'It would be less obscure to a Maori or an ancient Greek. One has to get de-educated to understand any poem well' ('Poetry and Education').

It can be argued that there is a degree of self-deception in Baxter's position—a barman who knew the word 'omnivorous' cannot have been all that uneducated; and poems on Hekate or Sisyphus or Antaeus are unlikely to make a strong emotional connection with readers who do not know the stories or even how to pronounce the names. But the problem is not 'phoniness' or 'disingenuousness' so much as a passionate belief in the power of myth to communicate on a deep, unconscious level. In a famous passage Baxter declares, 'Biology, mythology, / Go underground when the bookmen preach' ('Letter to Robert Burns', *CP* 289–91). For him 'biology' and 'mythology' are exactly parallel: the psychic facts embodied in myth are as fundamental to human existence as the physical facts of birth, reproduction and death, and they merely 'go underground' when intellectuals try to rationalise them away.

The second and larger assumption concerns the acceptable mode of twentieth-century New Zealand poetry, defined in the mid century by the dominant school of thought associated with Allen Curnow, and encapsulated in his assertion that 'Reality must be local and special [. . .]. Whatever is true vision belongs here, uniquely to the islands of New Zealand' (*Penguin Book of NZ Verse* 17). This poetic ideal is incompatible with imported traditions, inherited language and derivative imagery. The contingent nationalist myth-making relegates classical myth to the dustbin of empire. All of which profoundly complicates Baxter's position at the heart of New Zealand poetry. Curnow's marvellous boy, who in 1945 'proved so early his power to say and his right to speak' (*A Book of NZ Verse* 55), was by 1960 producing poetry 'muffle[d] in literary tissue', displaying 'a throwback to the make-believe art of earlier generations' (*Penguin Book of NZ Verse* 61, 62). It was a view that became, with repetition, orthodoxy—that Baxter's verse was inclined to the histrionic, oracular and melodramatic at the expense of clarity and precision; that he 'uses the hammer of his verse much more often to bang resonantly on the mahogany than to hit the nail on the head' (Witheford 52). And even after Curnow's views in general were challenged, the orthodoxy about Baxter survived.

The problem for Baxter was that the consensus formed in opposition to Curnow's views consolidated into another sort of orthodoxy from which he was also excluded. The poets challenging Curnow embraced a broader and more diverse view of New Zealand. However, there was still no space for Baxter's

Romantic and Dionysian approach. Ironically, when New Zealand poetry divided camps, Baxter found himself outside two tents, not just one. To quote Kai Jensen: 'Evidently no one knew where Baxter was coming from' (*Whole Men* 146).

In the late 1940s the young Baxter had learned that writing according to any other poet or critic's formulation caused his inspiration to dry up. Many poems in his first collection, *Beyond the Palisade* (1944), had been selected for him by the Caxton Press from the idiosyncratic section of his work which met with the approval of the developing Caxton orthodoxy. When, two years later, he attempted his own selection from the heavily mythologised and symbolic poems that were central to his work over the last four years, the manuscript was rejected. But Baxter had learned that he needed to listen to the promptings of his own troublesome Muse, and although he attempted compromises that brought him more closely into alignment with his fellow poets, mythic elements remained at the heart of his writing—although an increasing proportion of such poems remained unpublished.

One reason for the critical neglect of Baxter's mythology, then, is that critics have dealt almost exclusively with his published canon. But that is only about a third of Baxter's total output; another two thirds remains buried in his twenty-eight black-bound manuscript notebooks in the Hocken Library, and in other scattered places. It is tempting, if fanciful, to mythologise this unpublished material in Baxterian style—an underworld, a textual unconscious, a cellblock in the basement of the *Collected Poems.*

This is the first study to mount any sustained investigation of the unpublished poetry. When it is taken into account, the sheer scale and depth of Baxter's engagement with classical myth becomes much clearer. We have deliberately made no sharp divisions between the published and the unpublished material, attempting to trace Baxter's use of mythology across his full corpus, and—in the 'Mythological Who's Who' that constitutes the final section—to catalogue all of his classical references, published and unpublished. We have attempted to enter into his mythological frame of reference and understand what he was trying to do. While we offer some evaluation, it is for subsequent critics to judge the success of his project and its importance to his overall achievement.

Not all earlier critics, of course, have been hostile to Baxter's use of myth, and our project in this book has important critical predecessors. These include Baxter's close associates Frank McKay and John Weir, who, though both understandably emphasising Baxter's Christian over his classical themes, have written sympathetically about his mythmaking—McKay in the introduction to his selection *James K. Baxter as Critic* (xii-xv); Weir in his discussions of 'the poetry of myth' in his 1968 thesis and his published study *The Poetry of James K. Baxter* (16–20). Lawrence Jones' 'The Mythology of Place', though dealing only in passing with classical myth, is a penetrating analysis of Baxter's mythologising habit of mind and how it imbues the Otago landscape with mythic significance. A series of articles by one of the present writers, John Davidson, have explored Baxter's overall relationship with 'the classics' and his treatments of Odysseus, Dionysus, Philoctetes, Oedipus and Venus; and Goulter's 1980 thesis, already noted, conducted a broader survey of Baxter's classical mythology.

Two critical discussions stand out. The opening chapter of Vincent O'Sullivan's short book *James K. Baxter* is the most eloquent and perceptive argument for the centrality of myth to Baxter's thinking and writing:

> To think mythologically means simply that any event may become a symbol, any relationship may put one in mind of similar relationships, so all that *they* carry may be transferred to one's own. [. . .] The particular form of one's mythology finally depends upon what one draws from one's unconscious mind, or from that part of the human past which each man carries in himself. It becomes a matter of art if the relationship is with the more permanent figures in human imagination, and if they are expressed by a man of very considerable gifts. (*Baxter* 6)

O'Sullivan's discussion is the starting point for our argument, though we would place less emphasis than he does on the Campbellian 'myth of separation, death, and rebirth' as Baxter's central monomyth (9).

The other ground-breaking contribution is Kai Jensen's Jungian reading of Baxter, in his 1995 essay 'The Drunkard and the Hag' and his 1996 book *Whole Men*. Earlier critics such as McKay and Goulter had noted Jung's influence, but Jensen goes further in seeing Jungian psychology as central to Baxter's world view and poetic practice. His argument is brilliant and challenging but in some ways problematic in its absolutism, making both Baxter's personal experience and his Christianity subordinate to his Jungian mission. To declare that 'Our critics would far rather continue seeing Baxter as a death-bound, troubled natural man than as a therapeutic writer who based his life and work on the writings of a Swiss psychologist' (*Whole Men* 130) is to set up an unnecessarily binary choice: Baxter is surely *both* troubled and therapeutic. Jensen tends to drain out of the poetry the 'blood' and 'wounds of the person' that Baxter considered essential (Weir interview 244), making it sound too comfortably didactic; ironically (in view of Jung's principles) this Jungian version of Baxter suffers from 'undue cerebration'. Nevertheless, Jensen does demonstrate beyond reasonable doubt the profound influence of Jung on Baxter's approach to myth, and our analysis is substantially indebted to him.

Excavating the mythical stratum: Baxter's idea of myth

The best concise summing-up of Baxter's own view of the significance of classical myth is the opening sentence of his 1971 Introduction to the two plays based on Sophoclean tragedy, *The Sore-footed Man* and *The Temptations of Oedipus*:

> As a writer of verse with a mind to be a playwright, I think I brought with me to the theatre a subconscious certainty that the Greek myths and legends are never out-of-date since they form that mythical stratum in the mind of modern man which enables him from time to time to make a pattern out of the chaos of his experience. (*CPlays* 334)

There are several claims here, explicit and implicit. The first is that classical myth offers a way of making a pattern out of chaos. Baxter expanded on this idea in his *Landfall* interview with

John Weir in the same year, when Weir challenged him with the suggestion that his use of myth contradicted his aim of 'reflecting the world as it *is*'. 'When you are dealing with the world,' Baxter responded, 'you tend to see it as Chaos.' The task of the poet, he argued, like that of the scientist, is to discover an order which underlies and structures this apparent chaos; but where the scientist uses mathematical formulae, the poet uses symbolism and myth. 'The myth is the form that the poet uses to crystallise experience' (Weir interview, 242–43). The poet's mission is, in a phrase from 'Notes on the Education of a New Zealand Poet', 'the discovery of a sacred pattern in natural events' (*MH* 132).[3]

The same idea lies behind Baxter's most famous and resonant statement about myth, which virtually every critic writing about his work feels compelled to quote: 'What happens is either meaningless to me, or it is mythology' ('Education', *MH* 122). Mythology, in other words, is what makes life meaningful, rather than a random and chaotic sequence of one damn thing after another. To make sense of your life, you have to see how it embodies the fundamental, archetypal patterns that are reflected in myth. That is what his 'alcoholic grave-robbing friend' is doing when he describes his fall from grace in the words, 'I took the wrong turn round the cabbage tree [. . .] a long time ago.' Given Baxter's reference a few lines earlier to 'Original Sin', we could see the cabbage tree as a vernacular Kiwi reflection of the Tree of Eden, where we all took the wrong turn a long time ago. And it is relevant that Baxter's alcoholic friend is presumably not an artist or an intellectual, but just an ordinary Kiwi bloke: mythologising one's life as a way of making sense of it is a natural, spontaneous, instinctive human process. Baxter goes on to quote a passage from 'Letter to Robert Burns', which he offers, with wry oxymoron, as 'the exact mythological record of my birth'. The poet's mythology

3 Baxter's view here is strikingly similar to T. S. Eliot's famous 1923 comments on Joyce's *Ulysses*: 'In using the myth, in manipulating a continuous parallel between contemporaneity and antiquity,' Joyce had created 'a way of controlling, of ordering, of giving a shape and a significance to the immense panorama of futility and anarchy which is contemporary history.' Joyce's invention of this 'mythical method', for Eliot, had 'the importance of a scientific discovery' ('Ulysses, Order, and Myth', in Eliot, *Prose* 177–78).

can be as 'exact' and truthful as the more literal statements of the scientist or the historian.

The second claim is implied in Baxter's reference to 'that mythical stratum of the mind'. Consistently Baxter imagines mythology as belonging to, arising from, and appealing to a level of the mind deeper than rational conscious thought, a level which he would have identified with Jung's 'collective unconscious'. (He characteristically prefers the term '*sub*conscious', emphasising the image of something *underneath* consciousness.) Only by appealing to readers on this deeper level, whose images are shared by all of us, can poetry communicate fundamental truths: it 'presents the crises, violations and reconciliations of the spiritual life in mythical form because this is the only way in which the conscious mind can assimilate them' ('Conversation', *MH* 23). Therefore the writer's necessary task is 'not moralising but mythologising, rediscovering his or her own buried natural self' (22). Earlier, in 'Symbolism in New Zealand Poetry', Baxter explains the working of symbolism in terms of the excavation of a buried city:

> It lies at the roots of a poem where art form and suffered reality coalesce, and may be more apparent to the critical reader than to the author himself, as archaeologists unearth city after city from underneath a mound of simple rubble. [. . .] A symbol is often more vigorous when unsuspected by its author; as when a child relives in its play and fantasy the totemism of primitive man, or a civilised adult governs his life by an intricate ritual. (*FA* 56–57).

Again and again Baxter envisages this 'mythical stratum of the mind' as something which lies under the surface, perhaps unsuspected, but profoundly important. The level on which we make sense of our lives is one which lies beneath the reach of reason. 'A symbol cannot be explained; rather, it must be regarded as a door opening upon the dark—upon a world of intuitions and associations of which the poet himself is hardly conscious' (58). And—as Baxter's perhaps only half-conscious allusion to the excavation of Troy suggests—classical myth is one of the most important constituents of that mythical stratum.

A third and final point is Baxter's specification of 'the *Greek* myths and legends' (our emphasis) as having this profound significance. He is not necessarily claiming that Greek myth has an intrinsic profundity which is lacking in (say) Norse or Maori or African myth. Rather, it is important because it is part of Pakeha New Zealand's cultural tradition as the inheritor of western European civilisation. Figures like Oedipus and Odysseus are among 'the more permanent figures in human imagination' (in O'Sullivan's phrase), and are part of a vital living language for us—so, at least, Baxter would maintain, in the teeth of his critics. The early Baxter in particular is emphatic and even prickly in his defence of the relevance of classical myth to a New Zealand audience. When Noel Hilliard in 1952 criticised Pakeha writers for failing to write about Maori, Baxter assumed (perhaps wrongly, but characteristically) that Hilliard meant Maori mythology, and retorted that writers 'would find (as I have found) the myth of Odysseus just as applicable to New Zealand as the myth of Maui, and more familiar to an English-speaking audience' ('The Maori Motif'). Similarly in 'Symbolism in New Zealand Poetry' he criticises the use of indigenous myth by Pakeha poets as stiff and unconvincing, and argues that 'There is no reason, actually, why a New Zealand poet should use Polynesian symbolism rather than the Greek myths of Orpheus and Prometheus, or the medieval legend of Faustus. A correspondence with Polynesian culture should occur naturally; and can only succeed when the symbols are an integral part of the poet's mental equipment' (*FA* 62). Baxter's later wholehearted embrace of maoritanga casts an ironic light on the cagey defensiveness of these early pronouncements. Nevertheless, his praise in the same passage for Keith Sinclair's poem 'Memorial for a Missionary' represents an ideal that he never abandoned: 'Polynesian and European symbolism merge, as they must inevitably do in the mind of a New Zealander of European extraction.' There is a similar merging, or creative coexistence, of the Polynesian and the classical in Baxter's late poetry.

In the twentieth century, as Lillian Feder says, 'Psychoanalytic approaches [. . .] have been chiefly responsible for the reincarnation of myth as a new and potent symbolic language' (59). Kai Jensen has persuasively demonstrated that, for Baxter, one of the most crucial influences was the psychology of Jung. Baxter read *Modern*

Man in Search of a Soul during his adolescence, and singles it out in 'Notes on the Education of a New Zealand Poet' as one of the three books which helped him survive that period of his life (*MH* 127). At Otago University in 1944 he was fascinated by psychology: 'He was reading [. . .] texts of Freud, Jung, and Adler, not in potted versions, but in full. He knew them well enough to be able to argue with the lecturers over their interpretations' (McKay 72). He underwent analysis with a pupil of Jung's, Grete Christeller, in Christchurch in 1948. Jung became a touchstone that he returned to repeatedly throughout his life; as late as the Jerusalem period an unpublished essay, 'Things and Idols' (Hocken MS-0975/160), contains a lengthy exposition of the Jungian concepts of anima, animus and spiritus.

Baxter was also acquainted with Freudian psychoanalysis, and well aware that the mythic furniture of his imaginative life—Oedipal conflicts, devouring mothers, snaky temptresses—could be subjected to Freudian readings. Looking back years later on his poem 'The Unicorn' (*CP* 10–11), written at the age of sixteen, he acknowledged that its unicorn and archer could be read as a projection of his Oedipal relationship with his father Archie—'But the boy has read Freud, and these implications were fully in his mind. He was not wholly devoid of iconoclastic humour' ('The Unicorn: a consideration of adolescence', in *Spark* 539). Though capable of psychoanalysing his own work, and even of consciously building Freudian symbolism into it, Baxter is sceptical of the value of such analysis. An unpublished poem ironically titled 'The Advantages of Analysis' describes how 'The analyst unwinds it all, / That something happened on a bed. / He saw his mother's vulva, black / As anthracite, a gorgon's head'—yet at the end of the session the patient goes home, 'And at his ear the demon talks, / And still his heart is deaf and blind, // Because the uninhibited man / Can with his knowledge do no good' (1960, N20.68). Freud's psychology, in its narrow focus on personal sexual hangups, does not (in Baxter's view) get near the central malaise of the human condition. It is because Jung's comes closer that Baxter maintains throughout his life the view he expressed to Noel Ginn during his undergraduate days that 'in general [Jung] is one above Freud in my hierarchy' (8 April 1945, *Spark* 400).[4]

Baxter's preference was largely due to the much higher value that Jung places on the unconscious, imagination and myth.[5] *Modern Man in Search of a Soul* 'offered the possibility that my subconscious mind might contain sources of peace and wisdom as well as ghosts, werewolves, hags, demons, and the various zoo of the living dead who crowded round my bed at night' (*MH* 127). Whereas Freud—to grossly simplify—sees the unconscious as a container for repressed psychic detritus which must be decontaminated by exposure to the light of reason, Jung sees it as the submerged four fifths of one's true self, which must be understood and fully absorbed into one's personality. In particular, beyond the individual unconscious lies the 'collective unconscious', the source of the archetypal images which all human beings share and which are the raw material of our dreams, myths and fictions. Because of this, myth is a universal language: 'myths and symbols [. . .] can arise autochthonously in every corner of the earth and yet are identical, because they are fashioned out of the same world-wide human unconscious' (Jung, *Psychological Types*, *CW* 6: 120–21). Jung's defence of the poetic use of mythology in 'Psychology and Literature' would have strongly resonated with Baxter:

> It is therefore to be expected that the poet will turn to mythological figures in order to give suitable expression to his experience. Nothing would be more mistaken than to suppose that he is working with second-hand material. On the contrary, the primordial experience is the source of his creativeness, but it is so dark and amorphous that it requires the related mythological imagery to give it form. In itself it is wordless and imageless, for it is a vision seen 'as in a glass, darkly'. [. . .] Since the expression can never match the richness of the vision and can never exhaust its possibilities, the poet must have at his disposal a huge store of material if he is to communicate even a fraction of what he has glimpsed, and must make use of difficult and contradictory

4 More forcefully he told Ginn in 1950 that 'Jung is my Bible' (qtd in Jensen, *Whole Men* 129).

5 Segal, *Jung on Mythology*, is a very useful compilation and analysis of Jung's writings on myth.

images in order to express the strange paradoxes of his vision.
(*CW* 15: 96–97)

Two Jungian concepts in particular were profoundly fruitful for Baxter. The first was the 'shadow', the aspect of one's mind that represents all the qualities which one hates, fears and rejects, and which (in Jung's view) must be confronted and accepted into one's self in order to achieve full integration of the personality. This concept—that what is rejected in the self is the true source of value and imaginative power—is close to Baxter's heart. He draws on it in 'Conversation with an Ancestor', when he talks of 'my collaborator, my schizophrenic twin, who has always provided me with poems', who lives in 'the cellblock in the basement of my mind'. Ironically, however, the figure Baxter describes in this passage as 'my shadow, my enemy, my monster' is not the prisoner in the basement but the respectable public self (what Jung would call the *persona*) who 'would destroy if he could whatever gifts I possess' (*MH* 17, 19). The slippage is suggestive: while Baxter frankly owns his 'dark' side—the Bohemian, the drunk, the dropout, the 'other convict self' ('Pig Island Letters' 9, *CP* 282)—it sometimes seems to be his bourgeois domestic side, 'the poet as family man', that is truly his Jungian shadow, feared and rejected.[6]

The second crucial concept is that of the anima, the female aspect of a man's psyche (its male counterpart in a woman's psyche, less important to Baxter, is the animus), which serves as a bridge to and personification of the unconscious. As experienced in dreams or imagination, or projected onto women in the man's external life, the anima may be seen both as irresistibly attractive and as fearsome, monstrous or evil. Baxter describes it as 'archaic, natural, by turns beautiful and terrible, located at a deep unconscious level. The *anima* represents, to my mind, all that is not-self' (*MH* 116–17). The description comes from 'The Man on the Horse', Baxter's extended Jungian analysis of Burns' 'Tam o' Shanter', which (as Jensen comments, 134) is as much a commentary on Baxter himself as on Burns. He identifies the young witch in that poem as 'Burns's only real Muse—one of the

6 Compare the similar slippage in the last line of 'The Seagirl and the Poet' (N17.79), discussed in chapter 3.

most powerful evocations in literature of the *anima*, that mysterious archetype who has been called variously Venus, Cybele, Artemis [or] Hekate' (*MH* 116). As this implies, many of Baxter's own female mythological figures, along an unbroken continuum stretching from the irresistible Venus to the hideous Gorgon, can be seen as representations of changing aspects of the anima. It is also possible, as Jensen argues, to read the 'real' women in his poetry as anima figures, though such an approach risks tidying away too much the painful complexities of his relationship to the actual women in his life—mother, wife, daughter, lovers.

Finally, Jung illuminates a characteristically paradoxical quality in Baxter's handling of mythological images. In *Science of Mythology* Jung suggests that 'It is an essential characteristic of psychic figures that they are duplex or at least capable of duplication; at all events they are bipolar and oscillate between their positive and negative meanings' (Jung & Kerényi, 186). His collaborator, the mythologist Carl Kerényi, develops the point in relation to the classical gods: 'In *Apollo* sublimest clarity and the darkness of death face one another, perfectly poised and equal, on a borderline; in *Dionysus*, life and death; in *Zeus*, might and right'; these deities have 'contradictory aspects for the very reason that their structure combines contradictions in perfect equilibrium' (123). Baxter's major mythological figures almost all show this duality—an ability to stand, alternately or simultaneously, for diametrically opposite things. Prometheus is both the artist-liberator, and the power of technological civilisation which perverts art; Dionysus is both imprisoning alcoholism and festive release; Odysseus's return to Ithaca is both a humiliating failure and a triumphant completion of his quest; both the underworld and the Labyrinth can signify the spiritual death created by modern civilisation, and the unconscious mind which is the source of spiritual renewal. These apparent self-contradictions recall the medieval practice of allegorising classical and biblical stories *in bono* and *in malo*, in a good sense and a bad sense, so that the same figure could in different contexts represent either Christ or Satan.[7] Baxter's

7 For the multiple interpretation tradition, see Brumble xxi–xxiv and Miles, *Classical Mythology* 10, 64–65; on *in bono/in malo* see e.g. Kaske 23–26, Minnis 14.

practice is too consistent to be dismissed as merely muddle-headed: in Jung's words, he is using 'difficult and contradictory images [. . .] to express the strange paradoxes of his vision'. It reflects his sense of the union of opposites, his tendency to locate value and the possibility of renewal precisely in what he finds most frightening and alien—death, personal degradation and dissolution, the gap, the void.

'The classical referential spread': Baxter and myth 1926–72

Classical mythology was a presence in Baxter's life almost from the beginning. His mother Millicent records his earliest literary influences:

> It was a great joy to Archie that Jim, long before he went to school, listened to his recitals of Burns and the English romantic poets, and quickly got them off by heart. Jim imbibed all this Keats and Shelley and Byron poetry and became immersed, and also in classical and Scandinavian mythology. He was devoted throughout his childhood to the classical fairy tales of Andrew Lang[8] [. . .] and was really deeply steeped in classical mythology. He made Odysseus part of himself, as anyone can tell by reading his poetry. (M. Baxter 69)

Baxter himself recalls in 'Notes on the Education of a New Zealand Poet':

> Waves, rocks, beaches, flax bushes, rivers, cattle flats, hawks, rabbits, eels, old man manuka trees, meanwhile provided me with a great store of images that could later enter my poems. Among the books at home there were one or two of Norse and Greek mythology. I became the companion of Odin and Thor and Jason and Ulysses. That was an indispensable education.
>
> (*MH* 132)

The most striking thing in Baxter's account is the way in which he segues, without even a paragraph break, from the childhood landscape to the books of mythology. The two great ingredients

8 By 'classical' Millicent here means 'classic': Lang's collections mainly draw on post-classical fairy stories and folktales, though the *Blue Fairy Book* does include the story of Perseus.

of his imaginative life are here set side by side, and both linked to the kind of education which he valued—'the discovery of a sacred pattern in natural events'—and contrasted with 'the acquisition of the lens of abstract thought, which sees nothing sacred in heaven or on middle earth'.

Unfortunately, neither Baxter nor his mother specifies what were the 'one or two' books of mythology, so we do not know where he first read the stories of Jason and Ulysses. It is clear that he soon moved on from retellings to encountering the heroes directly in the classical epics of Homer, Virgil and Ovid. In his adolescent letters to Noel Ginn he is able to refer casually to these as long-familiar, telling Ginn that one poem was 'composed from vague memories of Ovid' (*Spark* 332), that another is 'referring to the fable in Virgil's *Georgics*' (386), or (rather immodestly) that an image was 'annexed with improvements from Lucretius and Vergil' (373). At some early point—in adolescence, or in his brief time at Otago University, where he studied (and failed) Latin—he also encountered more recondite classical texts such as the *Homeric Hymns*, Hesiod's *Theogony* and *Works and Days*, and Apollonius's *Argonautica*. In addition to these classical texts, he must have absorbed a great deal of classical mythology, and the freight of poetic association that comes with it, from the English poets that he read or had read to him in childhood—Burns, Byron, Keats, Shelley and others.

It is this English poetic tradition that most strongly shapes Baxter's first references to classical myth, in the poetry of his early teens. In these juvenilia it would indeed be fair to describe his use of myth as stale and second-hand. He draws on the mustiest clichés of eighteenth-century poetese (a poet is 'a fount whence Heliconian waters flow'—'To My Father', N4.183), and on conventional Romantic images of landscapes haunted by tritons, centaurs, fauns, 'woodland gods' and the music of Pan's pipes. His most ambitious early mythological poem, 'The Gods of Greece' (N3.157), wistfully laments the departure of the ancient gods, and especially that of Pan, 'he who was once the voice / Of nature and the woodland solitude', now desecrated and destroyed by war—'For Mars, red Mars, has laid his hand on thee, / Thou who wert once the voice of Poesy!' Nevertheless, even in these derivative early poems, we can see themes emerging—the association of classical myth with the natural and spontaneous, its opposition to the constraints of modern civilisation, the image of poetry and imagination as water welling up from underground—which would remain constant throughout his work.

In adolescence, Baxter's poetry evolved quite rapidly away from this derivativeness to the production of work of increasing originality. His use of myth in adolescence, rather than being clichéd, performs a powerful role in this transition. He realised that certain individuals, foremost among them his father and various Romantic poets, could be both real people and mythic archetypes, and that specific figures from classical myth can serve as symbols of the self—an insight that underpins his most distinctive early verse. His contingent discovery of the writings of Jung informs his understanding of the fundamentally mythic operation of the human mind. Figures such as Icarus, Atlas, Prometheus, the salamander, Janus, Tantalus, Sisyphus, Jason and the unicorn represent Baxter's best efforts to clarify his sense of self. The intensely private nature of this symbolism accounts for the opacity of much of his early verse. The recurrent themes of childhood acquire definition and complexity in this period as he contemplates the risks associated with art, the dangers to selfhood posed by conformity and authority, and the suffering one must endure to live a principled life, all complicated by the terrors of developing sexuality.

During the central span of Baxter's adult writing career, from the late 1940s to the late 1960s, classical mythology is omnipresent in his work—as can be seen from a glance at the Mythological Who's Who. Some of the myths crop up only occasionally and incidentally; others are constant presences, touchstones to which Baxter repeatedly returns. The adolescent figures of self are joined by heroes and anti-heroes such as Odysseus, Hercules, Theseus and Oedipus, embodying aspects of the poet's character and the options available to him; divine and demonic beings such as Venus, Dionysus, the Gorgon, the Muse, Persephone and the personnel of the underworld embody the natural and psychic forces which act upon him, and which he embraces or fears or both. Though these key mythic figures in Baxter's work are complex, they are not hermetically private like the figures in his adolescent poetry; rather Baxter is working with the traditional, even 'archetypal' symbolism of the classical myths. What they stand for is often simple—death, sex, alcohol, freedom, worldly power, innocence. The complexity comes from Baxter's (and the reader's) ambivalent response to those things.

Baxter's handling of myth is poetic rather than scholarly. He is quite capable of muddling the details of a story, or creatively misremembering or reshaping it to suit his purposes—sometimes with irreverent mischief, as when he blandly explains to the readers of 'Pig Island Letters' that the satyr Marsyas 'competed with Apollo in playing the ukulele' (*CP* 628). (Of course, classical poets reshaped the myths in exactly the same ways.) When he reads classical and English accounts of a myth it is often a single charged detail or image that fixes itself in his mind and recurs in his poetry: for instance, Apollonius's image of the magical iceflower growing from Prometheus's blood on the Caucasian snow (*Argonautica* 3. 851–53), or the description in the Homeric *Hymn to Aphrodite* (5. 64–90) of the goddess entering the hut of the shepherd Anchises, or Marlowe's comparison of Leander making love to Hero with Hercules entering the garden of the Hesperides (*Hero and Leander* 1. 297–300). Despite the encyclopedic range of his references to classical myth, his mythic characters are often not sharply individualised. It could be said of Baxter's goddesses—Venus, Hekate, Cybele, Diana, Demeter and the rest—that, as Eliot said of *The Waste Land* (82), 'all the women are one woman'. The same is sometimes true of his male heroes: it is interesting for instance that a description of Orpheus as 'Sallow, small, with broken teeth' (N19.19) is taken over and applied to Odysseus (N19.22), and that both Sisyphus and Tantalus are imagined as a 'proud tycoon' with a 'pearl-handled revolver' ('Sisyphus', *CP* 202; 'The Descent of Orpheus'). These dream-like overlappings and conflations are appropriate to figures who emerge from the collective unconscious.

Perhaps the best point of entry to Baxter's mature use of

classical myth is to look at his treatment of a single figure, the one highlighted in the title of this book—the Muse. She is one of the most familiar of mythological allusions, the figure who traditionally embodies the art of poetry itself. The Muses, the nine beautiful daughters of Zeus and Mnemosyne who dwelt around the sacred springs on Mount Helicon or Mount Parnassus, are the patron goddesses of literature and the arts. Poets from Homer onwards have invoked 'the Muse' as the source and symbol of inspiration. For this very reason the image was, by the twentieth century if not before, looking somewhat threadbare. Coleridge's schoolmaster derided it in the 1780s: 'Muse, boy, Muse? your nurse's daughter, you mean! Pierian spring? Oh aye! the cloister pump, I suppose!' (*Biographia Literaria* ch. 1, Coleridge 10).

Baxter's first reference to the Muse is exactly this kind of schoolboy cliché: in one of his earliest recorded poems, 'At School I have no time to Dream' (N1.18; *NSP* 170), the thirteen-year-old poet earnestly proclaims that 'when at night my Muse awakes, / Then soaring wings my Fancy takes / Far to the land of Poesy.' But within a few years he has come to distance himself from what he later describes as 'the pastoral Muse and [. . .] childhood' (*MH* 135), and from the ideal of poetry as a flight from earthly reality. A more earthily irreverent note, influenced by the colloquial verse of Robert Burns, enters his invocations of the Muse. He associates her with drink—'the Muse of Alcohol', in 'Horatian Ode on the Banishment of Beer' (1944, *NSP* 173–75)—or with sex: 'But let him leave the jades, he'll find / His dictionary no use, / For woman, lovely woman, / Is the mother of the Muse' ('I remember, I remember', 1954). In *Aspects of Poetry in New Zealand* he cheerfully observes that 'The Muse after all is a tall girl. Sometimes all that a growing poet can do is put a bucket over her head and swing on the handle' (7).

At the same time, in the 1950s and 1960s, he is developing his own, very unclassical conception of the Muse. Again, Robert Burns serves as the vehicle for this new conception. In 'The Man on the Horse'—a passage cited earlier—Baxter contrasts the 'idealised', stiffly formal Muse described in Burns' poem 'The Vision' with the young witch in 'Tam o' Shanter' who represents

'Burns's actual Muse [. . .] archaic, natural, by turns beautiful and terrible' (*MH* 116). True poetry comes from the unconscious, and the only true Muse is the poet's unconscious mind as embodied in the feminine figure of the anima. This Jungian concept may have fused in Baxter's mind with Robert Graves' *The White Goddess* (1948), which celebrates a lunar Triple Goddess who is 'mother, bride and layer-out' to the poet–hero: 'a true poem is necessarily an invocation of the White Goddess, or Muse, the Mother of all living, the ancient power of fright and lust—the female spider or the queen bee whose embrace is death' (Graves 24).[9] Baxter's ambivalent view of this Muse-figure was captured early on in the unpublished 'To My Father' (1954, *SP* 54–56), where the moon is 'Of Dionysiac poetry / The Muse and mother', and perceived both as a witch-like 'deathshead' and a beneficent life-giving Venus. In later poems it is often her terrible or grotesque aspect that predominates. She is 'the man-killing Muse' ('A French Letter to Louis Johnson', 1966, N26.62), or—echoing Graves' 'spider' image—'an old black hag with red arachnoid eyes' ('The Muse', 1961, *CP* 234). Perhaps most memorably, in 'Letter to Robert Burns' (1963, *CP* 289–91):

> For when the hogmagandie ended
> And I lay thunder-struck and winded,
> The snake-haired Muse came out of the sky
> And showed her double axe to me.
> Since then I die and do not die.
> 'Jimmy,' she said, 'you are my ugliest son;
> I'll break you like a herring-bone.'

By a kind of mythological pun, Baxter gives the Muse (Greek *Mousa*) the snaky hair of the Gorgon Medusa. The gracious goddess who provides poetic inspiration is fused with the hideous monster whose gaze paralyses and kills; poetry comes from a face-to-face confrontation with what inspires fear, horror and revulsion. The

9 A casual reference to 'Robert Graves's white goddess' (*MH* 96) shows that Baxter knew the book and had it in his mind as he was writing 'The Man on the Horse'. It should be noted that Graves sharply distinguished his quasi-historical approach from Jung's 'humourless and watertight psychological system' which turned myth into 'a delightful timeless world-soup [. . .] reduced to a single fundamental, Germanic taste' (qtd in Pharand 185).

same duality is embodied in the Muse's double axe, which Baxter (according to Bill Manhire, 11) glossed as 'the double-bladed axe of sex and death', conferring both death and life ('I die and do not die' suggesting a Shakespearean pun on 'dying' as orgasm). It is a quintessential Baxter passage, in which he has moved from mere 'mythological allusion' to genuine myth-creation. And it is worth noting that it comes in an otherwise light-hearted, bawdy poem in Burns' octosyllabic couplets. These serio-comic poems, straddling the colloquial and the oracular, contain some of Baxter's most striking mythopoeic moments. As he said of Burns, his 'best unconscious wisdom is often hidden in his jokes' (*MH* 117).

This conception of the Muse is essentially unrespectable, anarchic and 'Dionysiac'. In 'The Muse (to Louis Johnson)' (1966, *CP* 352) a shrewish wife screaming abuse at her drunken husband is identified as 'the Muse, whom you and I / Unhinge by our civility'. Civility and respectability are the death of poetry: 'Neither God nor the Muses visit a man who has bandaged his wounds and settled down to fulfil the expectations of his relatives, his audience, his bosses and his religious advisers' ('Portrait of the Artist as a New Zealander'). Given the importance of Robert Burns in the development of Baxter's conception of the Muse, it is ironic that it was his tenure of the Burns Fellowship at Otago University in 1966–67 that made him fear being cut off from her: 'the Muse, that primitive and prejudiced old Lady, does not smile on Fellowship holders. Our good morals seem to bore her' ('On the Burns Fellowship', 244). Laying down this institutional role and dropping out of conventional society could be seen as a rededication to 'the grim Old Lady'. That is not how Baxter puts it, however. After 1968 the figure of the Muse—which had evolved with his poetic evolution over the past thirty-odd years—drops out of his writing.

This is symptomatic of a larger shift in Baxter's work. It has become a critical commonplace that classical mythology largely disappears from the late poetry. McNaughton, as we have seen, locates the change in the Burns Fellowship years, when Baxter 'found his new voice and laid the strong ghost of scholarship'; after this point 'the tone of classical reference becomes ironic or contemptuous, and the ideal of the classical hero is abandoned' ('Baxter's Strong Ghost', 64). There is undoubtedly an element of truth in this, but it needs to be substantially qualified. For one thing, Baxter was never seriously in thrall to 'the ideal of the classical hero': he shows little interest in the 'heroes' of Greek myth, and those who appear in his poetry are usually flawed, compromised or defeated. For another, irony and satiric debunking had been an element of his approach to classical myth from very early on, as his treatment of the Muse demonstrates. The swing between irony and seriousness is another aspect of Baxter's ambivalent and dialogic approach to myth, with a grave and orotund treatment of a mythic character often followed soon after by a carnivalesque parody.

It is true that Baxter's use of classical myth, at its height in the mid 1960s, drops off sharply after 1968. This is just a part of his general movement in these last years towards simplicity: a quest for spareness, directness and colloquialism in the poetry, a stripping away of inessentials in his lifestyle and his spirituality, a discarding of the old 'ikons' (*CP* 499). When he declares in 'Song for Sakyamuni' (*CP* 500–502) that 'My words are no longer the words of Apollo', it is not so much a rejection of myth as of formally crafted 'Apollonian' poetry—perhaps of poetry or literature altogether.

However, this is only a partial truth. Classical myth becomes rarer but does not disappear from his work, and in some ways becomes more striking because it stands out more sharply in its plainer setting. The late poems include references, explicit or implicit, to figures such as Theseus (*CP* 488–89), Atlas (*CP* 519), Rhadamanthus (*CP* 531, 554) and Medusa (*CP* 557, 578). Sometimes they are strikingly juxtaposed with images from other mythic traditions, as in 'Autumn Testament' 10, where Odysseus and Maui are set against the mission church at Jerusalem (*CP* 545), or 'Autumn Testament' 48, where, in a bravura display of mythological multiculturalism that demonstrates Jung's point about the universality of myth, a spider is hailed as 'tantric goddess', 'Kehua, vampire, eight-eyed watcher / At the gate of the dead, little Arachne', and 'a king crab / At the door of the underworld' (*CP* 564). The most obvious counter to the view that Baxter had abandoned classical myth is 'The Tiredness of Me and Herakles' (*CP* 595–97), a major poem written within a week or two of his death, which puts him in sustained half-serious, half-ironic parallel with one of his favourite classical figures.

'Ode to Auckland' (*CP* 597–600)—Baxter's last poem, except perhaps for the two 'wallpaper poems'—begins with the image of an art school where

> The statue of a Greek god lay on the floor
> With his prick and balls knocked off by a chisel.
> 'Alison,' I said, 'they've buggered the god of death,
> They've cut the balls off the god of love.
> How can their art survive?'

This is not an iconoclastic image, though it is an image of iconoclasm.[10] The nameless Greek god is not being mocked (unlike the images of traditional Christian piety, 'the bourgeois Christ' and the Holy Spirit which 'squawked and laid an egg'). On the contrary, he embodies the powerful forces of Eros and Thanatos, the life-instinct and the death-instinct, and Baxter's anger and despair are directed at the society which desecrates them. There is an almost ludicrous gulf in style and tone between 'Ode to Auckland' and Baxter's juvenile poem 'The Gods of Greece', which mourned, in wispy late-Romantic vein, the loss of the classical gods and what they represent from the degraded modern world. But there is an underlying continuity: 'the gods of Greece' still stand for the values Baxter believes in. Across his writing career of more than three decades he continued to carry his classical baggage, and he managed to pack a great deal into it.

10 Contrast Goulter's reading (68): 'The demise of the deity is illustrative of profound changes in Baxter's poetry and his attitude to Classical myth.'

CHAPTER 2

'AN INDISPENSABLE EDUCATION': MYTH IN BAXTER'S CHILDHOOD AND ADOLESCENCE

> I became the companion of Odin and Thor and Jason and Ulysses. That was an indispensable education. ('Education', *MH* 132)

In August 1940, a few weeks after turning fourteen, James K. Baxter wrote a poem called 'Before the Creation' (N1.46). The poem is only ten lines long, and at first there doesn't seem much to discover from it other than that Baxter had read his mother's copy of A. & E. Keary's *The Heroes of Asgard* (1891) and he was working hard on his iambic pentameter. Yet twenty-seven years later, with Baxter now one of New Zealand's most prominent poets, he quoted this piece of juvenilia at the beginning of an explanation of how as a child he 'broke out in words' (*MH* 122):

> Long, long ago, ere e'en the world was made,
> Was naught but chaos, the abyss of space,
> The deep Ginungagap—on one side lay
> Cold Niflheim, home of frosts and gloomy mists,
> And in it was the cauldron Hvergelmir,
> The source of twelve great rivers of strange waves
> That flowed into the space and chaos far
> To freeze therein [. . .]. (*MH* 123)

It is likely that he selected these lines to mark his point of beginning as a poet because they represent his first concrete use of what becomes a defining trope of so much of his poetry, namely the presence of 'the gap, the void' as a feature of 'all good mythologies' (*MH* 122).

But Baxter's selection of this poem also has broader significance, for the contexts of its production reveal a substantial amount about his early influences and poetic preoccupations. Most notable is the fact that the poem concentrates on the period *before* the creation of living beings. Although *The Heroes of Asgard* brims with mythical creatures and divine beings, which surely appealed to Baxter's adolescent love of the fantastic, few of the heroes make it into his poetry. His adult recollection of companionship with Odin and Thor never significantly translated into verse: Odin is entirely absent from the juvenile poems and Thor manages one brief cameo in a single poem written a few months after 'Before the Creation', called 'Thunder and Lightning' (N3.156).

The dearth of heroes in 'Before the Creation' also points to the very early genesis of Baxter's lifelong habit of plucking from every system of thought or belief he encountered only those elements that meshed with his personal convictions, practices or mythology. His symbols might change over his lifetime, but his symbolism remained remarkably constant. The appeal of Norse mythology's yawning void—the Ginungagap—to the fourteen-year-old poet anticipates the profound significance to the forty-year-old Baxter of 'Wahi Ngaro', the Maori 'void from which all life comes' (*CP* 542).

It is also likely that 'Before the Creation' is unpopulated because in 1940 solitude was the defining condition of Baxter's life. For most of his teens he felt like the singular inhabitant of a paradoxical void: a place of barrenness, isolated from mainstream society, whose very emptiness fertilised his mind into producing those profound expressions of selfhood and identity—his poems. Looking back on that period, he wrote:

> I think that various factors combined early to give me a sense of difference, or a gap—not of superiority, nor of inferiority, though at times it must have felt like that, but simply of difference—between myself and other people. [. . .] These experiences were in the long run very valuable, for they taught me to distrust mass opinion and sort out my own ideas; but at the time they were distinctly painful. I could compare them perhaps with the experiences of a Jewish boy growing up in an anti-Semitic neighbourhood. They created a gap in which the poems were able to grow. ('Education', *MH* 123–24)

Not only poems grew in this gap; Baxter's conception of himself as a poet grew there also, for this was the time when he developed an identity as a poet firmly rooted in an ambivalent relationship with his parents, an oppositional relationship with his society, and a symbiotic identification with the solitary sufferers of mythology. When he pronounced some years later that 'what happens is either meaningless to me or else it is mythology' (*MH* 122) he was speaking personally and subjectively, and without abstraction.

'Knowledge is not wisdom': opposing parental influences

It was Baxter's mother, Millicent, who introduced him to classical mythology. She gave him her own books of Norse and Greek myth, and encouraged him to read widely. He acknowledges this in the early poem 'To my Mother' (*Spark* 48):

> O friend and mother in one form combined,
> To thee I owe the pleasures of the mind;
> For the full knowledge that thou long had'st known
> To me narrated was; and I was shown
> The many tales and legends of the past—

But his thanks aren't entirely fulsome, for although his mother took an interest in his writing she preferred 'history, international affairs and politics [and] never read poetry for pleasure' (Lenore Baxter to Frank McKay, 7 July 1985, FM 10/7/32). Millicent had inherited a rational, forthright mind from her father, John Macmillan Brown, Canterbury University College's dynamic first Professor of English and Classics, whose 'narrative of history is unabashedly progressive [. . . N]ot even the ravages of World War I could dampen his attachment to a fundamentally Victorian narrative of progress' (Schouten, 116–17).

Baxter always had a difficult relationship with his maternal grandfather. Late in his life he struggled, and eventually failed, to edit for publication Macmillan Brown's memoirs. A brief introduction was the best he could achieve, one which primarily served to distance himself from his grandfather: 'I am haunted by this ancestral voice which insists that the intellectual and moral betterment of mankind is achievable and should be every sane man's goal and concern' (*Memoirs of John Macmillan Brown*, xxxvi). To Baxter, Macmillan Brown's 'centre of thought and motivation is mysterious, because of the nuance of largeness, the sense of a broad view from high country, which his historical and personal situation made possible.' Set this broad view alongside Baxter's sense of the inadequate systems for discovering order in life's chaos—'what happens is either meaningless to me or else it is mythology'—and the opposition between the two men becomes fundamental. Baxter surely recognised by the sixth page of his grandfather's memoir that their incompatibility was absolute, when the dogmatic ancestral voice proclaimed:

> I was never afraid of darkness and throughout my life I have continued the long task of jettisoning the superstitions with which the traditions of boyhood and the local environment saturated my mind. I saw how much they disintegrated the character and wasted the natural endowments. There is nothing so obstructs the development of the soul and its virtues as those crude beliefs that previous generations have collected and handed on. (6–7)

In a sentence tribal tradition, religious belief and myth—the keystones of Baxter's poetry—are jettisoned by Macmillan Brown as superstitious nonsense. His confident Victorianism is profoundly at odds with Baxter's conception of art bred by 'that level of hardship or awareness of moral chaos where the soul is too destitute to be able to lie to itself' (*MH* 17). Where Macmillan Brown pursued rational explanation, Baxter preferred mystery. Atlantis, for example, symbolised for Baxter a drowned Edenic childhood touchable only in memory and the imagination (see 'The Town Under the Sea', *CP* 252). But for Macmillan Brown Atlantis was no more mysterious than any other clue to prehistory. Thus his extended scholarly expedition to Easter Island, the fruit of which was *The Riddle of the Pacific* (1924), developed a myth-derived argument that the island was the remnant of an abruptly submerged archipelago—as if 'Westminster Abbey were left isolated on the only insular relic of submerged Europe' (1)—whose foundering drew beneath the waves the race that erected the island's massive monoliths.

Baxter was equally at odds with Macmillan Brown's view of the classics as a necessary evil of the modern academy, mere window dressing of the educated mind, in which 'even to the most enthusiastic student of ancient classics there is dead and foreign matter clinging round them that makes his enthusiasm an effort' (Macmillan Brown, *Student Life* 23). Baxter never viewed classical myths as ancient artefacts, riddled with decay and sullied by the accretions of history, and he never valued full knowledge of classical myth as any sort of signifier of scholarly learning or elite status. As already noted in chapter 1, his discussion of the poem 'Prayer to Hekate' directly contradicts his grandfather's attitude of mind: 'One has to get de-educated to understand any poem well' (FM 18/1/16, p. 13).

To counter the influence of his grandfather's mind, 'in certain important respects different from my own' (*Memoirs* xxxv), Baxter turned to other 'ancestral voices'; those of his Highland Scots ancestors upon whom he projected a communal ideal of a 'tribal matrix' which carries the individual 'through the narrow gate of dissolution, and beyond it' (*MH* 27). As early as thirteen he was mourning tribalism's passing—'Gone is the kinship of the clan, / The brotherhood of man to man' ('Time was when on Loch Seven's Shore', N1.21), culminating, in *The Man on the Horse*, in the mythical resurrection of a Gaelic-speaking great-grandparent, Chennor, who interrogates him about the fidelity of his tribal identity, his willingness to place the tribe ahead of the state, his ability to place morality before legality, his sense of marital and familial responsibility and, finally, his ability to balance boldness and prudence (*MH* 28–35).

Chennor is thus the antithesis of Macmillan Brown, a mythical figure created by Baxter to illustrate a distinction, first articulated in adolescence, between wisdom and knowledge:

> Knowledge is not Wisdom, 'tis a tool
> That wise men use to make their words express
> The thoughts that teem within the busy brain.
> Thou [Wisdom] shinest oft where Peace and Quiet dwell,
> Far from the worldly turmoil and the strife [. . .].
> ('Wisdom and Knowledge', *Spark* 87)

Baxter considered the wisest man he ever knew to be his own father Archie, the model for Chennor, whose heroic pacifism demonstrated that mythical figures could exist in the present and be embodied as real people.

To be fair to Millicent Baxter, both father and mother were sufficiently strong-minded, non-conforming and unconventional to assume mythic status in young James' consciousness:

> My mother had a Newnham M.A. degree in Old French; and my father was a self-educated Otago farmer who recited Burns and Shelley and Byron and Blake and Tom Hood and Henry Lawson when the mood took him. Somewhere back in the Freudian fog belt these two strong influences began to work on me [and] I broke out in words. (*MH* 122)

But their strong influence tended to function in opposition in Baxter's life and writing, for he clearly associated his mother with knowledge and rationality, while his father represented the more important gifts of wisdom and poetry. Millicent's determined efforts to shape her adolescent son intellectually caused him to see her as a figure of constraint. Despite her own history of rebellion against her father, her aspirations for her son conformed to the standards of Macmillan Brown—the ancestor who valued education in classical myth only as a signifier of learning and elite status. Archie, by contrast, embodied a view that Baxter would develop into a fully realised schema, in which certain mythological figures, with whom he identified as key protagonists in the foundational narratives of collective humanity, are agents of progress and instruction.

Baxter knew that his father as a young man had written poetry, for he copied a number of these poems into his own notebooks. But he also knew that his father's art had been sacrificed for his pacifist convictions; his suffering in the First World War crippling him—'a poet whom time betrayed / To action' ('To My Father', *CP* 65–66). As Baxter explained in a letter to a friend, the 'war knocked all [. . .] poetry out of him—even now he can only appreciate, not write' (*Spark* 50). 'Pig Island Letters' 8 begins with Baxter's encapsulation of Archie's heroic pacifism:

> When I was only semen in a gland
> Or less than that, my father hung
> From a torture post at Mud Farm
> Because he would not kill . . . (*CP* 281).

But the poem moves quickly and characteristically from the personal to the mythical, universalising Archie's lonely torture as a lesson for, and about, humanity, in which his 'black and swollen thumbs' explain 'the brotherhood of man'. This convergence of the individual and the mythical originates in the adolescent Baxter's close observation of the writing of Archie's pacifist memoir *We Will Not Cease*, which occurred in the late 1930s while the family was travelling through Europe. Archie's narrative of unwavering conviction in the face of brutal persecution was the stuff of myth, and one myth in particular: that of Prometheus, who resisted dehumanising authority in full knowledge of the suffering he must endure. The fact that such suffering had happened not to a remote mythic figure, but to the gentle man Baxter knew and loved, showed him how myth could be embodied in an actual person—and perhaps even in himself.

'The heavens under his lucid gaze': the Romantic poet as myth

Poetry, too, is entwined in the understanding Baxter developed of his ordinary father's extraordinary story. It was through Archie that James discovered a relationship between certain kinds of poetry and the types of myth that spoke to his personal situation. Although Archie no longer wrote poetry, most of the poets he read and quoted had a mythical dimension, and most had experienced Promethean suffering.

Archie Baxter's passion for Robbie Burns was an early revelation. Listening to Burns' poems at his father's knee, Baxter came to understand that not only had the poet constructed myth in verse, he had himself become mythical:

> Burns walking bewildered from the wood of lies
> With poetry a gold and guarded flower;
> Evangelist of green among the charted deserts
> Of sad Mosaic stone;
> [. . .]
> Or rather the sinner grave and repentant behind
> A clown's mask (ill companions snared him):
> [. . .]

Choose what you will. The poet womanly, slender,
Spinning his pretty songs, watching a cloud.
The man who wrote with a diamond on heaven.
The ranting rhymer bawdy in a tavern [. . .].

('Burns', *Spark* 497)

The eighteen-year-old Baxter's catalogue of Burns' differing personae is closely related to the contradictory ways in which he later mythologised himself and was mythologised by others. By October 1944, when he penned his homage to Burns, Baxter had grown sufficiently confident in his own poetic destiny to make explicit comparison of himself to the 'Ayrshire ploughman', a Prometheus, repeatedly wounded by Calvinism for carrying the fire of poetry:

I would set before the throng

This epitaph of one living.
The crystal of Calvin wounded and oppressed
His lion breast;
But he who carries a fire in the heart and eyes
Dies not till the world dies.

(*Spark* 498)

On 29 October 1944—the day Baxter entered 'Burns' into his thirteenth notebook—he also copied an equally long and admiring homage to Byron, another of his father's favourite poets ('Byron', N13.820). Again both father and son admired Byron's nonconformity, his Promethean willingness, verging on compulsion, to stand apart from popular and political opinion, separate from society's 'viper host', which Baxter represents in the poem as a contaminated bird of prey: 'Age-bald his skull, withered each terrible claw— / Loathsome disease and the foul stench of tombs / Under those preyless talons.'

Initially, the poem argues, Byron is captured by the throng—becoming 'Society's tame lion and their boast'—but his 'pride', a synonym for poetic truth and artistic integrity, is an 'immortal diadem' which reanimates Byron 'the sot and knave', who shapes through his poems 'A giant chained whose bleeding entrails / By War's ruinous vulture torn, drag down the walls of sky.' Prometheus, as discussed later in this chapter, had become one of

Baxter's central figures of the self some time before the writing of 'Byron'. The crucial difference in this later poem is that the Promethean Byron doesn't remain chained to the rock in any essential fashion; rather, a dualism is proposed which detaches the poet from his poetry. Just as the crucified Christ dies leaving his physical body upon the cross, so the poet leaves behind his poetry—Baxter's 'empty lion-skin' (*CP* 27)—so that he can be resurrected as something altogether greater. Byron's 'hot heart and his cold remorse [. . .] show / A birth [. . .]. The man in his own effigy is lost / By transmutation perilous and strange: / More human and more godlike for that change.' Baxter's reborn Byron is 'the Sun! fierce-burning and blood-red / In fervent blaze he rises. Phaeton-wise [. . .] the heavens under his lucid gaze.' By this stage in Baxter's adolescent development he identifies with the poet as Phaeton rather than the Prometheus poet of two years earlier. 'I know that the Promethean fire was pain,' the final stanza concedes, but pain is not the end, for far from destroying Byron, he is made greater—the solitary poet as ultimate Byronic hero: 'no windy flake / His soul—blown sorrowing in the world's wood' but 'a sun sphereless in solitude'.

Baxter would again draw on this configuration in the mid 1940s—the poet who apparently perishes in suffering, only to be resurrected as an artist more resilient and altogether greater—to manage his painful transition from solitary adolescent to social adult. This symbolism of the poet as a type of Christ-figure is one which he will later apply to his father in 'Pig Island Letters 8', and ultimately to his Jerusalem-period self.

As well as the work of poets Baxter heard his father recite, in these early years Archie Baxter's own poetry was a powerful influence. One poem in particular, 'Spirits of Harmony, Music and Love' (*Spark* 544), opens upon 'the elemental chaos / When the worlds were in the making', but quickly moves to celebrate the emergence of order: 'And we sang as we saw the earth leap from the main / And the plan of Creation before us made plain.' It is a poem Baxter long approved of and returned to more than once as a model of mythic thought; in 1943 he described it as 'fine and beautiful' (*Spark* 292), and nearly twenty-five years on he lectured on its 'vatic and inspirational' mode, noting its relationship to Shelley's chorus in *Prometheus Unbound* (*Aspects* 8–9). It is certainly linked with Baxter's earliest attempt at incorporating myth into poetry, by describing chaos in 'Before the Creation', with a developing view of myth as a set of universal symbols suitable for discovering some form of order out of experience.

Narratives of order: Baxter's early mythic poems

But as with his father's poem, Baxter's early interest in mythology soon moved from a fascination with chaos to a focus on narratives of order. He began introducing figures from classical myth into his work—tentatively at first, as in the poem 'Enchanted Night', which borrows directly from 'Spirits of Harmony, Music and Love' to describe 'Spirits of the earth and air' swelling 'in one majestic chorus', before settling in 'the time when the old Gods hold / Their long-forgotten sway' and Pan's pipes flute 'faint and shrill [. . .] o'er the hill' (N1.66). Pan—the first named classical figure Baxter ever invokes—by embodying the traditional Romantic image of lost pastoralism, establishes a common Baxterian theme in which the natural world is at odds with debased and deracinated modernity.

The seeds of myth that Archie Baxter planted in his son's mind found fertile ground and swiftly took root. At fourteen Baxter inscribed in his second notebook three poems in sequence—'Song of Morning' (N2.84), 'Who hath not heard' (N2.85) and 'Sea Temple' (N2.86)—which hold the key to much of his later thought on myth.

The first of these three poems, 'Song of Morning', is a juvenile celebration of poetic inspiration as external and elevated; an early attempt to account for the experience of poetic creation, which Baxter would later describe as 'that voice inside my head—not in the head, the mind—that makes my poems for me' ('Further Notes on New Zealand Poetry', 4–5). Here the poem links poetic inspiration with natural fertility through the image of 'the archer of song' who 'Fleeteth his bolts from above', stirring not creation but recreation through a 'Song of the golden rebirth, / Song of the green-growing earth'. That the archer in Baxter's poetry is a recurring association with his father makes this poem his first attempt to cast Archie Baxter in a mythical role. Baxter later wrote in his copy of *Beyond the Palisade*, in reference to the archer in 'The Unicorn': 'father born under sign of Sagittarius—Archie' (Hocken 975/25). And in 'Rain-ploughs', a poem linked thematically to 'Song of Morning', an angel-Archer bears 'Fire-feathered arrow-thought to set new sun on flare [and] green again the land' (*CP* 26–27). Later still, Baxter acknowledges the Freudian significance of the 'father-archer' who 'kills or castrates the unicorn-child whose auto-erotic [. . .] rebellion involves a return [. . .] to his mother's womb' (*Spark* 539), although a more useful Freudian reading might involve the fertilising power of the phallic arrows of poetry restoring life to the maternal body of the land.

The second poem, 'Who hath not heard', inaugurates Baxter's habit of combining a Romantic mindset with personal mythic preoccupations. In this mode he generates numerous poems, characteristically setting a type of Romantic animism—which binds the more perceptive soul and intellect to natural beauty and by implication the production of art—in tension with contemporary insensitivity and lack of vision. His introduction of Triton shepherding a roving herd seaward, for example, links to Wordsworth's sonnet 'The world is too much with us', which regrets the '[l]ittle we see in nature that is ours' because 'for every thing, we are out of tune', and longs to 'hear old Triton blow his wreathed horn' (Wordsworth 237). Like Wordsworth, Baxter laments the things that cut most of us off from nature, save the sensitive soul who chooses alienation over domesticity and community:

[Who] hath not felt, in silence then,
The spirit beat against the bars
That bind it to the ways of men,
To earth and to the ancient Lars?

The speaker, who wants to see the old gods in nature, employs the Roman Lares ('Lars') negatively as emblems of household, domesticity and the marriage bond which, taken together, represent a prison of conformity. Set against this is a yearning for the woodland gods: 'He is a man who ne'er can find the way [. . .]

To where the woodland gods hold sway, / To where old Nature reigns anew / In all her pristine majesty'. It is a highly sentimental view of nature, which will wax and wane over a lifetime of verse, conflicting with, but never fully vanquished by, the other sense of nature as harsh, inimical and revealing in poems like 'The Mountains' (*CP* 8) and 'High Country Weather' (*CP* 34).

The third of these early sequential poems, 'Sea Temple', focuses on natural inspiration—the music of the waves—which helps the poet fall into an attitude from which poetry arises. This type of poetic inspiration is not the Apollonian strike of a fiery arrow released from on high, but a thing far more unsettling arising from the depths of the oceanic consciousness, that region of enticing kelp forests as sinuous and potentially deadly as gorgon hair. This is the poem where the importance of the sea—which in Baxter's poetry will grow in symbolic value and significance as a primary source of creative inspiration—is first made explicit. The eponymous temple may be classical, with columns, peristyle and fluted arches, but the rising smoke of a sacrifice—suggesting current and contemporary usage, and a fruitful combination of the classical and the present-day—lessens the sense of it being ancient. Even so, there is no sign of human presence; worship is implied but all the poet takes from the place is a spirit of inspiration. 'Sea Temple' does, however, link to a number of important later poems. For example, the sea wind, which 'murmured through the tiers / Of terraced columns', leaving within the poet's brain 'Some vision of the spirit-deep', anticipates the lines in 'The Unicorn' in which 'Sea-music moves [the unicorn/poet's] mind / To reverie on an enchanted ground' (*CP* 10). There is an even more specific connection to the 1963 poem 'The Waves', where the 'muffled chanting of the waves' of the early poem becomes, in a way which nicely epitomises the development of Baxter's poetic style, 'The slow language of the waves' (*CP* 287).

Shortly after completing these three poems, Baxter began developing an idiosyncratic hierarchy of mythic figures, in which heroic gods, demigods and men are steadily devalued in favour of non-conformist individuals, figures of alienation and isolation, and those with some fatal flaw. The ancient, animistic gods are still venerated, as in 'The Old Gods' (N2.112), which celebrates Pan, who never dies, 'Not while a green tree sways / Beneath a laughing sky'. Venus, too, is venerated in 'The Birth of Beauty', not, as she will soon be, as the embodiment of conflicted adolescent sexuality, but as a non-sexual emblem: 'As Venus shining from the silver sea-foam came, / So is the birth of beauty still the same' (N3.127). Shortly after Beauty's birth, a death occurs, this time of Apollo, the god of truth and light, whose lively demise in a roundel titled 'Apollo is Dead' symbolises the death of poetry in modern New Zealand. Baxter reworks the poem more optimistically some time later as 'Apollo but Sleeps' (N4.203):

> For Justice shall rise on the outermost steeps
> With the voice of a trumpet and countenance gleaming,
> While Freedom-in-Art to the battle-front leaps [. . .].

Despite the focus of these two poems, the days in which Baxter will use Apollo in the standard allegorical manner as figure of poetry and poetic inspiration are numbered, just as a Keatsian ode 'To Hermes' places a weight of symbolic meaning onto the god, who is then hardly mentioned again (N4.175).

This disregard for symbolic figures of reason and control seems to anticipate the adult Baxter's evolution into a Dionysian poet, at odds with, and temperamentally opposite to, such Apollonian New Zealand poets as Curnow and Brasch. What is more interesting about 'To Hermes' is that, in line with sea music moving his mind, Baxter here appears to see poetry as much more instinctive and dark and emanating from the unconscious as 'the fiery, fierce, intense / Flame of my inspiration'. His dual appeal to Hermes is to keep the flame of inspiration hot, but also to help him control the dreams 'of demons and of fierce affray' that rise from the unconscious at night to terrify him. It is notable that this juvenile appeal for easy slumber free of Ixion terrors—'let no dreams disturb me in that sleep! / For must the wheel of mind eternally / Revolve within the cavern of my soul?'—is reversed a few years later when Baxter discovers Jung and realises that demons and walking dead are creatures of the mind that might offer wisdom and insight to blunt the edge of terror (*MH* 127).

Baxter's most ambitious early mythological poem—over

seventy lines long—is 'The Gods of Greece' (1941, N3.157), which includes references to Zeus, Theseus, Bellerophon, Pluto, Tantalus, Poseidon, Bacchus, Apollo, Artemis, Aphrodite, Vulcan, Pallas Minerva, Hera and Pan. More than than just a mythological catalogue, though, it inaugurates a new mode of writing in which the Romantic ode, suffused with nostalgia for a lost primal experience of oneness with a numinous world, becomes tied up with his pacifist hatred of the modern world and the war. It is strongly influenced by Milton's ode 'On the Morning of Christ's Nativity', in which creation abases itself before the Christ child's glory, and the shepherds, who are associated with an older, animist world, little dream that Christ, 'the mighty Pan / Was kindly come to live with them below' (Milton 97–113). Milton celebrates the demise of pagan gods and the accession of Christ. By contrast Baxter's poem grieves for the old gods, most sadly Pan, who was the voice of poesy until Mars killed him. The poem, reflecting Baxter's bleak perspective on the early years of the war, concludes with a plaintive exhortation to the Grecian gods to 'return / Invest the broken urn / With vanished splendour as in ages past', and a plea to men to 'forsake / The evils of the sword / Revive the power of art' and 'with the written word / Conquer the realms of earth!' What most characterises Baxter's juvenile attitude to myth in this poem is its prevailing notion that poetry is of the old world, opposed to war and mechanised modernity.

The first figures of self

Up to this point in Baxter's poetic development, his use of myth, while not entirely trite and derivative, has recycled a conventional second-hand type of mythology inherited from the Romantics. But along with his stock gestures to Helicon, Parnassus and Pegasus, certain early poems give hints of the development of more original preoccupations, which anticipate ideas that will grow into elaborated symbols. The next major shift occurs in the poem 'Eurydice' (N6.345), which adopts the voice of Orpheus, so that for the first time the classical figure speaks directly. Orpheus, here embodying poetry, addresses Eurydice, who represents lost art and beauty. Although the things of nature listen to him, she 'in whom they found most perfect speech, / Most true and beauteous expression, / Art gone, art gone from me!' He resolves to descend into the underworld, risking everything in search of his muse.

Orpheus's acceptance of the dangers and solitude an artist must be prepared to face, redefining loneliness as solitary courage and loss as a 'precious stone' (*CP* 83), spoke to Baxter's sense of difference between himself and other people, helping him to value the 'distinctly painful' experiences of growing up for having created 'a gap in which the poems were able to grow'. His mother's memoir attempts to skewer this attitude as an adolescent pose of Byronic alienation:

> In his teens Jim read romantic books [. . .] about the sensitive artist having an unhappy childhood, with an insensible, stultifying family. Jim had to be a stranger in his family. What nonsense! [. . .] He admitted, when he was mature, that he had had a happy childhood—which was hard for him, because happy families destroy poets. He had to have an interesting tragic background, his own mythology. (M. Baxter, 143)

This literalist misreading, worthy of the daughter of Macmillan Brown the extreme rationalist, fails to recognise that Baxter's constant argument is with an 'insensible, stultifying' society—and only with his family to the extent that they are sometimes superficially employed to represent sections of such a society. The character of 'gross' and 'stolid' Daedalus, for example, in one of the key mythical poems of Baxter's early adolescence, 'Song of the Sea-Nymphs at the Death of Icarus' (*CP* 5), represents an insensitive and unimaginative patriarchy, not Baxter's own father. Nevertheless, aspects of Icarus are clearly biographical, making this tragic character the first of a number of mythical figures of the self to populate Baxter's poetry.

It is with this 1942 poem that Baxter first begins to identify in a sustained and serious manner with certain types of mythic figures whose qualities reflect his developing identity. This process of constructing mythical figures of the self, initiated at sixteen and continuing through his remaining lifetime of writing, is a habit of mind essential for an understanding of Baxter.

The early examples of such poems tend to be egocentric and

difficult to penetrate because of Baxter's dense symbolism, which is both a personal language and private evidence of distinctiveness and superiority over the mainstream herds. The 'alien Unicorn', for example, is the poet/self who walks 'steadfast and alone' while the herds 'return to fold as tame beasts would' (*CP* 10). Later poems of this genre move toward greater clarity, immediacy and first-person participation, demonstrating increasing levels of ironic self-knowledge; for example in Baxter's identification with the demigod Hercules, whose nigh-impossible tasks embody personal struggles, or with voyaging Odysseus, the successful warrior and consummate trickster who is reduced as both man and artist by domestic duty.

What makes an understanding of Baxter's early poetry featuring figures of the self valuable is that behind the mythic symbolism lie a series of edicts developed in adolescence that will inform Baxter's thought, writing and actions for the rest of his life: artists take risks; conformity stultifies; resist authority; be prepared to suffer for your beliefs; suspect mainstream approval; expect loneliness and solitude; embrace your dual nature; inhabit the threshold; never abandon your principles.

As he moved from writing derivative juvenile poetry to more original adolescent verse, Baxter also moved from seeing the source of his poetic inspiration as objective and external to seeing it as subjective and internal.[1] Throughout his juvenile, adolescent and early adult phases of poetic development, he uses polarities (tribe vs nation, man vs woman, old vs young, rich vs poor) to generate tensions that produce poetry. These polarities are alternately individual and universal, with the opposing poles being either himself and 'the status quo', or 'myself and other people' ('Education', *MH* 122–23). In Baxter's juvenile verse the locus of tension where poems come from may be externalised as, for example, a cave positioned between sea and sky producing the tension Baxter referred to as 'natural contemplation'—'the intense effort of *listening*' from which 'the words emerged' (*MH* 124); or perhaps as a garden, a human attempt to control nature, positioned between the city and the wilderness ('The Garden',

1 This paragraph incorporates material earlier published in *Spark to a Waiting Fuse.*

N2.89). In his adolescent phase, however, the locus of tension shifts from the external world to mythical figures of the self. The use of such figures indicates that Baxter discovered in adolescence that polarities can exist within one individual, and that the locus of tension that generates poetry—which, if personified in the juvenile phase, would have been externalised in such figures as 'my Muse'—may therefore be wholly internal. Once Baxter had arrived at this idea of the poetic self as a composite of opposites dwelling within in a state of perpetual poem-producing tension, he never abandoned it. And at the same time as we see him fastening on individual mythic figures to represent personal experience, we also discover the emergence of certain mythological types, such as 'gross Daedalus', as representative of sections of society.

The figure of Icarus in 'Song of the Sea-Nymphs' is only imperfectly a figure of the self in the sense that it refers to Baxter the young poet. In 1942 Baxter's estimate of his own worth as a writer was high, even though he was unpublished. Doubtless he mentally exempted himself later when arguing that the 'archetype that best expresses the situation of New Zealand poets is [. . .] Icarus' who signifies 'the minor talent determined to be major' (*Aspects* 7). At the same time he aligns himself with two Modernist poets who had written poems about Icarus: Stephen Spender and W. H. Auden. In keeping with Baxter's pacifism, Spender's 'Icarus' embodies the folly of conflict, by attempting 'War on the sun' (Spender 11). Auden, in 'Musée des Beaux Arts', focuses on the indifferent ploughman, who turns away from Icarus's death because 'it was not an important failure' (Auden, *Another Time* 34), just as pragmatically as Baxter's 'stolid Daedalus / Flew onward to the far Sicilian town.' Thus Baxter's Icarus, in this time of global hostilities, most obviously represents a modernist regret for youthful lives destroyed by war rather than a youthful poet overreaching himself.

Lament ye for young Icarus,
    Lament again!
    For he is youth
Forever living and forever slain.

The personal symbolism in the poem is more obscure. In respect of the father/son relationship, for the reasons discussed above, Archie Baxter cannot be gross Daedalus. He is conceivably the sun, however, given the early poems where poetic inspiration comes from Apollo, and others in which the archer-figure is explicitly linked to the sun god. In this context the fall of Icarus/ the poet into the sea—representing both the unconscious and poetry—for flying too close to the sun, is a necessary death if Icarus is to become the tragic figure of myth and the poet is to enter into the world of adult knowledge. The sun must cause the death of Icarus much as the archer in 'The Unicorn' must slay the fabulous creature if the adolescent poet is to enter the 'iron wood' of sexuality and mature, individual poetic expression.

Baxter's developing identification with mythic figures sharpens in two poems focusing on Titans, those pre-Olympian deities integral in the creation of earth and humanity, who are sentenced to perpetual punishment for resisting Zeus's new order and who, importantly for Baxter's later verse, play key roles in the myths of Hercules (see chapter 5). In the first poem, 'Atlas' (N7.430), another anti-war poem, the eponymous Titan is conspicuously absent until the final stanza: 'In the same orchard steel and oaken still / Where Time's first dream dissolved to adamant rhyme / Atlas lost heart and will.' The classical orchard is the Garden of the Hesperides, home of the golden apples, and its biblical counterpart is Eden, but in this poem the orchard also signifies the natural and social worlds laid waste by mechanised conflict: 'Death dons the cloak of dawn on these / Metallic seas of magma.' The connection between the poet and Atlas is initially unclear because the 'I' of the poem is a loner reluctantly drawn into the consuming conflict: 'Unreckoning the mortal ants await. / And I am of them! by the bitter gate / Of fire and metal also I await.' Only in a footnote to the manuscript version of the poem does Baxter make an explicit link between the Titan and the poet through the symbolism of shared humanity and a collective responsibility for the future, with Atlas representing 'Man bearing human destiny on his shoulders'.

The iceflower of art: Prometheus

While Atlas represents collective humanity rather than any specific individual, Prometheus, his brother, figures powerfully and repeatedly in Baxter's writing as one of the central mythic figures of the self and, by extension, the Romantic artist. Baxter's central interest is with the elements of fire and ice in the Prometheus myth: how the Titan enraged Zeus by stealing fire from Olympus in a hollow stalk and giving it to humans; how, in punishment, he was chained to a rock in the Caucasus mountains, where a giant bird daily claws his side and consumes his liver, which then grows back during the night; and how his blood splashing onto the snow grows into the magical iceflower.[2]

While these aspects of the Prometheus myth exemplify tensions between organised, dehumanising society (represented by authoritarian Zeus) and human aspiration and solitary suffering (represented by the liberator Titan), such tensions also represent what Baxter had come to see as part of the process, and much of the price, of artistic creation. When Baxter identifies 'the Titan Prometheus, from whose wound grows the iceflower of art' as one of his first adolescent figures of the self (*Spark* 536), he equates the Titan's torture with his own suffering for poetry. In his first 'Prometheus' poem (1943, *Spark* 183), the Titan/poet is chained on the cusp of adolescence, torn by sexual desires which he cannot fulfil (enduring without the 'love of lover'). In contrast to childhood, where the present seems an eternal perfect moment, the adolescent discovers himself chained like Prometheus to a present 'both moving and still' which—sexual desire and the generative urge remind him—is inexorably moving towards death: Prometheus is mourning the memory of a lost Edenic childhood ('the bleak mnemonic crows perch on my liver'), and dismayed by a tormenting future ('soldier-ants advance [. . .] on the white marble of futurity').

2 While it still seems plausible that 'the idea of Prometheus, the creator of rude human figures out of chthonian mud, [. . .] appealed, as an analogue, to Baxter's idea of himself as the creator of poems out of the chaotic clay of the unconscious' (Millar, *Spark* 103), our survey of Prometheus references finds no mention in Baxter's writing of the Titan creating humans out of clay.

The potency of these associations for Baxter is demonstrated in the way the key themes are repeated in the following years. His second 'Prometheus' poem (1945, *Spark* 416–18, shorter version *CP* 35) identifies the Titan/poet 'bleeding on the cross of time' with Christ. But from a two-year advantage, Baxter also sympathises with his younger self, exhorting the tormented boy to 'raise your eyes where the great waters flow / And breathe and hear night's cloudy torrent chime / From those immortal citadels of snow.'

Repeatedly in later years Baxter returns to the image of Prometheus in looking back on his adolescent experience. 'Autumn Waking' (1948, *CP* 69), for example, imaginatively recreates the miasma of the experience, contrasting that 'black swamp where I have lain among / Serpents, or chained to the Caucasian rock' with the timeless Edenic experience of childhood. 'Recollection' (c.1951, N16.35) recalls both sympathetically and mockingly 'That paranoid Prometheus, blinded, bound / On time's rock', who each day conjured from 'semen-smelling sheets a new despair'. Much later, in 'At Day's Bay' (1965, *CP* 308–09), he associates Narcissus and Prometheus: 'I think of / adolescence: that sad boy / I was, thoughts crusted with ice / on the treadmill of self-love, // Narcissus damned, who yet brought / like a coal in a hollow / stalk, the seed of fire that runs / through my veins now.' His mature judgement on the adolescent Prometheus poems comes in 'Notes on the Education of a New Zealand Poet' (*MH* 126): 'The words [. . .] say only that life is an arid secular crucifixion between a tormenting past and a stonelike future; it isn't quite enough to make a poem out of. [. . .] I had no tools to deal with the central anguish of a child hurled into the adolescent abyss, at the mercy of his imagination and the impulses of his body.'

In late adolescence a new image of Prometheus had made its first brief appearance when the rocks around a bay, evidently but not explicitly Brighton, are seen as 'mutilated / titans [. . .] Promethean / limbs by the sea-vultures / shadowed' ('Seascape', 1944, N13.826). Compelling evidence of the centrality of certain types of myth in Baxter's thought and writing is provided by his return to this image in a series of poems from the mid 1960s: 'Letter to Papua I' (c.1966, N26.65), 'The Titan' (1963–66, *CP* 372), 'Words to Lay a Strong Ghost (after Catullus)' 12 (1966, *CP* 356). The trials of adolescence that connected Baxter to Prometheus in the first place—'Calamity, time, deeply thwarted desire'—revisit the forty-year-old poet in midlife crisis, bringing him 'again to the place of the dark Titan'. Brighton bay, surrounded by 'Limbs of Promethean rock', is the place from which the older poet 'must make a journey' as it is 'that first place / where life and death contend like / wave and counter-wave.' The adolescent Baxter, fixed to time, endured a solitary suffering. The mature Baxter understands adolescent solitude to be an inevitable consequence of that phase, and values now the common condition as a link to past generations. In 'The Titan', Prometheus is seen as a culture hero, who 'brought / The fire of Zeus to us, // Lightening our chaos. For many aeons / Hour by hour the sea vulture / Has been tearing at his guts. We had / All but forgotten his pain and his gift.' In 'Notes on the Education of a New Zealand Poet' (*MH* 154) Baxter interprets this Prometheus as the 'principle of the rebellious energy in man that enlarges our order by breaking it and allowing it to re-form in another pattern—an energy that our way of life dismembers and disregards. It is necessary to honour him.' Hence his approval of the girl in the 'Ballad of the Runaway Mother' (c.1964, N24.63), who is impelled to save and keep her child by that Christ-like Prometheus which 'groans in us / Who will not drowse in any bed / Or make his peace with what is not.'

A much less positive view of Prometheus's gift to mankind, as a dehumanising rationalism, is suggested in another adolescent poem, 'Poem to Hoelderlin' (c.1947, N14.1014), which sees humankind cut off from the natural world by rational thought and material deed: 'Earth that was once our mother, shall we find / Again our infant peace? Your breasts are barren for / A mind at war. The eyes are blind / That look too long upon Promethean fire.' This critical view of Prometheus, which discounts the Titan as an adolescent figure of the self, is subsequently developed primarily in Baxter's prose. In 'Choice of Belief in Modern Society' (1952) he contrasts the 'genuine' artist's engagement with Prometheus—as a symbol of 'man chained to his Caucasian rock of suffering and isolation, and groping for self-understanding'—with a modern rationalistic and technological reading of the myth, which can 'conveniently symbolise the advent of modern science, and that popular belief which has accompanied it—that by biology, psychology, and science or -ism, man can master his remorse, banish his bad dreams, and to put it bluntly—be happy without being good.' Baxter associates this 'Promethean' myth with the Faustian one: 'the dilemma of the modern Faust, whose magical discoveries presuppose a new pact with the power of death' (*Aspects* 27). In 'The Criticism of Poetry' (*FA* 28–29), Baxter cites a parable in which Prometheus is 'the technician or political man who manipulates the world of things to his own advantage. Orpheus is the poet, able to be bribed, but well aware that if he gives his audience the poems they ask for, he will forfeit his gift.' Prometheus's punishment is extreme boredom, which he continually asks Orpheus to dispel; when Orpheus refuses to play the song Prometheus requests, he is sacked as court poet.

The same satirical attitude to Prometheus occurs in the play *The Bureaucrat* (1967, *CPlays* 161–89), Baxter's adaptation or parody of the pseudo-Aeschylean *Prometheus Bound*. The name of Baxter's hero, Fireman, ironically suggests his role as a quencher rather than kindler of the sacred fire. According to Baxter's programme note, he is 'a modern Prometheus chained to a desk instead of a rock, under the disastrous impression that the advance of technology, science and education is going to make human lives more meaningful, even though it has evidently made his own life more meaningless' (*CPlays* 336). In *The Temptations of Oedipus* (1968, *CPlays* 229–91), references to the cult of Prometheus the Fire-Bringer (taken over from Sophocles) suggest an identification of the technocratic ruler Theseus as a Promethean figure in this sense (234, 235).

A world-embracing solitude: the unicorn, Narcissus and Janus

The complex use Baxter made of Prometheus—the evolving connotations attached to a single mythic figure—was not some effort of adolescence that he matured out of, but an essential practice of involving idiosyncratic figures from classical myth in a lifelong production of intricate, relatively consistent structures of meaning. The key argument of this chapter is that the profound changes occurring in Baxter's life, thought and poetry during adolescence were the catalyst for a process which began around 1941, when

> at fifteen a world thundered without,
> Strange pebbles laid at the feet; but girded about
> With a world-embracing solitude there stood
> Narcissus, master of the iron wood.
>
> ('Autobiographical', N10.634)

The references here to Narcissus and the 'iron wood' look marginally ahead in time to the writing of 'The Unicorn' (1942, *CP* 10–11), which Baxter would identify in the 1960s as his most complete representation of the claustrophobic 'iron dream' of adolescence. He described its composition by

> a precocious boy of sixteen. A quiet lad, who lived too much in his own head; a constant beach-walker and word-builder, with the makings of a drunkard or intelligent schizophrene. The torments of the adolescent furnace are threefold: unnatural solitude, ignorance of life, and sexuality without love.
>
> (*Spark* 536)

Baxter's unicorn represents 'the soul of a man-to-be [who] wakens at puberty when the torments of the flesh begin and he is isolated for good from the fraternal universe of childhood'. But the poem's particular concern is with the effects of hybridity and solitude on an adolescent who is also an artist:

> Because poetry is conceived in the order of natural contemplation, it requires an interior solitude as its element. But the unicorn exists in a double solitude—a natural contemplative solitude, resonant with the correspondences of nature, and the terrible solitude of the boy himself, a child becoming a man and regarding himself as a monster.

Two ambivalent figures help the unicorn/poet survive adolescence and escape its aridity. The first is the Archer—symbol of Baxter's own father—whose actions in slaying the creature exemplify the type of paradox Baxter's poetry embraces: 'hound and Archer are secretly welcome to the unicorn, who knows that he must die for the adolescent to become a man' (538). The second figure is Venus/Aphrodite. In the early poem 'The Birth of Beauty' (c.1941, N3.132), Venus, rising from the sea foam, represents not the growth of sexual awareness so much as an abstract Romantic ideal about the conditions for writing beautiful verse: 'But new-born images to beauteous life / Can only rise if in the poet's brain / A calm tranquillity in quiet repose doth reign.' By contrast, the Aphrodite of 'The Unicorn' is not an abstract figure of beauty but the fully formed locus of desire moving the adolescent into adulthood. As Baxter put it, 'a prophetic intuition [. . .] enabled the boy to see beyond the furnace an image of cold waves breaking and the figure of the sea-born Venus' (539):

> O perilous unicorn!
> Death slays thee not—but see
> From the cold surf's futurity
> Aphrodite Anadyamone [*sic*]
> Arise in birth thou would'st extinction deem:
> Arise and bind thee to an iron dream. (*CP* 11)

Baxter goes on to suggest that Venus clasping 'the chains of manhood on [the adolescent's] limbs [. . .] is perhaps the true death of the unicorn, by the attachments that remove solitude, give human knowledge, and mercifully crucify [. . .] our passions' (539).

Given that 'sea-music'—Baxter's synonym for poetic inspiration—moves the unicorn's mind, it is relevant to note that one further aspect of the birth of Venus, which bears in important ways on Baxter's future poetry, has to do with the medium from which she emerges. The sea which produces the goddess is the same sea—deeply symbolic of the unconscious—that the adult Baxter will set sail on as the voyaging Odysseus/Ulysses figure, in search of the unattainable ideal which will see Venus evolve from young and desirable to aging and sad.

In the two years after Baxter's writing of 'The Unicorn' further mythical figures of the self appear as his poetry matures and develops originality, and his sense of vocation solidifies.

In 'Where nets of time encircle and destroy', for example, the figure of the poet navigates between life and death as Charon, the 'careless helmsman' who 'steers between / Shoals where yet lurk Scylla of cynic wit, / Charybdis of sweet sentiment' (*Spark* 286). The mythic salamander, which Aristotle asserted 'cannot be burnt' and 'puts the fire out by crawling through it' (Aristotle 5.19), becomes another figure of the self, for whom the sustaining fire of poetry is also a sentence of solitude. The salamander cannot survive in society—only the fire of poetry sustains it, but the cost is a 'cloistered meditation in clear flame' and grief because it 'has no mate' (*Spark* 241). In a number of poems from Baxter's late teens, Narcissus also features as a figure of the adolescent self, although this image is most fully developed in the late poem 'At Day's Bay' (1965, *CP* 308–09) in which Narcissus doubles as both the tormented adolescent and the (necessarily) self-absorbed artist.

The process by which certain mythological figures came to represent Baxter's adolescent efforts to 'mythologise' his own experience culminates appropriately in the figure of Janus, the Roman god of doorways—and hence of beginnings and transitions—who is depicted with two faces, one looking backwards and one forwards. Baxter's Janus represents the mediated self: on the one hand the individual enticed by the past—which is idealised as a mythical and Edenic childhood—and by the seductions of inwardness, where the mind can contemplate, write poetry, and have no allegiance to a social, human-constructed world; on the other hand, an individual who recognises that there is a world out there, and that he needs to participate in it or become a recluse and hermit. Related to this discovery, Baxter's Janus-self must choose—and choice is the key—between being a New Zealand poet or a transplanted British poet. Janus first appears as a figure of the self in 'Of Future Serenity' (1944, N9.537), associated with the transition from adolescence to adulthood, and from pastoral to political verse: 'The sallow Janus of my manhood year / will not sing of crisp leaves, thrushes' nests, / nor sleep on the floor of a snow-line hut.' But this poem is negligible alongside the strenuous 426 lines of 'Janus Unheard' (1944, *Spark* 457–67), in which Baxter attempts a contextual geopolitical survey of the contemporary world, combined with a fully realised self-analysis, incorporating his philosophy of art and manifesto for adulthood. To achieve personal and poetic maturity, rejection of the Romantic animism of adolescence is an immediate necessity:

> And I must rear again
> My Janus-head out of a country coma
> Of pastoral falsity, of rain on leaves;
> Hear history's abstract music thunder
> Her breves and semibreves. (457)

Although solitude remains the anticipated condition, the poet expects that a strong sense of self-worth and inner integrity will provide him with armour against the pain of social ostracism:

> I can endure
> the civic threat, the public hate
> Self-approbation remaining
> enwhorlèd, secure. (466)

Crucially, Baxter's prescription for salvation in a world intent on killing is poetry: 'The personal insight, the poet's vision / Would save them then . . . will save them still' (467).

Janus receives one further mention of significance in 'Crossing Cook Strait' (1947–56, *CP* 159–60): 'In the dark bows, facing the flat sea, / Stood one I had not expected, yet knew without surprise / As the Janus made formidable by loveless years.' While this Janus identifies himself with leftist politics embodied by 'Seddon and Savage, the socialist father', he is more familiar to the poet's heavy-drinking 1940s self: 'You have known me only in my mask of Dionysus.' The symbolism surrounding Janus in this poem remains associated with the end of isolated individualism and the transition to social adult. Significantly, the encounter takes place at sea while travelling between New Zealand's two main islands, with the South Island representing childhood and the North Island representing adult social engagement. The poet comes on deck hoping to encounter Venus, wishing a return to the first flush of adolescent desire. Instead he is brought short by an encounter with political reality, and a social rather than personal or sexual engagement with life.

Conclusion: 'I must Create a System'

Even in childhood and adolescence, James K. Baxter never employed classical myth simply in an academic or canonical fashion; mythic figures embodying some classical ideal were of little interest to him and classical heroes were treated with mounting scepticism. But classical myth, which Baxter linked to a primitive tribal view of a world experienced with the guts rather than the intellect, was central to his poetry from the outset. In myth, as in life, his identification was with rebels and outsiders, and always the mythic figures of most importance were imbued with distinct private meaning. It is worth recalling, in this context, that one of the young Baxter's great passions was the poetry of William Blake, that most marginalised of the Romantics, whose entire corpus represents a sustained attempt at personal myth-making. Baxter once remarked in a letter to Ginn that having reread Blake in the light of criticism of him he could find 'no trace of madness but only the workings of a clear, strong, imaginative mind and faculty [. . .] of poetic expression rarely equalled' (*Spark* 106). In important respects Baxter's own myth-making—with its consistent themes and messages, and transformational cultural politics—embodies the Blakean principle, 'I must Create a System, or be enslav'd by another Man's' (*Jerusalem* 10.20, Blake 435). There is a point in Baxter's adolescence when his poetry moves beyond imitation to begin displaying a unique personal language of and about the self. It is at this point of self-creation that the lifelong practice of employing highly original mythological figures to represent experience originates. The contention of this chapter is that, to fully understand Baxter's work, one must see the connection between the heavily symbolic adolescent myth poetry and (for instance) a poem that comes near to being Baxter's last, 'The Tiredness of Me and Herakles'. In adulthood Baxter no more eschewed myth than he eschewed adolescence, and before we dismiss the mythic elements in his poetry as hardly worth consideration we should recall Baxter's comments on the importance of his formative teenage years:

the man I see in the shaving mirror [. . .] has come a good way and knows less than when he began. The most dangerous time for him is the day he first uses the word 'adolescent' to describe the things he does not like; when he rejects one half of his universe to make the other half safe. ('Outlook for Poetry', *NZPY* 1955)

CHAPTER 3

VENUS IS RISING—OR IS SHE?[1]

> It seems likeliest that I will be in Jerusalem at the latest by mid-February—leaving 4 generations of women-folk, my mother, my wife, Hilary and Stephanie—groaning behind me, and there will settle down and try to live on nothing. Whether or not you come up there to stay, come anyway to see me and bring the plaque of Our Lady with you [. . .].
>
> (18 Dec 1968; Olds 6)

Baxter's letter to Peter Olds brings into unconsciously ironic juxtaposition two aspects of his difficult and contradictory view of women. A reverence for the idealised feminine principle embodied in the figure of 'Our Lady' (see e.g. *FC* 12–16) goes along with deeply fraught relationships with the actual women in his life, embodied here in the four 'groaning' generations of mother, wife, daughter and granddaughter, whom he is thankfully escaping as he sets off on his journey to Jerusalem. McKay's biography, though discreet, supplies abundant evidence of Baxter's at times difficult relationship with his domineering mother, his various sexual liaisons as both a young and a mature man, and the often stormy or bitter (though fundamentally loving) quality of his marriage to Jacquie. Not surprisingly, the treatment of women in his poetry has often been seen as problematic—'which,' Dougal McNeill remarked in a recent review of the *Selected Poems*, 'is an academic and coy way of saying appalling' (McNeill 4).

Undeniably, Baxter approaches women from an almost exclusively male perspective. They are seen in terms of their real or symbolic relationships to men, as mothers, lovers, wives,

1 A much abbreviated version of the material in this chapter can be found in Davidson, 'Venus/Aphrodite and James K. Baxter', in Wilkinson et al.

muses, temptresses, hags; it is very rare for Baxter to consider female experience for its own sake or attempt to get inside the mind of a female subject.[2] There is an uncomfortable truth in his wry confession that only middle age and the waning of the sexual drive had enabled him 'to make the shattering discovery that women also are people' (*FC* 170). Moreover, he casts the feminine in starkly binary terms, repeatedly contrasting the good with the evil, the beautiful with the ugly, the sacred with the mundane—virgin vs temptress, Venus vs Medusa, Our Lady vs the groaning womenfolk of his family. In a revealing passage in a letter (FM 27/1/8) he attempts to account for the fluctuations in his feelings towards Jacquie, and can do so only by representing her as a compound of two different women, the biblical sisters Rachel and Leah: 'Most men stomach Leah for the sake of Rachel. Rachel and Leah in the same woman. I could ask nothing better than J's Rachel—you would need to go into Greek mythology to describe the full force of her Leah side; for seven years or more I just couldn't take it.'[3]

Kai Jensen has sought to explain, and to some extent excuse, these 'problematic' features by severing the link between the actual women in Baxter's life and the female figures in his poetry. He rejects as naïve (*Whole Men* 144–45) the approach of a biographical critic like W. H. Oliver, who suggested in his 1983 'portrait' that Baxter's view of women was fundamentally shaped by his early, traumatic affair with Jane Aylward.[4] 'As Baxter dwelt on these experiences,' Oliver argued (43), 'he was led to a view of sex which linked it inextricably with death. [. . .] Woman became the temptress, the bitch-goddess, the destroyer of men—and memory and imagination populated his pages with Circe-

2 'Thoughts of a Remuera Housewife' (*CP* 314–15) is perhaps one of the rare exceptions.

3 In Genesis 29, Jacob agrees to work for his uncle Laban for seven years to win the hand of Laban's younger daughter Rachel. At the end of the seven years Laban tricks Jacob into marrying the elder daughter Leah instead, and requires him to work another seven years to win Rachel as a second wife. Understandably, the three-way marriage is a troubled one.

4 On the Jane Aylward affair see McKay 95–97 and Oliver 40–43. (McKay mistakenly calls her 'Aylmer', an error corrected by Pearson 46–47; see also Millar, *No Fretful Sleeper*, 99–100).

like figures.' Jensen proposes instead that Baxter's female figures are not representations of real women but aspects of the Jungian anima, personifications of aspects of the (male) psyche. Such a reading makes Baxter's sexual stereotyping and misogyny appear more palatable; but it is arguable that Jensen also oversimplifies the intimate connection in Baxter's world view between the realist and the symbolic. Baxter's affair with Jane Aylward coincided with his reading of Jung and was closely followed by his move to Christchurch to begin Jungian psychoanalysis. It is not at all surprising that, in this period of intense emotional and artistic self-shaping, he should have come to see Jane as an embodiment of the anima, and developed the habit of reading both this and future relationships in Jungian symbolic terms.

However deep its roots in his personal psychology and experience, Baxter's treatment of women in his poetry does lend itself to Jungian interpretation. Baxter himself, in a crucial passage from 'The Man on the Horse' already cited in chapter 1, draws attention to the concept of the anima, the archetypal figure of the feminine sited deep in the male unconscious, which 'changes shape according to the motives of those who approach her—a violent man will see her as a wolf; a sensual man, as a temptress; a Puritan, either not at all, or as a poisonous reptile; a saint, as a helpless child who needs to be looked after; a poet, as his difficult Muse' (*MH* 117–18). The anima is not a woman but an aspect of the male mind; it is femaleness as perceived by the male, and its forms are therefore shifting and prone to sexual stereotyping and binary oppositions.

In the same passage Baxter 'goes into Greek mythology', noting that the anima 'has been called variously Venus, Cybele, Artemis—but in Burns's case, one could say definitely, Hekate, patroness of witches, the goddess of the underworld' (*MH* 116). It is worth noting the startling range of the figures here heaped together: Venus, goddess of love and beauty; Cybele, earth mother and emasculating lover; Artemis, chaste moon-maiden and fierce huntress; and the witch-queen Hekate—all seen as avatars of a single divine archetype. Maternity, beauty, erotic love and sexual torment, chastity, fertility, death, are all tied together in Baxter's conception of the feminine, and all inextricably linked with poetic creativity, embodied in the figure of the Muse.

To try to disentangle the various strands in this conception is extraordinarily difficult. In this chapter and the next we shall attempt to do so by laying down a continuum from Baxter's most appealing and benign to his most fearsome female figures. Inevitably, though, the continuum will tend to turn into a circle, since the apparently benign figures can turn terrifying, while the most terrifying figures (such as the Furies and the Gorgon) can paradoxically be seen as benign. Chapter 4 will focus on the dark and infernal end of the continuum; this chapter, however, will begin with the beautiful and explicitly sexual aspect of the female as symbolised by the Roman goddess Venus and her Greek equivalent Aphrodite.

Star, mother, lover and destroyer

Given that the Venus/Aphrodite figure can never be isolated from the wider context in which she is embedded, there is a further complication. Venus may be the planet, sometimes seen as the morning or evening star, and this in turn is often seen as the *stella maris* or star of the sea, symbolising the Virgin Mary. The sexual beauty of the pagan Venus may be distinguished from the spiritual beauty of the Virgin, as in the opening sequence of 'Traveller's Litany' (1954, CP 139–45):

> Waste sea and dark dawn.
> And over the bow-wash rising
> the yoked immediate birds, black-backed gulls
> her servants
> who is younger than the Cytherean.
>
> It is not proper a foul-minded man
> should praise the Queen of Heaven
> but who, Lady, in these lands will sing you
> outside the ordered liturgy? (139)

But they may also be merged with each other. At the start of 'In Fires of No Return' (1956, *CP* 165–66), for example, the poet climbs 'Barney's pulpit rock': 'To wave and bird I open wide /

The bible of my rimrock days, / [. . .] To Venus' holy star who smiles / Upon the lives she cannot save.' The poem ends on a rather different note: 'Among night dunes the moony lovers / In lupin shade far and near / Twined under Venus' carnal star[5] / Mock the power of the prince of the air. / Their doomed flesh answers an undying summer.' Beneficence of a sort has given way to erotic passion which brings death in its train, a connection which we shall investigate further below. The concept of simultaneously operative spiritual and carnal aspects of the planet Venus is similar to the double aspect of the Rapunzel figure, for example, made clear by Baxter's own annotation of a published copy of 'Traveller's Litany': 'Rapunzel in her holy aspect is the Virgin and the ladder of her hair is grace; in her delusive aspect the *femme fatale*' (*CP* 626).

An early poem which illustrates well another complication with respect to the Venus figure, while at the same time offering insight into the young Baxter's approach to mythology in general, is 'Aeneas' (*CS* 3; *Spark* 454–55). Baxter refers to it in a letter to Ginn (25 February 1944, *Spark* 331–33), justifying his flexible handling of mythology in another poem, 'Me Also': 'Don't think my mythology is out. I know Ulysses wasn't changed into a swine, at any rate not literally. But I've changed the picture, humanized or de-humanized it a bit as I always do, as I did in Aeneas—"for Venus was the mother in his mind . . ."' (*Spark* 332–33). For the purposes of this discussion, the poem is worth quoting in full, even though Baxter confessed in another letter to Ginn that 'AENEAS although of clear-cut structure, does not satisfy me' (2 October 1943, *Spark* 266).

Aeneas, the astute and priggish, driven
By half-loved duty on the seas of fame
Longed to forsake that fate but faltered, craven,
Fearing the wrath of gods or the after-shame.

5 Cf. a passage from 'The Rock-Born Stream', written in the same year 1956 (*CP* 167): 'Venus that ardent planet shone / As she did years ago. // A voice rang in the branches, / "How shall your coarsened heart / And tired body find again / The grove of love and art?"' The force of passion still manifests itself, it seems, but advancing age makes the marriage of sensuality and poetry more difficult to consummate.

Aged Anchises on his shoulder borne
From the red ashes of a broken city . . .
'The shrunken child; his godhead cannot return.'
No reins but those of pity and self-pity.

But Venus was the mother in his mind
Who could not age; thus he could not forsake her
Like elder whores grown wearisome and blind.
Italy she, and the shoreward groaning breaker.

Yet once with Dido in the storm-hid cave
Found himself, unclothed by destiny;
Knew he'd not won but lost when the harbour gave
To an inhuman unrepentant sea.

Aeneas is evidently another figure of self, used to represent the transition from adolescence to adulthood (see *Spark* 114). What is more relevant here, however, is the Venus figure and Aeneas's relationship with her. In the myth, most famously recorded in Virgil's *Aeneid*, the goddess is the divine mother of the Trojan hero who helps him on his destined journey to a new home in Italy. Ironically, though, Venus is also responsible for a dangerous interruption to the journey since, fearing the machinations of Juno, she engenders a love between Aeneas and Dido, queen of Carthage, the city where Aeneas is driven by a storm at sea, the city loved above all by Juno, sworn enemy of the Trojans. The last stanza of Baxter's poem alludes to the mating of Dido and Aeneas in the cave in which they sought shelter from a storm during a hunting expedition. This was ultimately to lead to tragedy for Dido.

Venus in Baxter's poem is thus both the protective mother figure whose beauty is ageless, and the unseen initiator of that sexual union which will threaten to strike at the very heart of Aeneas's mission in life. Moreover, Dido is in a sense also the human manifestation of Venus herself, the Freudian subtext being uncomfortably close to the surface. If we apply this to Baxter's own personal development, we appear to have the classic tension between a mother who presides over the comparative 'safety' of boyhood leading into adolescence, and who continues to retain a maternal hold, and a sexual figure who is in fact another aspect or extension of the mother figure who beckons him to the nakedness of adulthood and ultimate death. The concept of Venus as 'the mother in his mind' also hints at the idea of a 'female' source or birthing place of the poetry which expresses the angst of developing maturity.

Another important reference in this poem is to Aeneas's famous act of filial *pietas* in carrying his aged father Anchises on his shoulders away to safety from the burning city of Troy. A later version of the poem (N15.46), along with making some minor changes of wording, rewrites the last two lines of the second stanza, as follows: '(Mate of a goddess once—that hour cannot return / But leaves the rack of pity and self-pity.)'. This clarifies a reference to the incident described in the so-called Homeric *Hymn to Aphrodite* in which the goddess claims to be a mortal woman and thus tricks the humble herdsman Anchises into making love to her in his hut on Mount Ida near Troy. When she afterwards reveals her true identity, Anchises is terrified, since disaster of one kind or another always strikes a mortal man who has slept with a goddess. Aphrodite, however, reassures him and predicts the birth of Aeneas as a result of their encounter.

Although it is not explicit in this particular poem, Baxter clearly absorbed into his consciousness a version of the myth, alluded to by Anchises himself in Virgil's *Aeneid*, in which the mortal man broke his promise to Aphrodite/Venus to keep their liaison secret and was therefore blasted and crippled by a thunderbolt from Zeus/Jupiter. In the Homeric Hymn the goddess warns Anchises of just such a consequence of any violation of confidentiality. She also explains why she will not request immortality for her mortal lover, citing the tragic story of Tithonus who *was* granted immortality but not eternal youth. Baxter comes up with a kind of amalgam of these two stories, while following the Anchises storyline as such, in the course of a semi-autobiographical story which comprises a part of 'Notes on the Education of a New Zealand Poet':

> With high forehead and full mouth, with doves about her feet, small-breasted and wide-thighed, her hair a bright cloud at her shoulders, Venus trod swiftly over the wooded slopes on yielding

> air. The blind earth kindled. Bull and heifer, stag and hind, all beasts and birds coupled in her path, each according to its species, so strong was the influence of the goddess. To the hut of Anchises she came, entering to the fume of woodsmoke, and lay that night in his arms on a rough sheepskin. There the Trojan shepherd drank from her embracing limbs the medicine of immortality, bitter to men. For he grew old, chewing the cud of knowledge, and when he wished for death the earth barred its gates against him. But she lived on, without remorse, for her nature was not subject to decay. ('Education' 144)

From Baxter's perspective, an encounter with Venus leads inevitably to disaster, and he clearly found the Anchises myth to be the most graphic way of illustrating this.[6]

Baxter's engagement with the Venus/Anchises story in his second Dunedin period can also be seen in an unpublished sestina entitled 'The Climber' (1967, N28.9). The poem follows closely on two other sestinas, each entitled 'Thinking About Mountains', which contain meditations on nature, the human soul, ageing and death, including a reference in the first sestina to a friend who had been killed in the mountains at the age of eighteen. 'The Climber' is a reflection on the fall and death of the title figure, concentrating on a dream which he is imagined as having had in his hut on the night before his death. The first stanza finds him putting on his climbing gear, having already 'climbed from a racking dream / in which he saw but could not grasp a woman / with limbs like a waterfall'. The dream itself is treated in more detail in the third stanza, with some spillover into the fourth:

> The darkly recurrent and improbable dream
> By which the heart is nailed to its own folly,
> Believing the earth could take the shape of a woman
> (As if some cosmic engine shifted a gear)
> And Venus enter dull Anchises' hut,
> He in the sweat and stink of selfhood lying
>
> And she bend over him so fetid lying

6 The 'fume of woodsmoke' echoes 'Charm for Hilary' (1949, *CP* 83), Baxter's invocation over his infant daughter; in the light of this later passage, 'Fume of woodsmoke leave thee / Whole' implies a prayer that she survive the torments of adult sexual desire.

And say—'See, I have come'—the common dream
Of boys and louts . . .

The introduction of the myth emphasises the idea of the ordinary man encountering in his fantasy an image of the goddess.

The word 'folly' is used seven times in the poem, traversing a wide area including human aspiration in general (and, by implication, mountain-climbing as a specific symbol of this) and the male sex-drive. Emphasis on the 'bare hut' with its 'foul blankets' draws attention to a reality starkly contrasted with the vision of the goddess. The climber is described as 'wisely' leaving the hut for the next stage of his climb and forgetting the dream, being 'rubbed clean of human folly / By the fingers of the mist that gripped his gear, / His head, his thighs, more closely than a woman'. However, the danger inherent in the mist leads immediately to the thought that the mist 'had in part the nature of a woman / When she has set aside both truth and lying / to grip the naked heart'.

The climber falls to his death, having found 'no dream / Accomplished, but the creek that washes folly / Out of his veins'. The poem concludes:

Shall I say the woman
Conquered, whose breasts are icefields, whom our folly
Pursues? It could be so. The body lying
Under the glacier wall, though, owns no dream
And has no use for foolish climbing gear

Or lover's gear. Just like the empty hut
In which he dreamt that dream about a woman,
It swears that truth is lying, and each heartbeat folly.

Thus nature itself, whose cycle includes human mortality, is virtually identified with the goddess, seen as the alluring yet deceitful Venus, who holds out a false hope of pleasure and satisfaction—the same goddess who, at least in Baxter's understanding of the myth, appeared to the humble Anchises in his mountain hut, only to leave him eventually maimed.

The seaborn Aphrodite

We have seen in 'Aeneas' how Venus may also be seen as the birthing source of poetry; and it is to another image of birth that we now turn. One of the most dramatic passages from Greek literature, in Hesiod's *Theogony*, describes the very birth of Aphrodite herself, symbol of female sexuality, from an act of sexual mutilation. The god Kronos, at the instigation of his mother Gea, castrates his father Uranus with a sickle and then casts the parental genitalia into the sea where, protected in a foam sac, they become the embryo of the goddess. This unusual piece of flotsam touches at the island of Cythera[7] and then proceeds to Cyprus where the now fully developed goddess, 'lovely and inviting reverence', steps ashore, bringing instant fertility with her. Famous representations of the myth in visual art include the now lost *Aphrodite Anadyomene*[8] of Apelles, which depicted the goddess wringing out her hair as she rose from the sea. Universally admired today is Botticelli's painting, in the Uffizi Gallery in Florence, which features the goddess floating towards the shore in a scallop shell, a detail already known from ancient art. Like many other poets,[9] Baxter responds to the poetic potential of the myth, and this is scarcely surprising in his case, given the prominent place the sea plays in his poetry.

We have discussed Baxter's early references to the birth of Venus from the sea. Whereas 'The Birth of Beauty' (c.1941, N3.132) reflects juvenile abstraction, the final stanza of 'The Unicorn' (1943, *CP* 10–11) looks ahead to the dominant role played by female sexuality in his life and writing. The idea of female sexuality heralding death and shattering the illusory comfort of an Edenic boyhood persists and becomes associated with a deepened emotional charge reflecting adult experience. A poem written in the early 1950s, 'On His Mistress Dressing' (N17.14), which perhaps takes a sidelong glance at John Donne's

7 This is why Aphrodite/Venus can be called 'the Cytherean' (cf. 'Traveller's Litany', *CP* 139).

8 The description *anadyomene* simply means 'rising'.

9 For a survey of some of the uses of the image in New Zealand poetry, see Davidson, 'Venus Is Rising'.

'To his Mistress Going to Bed' (Donne 12–13), neatly contrasts the ideal with the reality:

Though I know well that safe abed
She bears no trace of maidenhead,
For those firm legs have opened wide
To me and other men beside;
Yet now to see her standing there
I'm shaken by an old despair:
For so in ocean solitude
The seaborn Aphrodite stood,
The sunlight on her breast and brow
And naked as the mountain snow.

What is explicit now is the feeling of 'despair'. The concept of 'ocean solitude' is important too, because although it technically refers to Aphrodite it can also be applied to Baxter himself, especially through his Odysseus alter ego (discussed in chapter 6). Moreover, despite the fact that sunlight is said to fall on the goddess, the final image of her is characterised by extreme chill. Sexuality is exposed, as it were, as anything but beautiful.

Baxter's ambivalent attitude to sex, which he increasingly associated with death, is again well illustrated by two poems written twenty years apart, both of which in different ways use the 'birth of Venus' trope. 'Tunnel Beach' (*CP* 53), written as early as 1946 yet displaying greater subtlety and a marked change in register from 'The Unicorn', recalls a specific sexual experience.[10] The walk across fields on the way to the beach is forgotten, 'for the boughs of flame were seen / Of the first garden and the root / Of graves in your salt mouth and the forehead branded fire.' The third stanza of the poem contains the climax:

Through the rock tunnel whined
The wind, Time's hound in leash,
And stirred the sand and murmured in your hair.
The honey of your moving thighs

10 For a brief but sensitive analysis of this poem in the overall context of Baxter's writing on sex, see O'Sullivan, *Baxter* 24–25. Trevor James, 'Primal Vision' 89–91, discusses the presence of Venus/Aphrodite in this poem, but rather pushes the operative associations, including the goddess's own birth from the castrated genitals of Uranus.

> Drew down the cirrus sky, your doves about the beach
> Shut out sea thunder with their wings and stilled the lonely air.

The dove can often symbolise Venus/Aphrodite, and so the goddess is implicit here, beside the sea.[11] This is a moment of ecstasy. Yet even here Time is waiting to be unleashed and, as the final stanza goes on to show, the stillness immediately evaporates: 'But O rising I heard the loud / Voice of the sea's women riding / All storm to come.' The felicitous expression 'O rising' could belong grammatically to the 'I' of the poem. However, it more naturally refers to the 'Voice of the sea's women' which, in a Venus context established by the doves, hints at the goddess herself 'rising' from the waves. But the poem ends on a note of uncertainty and emptiness as the vision vanishes to be replaced by a cold evocation of the natural world: 'No virgin mother bore / My heart wave eaten. From the womb of cloud / Falls now no dove, but combers grinding / Break sullen on the last inviolate shore.'[12]

'Rhadamanthus' (*CP* 407–08), written in 1966–67, refers apparently to the same incident when the site of the sexual encounter is revisited many years later. But now the experience, already touched by melancholy in the earlier poem, is shot through with pain, and the speaker regrets the return. The goddess is here explicit, but the effect she has is recalled as a kind of dismemberment: 'Venus came over the sea to us / Lying (as so many do) / In one another's arms. She left us / Like shards of a dish the spade jars on.'

As in 'Tunnel Beach', the poem ends with a picture of inscrutable nature, but there is a difference: 'From some cleft / A pigeon scuttered out. Above the place of love / The cliff was a

11 The same associations recur in 'Jerusalem Sonnets' written 23 years later in 1969 (*CP* 455–74). In sonnet 19 (*CP* 464), referring to his wife, Baxter writes: 'this old bullock will kick / Once or twice, but offers himself again // To the knife of love—Te Kare, wave of the sea / On which the Dove moved before the world began.' The primary reference is to the Holy Spirit and the Genesis creation, but the 'birth of Venus' is a clamouring subtext.

12 As in a passage from 'Traveller's Litany' (*CP* 143), not even the dove escapes the taint of the deadly associations of love. Again in 'Songs of the Desert' 7 (*CP* 57) the woman's smile means that 'I am deceived / and gladly hail the murderous dove', and 'Poem by the Clock Tower, Sumner' (1948, *CP* 73) ends with the words: 'Again the dark Dove nestles in my breast.'

high stone Rhadamanthus / Washed by the black froth of the sea.' What we now have is an explicit death image brooding over the place and the poet. But Rhadamanthus is not just an underworld figure. He was one of the judges of the dead, so that a kind of anticipatory eschatological tribunal is implied. The moment of ecstasy, the Venus theophany, has dark longer-term consequences.

There are also more immediate consequences. In 'Letter to Robert Burns' (1963, *CP* 289–91) Baxter had already dwelt on the Tunnel Beach moment, emphasising the connection between the acts of sex and poetic creation through the appearance of the personified female figure of 'the snake-haired Muse' who, as noted in chapter 1, paradoxically offers both death and undeath. In between 'Tunnel Beach' and 'Rhadamanthus' we can also usefully place 'Be Happy in Bed' (1958–59, *CP* 199–200). Its opening line is 'One landscape, many women', and it takes the form of a reverie, with a strongly nostalgic tone. In an almost central position in the poem is the statement 'sex taught him sadness', and it ends: 'The age of sex, the age of centaurs / Returns to punish after-dinner sleep.' Most directly relevant to this discussion, however, are the words: 'Where the boats ride endlessly / Grip and hold the sea king's daughter.' This figure is not, strictly speaking, Venus/ Aphrodite of the sea, but she is closely related. Indeed, she belongs to a group of such female figures, all of whom are associated with water, all of whom bring sensual pleasure, but also danger.[13]

In classical mythology, one of the daughters of the 'sea king' is Amphitrite, the very sound of whose name recalls Aphrodite, and she appears under this name in the short poem 'Kelp' (1966, *CP* 343). She is, however, specifically ruled out by the poet as being symbolised by the kelp. Instead, the kelp is seen as a kind of 'double' of the 'snake-haired Muse', in this manifestation the literally petrifying Gorgon Medusa, whose role will be examined in more detail in the next chapter.

Limbs of the Kraken? The unplaited
Hair of Amphitrite? No;

13 Undine is one, the figure in the play *The First Wife* is another, and we can add sirens (especially as associated with Odysseus) and mermaids (see e.g. 'The Mermaid', N17.100).

The dark locks of the deaf Medusa,
Mother of my songs: who has turned me to stone.

Waiting for Venus: the absence of the goddess

This motif of monitoring the sea and identifying what comes from it recurs in Baxter and is often built around the possibility of an appearance of Venus/Aphrodite. Almost invariably, however, this fails to eventuate, so that the true vision of beauty, of female perfection, remains elusive. It has been lost, just as Eden has been lost.

The idea is strongly expressed in 'Elegy at the Year's End' (1953, *CP* 135):

One may walk again to the fisherman's rock, hearing
The long waves tumble, from America riding
Where mottled kelpbeds heave to a pale sun,
But not again see green Aphrodite
Rise to transfigure the noon. Rather the Sophoclean
Chorus: *All shall be taken.*

This is a sombre reflection on human mortality, triggered by 'an elder uncle's deathbed'. The dream of love remains just that, a dream, while life takes on the appearance of tragedy, almost tauntingly vocalised from more than 2000 years in the past. As Goulter comments, 'The absence of the goddess Aphrodite rising from the sea foam into a landscape which her presence would transform is a factor of the de-mythologised condition where "Spirit and flesh are sundered / In the kingdom of no love"' (40). Even the animal world seems preferable, so that one can 'envy the paradise drake his brilliant sexual plumage' and see the movement 'on maimed gravestones under the towering fennel' of 'the bright lizard, sunloved, basking in / The moment of animal joy.'

The seemingly vain search for lost love also features in 'Crossing Cook Strait' (*CP* 159–60), a poem transformed from its original draft in 1947 by the time of its completion in 1956. The poet tells how he came on deck with several mundane possibilities in mind—'To stretch my legs, find perhaps / Gossip, a girl in green slacks at the rail / Or just the logline feathering a dumb wake.' But the ship's movement coincides with an appearance from the sea:

'Dolphins!' I cried—'let the true sad Venus
Rise riding her shoals, teach me as once to wonder
And wander at ease, be glad and never regret.'

Once again, the vision of a longed-for regained innocence is expressed in terms of the 'birth of Venus' myth. It is not altogether clear why the 'true' Venus should also be 'sad', especially if, as seems quite possible, Baxter is alluding to D. H. Lawrence's basically optimistic poem 'Whales Weep Not' (Lawrence 2: 694). This poem begins: 'They say the sea is cold, but the sea contains / the hottest blood of all, and the wildest, the most urgent.' It concludes:

and all this happiness in the sea, in the salt
where God is also love, but without words:
and Aphrodite is the wife of whales
most happy, happy she!
and Venus among the fishes skips and is a she-dolphin
she is the gay, delighted porpoise sporting with love and the sea
she is the female tunny-fish, round and happy among the males
and dense with happy blood, dark rainbow bliss in the sea.

It is possible that in Baxter's case, the poet's own feeling of sadness, sparked by a keen awareness of the cycle of life which entails the death of lovers and of love itself, has been transferred to the goddess for whom he yearns.

In any case, the vision is not granted, in its place appearing the socialist apparition which is referred to in chapter 2 and discussed in more detail in chapter 7. This apparition may, in fact, be another reason, perhaps working in parallel with the Lawrence passage, for Baxter's introduction of dolphins. Goulter, in commenting on the passage, writes that 'Dolphins are not explicitly associated with Aphrodite's birth from the sea foam but they are in harmony with the other elements of that scene such as doves and sparrows that flew about the rising goddess' (43). He also notes the frequent appearance of dolphins in classical art and mythology, especially as the sacred companions of the sea god Poseidon, and their presence in the sixth-century BC painting by Exekias. However, he does not note in this context that Baxter was to allude to this very painting in his poem 'The Jar', or relate

Baxter's later use in 'Crossing Cook Strait' of the expression 'my mask of Dionysus' to the earlier mention of the dolphins. It is not beyond the bounds of possibility that it was precisely Baxter's knowledge of the Exekias painting with its Dionysus/dolphins juxtaposition which influenced the appearance of both dolphins and Dionysus, albeit separately, in this poem. The goddess Venus makes a pleasant mediatrix!

The 'birth of Venus' myth also finds a place in three poems written a decade later. In 'The Kraken' (1966, *CP* 335–36), any expectation of seeing the vision has apparently been dashed: 'You who stroll on cliff-top boulders and / The abandoned gun-pit, do not // Expect the sea to break its own laws, / Or any Venus to be born // Out of the gulf's throat.' Inevitably, no Venus is born, yet the still underlying yearning for her is evident, since in her place is the sound of the foghorn and the sight of 'the Kraken's wide // Blinding tendrils'.

A somewhat more positive substitute for the missing Venus is found in 'At Brighton Bay' (1966, *CP* 371). This is a further poem in which the poet returns to one of the places he had once frequented where, in fact, in the grip of 'that grotesque adolescent fury // We never grow beyond', he had contemplated suicide:

No squid-armed Venus rose

Out of the surf, but through the smashed gate
Of many winters, from the hurdling water

Came to my heart the invisible spirit
These words have given shape to.

Poetic inspiration seems a reasonable compensation for the absence of the vision of beauty and love, and the epithet 'squid-armed' applied to the non-existent Venus in this context perhaps carries with it connotations of smothering in any case.

'Apparition of the Goddess Venus to a Sleepy Man' (1967, *CP* 384) appears to demonstrate once and for all the impossibility of the ideal. The setting is once again the seaside, and the poet relates how he

Saw rise, merciful between
Breakers and heaps of bladder-weed

That stank at Long Beach, one tall sail, rudder
And wheel of a sand-yacht where children ride.

Nothing apparently could be further from the vision, yet ironically this proves to be stimulation enough, so that 'my dull ease / Was broken, and venereal thought / Constructed out of air or nothing.' And the object of the 'venereal thought' turns out to be 'A girl like a green hard stringy lupin pod'. Thus the goddess Venus can still manifest herself, but not in person from the waves which can produce only a sand yacht, while her human embodiment links directly to the consummation of adolescent desire under the lupins at Brighton, site of Baxter's first sexual experiences, repeatedly referred to in his writing.

Lawrence Jones (76–79) has most insightfully demonstrated how these and other appearances, non-appearances and quasi-appearances of Venus are intimately connected with the coastline of Otago. As he puts it, Baxter 'relates sexual adventures to a complex of recurring images involving lupin, sandhills, the Brighton bathing sheds, the Brighton boathouse, summer, Venus personified in girls in bathing suits, frustrated or exploitive sexuality, condoms, and masturbation' (78)—to which list 'kelp' among other things could be added.

A halo of scum: the goddess subverted

In some ways, the most intriguing out of all this group of poems is 'Encounter with Venus' (*Landfall* 1965). This time the poet is 'Walking Tait's Beach' and reflecting gloomily on the current state of his country:

I thought how the sweet flagon
had brought death to many loves,
of Hell and the Police State,
but most how great Venus rose
from roots of kelp to fill our
barns with hay, our beds with heat,
our books with ballads, who has
lately abandoned our shore—

Once again, the regret is that Venus has disappeared. She had once risen in all her beauty, apparently, to stimulate farming, sexual and poetic activity. Now she is gone without trace. Or is she?

The poet now catches sight of a curious object floating a short distance out to sea and he wades out, afraid that it might be human remains:

> Nymphs and gods, it was a vile
> corpse, with a great swollen gut,
> putrefied, nibbled by ten
>
> Jerking fish, in a halo
> of scum—our island's emblem,
> a dead sheep . . . . Yes, mate, indeed
> a sacred occasion! Through
> the surf I stumbled back, dumb-
> Struck by shades of nationhood.

The tone of this is very different from that of the previous poems discussed, being a humorously expressed piece of social satire. In a way, however, it encapsulates the essence of all of them, albeit as caricature. The only equivalent now for the 'birth of Venus' image is a dead sheep, with all that this implies, symbolically, for New Zealand. A piece of Baxterian wizardry, even down to the detail of the 'halo of scum' which appears to be the final insult to the 'sac of foam' in which the embryonic Aphrodite of the Greek myth floated towards Cyprus.[14]

This poem, in its humour, its social comment, and its use of the 'birth from the foam' idea, has affinities with one written a decade earlier, 'The Seagirl and the Poet' (N17.79). Once again the setting is a saunter along the beach:

> I walked in windy autumn
> Beside the Parson's Rock
> Observing with a bloodshot eye
> The gaunt birds gape and shriek.
> A greenhaired girl rose in the foam
> And thus to me she spoke:

14 It is instructive to compare this poem with Lawrence Durrell's serious, harsh poem 'Aphrodite', whose opening lines run: 'Not from some silent sea she rose / In her great valve of nacre / But from such a one—O sea / Scourged with iron cables!' (Durrell 285).

On this occasion, then, the genuine article, albeit not Aphrodite as such, does rise from the sea, and it transpires that she likes 'a roughneck runagate sailor boy', but that 'for a poet, a spongy poet' she has 'no time at all'. Those modern poets who took up an invitation to visit her at home proved most uncongenial company—Shelley quoted Plato and Hart Crane clamoured for rum, both remaining unmoved by her 'feminine attractions'. In striking contrast, Homer and the other Greeks had reverenced her and her family as gods. The final three stanzas of the poem run as follows:

I said—'My dear young lady,
I certainly agree.
The times are not propitious
For either you or me;
But with my weak digestion
Salt water won't agree.

Not for a submarine romance
Or any other date
I haunt the weedy ledges
Where small-mouthed greenbone bite,
But to sweat out in quietness
The beer I drank last night.'

The seagirl dived into the wave
Which heaved an angry sigh;
And gaunt gulls rose on stoic wing
To wrangle in the sky
While on the autumn beaches strode
My sober self and I.

Inspiration allied with allurement again rises from the sea, but on this occasion the poet, while deploring modern attitudes and lack of receptiveness, is unable to do better himself since he is wrestling with his own down-to-earth drinking problem.

There is something especially noteworthy about the last line of this poem, given that we have an abortive encounter between the hungover poet and a symbol which combines artistic creativity and female sexual appeal. In his notebook, Baxter originally wrote 'My shadow self and I'. This draws attention to his ongoing relationship with an artistic well-spring and anticipates his later description of this as his 'schizophrenic twin' to whom, he said, the Burns Fellowship should have been awarded ('Conversation', *MH* 17).[15] Thus the drunken artist or shadow self is contrasted with the 'I' who is the family man walking along the beach in an effort to sober up and face a day of respectability and domesticity. However, by crossing out the word 'shadow' and replacing it with 'sober', Baxter has inverted the relationship, the 'I' now becoming representative of the alcoholic creative genius. This can be seen as a clear reinforcement of the point about the tension within Baxter noted in chapter 1.

The romantic, the carnal, and the elemental

It is a quantum leap from poems like 'The Seagirl and the Poet' and 'Encounter with Venus' to the sensitive love poetry that Baxter wrote throughout his career, ranging from the series of poems with the title 'Love-Lyric', written when he was in his late teens (four of them in *CP* 22–26) to poems like 'My Love Late Walking' (*CP* 164–65), whose composition spanned the years 1953–56. The love experience is often not expressed through mythological symbols in such poems, although 'Love-Lyric III' (*CP* 22–23) contains a reference to the Venusberg's attraction to the young Tannhäuser, a scenario popularised by the Wagnerian opera.

When Venus or Aphrodite is named in erotic contexts, she is sometimes no more than a synonym for 'sex', and the contexts themselves vary greatly in tone. Thus we can find a simple, neutral allusion such as in a couplet of 'Song of the Years' (1958, *CP* 188–89): 'When my childhood days were spent / To Venus I grew suppliant.' Totally different is the designation of a sexual partner in 'Letter to Sam Hunt' (1968, *CP* 429–31) as 'One of the best of Venus' nuns, / A girl with tits like ack-ack guns'.

Sometimes the goddess is presented in more elemental dress. In 'The Return' (1956, *CP* 179), yet another of the nostalgic poems memorialising a revisit to haunts of earlier years, in this

15 See also the discussion of Dionysus in ch. 7.

case childhood, the poet is aware of her presence: 'Venus with her thunder slept / On tired dunes, in grey maternal / Macrocarpa branches.' Here the goddess is identified with the land, the earth. Her sexual power in childhood was potential only, and it was the maternal aspect that dominated.

She is very different in 'Husband' (1965, *CP* 327–28), which finds the poet's wife as her embodiment:

My wife in a black jersey and a brown skirt
Dawdled round the kitchen repeatedly arranging
Sprigs of japonica. To my eroded
Sight she resembled the earth itself, the long-haired
Daughter of Zeus who likes whatever happens
Because it happens to her. I had to
Grit my teeth, shut my eyes, in order
Not to arrange her on the seagrass matting
And father an unplanned child.

The vision involves domestic woman, elemental woman and sexual woman all in one, bound together through the mythological concept of mother earth. Thus she is not named Venus here, but this aspect of her is still prominent, and her birth from the waves is again hinted at in the desired site for sex—'the seagrass matting'.

Yet another angle on the elemental goddess can be seen in 'Waipatiki Beach' (1963, *CP* 263–65). Again, the setting is the seashore, and again the goddess is the elemental force to whom the poet's words pay homage:

If anyone, I'd say the oldest Venus
Too early for the books, ubiquitous,

The manifold mother to whom my poems go
Like ladders down—at the mouth of the gully

She had left a lip of sand for the coarse grass to grow,
Also the very quiet native bee

Loading his pollen bags.

The fertility of nature is also evoked, but fertility is just one part of the natural cycle, and this is soon made obvious as another face of the goddess puts in an appearance: 'Her lion face, the skull-brown Hekate / Ruling my blood since I was born'.

The Ace of Death upon Queen Venus

This brings us back to Baxter's already mentioned and almost obsessive association of sex with death, an association expressed in many different ways, and at least to some extent related to the Freudian concept of the 'life-instinct' (Eros) and 'death-instinct' (Thanatos).[16] In 'Love Sonnet' (1960, *CP* 221–22), for example, the poet, in a tone of bitterness, advises the poem's addressee to hide her beauty from the wind and the sky: 'They'll remind you how your bones'll / Be at length an empty honeycomb.' Often Venus/Aphrodite is directly named, as a way of universalising the specific through the mythologising process: in 'Bar Room Elegy' (1951, *CP* 119), 'Angst lays the Ace / Of Death upon Queen Venus, the black Spade.' Even in a context where the dark aspect of the goddess is deemed to be inoperative, her presence can be captured through the very mention of her absence, as in the short 1967 poem 'Spring' (*CP* 404):

> Girls like red-hot peonies (how nakedly they dress!);
> Invisible fingers tugging at my fly;
> The sense of being in a bent glass funnel—
> Is it the devil? No;
>
> It is the Lord's female lieutenant,
> Venus, for once without her brother Death,
> Who makes the hard twigs burst—who makes me notice
> My own woman's dark mane of hair.

Here it is noteworthy that the classical goddess is classified as a subordinate co-worker of the Christian God. This clearly indicates that sexual arousal is here not felt to be a manifestation of evil or sin; on the contrary, it is part of a saving, life-affirming process that excludes the devil and Death itself.

The close connection between sex and death is again made explicit, however, in 'Summer 1967' (*CP* 408–09), written in the same year. The optimistic connotations of the season are soon clouded over. The poem begins: 'Summer brings out the girls in their green dresses / Whom the foolish might compare to daffodils,

16 For Baxter's own use of these personifications, see, for example, 'Traveller's Litany' (specifically *CP* 143).

/ Not seeing how a dead grandmother in each one governs / her limbs.' Later in the poem, we find: 'To want nothing is / The only possible freedom. But I prefer to think of / An afternoon spent drinking rum and cloves / In a little bar, just after the rain has started, in another time / Before we began to die—'. And the poem ends: 'Herbs of oblivion, they lost their power to help us / The day that Aphrodite touched her mouth to ours.'

This sort of thought, prominent in the poetry of the second Dunedin phase, is also expressed less poetically in the lectures collected in *The Man on the Horse* written during the same period. In 'Conversation with an Ancestor', for example, Baxter relates how he was able to craft a poem out of the phrase 'Suffer the autumn of the succubus'. He quotes the poem ('The Succubus', *CP* 330–31) and then comments: 'I can't interpret my own poems infallibly; but the message of this one seems to be that the Venus of the greengrocer's calendar who gives life becomes in the long run the succubus who gives death' (*MH* 20).

Even more enlightening is Baxter's commentary ('Conversation', *MH* 24) on the poem 'At Aramoana' (*CP* 330–31). He picks up key images:

> I describe the sheaves of water bowing as if to the sickle, an image of the obedience of nature that does not resist death; and the young lads on the sand construct their sensual fantasy which is also sacred, each observing the image of Venus not rising from the sea but going out into it. The hanging gardens of her hair I took directly from the words of my wife; yet this Venus is in some degree an artificial image, she is half woman and half surfboard, the modern Venus who is so much an object, made of blood and fibreglass; and my own dream, my way of hiding myself from death, from the lack of spiritual support in all created things, is to turn to the least demanding and most supporting reality, Gea, the earth herself, the oldest of the tribe of gods. The sandhill cone is her breast, the mats of cutty-grass cover her ancient vagina—my words, if they are to make sense, depend on her and return to her as the symbolic ground of existence—away from her I feel lost; yet because all men die, she can only comfort, never save, and I go on from her towards the sea, which is the image of death, the separating and dividing void, which nevertheless is the source of my joy. (*MH* 25–26)

Jungian thought and classical mythology come together here but are laced with Christian overtones. The classical goddess, in her guise of mother earth or Gea, can only provide comfort in the face of the inexorable path towards death, here symbolised by the sea. Since in terms of Jungian thought the sea stands for the unconscious, we are also dealing with the process by which the conscious mind is to be united with the unconscious. But salvation as such is the exclusive gift of Christian belief. Without such a Christian prospect, we are left with the bleak thought expressed in the final section of 'Notes on the Education of a New Zealand Poet': 'When Venus leaves us to ourselves, her uncle Hades enters the door of the heart' (*MH* 154).

Baxter may have become increasingly reconciled to the death aspect of the goddess, but there is also a definite note of regret for her as the erotic and stimulating Venus who is now beyond his reach. As he expresses it in 'At Goat Island (for Hoani)' (1968, *CP* 426):

> There is no other
> Language that I understand
> Now that the Queen has closed her door to me
> And the young girls in their pink blouses
> Shouting along the sandy track
> Belong to other men.

The same regret is recorded in another short passage from 'Notes on the Education': 'That girl in her beach suit loitering among the dunes is no longer a figure of Venus to me. The change is not in her, but in myself. Over twenty years I fought the wars of Venus, the bitterest of all to lose' (*MH* 153). Baxter may have lost, but he was at least not party to the unconditional surrender expressed in a passage from D. H. Lawrence's poem 'Spiral Flame' (Lawrence 2: 169–70):

> And that poor late makeshift, Aphrodite emerging in a bathing-suit from our modern sea-side foam
> has successfully killed all desire in us whatsoever.

For Baxter, the desire seems always to have been there, even if it was increasingly complicated by a range of other significantly less positive feelings. What is most striking, however, is how the 'birth of Venus' myth came to play such a role in his thinking. The sea itself may be the key here, given the prominence with which it features in his writings in general, as a symbol of both the elemental and the subconscious. Thus it can be seen as the natural place for Baxter to look for and sometimes see—but more often not see—the hoped-for idealised female. The classical myth could then provide him with a creative mode for the expression of his often frustrated response.

It is apt to conclude this discussion by quoting a passage from Baxter's unpublished play *Tiger Rock.* In the sitting-room of a seaside bach, a young woman is attempting to show an older man how he should respond to his estranged wife who, she claims, really loves him as he loves her. She engages in role play, replicating the imagined entrance of the wife:

> Now I am a different Sharon. I am Venus come out of the sea. My hair is dripping and the salt dries on my skin. I am terrible and beautiful. The birds and the horned animals are mating when I go through the forest. And you are the shepherd Anchises. I will come to your house and lie down with you on a sheepskin rug in front of the fire. I am the goddess Venus—because you love me, John.

This is both a more positive take on the Anchises myth than that given in the passage quoted earlier from 'Notes on the Education of a New Zealand Poet', and also a hint that Venus *can* be manifested in the form of a real, flesh and blood woman, and a wife at that. The play ends in the reconciliation of husband and wife and the husband's new awareness of how his concentration on intellectual abstractions has blinded him to the overriding importance of proper human relationships. On one occasion at least, then, Baxter's flirtation with the Venus myth points to a happy ending. In the next chapter, however, we shall see that when the beauty of Venus's face and form is distorted and twisted to its opposite, no ending can be happy.

CHAPTER 4

THE INFERNAL FEMININE

We have seen in the previous chapter how Baxter was able to articulate, in terms of the biblical figures Rachel and Leah, what he identified as diametrically opposed aspects of his own wife. We have also seen that such binary thinking lies at the heart of his response to the female in general, as well as to the sexual act. With regard to the latter, he himself puts it this way:

> Again, there was the stumbling-block of sex. Here I tended to oscillate between two extremes. Either I thought that the sexual instinct was itself the source of meaning in life; or else, in sour and baffled moments, I entertained the suspicion that God had played a bad joke on the human species by giving them sexual equipment. (*FC* 169–70)

Much of his poetic output, indeed, reflects this 'oscillation' as he wrestles with such polar opposites—on the one hand the sexual allure of the female who torments him with desire, persuading him that true happiness is carnal (and thus possible in this life) and that permanent and transcendent bliss lies between a woman's thighs, and, on the other hand, the emptiness and misery resulting from disappointment and lack of fulfilment which tells him to distrust carnal pleasure and seek transcendence elsewhere. Emptiness and misery itself then assume even darker and uglier guises.

This chapter explores Baxter's sense and expression of the darker side of the female. There is a much higher degree of complexity here, since what is already partly implicit in Venus/ Aphrodite as an alter ego, so to speak, is in fact a *series* of classical mythological figures, overlapping to some extent but each having a distinctive function or functions. Collectively they can embody sexual bondage and dehumanisation, death itself, and the rigid malaise at the heart of New Zealand society. Yet they can also function as anima figures, connected with the agony of the creative process welling up from the subconscious.

The figures range from Circe, who possesses the sexual attractiveness and promise of fertility of Venus/Aphrodite, but who is more obviously dangerous on account of her transformative power and her ability to reduce men to the level of animals, to the Gorgon Medusa, whose outward appearance is hideously ugly and who has the power to turn individuals and indeed societies to stone, but who is also ironically associated in Baxter's thinking with the Muse and the creative process. Close to Circe in one sense is Hekate, another witch-figure who can smell strongly of sex, but different in that she can more explicitly open the door leading to death. Cybele can have sexual allure like Circe, but she is also the one who specifically emasculates and imposes bondage. Closest to the Gorgon Medusa are the Furies, who inspire terror, who are infertile and life-denying, and whose very breath has the odour of death as the only meaning of existence, yet who also seem to be at the heart of the creative process.

Acting as something of a mediatrix, and thus serving to at least partly break down the binary oppositions, is the figure of Gea, the ancient earth mother. As a maternal figure she nurtures and, although she also represents the physical reality of the grave and therefore death, her face of death is more benevolent and welcoming than that of some of the other figures. As the archetypal mother she coincides too with one aspect of Cybele, personifying nature. We will not deal with her in detail in this chapter, but she must be understood as underlying the other figures, all of whom are inseparable from Venus/Aphrodite, and all of whom are also inextricably interwoven with the fundamental figure of the Muse. We will begin our more detailed examination with Circe.[1]

1 It should be noted that there is a range of other related figures not discussed here, such as Scylla and Charybdis, the witch in general, Arachne and the spider in general, Tisiphone, the Sphinx, and Kali. The Sirens are dealt with in chapter 6.

Circe was not to blame

The witch Circe, like the Sirens, is both extremely attractive and dangerous; like Greek mythology's first created woman, Pandora, she is a 'beautiful evil' (Hesiod, *Theogony* 585). It was Circe who drugged some of Odysseus's men and literally turned them into swine. She tried the same medicine on Odysseus himself, but he was forewarned and forearmed, and so was able to subdue her. As a result, however, he did dally with her in a sexual relationship, delaying his homeward journey for a year, so that in another sense he was at least temporarily drugged by her as well. Significantly, though, it was Circe who gave him instructions for the next stage of his wanderings, his visit to the land of the dead. With her power to dehumanise but also to guide a man to discover his spiritual direction through the chaos of the land of death, Circe would be an obvious candidate to represent the Jungian anima. To what extent do we see this in Baxter's treatment of her?

At the level of actual human relationships,[2] Circe can be paired by Baxter with Calypso, as a female who offers illicit pleasure to a man while distracting him from his duty or responsibilities—as symbolised by Penelope, the faithful wife waiting at home. His application of this idea can be seen in a letter written to a female correspondent on 20 October 1961 (FM 27/1/11), in the course of which he comments: 'It can't give you much joy to be shoved into the Calypso or Circe role, any more than it would be for [your lover]'s wife to be typed as Penelope, one of the most unattractive characters in fiction.' As is so often the case with Baxter, domesticity is seen as distinctly less appealing than allure, problematic though allure itself may be for those concerned.

There is a somewhat more sinister touch to the Circe concept in the 1952 poem 'The Homecoming' (*CP* 121). Critical discussions of this poem tend to ignore Circe, which is not altogether surprising, since more emphasis is placed on the mother/Penelope figure. The poem can certainly be read in Jungian terms: an encounter with the anima in different guises. At the same time, the surface level of life experience cannot be glossed over. From a

2 Leaving aside Baxter's humorous description of a girl at one of the schools he attended as 'a large, square-built Circe' ('Education', *MH* 135).

mother love 'demanding all' the hero had escaped into the wide world, only to find more of the same there. It drugged him 'in Circe's hall', and now it is 'more relentless' when he returns home. There thus appears to be nowhere in which he can be free of this constricting and energy-sapping force with its Freudian Oedipal overtones.

Charles Doyle (54) usefully applies Baxter's own comment on the much later poem 'Henley Pub' (*CP* 324–25) to this poem as well: 'My hero is a man who has not travelled far from the gates of the womb; hence, his extreme vulnerability to the faults of the flesh. There is an undeveloped Oedipal quality in his relation to his mistress, in his closeness to water and earth, in the complete passivity of his Marian devotion. Women are all mothers to him' ('Virgin', *MH* 75).

Circe is made part of this, her foreign environment proving little better than that of his home—a point reinforced by locating her in the domestic space of a prosaic 'hall' rather than in a cave, which would carry overtones not only of her Homeric context but also perhaps of oracular wisdom.[3] Rather than embodying a new spiritual direction, she functions as a sort of cloying opiate, with effects akin to those found in the land of the Lotus-eaters. Circe might at least have offered Odysseus some excitement before tedium or disenchantment set in, but her deeply negative treatment here makes it clear that she provides no real alternative to his deep-seated restlessness and discontent. Nor is there much hope that the 'sea's hexameter' which he hears 'beyond sparse fields / On reef and cave' will yield anything like a lasting satisfaction.

Even more sinister, as far as Circe is concerned, is the stage after the drugging, as experienced by Odysseus's unfortunate companions. This is adumbrated in the poem 'Beatrice' (1961, *CP* 228),[4] in which the male subject, leaving the 'female town' in search of a Muse to guide him to spiritual insight, finds instead 'the image he has made, / One who holds the judgement prism, / Who sees the swinish bristle sprout / On his rough jowl in Circe's

3 It is notable that a cave *is* made by Baxter the home of Calypso, who is discussed in chapter 6.

4 Also published in *Image* 8 (Aug. 1961) under the title 'For a Sexual Idealist'.

cage, / And will accuse, and will accuse, / Till he can tear the heart out of his side.' He is unable to shake off the sense of his own humanity as locked into a sexuality that drags him down to a subhuman state. It appears to be impossible to escape the sense of guilt stemming from the theriomorphic effects of female sexual control and a caged environment. All that is left to him is futile and destructive protest and the pain of creating a poem.

In the narrative of the *Odyssey,* the hero's journey after he leaves Circe's island of Aeaea leads, as we have seen, to the far west and the land of the dead. This transition is evoked in the early Baxter poem 'The Journey' (*CP* 127), further discussed in chapter 6. Circe is naturally present too in other poems dealing with the experiences of the Odysseus figure. At the end of 'The Watch' (*CP* 273–74), for example, the poet narrator quotes the words of the dead Elpenor, whose spirit accosts Odysseus pleading for burial: 'In Circe's palace I fell drunk / Missing the steep ladder; I came before you to this den.' (More or less the same lines had already been used by Baxter in 'Traveller's Litany', *CP* 139–45). Danger was still present for Odysseus's companions even after their human shape was restored. Elpenor became 'drugged' through an excess of alcohol and paid the ultimate price. Death, then, is the close companion of Circe—as we might expect it to be, given Baxter's preoccupation with the link between the female, sex and death. In a sense, there is nothing left, when weariness kicks in so quickly after 'Circe's bed of stone' featuring in 'What the Sirens Sang' (N16.15), which provides a nice link with the Medusa figure to be considered shortly.

Baxter wrestled continually with the Circe concept, yet from the beginning did not altogether blame what she entailed, as can be seen from the final stanza of the very early poem 'Me Also' (N12.725):[5]

> Circe was not to blame, Ulysses' brain changed her
> From the elusive beauty, daughter-of-Sun divine;
> Saw from the eyes of beast, no, not beast but swine,
> Tears running down the snout for the irretrievable vista.

5 For Baxter's own comment on this poem, see *Spark* 332–33.

This is a little obscure in its detail, but is certainly closely related to the idea later to be expressed in 'Beatrice', which is well illustrated by the passage already quoted in the previous chapter from Baxter's discussion of Burns' poem 'Tam o' Shanter' (*MH* 117–18). It is worth repeating:

> The *anima* changes shape according to the motives of those who approach her—a violent man will see her as a wolf; a sensual man, as a temptress; a Puritan, either not at all, or as a poisonous reptile; a saint, as a helpless child who needs to be looked after; a poet, as his difficult Muse [. . .].

The point is that the anima, and therefore the poetic expression of it, changes appearance in accordance with the way in which the male poet approaches it. Thus in 'Me Also' Baxter/Ulysses changes the shape of Circe into something unpleasant so that she in turn turns him into a beast.

There is some variation, then, in Baxter's use of the Circe figure in the course of his career. Judith Yarnall, in her thoughtful study of the figure from Homer through to the twentieth century, writes: 'Though she is herself the veteran of many transformations, the archetypal core of Circe's power remains unchanged: she is the female figure who possesses the ability to *transform*, to give shape to others or to take it away. She offers both debasement and deliverance, a new life in the flesh' (Yarnall 6–7). Yarnall's moderate feminist perspective deliberately eschews a Jungian approach to her subject, arguing that:

> It is more helpful to think of Circe simply as an archetypal woman of power, whose potency is grounded in her disturbing ability to give form to flesh and blood, than as an anima figure. She is as compelling to modern women seeking to explore the range of their own natures as she has been to male poets and dreamers in the past. (5)

Baxter, of course, is one of the 'male poets and dreamers', and quite clearly does use Circe as an expression of the anima; yet his response to her, albeit from a male perspective, seems to have much in common with Yarnall's.

Hekate taught him love

Like Circe, Hekate is a witch-figure, but of a much more complicated kind in Greek thinking; powers extending to the whole created order have already been allotted to her according to an extended passage of Hesiod's *Theogony* (411–52). She is also clearly a liminal figure, being associated with the crossroads, and she has very strong underworld connections. In addition, she has associations with the moon, in this aspect being almost a double of Artemis/Diana.

In Baxter, Hekate makes a significant appearance in 'The Goddess' (1966, *CP* 351–52), in which he recalls the moment in childhood when a woman neighbour, at whose house he was spending the night because his mother was away, tied up his pyjama cord 'properly'. This woman, 'mother of eight', used to beat up her husband and then 'come out and sit / Crouching on the back step, // As if Death was the next child in her womb.' The rumour was that she was 'wicked' and that 'she did it with soldiers—what, I wasn't sure'. The point, though, was that the action of tying the pyjama cord produced a strong reaction:

> and like a door opening,
> A smell, a touch, a wave of the sea,
> It reached me—what, I couldn't tell you—
> Earth, great trees, a nature saying 'Yes'
> Beyond all bargains . . .
> I'd say, Hekate taught
> Me to act, fight, groan, give.

Here we have mother (evoking Gea specifically as 'Earth'), sexually active woman (reflecting Venus/Aphrodite) and Death (strongly implied by Hekate) simultaneously encapsulated in this goddess/woman, well illustrating the contradictory feelings about the female. Baxter recalled the same incident, and made the same association with Hekate, in an earlier poem, 'Blue Notes for Mack' (1965, N25.31). It was a somewhat rambling effort, much of which Baxter crossed out; however, the final section, left more or less untouched, contains the seeds of what was shortly afterwards to become 'The Goddess':

yet, at five
Or thereabouts, had my pyjama cord
Tied up by the wicked woman of the town
(My mother being absent); smelt the sweat of
Earth, great trees, a nature saying 'Yes'
Beyond all bargains—and, in a child's ear,
'You have no longer any need to fear;
You'll do just as you are.'
All this
lay in the movement of a hand,

And without this first touch, how could the mind
Conceive it possible to act and live?
Above the last jail on the flat stone write:
'Hekate taught him love.'

As Baxter reflected further on his experience, the Hekate figure ended up teaching much more than just love. She had in fact taught him the agony of being an active agent, of striving, and of committing himself fully to all that life has to offer.

Another unpublished poem, 'The Strong One' (1963, N23.98), is also most instructive in this context. The poem begins: 'That woman I carved from a bit of pumice stone / Pushed up on the shore like floating sodden bread'. This artistic creation, with her 'hanging dugs, great belly and panther head', is then made a point of comparison with the woman the poet is sleeping with at the time. The real woman has a straight back and a slim body and wears 'no grim beast-mask to cover / Brow, cheek or mouth'. However, after the sexual act 'my dreams have told me I am Hekate's lover'. The final stanza of the poem, however, is surprising:

Praise be!—and your dark strength will be mine to withstand
Slow snares, quick knives, and the poison that eats at the marrow
On that day when men grope through the streets of a blind land
Because the sun's eye has been struck by an enemy arrow.

Baxter clearly had an affection for his figure carved with a nail out of pumice, because it reappears a few years later, still in Hekate guise but with a twist—it becomes assimilated to the figure of a protective Christian saint. This association had already been made in 'A Girl's Invocation' (1963, *CP* 271–72), which echoes a Catholic 'Litany of the Saints':

From the ghost behind the mirror,
From the blood on an old coat,
From the bite of the cave weta,
From the claws of the thin cat,
Hekate, save me.[6]

The same liturgical resonance, with a rather startling hint of an association with the Virgin Mary, appears in 'The Rostrum: a memorial ode on hearing the news of my appointment as a Robert Burns Fellow' (1965, N26.12), this time being explicitly linked with the pumice carving. The poet has been reflecting on the ageing process and the prospect of holding down an academic post:

Blind Hekate,
Mother of drunks and fools,
whom I once carved
Out of seastone pumice, with a great
Belly and the head of a beast,
To outlast Varsity pundits, bureaucrats
Or nuclear plague—
Have mercy!

As with the other related figures, death is never too far away from Hekate. This can be seen most clearly in 'Waipatiki Beach' (1963, *CP* 263–65). Baxter sets a graphic scene of wilderness to which, along with his son, he has gained access by car 'by a bad road'. He finds himself in the presence of 'the oldest Venus / Too early for the books, ubiquitous, // the manifold mother to whom my poems go / Like ladders down'. Then, walking down to the bank of the creek, he sees 'in the dune's clasp the burnt black / Trunk of a totara the sea had rolled back.' This comes at the end of the second section of the poem, and the third section begins immediately: 'Her lion face, the skull-brown Hekate / Ruling my blood since I was born, // I had not found it yet.' The natural world involving birth and its inevitable consequence, death, finds compelling expression through the enigmatic figure of Hekate,

6 Compare e.g. 'From all evil, DELIVER US, O LORD / From all sin, / From thy wrath, / From sudden and unprovided death, / From the snares of the Devil, / From anger, hatred, and all ill-will, / From the spirit of uncleanness [etc]' (*Layman's Missal* 1266).

who can show her death mask at any time. As Weir puts it:

> Having penetrated outwards in space and inwards in time, Baxter has completed the mythological presentation of the event, so that what we are left with is not so much a nature poem as a parable of life and death. What Baxter found in the natural scene of Waipatiki Beach was an unmistakeable sign of the presence of death, that event which brings a final order to the chaos of living.
> (Weir, *Poetry* 31)

Bondage and discipline: Cybele

The description of Hekate's 'lion face' links suggestively to another of Baxter's fearsome goddess figures: Cybele, the Anatolian Great Mother or earth mother goddess, who demanded emasculation of her male priests. She appears most famously in a narrative poem by the Roman poet Catullus, who describes how the young man Attis sails across the sea where, in a frenzy, he castrates himself, becomes enslaved by the goddess, and is pursued by lions, the symbol of her power in nature.

Not surprisingly, Cybele features in Baxter's poem sequence 'Words to Lay a Strong Ghost (after Catullus)' (*CP* 356–64), almost all of which was written in 1966 after he returned to Dunedin to be confronted with the ghost of 'Pyrrha'. The Cybele imagery is used most extensively in 'The Wound' (*CP* 360, no. 8 of the sequence). The poet compares himself to Attis, his response to 'Pyrrha' being like an emasculation, with the wound still aching, though he hears 'the flute-players / And the rattling drum', the signature tune of the ecstatic worshippers of the goddess. He describes his life as 'Exile from the earth I came from', an exile in a metaphorical Mount Ida, which was Cybele's Phrygian home. The final stanza of the poems runs:

> No longer a man—Ah! don't let
> Your lion growl and run against me,
> Cybele's daughter—I accept
> Hard bondage, harder song!

The bondage to a daughter of Cybele thus entails the enforced torture of the creative process.[7]

The Cybele figure was, however, in Baxter's mind at least a decade before this: in 'Letter to Australia' (1955, *CP* 151–52) the poet speaks of resting his head 'upon the cancered breast / Of Cybele who is the dream's mother.' The goddess here appears to symbolise the unconscious and the source of the imagination, almost another face of the Muse. Her association with disease and pain again highlights the torment of the creative artist.[8]

In 'Reflections at Khandallah Baths' (1963, *CP* 288–89), Cybele's sphere of influence, like that of all the other similar female figures, extends to death. The poet has climbed a hill behind the bathing sheds and the cacophony blaring from transistor radios, and has dark thoughts about the life of the city. By contrast, he was in a place where 'punga ferns and boulders gave / The shelter of a green gully, / And the leaves rattled quick and blind / In the shade of the multiple Cybele / Whose gate of love is an open grave.' The goddess is here the earth mother, but also the entrance to sexuality and, inevitably, death.

'A Little Letter to Auckland Students' (*CP* 291–93), a satirical poem written in the following year, 1964, focuses on a somewhat less universal application of the goddess. The poet has supposedly had some rather risqué poetry banned by the university authorities, and he responds with typical energy. At the end of the poem he draws a contrast between 'You varsity maidens, sweet, refined' who can look forward to a life of deadly boring respectability, and himself:

> But as for me, my doom is plain;
> Outside the window I'll remain
> With callgirls, jockeys, spades and drunks,
> Who read no Milton in their bunks,
> Describing in barbaric verse

7 In 'The Friend' (*CP* 361, no. 10 of the sequence), the poet affirms that the friendship offered by the addressee (called Allius after a friend featuring in Catullus's poetic corpus) 'Has lifted for a half day from me / The manacles of Cybele.'

8 Just prior to this, in the same stanza of the poem, there is reference to 'The rose that opens like a wound / Where our blood upon the ground / Denies the existential night.' This is reminiscent of the same set of associations that Baxter was to apply to Cybele in 'The Wound'.

A non-Platonic universe
In which Pope Paul or I may be
The natural son of Cybele,
Digging in my private dunghill
Outside, outside the culture mill—
But soft! These verses will be read
When the inquisitors are dead.

He thus situates himself outside the 'artificial world' of refinement and culture in the 'real world', where everyone in the end is simply a human being, subject to the terms and conditions of humanity which owes its very continuation to sexuality. It is Cybele who symbolises this 'natural world'.

Two further poetic appearances of Cybele merit attention. The first of these occurs in the short, unpublished 1966 poem 'Epithalamium' (N26.48):

After a hundred tasks you lie down calm
    As if our bed were a grave,
And no bullheaded man invades your dream
    Of just platonic love,

But I remember, splitting rocks at dawn,
    The day you handed me
The altar knife by which my sex was torn
    And thrown to Cybele.

We are here dealing with the same imagery as that featured in 'The Wound', a poem written later in that same year, but applied to another, earlier relationship. The initiation into sex with a woman is seen as an emasculation and concomitant bondage. The irony is that the woman is now preoccupied with mundane tasks, so that a bed *without sex* becomes seen as a grave from the point of view of the man whose transformation into bestial Minotaur form is thwarted.

Cybele can represent little more than female domination seen in a negative light, as in 'The Eccentrics' (1968, *CP* 434), where 'Queen Cybele's grip' is placed alongside 'the shape in the cellar', 'the choirboy's bellow of rape', 'the whack of Caesar's whip', and 'the excellent electrode' as part of a catalogue of the unpleasant aspects of life from which escape is a boon. However, when one considers the roles she plays across a range of Baxterian contexts, it is clear that she is much more than this. She does provide sexual pleasure, even if the price to pay for this is a kind of emasculation and servitude. At the same time, she is the key to the 'natural' world that is portrayed as far preferable to the world of 'refined' urban culture. And she is the mother spirit of the earth who calls all her children back to her in death. Perhaps most importantly for Baxter, however, she is the source of dreams and the poetic impulse, agonising though this may be at times.

This final aspect of Cybele aligns her closely with the Muse herself, as can be seen from Baxter's already-quoted inclusion of her (along with Venus, Artemis and Hekate) in the list of names given to the anima (*MH* 116). As we have seen, this offers a valuable insight into the workings of Baxter's mind. It brings together the aspects of the female discussed in the previous chapter as well as this one, and it shows Baxter applying Jungian terminology to concepts which, although with an undeniably Jungian flavour, also have roots in the literary expressions of classical myth as well as in Baxter's personal encounter with the female.

The glare-eyed Eumenides

Moving further into the dark end of Baxter's feminine spectrum, we come to the Furies—in Greek, Erinyes or Eumenides. In the earliest Greek literature they could be a single entity, the Erinys, but it is the collective who became dominant, and it is as a group that they act out their role on Baxter's poetic stage. Originally, they were spirits of vengeance in a broad sense, but they came to be in particular avengers of the spilling of kindred blood. Most famously, in the hands of Aeschylus in the trilogy the *Oresteia*, they were the spirits who tormented Orestes, son of Agamemnon, for the crime of matricide, a crime which the divine authority of Apollo had ordered because Orestes' mother Clytemnestra had murdered his father. Orestes' reward was to be driven mad and pursued by the Furies, portrayed as women of hideous appearance with writhing snakes for hair (in this respect Gorgon-like). The final play of the trilogy then dramatises Orestes' trial at a court of law in Athens and his acquittal by a casting vote. The Furies, though mortified by the result, are offered compensation by being accorded an honoured dwelling place in the city; they are given the role of guardians and bringers of blessing and are renamed Eumenides or 'kindly ones'. They feature in other Greek tragedies, too; most importantly, for Baxter, in the drama of Sophocles' old age, *Oedipus at Colonus*, where their unseen presence is felt in the sacred grove into which the blinded Oedipus stumbles as he seeks shelter and asylum in the environs of Athens after his exile from Thebes and period of stateless wandering.

In *The Temptations of Oedipus*, Baxter's 1968 adaptation of Sophocles' play, the Furies appear in person without speaking and cast a shadow over the entire action. Oedipus's first mention of them at the start of the play associates them with death ('the power of the Furies and the ice-cold region of Persephone!', *CPlays* 232). After this, throughout the play, there are many references to them, often couched in the positive language of appeasement (234, 236, 238, 241, 242, 244). It is the sheer power of these goddesses and their almost unlimited potential to cause destruction that lead them to be addressed so often in this propitiatory manner. Oedipus himself, in a prayer to them early in the play, calls them 'Dear ladies' almost in the same breath as he has just called them 'you terrible Mothers' (237). This same ambivalence is also reflected in Theseus's words when Polyneices has abducted Antigone and Ismene: 'Let the Furies—no—I trust the Gracious Ones will accompany them' (255).

At the end of the play, when Oedipus's earlier thoughts about the chaos of existence appear to be confirmed by Theseus's decision to sacrifice Antigone's baby to avert the plague, he kneels to the Furies and addresses them with these bitter words, which bring to the surface the fear and loathing that have been masked by all the soothing gestures towards the 'Dear Ladies' or 'Gracious Ones':

> Old, foul nurses—daughters of Chaos—now I feel the grip of your teeth! You must have your blood—blood out of the soul itself! Now Oedipus is broken. Child-killers! Child-killers! Old hags! I deny you. I give you no more worship. Feed on the living! All men belong to you. What is there left in me for you to take? Now the parricide will die—the incestuous son—incestuous

> father—he will marry the Earth. You have lost your power. (260)

The operation of the Furies, who basically exist to harass the living and drive them to death, is only terminated by death itself and the return of a human being to mother earth. This passage, at the climax of Baxter's play, provides an ideal context in which to situate Baxter's other uses of the Furies concept throughout his poetic career.[9]

The unseen Furies are already threatening in 'A Rented Room' (1950, *CP* 93–94). A young man wakes in 'his own place', feeling quite content with what life is apparently offering him and even believing that he has 'all that the young require / To walk Niagara'. But the last two lines of the poem show that it is all a delusion: 'Not seeing the handsized cloud in the clear sky / And the door ajar to let the Furies enter.'

What is here only a vague threat is a much more immediate reality in the slightly earlier 'prose-poem' 'Eumenides' (N15.26, published as 'The Furies' in *Canta* 1948).[10] The Furies are portrayed here as having the function of haunting humans, punishing the 'crime' of being born in the first place. Baxter goes on:

> Their cry is an echo of that first cry of horror which rose at the breaking of the virgin sleep of Mother All. Our immortal companions, they are those forms to whom the child stretches his hands with his first inarticulate croaking, and the last mourners visible to his dying eyes. Especially they haunt the bed of love, with its mirage of Freedom beyond the last horizon—Fear, Guilt and Pain, the guardians of an imagined Eden never known in the act but anticipated in dreams.

Baxter provides an insight into his own thought process here in the discussion 'Notes on the Making of "The Martian"' (FM 20/4/19). He quotes from this poem ('He has chosen / To die

9 As with almost anything, Baxter could use the Furies in humorous contexts too, as, for example, in 'The Wheel' (1967, *CP* 386), in which a friend's mistress is said to be a woman 'Whose brass eyes and brass hair could keep / The Furies at arm's length'.

10 This is one of a series of prose-poems in notebook 15, several of which were published in *Canta*. Baxter himself says (FM 20/4/19) that the sequence had been published in the Victoria University student periodical *Salient*; his memory, however, seems to have let him down here.

in the lap of the cruel virgin / We call Reality') and comments:

> This statement is the metaphysical core of the poem. Who is the cruel virgin? I suggest—Diana, the moon-goddess—though in my early poem, 'The Unicorn', she was Aphrodite—'. . . but see / From the cold surf's futurity / Aphrodite Andyomene [*sic*] / Arise in birth thou woulds't extinction deem, / Arise and bind thee to an iron dream . . .'

He then proceeds to quote the first sentence of the passage from 'Eumenides'/'The Furies' (the cry of the Furies as 'an echo of that first cry of horror which rose at the breaking of the virgin sleep of Mother All') and comments: 'this Unblessed Virgin is creation seen as chaos, the emptied and non-sacramental universe which modern man has to try to penetrate, master and understand.'

Although the idea of the Furies appears comparatively early in Baxter's thought, he was clearly also carrying it with him throughout the 1960s. We can see this, for example, in 'Prayer for a Duck-Shooting Uncle' (1961–64, *CP* 304–05), where it seems clear that 'the Fury squatting there' is a symbol of death heralding the return of one of earth's children to herself. Then again, a poem dating to the period 1962–63 and explicitly entitled 'The Eumenides' (N 23.67) begins with the words:

> A man late at night on his own
> Whittles a fear to a fine edge
> On the mind's lop-sided grindstone:
>
> Shuffle, behind an antique hedge,
> Of the glare-eyed Eumenides
> Felt at the darkest fringe of knowledge,
>
> Blood-born.

This nicely evokes the primitive siting of the Furies—what Baxter goes on to call 'the snake-haired Daughters'—on the margin of the intellect yet part of the very essence of the human condition.

'Ancestors (I)' (c.1963, N24.7) imagines dead family members, evoking them as 'Images from nowhere [that] darken my pillow / with ghostly circumstance'. The source of such imaginings is then described as follows:

The fire-bred Furies
Spew such phantoms, aiming to divert
Us from knowledge of the Atridean pain
They battened on, like fleas in an old shirt,
Our fathers and their houses, or how the stain
Of sweat and sorrow, spreading under the frames
Of photographs, first made their names our names.

This take on the Furies' function as senders of dreams—in which the term 'Atridean' (referring to the myth of Orestes, grandson of Atreus) basically means 'ancestral'—is reminiscent of a passage in the novel *Horse* (written in the 1950s but published posthumously in 1985). The title character attends what is supposed to be a lecture at the Literary Club but realises 'with sudden joy' that Mr Grummet the lecturer is extremely drunk. Mr Grummet indeed acts out the role of the hero of Sophocles' tragedy *Oedipus at Colonus*, addressing the audience as though they are the citizens of Colonus:

> 'I myself am blind!' Mr Grummet gripped the table and stared at it. 'I am Oedipus the King of many-gated Thebes. This slab of wood, or it may be stone, is, I believe, the doorstep of the goddesses who send us dreams of damnation, the powerful Eumenides. (*Horse* 85–86)

We are back in the territory which Baxter was later to colonise with his play *The Temptations of Oedipus*. Although the register of *Horse* is satirically comic, the role of the Furies remains the same as in many of the serious contexts already discussed.[11] 'Dreams of damnation' is precisely what Baxter has consistently been subjected to.

It is clear, then, that the Eumenides or Furies represent an extremely important aspect of Baxter's world view, emerging as they do from the darkness of the subconscious and the primeval past of humanity. He was always wrestling with them, finding it extremely difficult to come to terms with them. He even attempted to make them servants of his Catholic Christianity, as the following statement from a letter to John Weir dated 4 March 1967 (FM 20/4/7) illustrates:

11 Baxter discusses the story of Horse and his girlfriend Fern in 'Further Notes on New Zealand poetry', including a reference to this lecture by Mr Grummet (11).

> THE FURIES—what is most feared, rising from the subjective abyss—are the image of the love of God—the devourers of the relics of sin in the soul—to fall into the hands of the living . . . again an intuition I cannot fully achieve, but which represents a boundary of my art.

In the end, though, like so many other similar figures, the Furies can be situated at the heart of the poetic impulses which Baxter experienced. As he once expressed it: 'The Furies, those Muses of black-humour poetry, roosted on my doorstep like great scraggy chickens, and never left it again. It is, after all, their proper home' ('Essay on the Higher Learning' 62).

Medusa, image of the soul's despair

The Gorgon is the most ubiquitous of the infernal feminine figures in Baxter's writing, and also perhaps the most complex. According to the myth there were three Gorgons, two of them immortal and one mortal, depicted in ancient art as horrendously ugly although, according to one branch of the tradition, the mortal one at least had once been exceedingly beautiful but had been punished with a degrading metamorphosis for offending the goddess Athene.[12] This mortal one, called Medusa, became the most famous, and the term 'Gorgon' more often than not refers just to her. The spectrum of what she has come to represent is well captured in the following description:

> Poets have called her a Muse. Feminists have adopted her as a sign of powerful womanhood. Anthropologists read her image as embedded in the paradoxical logic of amulets, talismans, and relics. Psychoanalysts have understood the serpents wreathing her head as a symbol of the fear of castration. Political theorists have cast her as a figure for revolt. Artists have painted her in moods from sublime to horrific. The most canonical writers (Homer, Dante, Shakespeare, Goethe, Shelley) have invoked her story and sung both her praise and her blame. The most adventurous of postmodern designers and performers see her as a model, a logo, and a figure for the present age. (Garber and Vickers 1)

12 For a full account, with all the ancient sources, see Gantz 20–22.

Medusa was generally portrayed with writhing snakes for hair, boar's tusks and a lolling tongue—a hideous visage that immediately turned to stone any living creature that looked upon it. She could be killed safely only by the hero Perseus, because he looked at her reflection in his shield as he decapitated her. He then flew away courtesy of his winged sandals, after placing her head in a pouch attached to his belt. He would subsequently use the lifeless head (which still retained its petrifying power) on his enemies. This face or mask of the Gorgon has been used by Freudians as a symbol of the vulva, which supposedly generates in a male the fear of castration. Baxter used it in this way (as noted in chapter 1) in 'The Advantages of Analysis' (1960, N20.68); but he also gave it a range of other negative applications.

Sometimes in Baxter's work the word 'gorgon' simply stands for something unpleasant. We can see this, for example, in 'The Surfman's Story' (1950–52, *CP* 124–25), where a 'narrow rip' that has claimed the lives of 'a few / Fool bathers' gets a bad name which has grown 'to a gorgon myth'—though there is also an implication here of the paralysing fear involved in the drowning process. In 'Songs of the Desert 2' (1947, *CP* 54–55), a place of respite after strife is described in these terms: 'The sun is not darkened / with brazen wings / and the face of the gorgon / is hidden.' And in 'The Fallen House' (1950, *CP* 97–98), the doom haunting a house 'daunted / The heart with a lidless gorgon stare.'

More commonly, Baxter specifically identifies the Gorgon with the dangerous, angry or warped aspect of the female,[13] as in a passage from 'Poem on a Clay Tile' (c.1959–60, N20.76): 'Perhaps a brown Etruscan figurine / Of angel self and gorgon self / Dug from beneath the lintel of the senses'. The opposition between Christian angel and classical Gorgon points towards the poem-producing tension between Baxter's respectable and anarchic twin selves.[14] Baxter's sense of the dangerously double nature of the feminine is encapsulated in a prose passage, which

13 On one occasion Baxter masculinises the Gorgon: 'when a maid is a-weeping no gorgon am I.' This occurs in a sea shanty sung by Charlie Bird in *Jack Winter's Dream* (*CPlays* 9).

14 Baxter reused these lines in 'Tuatara Poem' (N20.77), the very next poem in this notebook.

perhaps references Medusa's own transformation from beauty to life-destroying hideousness: 'A young man who has married a vivacious and flirtatious girl may be scared out of his wits by her transformation into a neurotic and life-hating gorgon. He doesn't know that it's happening to everybody; that it's the way our society digests its members' (*FC* 96).

But applications of the Gorgon figure go even further. As already noted, the Gorgon of myth had the power to literally petrify any creature that saw her face. Thus Baxter, metaphorically, can see her agency behind any case of coldness, lifelessness, or inert stupidity. Thus he can write: 'It seemed to me (old enough to know better) and other admirers of their own words in print, that those thousand upon thousand mysterious lives that suffer and exalt, dread and endure behind the lights on the Wellington hills had inexplicably become a Gorgon's head, a stone mask of stupidity from which we are prepared to run screaming' ('The Phoenix and the Crow'). In 'Design for a Mural' (N25.66) he can speak of a time when 'the Gorgon's face / Across millennia smiling a stone grimace / Freezes our hearts that would cry peace, / Cry mercy, but from habitual pride are drunk.' And in the context of a lover's quarrel ('Discussion of the Heart's Infirmity', N17.101) we find: 'As lovers grow in natural cruelty / bodily love imparts no remedy. // Nor spiritual; for the spirit turns / Medusa-head, enraged at love's defeat.'

The proper name Medusa is used here, as it is in a very different application of the idea of the deadening process in 'Letter to Robert Burns' (*CP* 289–91). Baxter is communing with the Dunedin statue of the Scottish poet, reflecting on his experiences in the city, including drinking binges, and speaks of 'the blank / Medusa conscience of a drunk / That hankers for the purity / Of an imagined infancy'. Quite differently again, we find in 'Autumn Testament' 33 the thought that 'Our Church looks to the young / Like a Medusa' (*CP* 557). The implication is that the church, which should have a life-giving message, appears to be offering the opposite and to have had a paralysing effect on society, so that a younger generation, seeing this, choose to turn their faces away from her.

Indeed, it takes great strength and moral courage to resist the deadening forces to which one is exposed. As Baxter writes in the notes following the poem sequence 'He Waiata Mo Te Kare', the first section of *Autumn Testament*: 'Depersonalisation, centralisation, desacralisation: the three chief scourges of the urban culture. One has to look squarely at the Medusa's head that turns so many into stone before one can even begin to smile again' (*AT* 9).

In one early poem ('To the Moon', N15.74), the coldness of the moon, in comparison with the life embodied in a sleeping wife and child, is expressed through this same image. The poet asks the moon to turn away her face, a face that is 'unchanging', yet 'furrowed with age, but never tears'. She is 'not the virgin huntress' grace / Of glimmering limbs, rather the Gorgon's eye, / Whose loveless brow must burn and petrify / Washed by the sterile winds of outer space.'[15] Three human lives are thus set against the impersonal universe as represented by the moon. Interestingly, the poet, rather than averting his own gaze, requests the moon to avert hers, with the comment, 'I am no Perseus.'

Given that the Gorgon petrifies, it is hardly surprising that Baxter takes the ultimate step of associating her with death itself. In the poem 'At Rotorua' (1961, *CP* 228–29), it is the moon which provides the link: 'I see the skull moon reddened by / Scrub fires, a summer gorgon'. Perhaps the hardest hitting application of the Gorgon figure to death, as well as to the idea of New Zealand society as a death-dealing institution, however, appears in 'Letter to Peter Olds', a poem written in the last year of Baxter's life (*CP* 578–81):

> So hard to focus the ball of the human eye
> On our terrible Mother, that stone Medusa
>
> Sitting on her hill of skulls—suicides, abortions,
> Gang-splashes, bloodstained mattresses, a ton of empty pill bottles,

15 A similar idea can be found in 'The World of the Creative Artist', in a discussion of Roy Fuller's poem 'Harbour Ferry': 'The moon, a customary symbol of fertility, brings rigor mortis to the war-broken ships and the men on the battlefields. Like the archaic Gorgon on the wall of a Greek temple, with "furious steps" she scatters death and poison, a devouring force of blind causality; and love as well as war comes within her orbit' (24).

And whatever else the wind may blow in the doorway,
Including, one may hope, the tired dove

Of the human spirit, raped again and again in the skyway
By the mechanical hawk.

The aspects of the Gorgon imagery come together most strikingly in contexts concerning poetry and poetic inspiration. As noted in chapter 1, Baxter often depicts his Muse as a terrifying, ugly female figure. Thus she can be 'An old black hag with red arachnoid eyes' ('The Muse', *CP* 234). She can be 'a woman in a sack or shroud' berating a returning drunkard with the words: 'Husband, liar, drone, / What scissor cut the cord and brought you home? / Has the pub burnt down?', after which Baxter concludes: 'I think, / Johnson, it was the Muse, whom you and I / unhinge by our civility' ('The Muse (to Louis Johnson)', *CP* 352).

In a letter to Fleur Adcock dated 11 September 1961 (FM 27/1/3), Baxter discusses the first of these poems, making specific a connection with the Gorgon as well as with the Jungian archetype: 'The hag is of course the Bad Mother of the psychologists. You would probably have a different kind of Gorgon.' It is specifically the Gorgon/Muse who appears in 'Inscription' (1965, *CP* 329): 'It is hard to master the verbs of the body, not easy / To frame for the Gorgon a decorous speech.' And the short 1966 poem 'Kelp' (*CP* 343), as we have already noted, identifies the seaweed as 'The dark locks of the deaf Medusa, / Mother of my songs; who has turned me to stone.' The same idea appears already in 'Mandrakes for Supper' (1959, *CP* 200), an exploration of the unconscious and the source of poetic inspiration:

The white Antarctic Gorgon was my mentor:
Her cloudy arms, her eyes of desolation

Sisterly gazing from the whirlwind's centre,
Received, embraced my naked intuition.

And in 'Letter to Robert Burns' (*CP* 289–91), as we have seen, the Gorgon/Muse is specifically given credit for transforming a life experience into poetry.

Baxter's most extended exploration of the figure of Medusa, however, is found in the early 1952 poem 'Perseus' (*CP* 129–30).

It would certainly be possible to interpret this poem in Jungian terms as a vignette of the battle against the mother image. At the same time, other approaches are also relevant. The narrative follows the hero's journey eastwards[16] until he reaches 'the stone kingdom where no life / Startled,' where he encounters the Gorgon:

> Fair smote her face upon the burning shield,
> Medusa, image of the soul's despair,
> Snake-garlanded, child of derisive Chaos
> And hateful Night, whom no man may
> Look on and live. In horror, pity, loathing,
> Perseus looked long, lifted his sword, and struck.

This brings us back to Baxter's conviction that the mythologising poet can impose some kind of order on the chaos of existence. But there is also a more specific angle to this, as O'Sullivan rightly emphasises (*Baxter* 40). Baxter saw it as the artist's duty to rid urban society of the monster that turns its inhabitants to stone, as it were, by deadening their souls and enslaving them to the material. In this poem, he does so by assuming the heroic role and beheading the 'image of the soul's despair', but he must then travel home with 'the pouched Despair at his girdle hanging'. Moreover, awaiting him, once his heroic foray is over, is the reality of domesticity as he gives back to his divine sponsors 'the borrowed sandals of courage and the shield of art'. This Perseus figure, then, travels in parallel with the Odysseus figure.

Baxter was still thinking in these terms a decade and a half later when, in discussing John Henry Newman's views on Christianity and literature, he quotes what he calls 'the positive core' of Newman's argument: 'it is not the way to learn to swim in troubled waters, never to have gone into them'. And Baxter continues:

16 In a letter to Charles Brasch of 31 March 1953 (FM 20/2/3), which accompanied his submission of 'Perseus' and 'Seraphion' for publication, Baxter commented that the second stanza of 'Perseus' had echoes of Aphrodite's passage over the Greek hills in Hesiod. His memory seems to have let him down here, since what he had in mind is more likely to have been the passage from the Homeric *Hymn to Aphrodite* in which the goddess is on her way to visit Anchises in his hut. This incident, as we have noted in ch. 3, made a lasting impression on Baxter, and he referred to it in a number of contexts.

I would interpret this to mean that Newman thinks an intellectual knowledge of evil is a safeguard, not a handicap, in coping with actual evil, and that it is one of the functions of literature to supply this knowledge by holding up an exact mirror to human nature. The face of Medusa did not turn the Greek hero to stone when he saw it reflected in his shield. To throw away the shield of art is a great folly. ('Literature and Belief', *MH* 44)[17]

It is clear, then, that the figure of the Gorgon Medusa was useful to Baxter for expressing a number of central ideas. In the first place, Medusa represents all that is ugly and terrifying, the manifestation of chaos which turns the human heart to stone, whether this stems from modern urban society in general or from a church that appears to have lost its way. Ironically, however, Medusa's head also appears from the chaotic unconscious to stimulate that very artistic creativity designed to keep her in check.[18]

When we place Medusa alongside the other figures discussed in this chapter, we can see that 'the infernal feminine' fulfils a variety of functions in Baxter's writing, and cannot be reduced to a 'monomyth', Jungian or otherwise. The same is true of his versions of Venus/Aphrodite, and indeed of the whole female continuum traced in the last two chapters. Baxter's mythic images of the female may appear problematic—even 'appalling'—if they are viewed as statements about the nature of women; but that is not necessarily their function. Viewed as statements about Baxter's mental landscape, about the human (male) condition, and about the forces which goaded or scourged him into poetry, they are very close to the heart of his creative process.

17 There is a slightly different angle on this in 'Further Notes on New Zealand Poetry' (FM 18/1/4 p.21) where Baxter claims that the young 'endeavour from time [to time] to hold up a mirror to the inhuman pattern of public events, as Perseus held up a shield to the Gorgon'.

18 It is interesting to find many of the elements of Baxter's treatment of the Gorgon imagery already in 'Resurrection' (c.1944, N13.792). This rather rambling piece, about war and various other topics, includes expressions such as 'Medusa she', 'the snakes of fear' and 'Man's heart is stone'.

GORGON AND TANIWHA

CHAPTER 5

THE GARDEN AND THE LABYRINTH: HERCULES AND THESEUS

Baxter and the heroes

'I became the companion of Odin and Thor and Jason and Ulysses' ('Education', *MH* 132)—so Baxter recalls his first acquaintance with Norse and Greek mythologies. His fond roll-call of childhood friends suggests one difference between the two bodies of myth: whereas the most memorable Norse myths concern the battles and tragedies of the gods, Greek myths characteristically focus on the deeds of heroes. 'A class of being between man and god', usually though not invariably the half-and-half offspring of a god and a mortal woman, Greek heroes are larger-than-life warriors, monster-slayers, establishers and defenders of civilisation. They also tend to be marked out by turbulent personal lives and tragic deaths; 'heroes in myth have a nasty habit of living hard and dying young' (Dowden 156). In Greek religion, they are defined by the semi-divine honours that are offered to them at their (supposed) graves. In art and literature, classical and post-classical, they become icons of the nature and limits of human achievement.

For the mature Baxter (rather than the excited boy reader), heroes as such were of little interest. As a lifelong pacifist, he saw no appeal in warriors or conquerors; it is symptomatic that whereas the wanderer Odysseus/Ulysses recurs constantly in his work, Achilles (the glorious warrior hero of the *Iliad*) is conspicuously absent. With an almost anarchistic disdain for the arena of worldly power and government (the world of 'Caesar'), he was not interested in hero-kings or lawgivers. And as a Christian whose world view is dominated by a sense of the Fall, he was deeply sceptical of the pagan ideal of worldly glory; as his sister-in-law noted, 'He may have known all his Greek legends but he never subscribed to the Greek philosophy of the glory and immortality of human achievement' (Lenore Baxter to Frank McKay, FM 10/7/32). The nature of heroism is a subject that his poetry rarely explores.

Nevertheless, certain classical heroes do recur in Baxter's work. Odysseus, the most important of these, demands a chapter to himself. This chapter will focus on two other major figures: Hercules and Theseus.[1] Despite the similarities between their classical stories, these two heroes become for Baxter in effect symbolic opposites. Each is associated for him with a place which has deeply symbolic associations: Hercules with the Garden of the Hesperides, Theseus with the Labyrinth. And they take on meaning in relation to Baxter's central myth of the Fall—Hercules associated with the desire to return to the unfallen innocence of childhood, Theseus (an anti-hero, for Baxter) with the fallen and compromised world of adult experience.

Hercules

Herakles—or Hercules, in his more familiar Roman guise—is the greatest of the Greek heroes, the only one to cross the hero/god divide by becoming a full god when he dies.[2] In Greek myth he is a rather equivocal figure. Wandering all over the known world and beyond, performing countless feats of strength and daring on top of his famous Twelve Labours, he is the greatest of all monster-slayers, a champion of civilised humankind against the threats of the wild and the monstrous. Yet his superhuman strength, size, and courage are matched by equally superhuman physical and sexual appetites, and by fits of titanic rage and madness in which (among other crimes) he kills his wife and children. Clad in a lion-skin and wielding a huge club, or dispatching opponents with his bare hands, he is a primitive figure, as much the antithesis

1 Jason, who appears almost exclusively in Baxter's unpublished work, is discussed in Miles, 'Baling the Golden Fleece'.

2 Baxter's usage is divided about evenly between Greek *Herakles* and Latin *Hercules*; the more familiar Latinised name is here used as the standard form. For a brief summary of Hercules' career, see the Who's Who.

as the champion of civilisation. However, Stoic philosophers and Christian moralists found it easy to simplify his contradictions into a simple embodiment of virtue (the 'choice of Hercules' between easy Pleasure and strenuous Virtue became a popular allegorical theme). For Christian writers he even becomes a type of Christ: a son of God who comes to earth to labour tirelessly on behalf of mankind, who dies a painful death as a result of human betrayal, but rises again to join his Father in heaven.[3]

Allusions to Hercules, both explicit and covert, appear in Baxter's writing throughout his career—though, for reasons which will be explored later, they tend to cluster around two particular periods of his life, in the years 1946–47 and 1966–68. Hercules is never such a consistent 'figure of self' for him as Odysseus, however, and there is an ironic distance in his self-comparisons, from the disparaging allusion to his 'empty lion-skin' in the 'Letter to Noel Ginn' (*CP* 27–29), written at the age of eighteen in 1944, to the bleakly comic incongruities of 'The Tiredness of Me and Herakles' (*CP* 595–97), written not long before his death in 1972.[4] Like Hamlet (1.2.152–53), Baxter is most conscious of his ludicrous unlikeness to the great hero.

Hercules is also a strangely 'absent presence' in Baxter's poetry, most often invoked as absent, or dead, or unable to help—'For us no Theban Hercules / Can raise again the fallen sky' ('As we have sown', N15.7).[5] In his first explicitly named appearance, in the unpublished 'City of Desolation' (1946, N14.697), he is an undead, skeletal figure: 'And Herakles laying his bony breast / upon the careless marble turns and sighs'. The image is echoed in *The Sore-footed Man* (1967, *CP* 127-59), where Baxter omits the deus ex machina appearance of the god Herakles which is

3 For an excellent survey of Hercules' changing incarnations see Galinsky, *The Herakles Theme.*

4 The 'empty lion-skin' could also allude to Aesop's fable of the ass in the lion-skin; Baxter may have had both images in mind.

5 The elusiveness of Baxter's Hercules may owe something to the haunting final image of him in Apollonius's *Argonautica*, where the Argonauts arrive at the garden of the Hesperides only to find he has already departed, and only the keen-eyed Lynceus 'fancied / that he could see Herakles, off in the farthest distance, / the way a man, when the month's new, sees—or imagines / he sees—a sliver of moon through the obscuring clouds' (4.1477–80).

the climax of Sophocles' play, and substitutes Philoctetes' moving description of the mortal hero's death: 'He asked me to carry him to the top of the mountain and throw his body into the crater—I say "his body"—he was almost a living corpse' (*CPlays* 139–40). In the same speech Philoctetes describes Hercules as 'A great man [. . .] But somehow childlike'. 'Childlike' is not perhaps the most obvious word one would choose to describe Hercules; but the primitive, pre-civilised quality of the Greek hero and the Christ-like associations of his later tradition come together for Baxter to suggest a figure who is associated with the innocence of an unfallen world, and who cannot exist in the fallen world that we inhabit.

Baxter's Hercules and the Garden of the Hesperides

One episode in Hercules' eventful career is overwhelmingly most significant for Baxter: his quest for the golden apples of the Hesperides. These apples were a gift from the earth mother, Gea, for the wedding of Zeus and Hera. They grew on a tree in a magical garden beyond the bounds of the known world, somewhere in the far west, where the sun sets. The nymphs known as Hesperides, daughters of the evening (the Greek *hespera* means both 'evening' and 'west'), sang and danced around the tree, and it was guarded by a great serpent or dragon. Hercules, as the eleventh of his (increasingly difficult) Twelve Labours, had to steal some of the golden apples. In some tellings of the story he simply killed the dragon and seized the apples. The more popular version, however, had him seek the help of the Titan Atlas, who stood in the far west perpetually holding up the sky, and who was a kind of gatekeeper for the garden. Hercules took the load of the sky on his own shoulders, while Atlas, grateful for the relief, fetched the apples for him (he then tried to cheat Hercules and leave him holding the sky, but Hercules, with unusual quick-wittedness, tricked him into taking on the load again).

It will be clear how this myth echoes the biblical Garden of Eden: a paradisal garden, an apple tree, a serpent, a theft of fruit. The Garden of the Hesperides is linked with other unattainable paradisal places in Greek myth—the Golden Age at the beginning of human history; the Islands of the Blest or the Elysian Fields where the souls of the specially favoured enjoy eternal bliss after death. The golden apples may originally have granted immortality or godhood, like their counterparts in Norse and Celtic myths—though this significance has faded from the received version of the Greek, where Hercules rather anticlimactically hands the apples back to Athene after showing them to his king (Kirk 193). Richard Caldwell, in his Freudian analysis of Greek myth, suggests that the Garden of the Hesperides and its counterparts are symbols of the womb, that meadows and gardens are associated in Greek literature with female genitalia, and apples (golden or otherwise) with the female breast; the myth thus embodies a human longing for return to the infant state of 'symbiosis' with the mother (156–61).[6] It is a reading which seems plausibly applicable to Baxter's use of the myth.

The appeal of the Hesperides image for Baxter is obvious. Even before his conversion to Christianity and his intellectual acceptance of the doctrines of the Fall and original sin, he was strongly drawn towards the image of Eden: an original condition of innocence and harmony with nature, still partly accessible to us in childhood but lost with the entry into adult experience and the knowledge of sexuality and mortality. This vision is at the heart of many of the poems of his earlier, more lyrical period: 'the bay that never was' in 'The Bay' (*CP* 44), 'the undestroyed / Fantastic Eden of a waking dream' in 'Virginia Lake' (*CP* 74), the 'wild children, stranger than Atlanteans' in 'Poem by the Clock Tower, Sumner', for whom 'rises yet / From earth's still centre the heaven-bearing / Immortal Tree' (*CP* 73). And in a whole series of early poems, it is associated with the Garden of the Hesperides—'The last the first the day-forgotten garden / The fruit Hesperidean' ('Aubade', N14.948). (It is also associated with the Celtic Avalon, an enchanted island of apple trees.) Baxter wholeheartedly identifies with the dying words of Dylan Thomas,

6 The breasts/apples analogy, suppressed in Baxter's serious verse, is made explicit in the bawdy 'Ballad of the Venus Man-o'-War' (N22.59), as the hero Willy swims naked with his beloved: 'Two golden apples on a dish / In Eden's grove he saw; / He did not see that jellyfish, / That wily man-o'-war.' The whole poem is a carnivalesque parody of the Eden myth, with the jellyfish standing in for the serpent.

quoted in 'Conversation with an Ancestor' (*MH* 20): 'I want to go back to the Garden of Eden.' This, for Baxter, is the primary significance of Hercules: he is the man who wants to go back to Eden, and who, because he is a hero rather than merely a man, might be capable of realising that desire.

The figure of Atlas is also drawn into the Edenic imagery. (The connection between Atlas and the 'Atlantean' children in the 'Clock Tower' poem is perhaps not just a verbal coincidence.) In 'The Giant's Grave' (1951–55, *CP* 153) he is a guardian and gatekeeper figure, protecting the earthly paradise where the poet and his brother played as children—

> Some heavens ago, when the wind blew from a calmer
> Airt,[7] and stood yet Atlas, benignant Titan,
> At the winged horizon's gate, his locks of cloud unshorn,
> Heaving the sky on his shoulders [. . .]

—and twinned, in a sense, with Antaeus the earth giant, whose grave-tumulus is at the heart of the paradise. In 'Atlas' (c.1942, *Spark* 447–48), on the other hand, the Titan seems to be himself suffering the consequences of the Fall:

> In the same orchard steel and oaken still
> Where Time's first dream dissolved to adamant rhyme
> Atlas lost heart and will.

The poem, in Baxter's early 'obscurist' style, is hard to interpret in detail, but in a pencilled note Baxter identifies Atlas as 'Man bearing human destiny on his shoulders'—an Adam figure, perhaps. The association between Atlas and Adam will resurface nearly three decades later in 'The Tiredness of Me and Herakles'.

At the same time that Baxter associates the Hesperidean garden with pre-pubertal childhood innocence, he also insistently associates it with love and sexuality. This paradoxical connection—not so paradoxical, if one accepts Caldwell's psychoanalytic reading of the myth—may originate from a seminal (as it were) passage in Marlowe's *Hero and Leander*. Describing the first sexual encounter of the young lovers, Marlowe writes:

7 'Airt' (a Scots dialect word): direction, point of the compass.

> Leander now, like Theban Hercules,
> Entered the orchard of the Hesperides,
> Whose fruit none rightly can describe but he
> That pulls or shakes it from the golden tree. (1. 297–300)

The first of these two couplets seems to have lodged irremovably in Baxter's mind. He quotes it in *Aspects of Poetry in New Zealand* as an example of the difference between male and female uses of symbolism: whereas a female poet will tend to use the image of a garden as a reflection of her own self, 'a man [. . .] will tend to see it as a private paradise, a sacred place, a womb perhaps, which he enters from the outside' (30–31).[8] The phrase 'Theban Hercules' becomes Baxter's quasi-Homeric formula for referring to the hero. It appears, for example, in the 1962 poem 'The Betrayal' (*CP* 254–55): 'his body between her knees, / In the place we begin at, like Theban Hercules'. The allusion to Hercules here is mysterious unless one recognises the Marlovian echo, and hence the equation of entering the Hesperidean orchard with entering the vagina/womb.

Hesperides regained: the 1946–47 love poems

This erotic reading explains the sudden prominence of the myth of Hercules and the Hesperides in Baxter's poems of 1946–47. In these years Baxter, aged 20–21 and a student at Otago University, was having his first, intense love affair with the medical student Jane Aylward, whom he later recalled as 'Cressida' (*CP* 101–11) and as Pyrrha in 'Words to Lay a Strong Ghost' (*CP* 356–64). One can trace the progress and decay of the affair through Baxter's use of the Hesperidean image through these (mostly unpublished) poems.

The first poem of the sequence, 'Ode to the New Zealand Summer' (N14.916, dated Christmas Eve 1945), is not a love poem but a lament for a loveless society. Here the eternal summer and bliss of the Hesperides is contrasted with New Zealand's 'antarctic age of wrath and hunger'. As Maori used to huddle

8 A small verbal slip (substituting *then* for *now*) indicates that Baxter is quoting from memory.

in caves, we take refuge in pubs or Calvinist churches: 'Who now the inviolable garden may / Force, to the rich Hesperides and peace?'[9] Yet even when winter gives way to spring and summer, 'the self-chosen captives lock their love / Hang chains on either wrist'. As often in Baxter's early poems, winter, cold and rain figure a spiritual or psychological desolation.[10] Hercules makes his first explicit appearance in a poem built around similar images: 'City of Desolation: A fantasy of the winter world' (N14.697, dated 7 May 1946). The 'city' is an urban version of Eliot's Waste Land, a place of spiritual death and acedia where the 'green fountain' of life at the city centre has dried up, where love is extinct and even Hercules impotent, 'laying his bony breast / upon the careless marble'. Here it is the serpent, 'the great python coiled', which is the latent principle of life: 'could he rise erect and golden-mailed / then were the world renewed and the frozen wells of Eden'.

In 'Night Song' (N14.923, dated 1 January 1946) the garden is still inaccessible:

And sworded angels guard
Th' Hesperidean tree—
Man homeless in the wood
Of immortality.

But this time the poet addresses an imagined future lover—'Sweetheart I have not seen / Child or woman', 'whom the heavens keep / Unborn or underground'—whose happiness he prays for even in the winter world. In the poems that follow the potential lover becomes an actual one, and love, it is claimed, can indeed force open the inviolable garden and restore us to Eden. In 'Aubade' (N14.948, early 1946):

9 The idea of the pub as an inadequate surrogate for the Edenic garden suggests that there may be an ironic allusion to the Hesperides in Barney Flanagan's Hesperus Hotel (*CP* 136–37). (It was the 'Covenant Hotel' in the notebook draft, N17.79; both names are fictional, Flanagan's real-life original being licensee of Wellington's National Hotel (McKay 150).)

10 Compare, for instance, 'Rain-ploughs' (*CP* 26–27); 'The Snow-Bird' (N14.942—'cruel winter' vs 'Eden freshness'); 'Songs of the Desert' 6 (*CP* 57—'My winter world can smell the spring returning').

O in the mountain of
My anguish you are Spring;
And the rose of peace, my love,
At day's awakening
The green buds burst and sing.
[. . .]
For you the brazen
Impenetrable gates may swing:
To man's love open
The last the first the day-forgotten garden
The fruit Hesperidean.

And in 'O do not strip' (N14.987, 28 July 1946) love is available to all of us and, though brief, gives us a glimpse of the eternal happiness of Eden:

There is no truth but in the tenuous
Moment of love that everlasting shows;
The heart moulds all—in every garden grow
Hesperidean apples cankerless.

The apples of the Hesperides—and of Avalon and Eden—are repeatedly associated in Baxter's poems with his love affair with Jane. In 'Songs of the Desert' his lover has 'the scent of apples on [her] skin' (7, *CP* 57), and is '[f]resh as an apple blossom' (13, *CP* 61). In 'Cressida', more ominously, 'cigarette ash and apple core' litter the floor as the lovers 'smoke, smile, sport, // With not an eye for the snake twined / Old on the garden-tree' (*CP* 102). All these apples are fruit of 'that high apple-tree [. . .] / That somehow bent in Eden' ('The Apple Tree', *CP* 220–21).

The moment of love, however, is indeed 'tenuous'. As early as May 1946, in 'Loved face my own and not my own' (N14.953), Baxter tells his lover that she cannot 'lead [him] to Hesperus again / Where charmed rivers nightlong fill the night'. By November or December, in 'Hesperides was growing' (N14.1004), the image of the Hesperidean garden has 'put on / An elegiac colour', associated now with childhood memories and dreams. And by the time Baxter is writing the 'Songs of the Desert' in mid 1947, the affair is clearly over: 'My shadowless familiar / Long since sucked dry the apples of my summer' (3, *CP* 55). The lovers are once again in the fallen world, and no Hercules can give them access to the garden:

> As we have sown the changing breeze
> And squandered our heart's charity,
> For us no Theban Hercules
> Can raise again the fallen sky—
> Nor shall the great angelic throng
> That trembled at an infant's cry
> Echo anew our broken song.

Baxter sums up their fallen condition: 'Heart as blind as a darkened room / And our every act a vain / Hieroglyph in a desert tomb' (8, *CP* 58). The desert is the barren antithesis of the Edenic garden; the tomb even more emphatically signifies entrapment in mortality—'the bloody / Sarcophagus of this a dying body' (3, *CP* 55).

Hesperides lost: young love in retrospect

When Baxter, in later years, recalls the affair with Jane, images of Hercules and the Hesperides recur. One example has already been cited: 'The Betrayal' (1962). This is a revised version of 'The Dream' (1961, N22.3) which relates the dream more nakedly in first rather than third person. In the earlier version Baxter describes how 'Last night I slept with Pyrrha / In an orthopaedic surgery', while a 'fat hoggish landlady' glares through the window—a surreal dream-transposition of the bone-cluttered flat and suspicious landlady recalled in *Horse* (58). The lovers are on the floor, 'Her arms behind her head, and I between her knees, / In the place we begin at, like Theban Hercules'. This highly compressed line evokes Marlowe's comparison of Leander making love to Hero with 'Theban Hercules' entering the 'orchard of the Hesperides'; at the same time 'the place we begin at' suggests both a return to the original Garden of Eden, and a return to the maternal womb. The moment of erotic triumph is brief; when the dreamer asks Pyrrha, 'Where have you been, all these years?' her head rolls sideways and she looks at him 'with a yellow corpse's eye'. The consolatory fantasy of the garden gives way, again, to the tomb.

The most revealing later treatment of the theme, unexpectedly, is in Baxter's largely comic autobiographical novel *Horse* (posthumously published in 1985). *Horse* was probably written in the early 1960s,[11] but it first surfaced publicly in 1966, when Baxter discussed and quoted from his 'unpublished and unpublishable novel' in the Otago University lecture 'Conversation with an Ancestor' (MH 17–20). It thus becomes associated with the Burns Fellowship period in which Baxter 'wrestled with the ghost of an ancient mistress who came back to haunt me, and got a number of written lectures and some grim, dry poems out of the encounter' ('On the Burns Fellowship', 244–45). Earlier and much lighter-hearted than the Catullan sequence 'Words to Lay a Strong Ghost' (mainly 1966, *CP* 356–64), *Horse* nevertheless also springs out of Baxter's 'wrestling' with the Jane Aylward experience.

In 'Conversation with an Ancestor' Baxter presents Horse as a Hercules figure: 'His public name is Timothy Harold Glass, granted to him by me in honour of his glass belly and the twelve labours of Hercules' (MH 17). It is at first sight a puzzling assertion, with a touch of the professor-baiting mischief to which Baxter is prone when talking about his classical sources: the resemblance of the names is hardly obvious, and the comically shambolic and ineffectual Horse seems to have nothing (apart from his appetite for liquor) in common with Hercules.[12] Baxter's working notes

11 McKay (*Life* 191) dates it to 1962 (the same year as 'The Betrayal'), citing letters to his mother in October and to Weir in November in which Baxter reports 'recently' writing the 'prose sketches' which would become the novel. The assertion on the back cover blurb of the 1985 edition that it was 'written in the fifties' is thus presumably wrong. However, a notebook in the Hocken Library (MS-0975/109) contains preliminary notes for the story alongside records of Baxter's Indian travels of 1958–59, so Baxter may have been planning it in the late 1950s; it seems plausible that he continued to tinker with it over several years.

12 The phrase 'glass belly' is also puzzling; it sounds like a piece of drinker's slang, but parallels are hard to find. It may work on the analogy of 'glass jaw' or 'glass chin' for a boxer's vulnerable point, implying that Horse's belly (his appetite for drink) is his fatal weakness; Lighter's dictionary of American slang cites a 1970 reference to a fighter with 'a glass gut from too much drinking'.

Baxter's explanation for the nickname 'Horse'—that 'he is frequently being ridden by everybody he knows' (*MH* 17)—also seems a little disingenuous. The sexual implication ('hung like a horse') is obvious (and made even more so by the cover of the 1985 paperback). More profoundly, Baxter is probably influenced (as McKay suggests, *Life* 191) by Jung's treatment of the horse as a 'libido-symbol',

in the Hocken notebook make the connection clearer. There the draft title is 'The Adventures of Harry Glass'—a more obvious pun on 'Heracles'. And there is a list of 'The Labours of Harry Glass', in which Baxter enumerates nine of Hercules' exploits and begins to sketch in their parallels in his planned story. The 'Stymphlegalian Birds'[13] are a meeting of the Poetry Society; the battle with the Amazon queen Hippolyta is the hero's sexual encounter with lecturer's wife Hippolyta Goode; and—first on the list and most important for our purposes—the 'Apples of the Hesperides' are paralleled with a 'Visit to Women's Hostel—"Leander then like Theban Hercules"'.

Clearly, at this stage, Baxter was planning a novel on the lines of Joyce's *Ulysses*, in which his hero's bawdy and undignified adventures would be set in mock-heroic counterpoint with the classical myth. The plan was not fulfilled. Baxter abandoned his notebook list of parallels after only four items, and in the published novel the Herculean connections have almost disappeared from view: Timothy Harold Glass is never referred to as 'Harry Glass', Hippolyta Goode has become Zoe Virtue, and Horse visits his girlfriend at her flat rather than at a women's hostel, eliminating the sense of his invading a sacred female 'garden'. Only Baxter's offhand and mysterious reference in 'Conversation' draws attention to the original mythic underpinning of the story.

The character of Fern, whose 'golden-brown hair hung like a rippling carpet to her waist' (*Horse* 58), is Baxter's fictional recreation of Jane Aylward. In her flat, 'Open textbooks lay on the table, surrounded by human fingerbones and Japanese teacups and apple cores' (58)—the apple cores because of her habit of 'swotting' on the sofa 'with her knees drawn up, eating apples till she got the skitters' (54). This clearly factual detail is perhaps

---

associated with 'the unconscious of man'; 'the hero and his horse seem to symbolize the idea of man and the subordinate sphere of animal instinct' ('Archetypes of Transformation', 5: 275–77). Baxter draws on this Jungian symbolism in 'The Man on the Horse', where Tam and his grey mare signify 'the double union of conscious and unconscious faculties in the difficult journey of life' (*MH* 108); and it presumably underlies Baxter's explicit reading of Horse as his own repressed 'natural' self (*MH* 19–20).

13 *Sic*—for 'Stymphalian'.

the piece of naturalistic grit around which accreted the pearl of Baxter's Hesperidean myth-symbolism.

The description of Horse making love to Fern is near the centre of the novel, and it is here that Baxter spells out most explicitly his reading of the Hesperides myth, in his half serious and half tongue-in-cheek summing-up of 'the tenets of the Horse religion' (49). Horse believes that intimate contact with the physical world around him gives him 'access to a sacred power'. In childhood he found that power in his father and in certain places in the natural world; but 'As the primitive paradise of childhood fell apart, Horse had been led [. . .] to look for the signs of this power in women'.

> A woman who carried this power was in a sense a goddess. Sex, seen merely as the fitting together of nut and bolt, did not interest Horse greatly. But when it occurred as the central act of the Horse religion, in conjunction with the goddess, sex conferred the same power on the believer. It led him through a low doorway to the only earthly paradise. (50)

So when Horse first slept with Fern 'he found for the first time in his life the gates of that paradise from which runs the great river Euphrates' (58). Now as they make love, and Fern's face glows with 'the nimbus of the goddess', Horse has an ecstatic vision of the dead emerging from their graves to shout praise, and all the outcasts of society—the mad, the lonely, the destitute—'gazing and stumbling with bottomless joy and sorrow towards the light they had never known, the rekindled torch of Eden' (63–64). Horse, then, is associated mock-heroically with Hercules because of his 'longing to return to the Garden of Eden' (45) and his conviction, in the spirit of Marlowe's lines about Leander-as-Hercules, that it is possible to do so through what Horse would refer to as a 'good bang'.

It is a conviction that the twenty-year-old Baxter seems to have shared, for a time; but the forty-year-old Baxter treats it with more scepticism. The drunken poet Grummet, a parodic version of Baxter's older self, warns Horse that women are 'Either Christ or the death goddess'. 'I would have said the love goddess,' Horse objects, but Grummet insists: 'The death goddess. The sacred earth. Maui entered her gate. It closed upon him' (93).

Grummet is proved right in Horse's comically appalling sexual encounter with Zoe Virtue, who in her jealous rage turns into a vision of 'Kali, the death-goddess' (111). Zoe, ironically, means 'life', but the source of life here becomes death—just as Pyrrha, in 'The Dream'/'The Betrayal', is nightmarishly transformed into a yellow-eyed corpse. Sexual love is no longer a way back to the Edenic garden; it may be a way to death.

The same dark view of sexuality appears in other versions of Hercules written in Baxter's second Dunedin period. In *The Sore-footed Man* (1967), as we have seen, Baxter keeps Hercules offstage, cutting his climactic appearance as a god in Sophocles' original play. He adds, instead, Philoctetes' description of his painful death, 'wearing the poisoned shirt that his wife gave him', victim of 'a woman's despicable revenge' (*CPlays* 139). Philoctetes' account is somewhat unfair: in most versions of the story, when Hercules' wife Deianeira sent him a tunic dyed in the blood of the centaur Nessus, she believed Nessus's dying lie that the blood was a love potion which would restore her husband's waning affection. Instead it was a corrosive poison, which ate away his flesh until he had himself burned to death on a pyre (or in a volcano, in Baxter's version) to end the agony.

The image of the poisoned shirt of Nessus has appeared before in Baxter. In 'Songs of the Desert 10' (1947, *CP* 59), to 'wear in my own name / The terrible shirt of flame' is one of the purgatorial ordeals that he must undergo to become a true poet. In that context it may refer to the torment of lost love; certainly in 'Traveller's Litany' (1954, *CP* 140) 'Love is indeed the centaur shirt / That burns, burns to the bone'. Now in 1967 it makes its most powerful and bleak appearance in 'The Fiery Shirt' (*CP* 407):

In the garden by the river, walking
With one woman—clear night, a touch of fog—
The fiery shirt rose up from the turf we trod on
To wind around my ribs.
                                        We lay down
Without speaking. A writhing of worms
Under the sack dress,
And the moon's great ruined face
Gazing up at me from the roots of the grass.

The fiery shirt is clearly an image of sexual desire, and it is an irresistible and destructive force which degrades us to the animal level and reduces us—even heroes like Hercules—to worms' meat. We are at the furthest possible extreme here from the idea of sexual love as a way back to the Hesperidean garden.

Hesperides in Kiwiland

Before turning to Baxter's final Hercules poem we must backtrack briefly to the mid 1950s, and a version of Hercules and the Hesperides which sits outside the patterns we have been tracing so far. 'Threnos' (1956, N18.31) begins 'Reached, after Heraklean search, / The serpent-kept Hesperides'—and then abruptly drops from epic grandeur to bathos: 'We found a swamp, a wooden church / And Maori women felling trees'. The Hesperides, the fabled paradisal garden, turns out to be merely New Zealand, a country satirically depicted in the following stanzas as dull, complacent, and philistine. The poem concludes:

> And who will walk in Cressid's gown?
> And who will bend Ulysses' bow?
> Who'll pluck the golden apples down?
> I do not know. I do not know.[14]

Baxter's mythic theme is here transposed into social satire. The Hesperides still embody a vision of paradise lost, but the loss is of the good—or at least more *interesting*—society that New Zealand might potentially have been; and Hercules (along with the rather more morally equivocal Ulysses and Cressida) represents the kind of heroic glamour that 1950s New Zealand so dismally lacked.[15]

14 In 1959 Baxter recycled the opening stanza, slightly rewritten, as the start of a less effective poem, 'Landfall at the Hesperides (circa 1820)', N20.2. The opening stanza loses its allusion to Hercules and much of its mythic quality ('Found, after a twelve-month search, / The thunder-girt Hesperides'), and the rest of the poem focuses on the greed and exploitativeness of the American colonialists.

15 Cf. O'Sullivan, *Baxter* 11, who relates Baxter's fascination with Eden to 'that curiously New Zealand condition, where a finer and broader world is what our forebears sought, and yet is what many of their descendants felt was left behind.'

Hercules, Baxter, Christ: 'The Tiredness of Me and Herakles'

The sense of Hercules as hero and his contrast with the shabbiness of contemporary New Zealand is developed in Baxter's last and fullest treatment of the Hercules story. 'The Tiredness of Me and Herakles', written in early October 1972 only a fortnight or so before Baxter's death (McKay, *Life* 282), is one of the most elaborate and sustained of all Baxter's mythological poems, and it is unexpected, not only that he should turn so emphatically to a classical myth at a point in his career when he was more focused on Christian and Maori motifs, but also that the hero he chooses should be Hercules rather than (say) Odysseus. The Labours of Hercules here become a sustained metaphor for Baxter's own laborious struggle against a series of 'monsters' preying on New Zealand's society and spiritual life.[16] More than in any previous treatment, Baxter is drawing here on the tradition of Hercules as benefactor and champion of humanity, as exemplar of virtue, as Christian hero or even as type of Christ. At the same time, he brings out the darkly humorous incongruity between the invincible Herculean hero and himself, and between the heroic world of myth and the grubby Pig Island of racist cops, scandalmongering tabloid papers, and teenagers stoned on LSD.

Hercules is also presented as an innocent figure, 'somehow childlike' as Philoctetes said. There is a childlike quality in the simplicity of the poem's language (the flatness of the hero's response to Hippolyta's advances, for instance—'I did not like her'), suggesting the clear-eyed vision of a child. This is Baxter's version of a traditional concept of Hercules as the primitive man, 'the archetypal "man of nature"' as Galinsky calls him (69), confronting the unnatural corruption, hypocrisy, and intellectual sophistry of the civilised (adult) world. The clearest example is the cleansing of the Augean Stables (stanza 2), interpreted as the

16 Baxter does not strictly follow the classical Twelve Labours. Of the seven Labours described in the poem, five are from the traditional list (the Boar, the Augean Stables, the Apples of the Hesperides, the Amazons, the Hydra), one is a deed of Hercules not traditionally counted as a Labour (wrestling with Death), and one is borrowed from the story of Jason (yoking the fire-breathing oxen).

cleansing of the church of centuries of accumulated religious 'horseshit'—ritualism and false dogma—to reveal at last the simple basic essentials of Catholic faith: 'one iron crucifix / And a thin medal of Our Lady'.[17]

Likewise Baxter/Herakles defends the naturalness of the flesh and human sexuality against the religious puritanism of the Jansenist priest, 'the great boar', who believes that 'The christly do not have erections' (stanza 1);[18] and against the secular puritanism (and hypocrisy) of the sexually repressed feminist Amazons who label him a 'Pornographer' (stanza 4). He fights the more frightening vision of purity represented by the fascist policeman who is Death and who declares, 'Life is filth. I keep the world clean' (stanza 6). He defends the truth about himself against the lies of the media (primarily, ironically enough, in the newspaper *Truth*) and the prejudices of public opinion, which regards him as a publicity-seeker (section 5). And he struggles with the insatiable, exhausting, Hydra-like demands of his own followers (section 7). Unlike the original Herakles, he is not infallibly victorious; he is fought to a draw by the boar and by Death; is wounded 'above the right testicle' in the battle with the Amazons; and is still hopelessly attempting to kill the Hydra.

Among the labours of Baxter/Herakles, one stands out from the rest as not having a clear satirical reference to some aspect of contemporary New Zealand or Baxter's own life. That is—not surprisingly—the story of the apples of the Hesperides (stanza 3):

> The sky met the earth
> To the west of that marae.
> Great trees hung over the meeting house.
> The earth giant did not greet me gladly.
> 'Apples,' he grumbled, 'too many apples,

17 In an essay in *The Flowering Cross* Baxter allegorises the story (which he calls 'a favourite one of mine') differently, as 'a basic analogy of the spiritual life': the river represents God's grace, freely available to 'our Christian Hercules' in the Eucharistic sacrament, to cleanse the soul of sin that could not be removed by human effort (*FC* 179).

18 Compare Baxter on Burns' war against Calvinism: 'the struggle of the natural man against that inhuman crystalline vision of the total depravity of the flesh and the rigid holiness of the elect' ('Man', *MH* 92).

My troubles began with an apple.'
But he let me take the rigid weight
Of the firmament on the strap-hardened shoulder
I got as a city postman long ago.
The apple that he plucked from the oldest tree
Burned in his hand like a sun.

In this version Baxter/Herakles *can* 'raise again the fallen sky', in a mythic gesture beautifully brought down to earth by Baxter's wry reference to his old job as a Wellington postie. Atlas—whose description as 'the earth giant' fuses him with Antaeus—is again associated with Eden and the Fall; his grumble that 'My troubles began with an apple' suggests that, as in the early poem 'Atlas', he is to be identified with Adam or Mankind. The passage hints, then, at an unusually straightforward (for Baxter) Christian allegory of the Atonement. Herakles shouldering the firmament for Atlas is Christ relieving Adam/Mankind of the burden of original sin, enabling him to re-enter the Garden of Eden and grasp the golden apple of eternal life. Herakles/Christ is, in Milton's phrase, the 'one greater Man' who will 'restore us, and regain the blissful seat' (*Paradise Lost* 1. 4–5).

Baxter's implicit self-identification with Christ the Saviour may seem startlingly hubristic; as O'Sullivan dryly remarks, the histrionic imitations of Christ in his late poetry 'may be fairly hard to take' (*Baxter* 56). In this case the potential blasphemy is softened by its subtlety; the allegory we are suggesting here only becomes apparent after one has followed Baxter's treatment of Hercules, Atlas and the Hesperides through a number of largely unpublished poems. It is also softened by the sad irony that permeates the whole poem, emphasising the poet's sense of weariness and failure and his sheer unlikeness to the mythic hero-saviour whose role he assumes. Hercules–Christ might really be able to reopen the brazen gates and restore the day-forgotten garden; for Baxter, 'tired already' with five labours to go, it can be nothing more than a wistful fantasy.

Theseus

Theseus, in Greek myth, has a great deal in common with Hercules: both warriors, bare-hand fighters, monster-slayers, champions of civilisation against barbarism, tragically unlucky in their sexual lives. Indeed, it is a common view among scholars of classical myth that Theseus was built up by the Athenians, in historical times, into a national hero to rival Hercules (Kirk 152). Baxter, however, regards the two heroes very differently: his Theseus is almost an anti-type of Hercules, treated (for the most part) with hostility rather than veneration. And the key image associated with Theseus, the Labyrinth, is precisely the symbolic opposite of Hercules' Edenic garden.

'Beloved monster O maternal maze': Baxter's labyrinths

The original Labyrinth, in Greek myth, was the maze underneath the palace of King Minos of Crete, an impenetrable knot of winding corridors at the heart of which lurked the bull-headed, man-eating Minotaur; Theseus, by following the ball of thread given to him by the princess Ariadne, was able to penetrate the maze and kill the monster. A historical origin for the story has been found by some scholars in the complex floor plans of the palaces of Minoan Crete. The name means 'house of the *labrys*', the Cretan double-headed axe, which has come to be seen (without much clear classical evidence) as an emblem of matriarchal power.[19] Beyond its context in Greek myth, however, the labyrinth is an extraordinarily ancient and widespread symbol, dating back to prehistory, and found in cultures from northern Europe to India and South America. Its original significance is dubious: perhaps an enclosure for the spirits of the dead, perhaps a site for rituals of initiation; modern mystics tend to read it as a female symbol, associated with the great mother goddess and the cycles of birth, death and rebirth. In literature and art, its symbolism is ambiguous and double-edged. Penelope Reed Doob, in *The Idea*

19 Baxter draws on this association in two 1963 poems, 'The Waves', *CP* 286–88 (the double axe associated with 'the horned and processional / Goddess of sexual pain') and 'Letter to Robert Burns', *CP* 289–91 ('The snake-haired Muse came out of the sky / And showed her double axe to me').

of the Labyrinth, argues that its positive or negative connotations depend on the perspective of the viewer. Seen from outside or above, the labyrinth is a feat of marvellously intricate, ordered complexity, reflecting the order of God's cosmos or the creations of human art and intellect; seen from within, it suggests merely entrapment and confusion, the frustrating complexities of human life and the danger of being lost in mazes of sin and error (Doob 64–91).

In modern psychology, the labyrinth is frequently a symbol of the unconscious. Freud said that 'Psycho-analysis simplifies life [. . .] it supplies the thread that leads a man out of the labyrinth of his own unconscious' (Viereck 33).[20] Jung, responding in 1941 to Kerényi's gift of his book *Labyrinth-Studien*, described the labyrinth as a 'primordial image' for 'the topography of the unconscious', often associated with the image of a descent to the underworld (quoted in Adams 273). The legend of Theseus and the Labyrinth lends itself particularly well to Jungian interpretation: as the Jungian psychotherapist Michael Vannoy Adams explicates it, 'Theseus (the ego) enters the labyrinth (the unconscious), [and] slays the Minotaur (a specific content of the unconscious) [. . .]. Ariadne [. . .] is the anima as psychopomp, the guide of the soul on the journey into and out of the underworld' (Adams 273–74). For Freudians the labyrinth-unconscious is a trap that must be escaped; for Jungians, it is a process which must be gone through to achieve full selfhood.

Although Baxter sometimes draws on this psychological symbolism, his treatment of the labyrinth image is rather different. For him it is primarily a negative symbol associated, like the tomb, with enclosure and suffocation.[21] (In more positive contexts he prefers the word 'maze', which perhaps carries more suggestion of

20 This quotation formerly appeared on the homepage of the Freud Museum, accompanied by a logo based on Freud's doodle of a labyrinth.

21 James, 'Poetry in the Labyrinth', reads Baxter's use of the symbol much more positively ('the search for a centre of ultimate reality', 79), but uses a much broader definition of what constitutes a labyrinth image, of which the examples discussed here are only a subset.

the open air.)[22] And his labyrinth is primarily external rather than internal. As in much medieval literature, Baxter's labyrinth is an image of the world: the fallen world that we live in, which we experience as a place of entrapment, confusion and frustration, in which it seems impossible to find the true path or the way out. If the Hesperidean or Edenic garden is the image of the ideal, unfallen world of childhood innocence to which we all long to return, the labyrinth is the fallen world of adult experience in which we are all trapped. In the final lines of one of his most famous poems, 'Virginia Lake' (1947–48, *CP* 74), Baxter powerfully brings the two images together, as the adult poet grieves for the loss of the vision of his childhood self:

O out of this rock tomb
Of labyrinthine grief I start and cry
Toward his real day—the undestroyed
Fantastic Eden of a waking dream.

Baxter's conception of the labyrinth is most clearly defined in an early unpublished poem (N14.1013):

Lost in the labyrinth no Ariadne
Can chart or penetrate, we fumble for
Clues, intimations—hear in memory
The groaning of the prisoned Minotaur,
That brutish god who tugs his chain of years
Beyond a vacant shrine and judgement throne
Crying 'I shall be free.' But bound in tears
Love powerless likewise, can reveal alone
A desert rainbowed by the polar lights,
An infinite regret in finite minds.
For what? for Eden? O that sounds and sights
Which thaw the universal frost that binds
Our unimaginable Spring, were plain!—
Not echoes, but the roaring of the shoreless main.

22 This is different from the strict technical distinction, by which a labyrinth is unicursal, with only one long winding path through, whereas a maze has multiple paths, false trails and dead ends. The labyrinth is a test of endurance; the maze a test of ingenuity or luck. By this definition Theseus's Labyrinth must have been technically a maze, otherwise Ariadne's thread would have been unnecessary.

The human condition is to be 'lost in the labyrinth' without a guiding thread, fumbling for 'clues' (Baxter plays on the original meaning of *clue*, a ball of thread). There is 'no Ariadne' and no heroic Theseus, and the Minotaur is not a threat but (as often in Baxter) a sympathetic fellow-victim of the labyrinth, an emblem of humanity's trapped condition. He is perhaps a figure of the 'natural man, [. . .] the fallen Adam who remembers, as in a dream, his first state', like Horse, whom Baxter imagines as a prisoner in 'the cellblock in the basement of my mind' ('Conversation', *MH* 19–20). The Minotaur groans for freedom, tugging at the chain of years which binds him to this world. But there is no help from religion (God's throne is empty); nor from love, which merely stirs an unfocused regret and longing for a condition—'Eden?'—which we cannot fully imagine, let alone achieve. All that we know outside the airless confines of the labyrinth is the roaring of the sea, which suggests an alien and unfriendly universe and, perhaps, death.

The labyrinth/world analogy is developed in the clotted (and at times incoherent) images of 'Letter to the World' (1955, *CP* 149–50):

Beloved monster O maternal maze
Where the innumerable dying tread
Sighing for sleep and for the womb denied,
Too long I deny you, you are my own voice.
Playing Russian roulette with the gun of a word
        I had forgotten your face
Of blood and dirt, your tears in the abyss
Making stone rainbows. Now I bleed from love's scar.
At the heart of your maze man's heart is Minotaur.[23]

In the first line 'the World' is identified, alliteratively and oxymoronically, as at once a maze, a monster, and a mother. It contains us like a womb—but not the 'womb denied' that we long for, the Edenic source of life, merely a labyrinthine enclosure

23 The later stanzas of the poem are hard to interpret, as the identity of the addressee disconcertingly shifts from 'the World' to a figure who suggests the Virgin Mary. Weir's judgement on the 'extravagant rhetoric [. . .] neither concrete nor coherent' (*Baxter* 48) of the poetry of this period seems a fair comment on this poem.

in which we are 'dying' from the moment of birth. Once again, 'man's heart' is the Minotaur at the heart of the labyrinth, both monster and victim. 'Letter to the World' makes explicit the crucial association between the world and the flesh. The body is a prison—'the soul sweating in its iron lung', 'the heaven's bird / Hopping and mowing in a bone cage'—and it is sexuality which both imprisons us and reminds us of what we have lost: 'How except when he wets his beak with blood / Can he tell Eden's huge / Indemnity?' The causal link between the labyrinth and adult sexuality is there very early in Baxter's poetry: in 'Reverie of a Prisoner' (N10.588), written at the age of seventeen, the 'mazes' seem to be the dreary torments of adolescence in which the Edenic vision of childhood is lost.

> I had forgotten all that I held dear—
> Captivity creates the world anew—
> And puny hate and puny fear
> Made mazes that I long must maunder through;
> Made mazes where no Minotaur will thunder,
> Nor spiral flame in purgatorial wonder
> Shake, flake to song.

In these poems the labyrinth is simply the condition of human existence—a 'prison-house' which (Wordsworthianly) closes round us at adolescence, and from which there is only one escape: 'Death is the one door out of the labyrinth!' ('The Rock', *CP* 362).

In other contexts—and increasingly in Baxter's later work—the labyrinth takes on a more specific and social meaning. It is not just 'the World' but human society, and more particularly modern urban, capitalist, bureaucratic society, as summed up in 'This Indian Morning' (1959, *CP* 198):

> This Indian morning brown as Icarus
> Flows guiltless to the vault of noon
> Not influenced by cent per cent,
> Obediences baggy at the seams,
> Outside the Cretan labyrinth
> Of money, conscience, work, glum dreams.

In 'The Ballad of One Tree Hill' (1963–64, *CP* 293–96) it is 'the labyrinth / Of time and money'. Often the labyrinth is associated with the city, its maze-like physical complexity mirroring the spiritually lost and alienated condition of the workers who inhabit it. In 'Wellington' (1949, *CP* 76) 'Power breeds on power in labyrinthine hives'; in 'Autumn Testament' 17 the 'dark angel of the town' (Auckland) tells the poet, 'Man, there's no way out / Of this labyrinth! I mean to grind your soul / And theirs, and spit you out like rotten cabbage' (*CP* 549); and in a prose passage from that book Baxter fears that visitors turned away from the Jerusalem community 'go back so often to a labyrinth from which there is no apparent exit' (*AT* 52).[24] The labyrinth is (in Augustinian terms) the soul-destroying City of Man, the domain ruled over by 'Caesar', as opposed to the City of God. So in another Indian poem, 'The Carvers' (1958, *CP* 195), Baxter prays to the 'Dark Spirit', God in his hidden aspect, to 'Shine in the casual labyrinth, / Explode the debris of our lives.' *Casual*, along with *debris*, suggests the meaningless quality of life in the labyrinth: a mere succession of random events, as one 'maunders' through the winding paths with no sense of purpose or goal. On both the socio-political and the metaphysical level, the labyrinth embodies the ordinary life which 'tends to be experienced as chaos' (*CPlays* 336), in which any sense of the 'sacred pattern in natural events' is obscured (O'Sullivan, *Baxter* 10, quoting *MH* 132).[25]

In a few poems, however, there are hints of a more positive reading of the image. In 'Christchurch 1948' (1960, *CP* 215), Baxter describes his younger self and Jacquie as 'Two children sighing in the labyrinth / For light, for the country of high noon'. On one level, this is again the labyrinth of the city: like Wellington and Auckland, Christchurch—'Murderous, choked by its cathedral stone'—is a prison for the human spirit. But this labyrinth may also be an internal one. 'Hunger for light sustained me there, / Under the sign of Dionysus-Hades': the young poet was enduring a dark night of the soul in an underworld ruled by

24 In another labyrinth allusion in 'The Ballad of One Tree Hill' (1963–64; *CP* 295), Auckland becomes 'the house of the black bull' where we are 'torn / By the bull's horn'—the Minotaur here a threat rather than a sufferer.

25 Compare a very early poem, 'Webs of Circumstance', N2.92 (c.1941), which refers to 'the labyrinth of chance' in which we seek 'solace for eternal discontent'.

the compound god of death, madness, drink, and inspiration.[26] Baxter in Christchurch in 1948 was undergoing Jungian analysis, and there is a hint here of the Jungian image of the unconscious as labyrinth, into which we must descend to acquire self-knowledge. Similarly, in 'For Kevin Ireland' (1957, *CP* 186), Baxter advises his fellow-writer to 'praise / The lion-headed incubus / That grips your life and mine within / Its strict Egyptian maze.' The 'lion-headed incubus' is one of Baxter's fearsome Muse figures, like the lion-headed goddess Hekate; and its 'Egyptian maze' (probably alluding to the Bible's 'Egyptian darkness') suggests, again, the dark labyrinth of the unconscious that poets must explore as they 'tread a pathway to the fire / Where affliction makes them whole.'[27] In these poems the labyrinth is not meaningless chaos but a source of poetic power, and to pass through it is a painful and frightening but ultimately creative process of initiation.

This psychological reading of the labyrinth symbol may seem logically incompatible with the more dominant Christian–existentialist and political readings. In some ways it is so: Baxter is drawing with medieval impartiality on both the negative and positive readings of the symbol. Nevertheless, there is a kind of emotional logic running through the contradiction. In all its guises, external and internal, the labyrinth is a dark, gloomy, fearful place, and the fear and horror it arouses is part of what (to adapt Auden's phrase about Yeats) hurts Baxter into poetry. 'Letter to the World' makes it clear that the poet's relationship with the 'beloved monster' and 'maternal maze' is vital to the sources of his poetry: 'the green / Song rises from your mystery of pain'.

The Commissar in his labyrinth: Baxter's Theseus

The ambiguities of Baxter's reading of the labyrinth both complicate and deepen his treatment of Theseus. Given his sympathetic view of the Minotaur as a representative of suffering humanity, he is

26 For further discussion of Dionysus-Hades see chapters 7 and 8.

27 Hekate: see 'Waipatiki Beach', *CP* 264. 'Egyptian darkness': Exodus 10:22; cf. 'Egyptian darkness staggers in the sun' in 'Air Flight to Delhi' (originally titled 'Flight into Egypt'), *CP* 193—a poem written around the same time (1958) which also refers to night terrors, demons and an 'incubus'.

not likely simply to celebrate Theseus as the heroic Minotaur-slayer. Baxter's more complex and ironic view of Theseus and the Labyrinth is summed up in an equivocal line in *The Temptations of Oedipus*, his 1968 adaptation of Sophocles' *Oedipus at Colonus*. Theseus, sympathising with Oedipus over what he calls (with grotesque understatement) his 'private difficulties', confides that his own life has had its difficulties: 'The matter of the bull. In a sense, you might say, cousin, that I entered the labyrinth and never came out.' The sense he has in mind, as his following words indicate, is that the man who came out of the Labyrinth was not the man who entered it: 'A young man went in. But an old . . .' (*CPlays* 244; the ellipsis, as often in this play, is Baxter's). We may hear, however, another ironic meaning to his words. In this deeper sense, Theseus is still trapped in the Labyrinth: he is the archetype and epitome of the man whose natural home is the World and who presides over the labyrinth of human society.

Apart from his youthful exploits as slayer of the Minotaur and of other monsters and bandits, Theseus is most famous in myth as a hero-king. Unlike Hercules, he spent most of his career on a throne; and the classical Athenians celebrated their national hero as founder of Athenian democracy, establisher of laws and traditions, protector of the oppressed at home and abroad, the archetype of a noble and just king. Baxter, with his ingrained suspicion of any kind of political authority, however well intentioned, subverts this mythic propaganda. His darker view of Theseus has some justification in the classical legend, in Theseus's callousness towards women (the abandonment of Ariadne, the rape of Helen, the attempted abduction of Persephone) and his dysfunctional family relationships (responsible for the deaths of his father Aegeus and of his son Hippolytus). Baxter's Theseus is essentially the embodiment of worldly power and *Realpolitik*, cold, ruthless and loveless.

This hostile view is most sharply summed up in 'At the Tomb of Theseus' (*CP* 199):

Bramble and couchgrass twine above
The tumulus of giant bones.
This king despised his mother's love,

Subdued bullheaded chaos, built
An aqueduct, a cenotaph.
His bones rot like other bones.
Human hatred, human guilt,
Fuel the engine of the State.
The legless beggar at the gate
Has freedom still to spit and laugh.
The twining couchgrass seeds above
Bones that were ignorant of love.

The poem was written in India in 1959, where the sight of extreme poverty and social injustice had hardened Baxter's attitude towards the political powers that be. Its 'tumulus of giant bones' is presumably inspired by Plutarch's story of how, in the fifth century BC, the skeleton 'of a man of extraordinary size' was discovered in a burial mound on the island of Scyros, identified as that of Theseus, and brought back to be entombed in honour in Athens (Plutarch, 'Theseus' 36.2; Ward et al. 157–58). For Baxter, however, the decay and neglect of Theseus's tomb becomes an 'Ozymandias'-like image of the vanity of worldly power. King Theseus, during his lifetime, subdued chaos (embodied in the Minotaur) and established order; his monumental achievements demonstrate his command over the sources of life (the aqueduct) and death (the cenotaph). But in death he is reduced to common humanity: 'His bones rot like other bones.' His ultimate failure is linked to the fact that he was 'ignorant of love'. The young Theseus's decision to leave his mother and seek out his royal father shows (for Baxter) that he 'despised his mother's love', and sets a pattern for his loveless and exploitative relationships with women, and indeed with people in general. Without love, political power is hollow and destructive; the state, however efficient and enlightened its intentions, becomes a mechanical 'engine' which runs on hatred and guilt. True value, freedom and happiness, as so often in Baxter, are to be found not in the powerful but in the despised outcast, 'the legless beggar at the gate'.

Theseus's denial of love appears again in 'Spring Song' (1953, *SP* 50–51), a poem unpublished in Baxter's lifetime, but powerful and significant. The innocuous title is ironic: this is a bitter poem about human destructiveness, surveying a post-Hiroshima world dominated by 'Machinery of war / And the worse war within'.[28] In the fourth stanza Baxter invites the reader to 'Turn inward then your eyes', from the external world to the inner roots of this destructive behaviour. As so often in Baxter, this psychological reality is expressed in an image from classical myth:

From Naxos' angry beach
Forgetful Theseus rows,
Love's lucid power to teach
Left in the Bacchic maze;
Stony his breastplate gleaming,
At his prow the black sail booming.

Abandoning Ariadne on the beach at Naxos, Theseus is also abandoning love, and its 'lucid power to teach'. His stony-gleaming breastplate reflects his stony heart, an image Baxter has borrowed from Ariadne's complaint in Ovid's *Heroides*.[29] The mention of his 'black sail' reminds us that he is again being 'forgetful': his failure to change the black sail to white, as he had promised, will lead to his father's despairing suicide. Theseus's callous indifference to other human beings creates misery and death wherever he goes.

The labyrinth here is characterised as 'the Bacchic maze'. On one level, the reference to Bacchus or Dionysus reminds us of Ariadne's connection with the god, who will descend to rescue her from the beach of Naxos and make her his consort. On a deeper level, it anticipates the connection in 'Christchurch 1948' between the labyrinth and 'the sign of Dionysus-Hades'. Here too the labyrinth is seen positively as a psychological realm of imagination and intuition, through which one must pass to achieve integration and self-knowledge. It is a strand of symbolism which sharply contradicts the association of the labyrinth with the World: here, paradoxically, Theseus's fault is to turn his back on the Labyrinth. Refusing to 'turn inward [his] eyes', unconcerned

28 The same ironic contrast appears in a very early wartime poem, 'The Voice of Spring (a rondel)', N3.152, c.1941: 'The voice of the Spring is heard as a desolation / To those who see no new awakening.'

29 'Your iron breast could not have been pierced by mere horn. / You had no armour, but your chest was safe from harm, / for there you wore the hardest stone, the hardest steel— / there you had *Theseus*, which is harder than any stone' (Ovid, *Heroides* 10.107–10, trans. R. Scott Smith in Trzaskoma et al. 321).

with self-knowledge, he is (in the jargon of the period) an entirely 'outer-directed' man.

The last (more obscure) stanza suggests that Theseus is a symbol for modern, warmongering, technological, materialistic Western man:

> The great ice-goddess of
> An abstract myth
> Contents our love
> Where, numbed by her blizzard breath,
> A climber's tactics have
> Meaning; for there's no backward going
> Alive to the grove of our spring denying.

Turning our backs on the unconscious and the wisdom to be found in myth, we have devoted ourselves to 'an abstract myth' of cold scientific rationalism, and an ideal based purely on economic and technological progress. The image of progress as a climb to icy heights may be inspired by Edmund Hillary's ascent of Everest in May of that year, a 'conquest of nature' that Baxter would have seen as hubristic.[30] It is this set of values, epitomised by Theseus, which has created the world of 'ashes blood-bedewed' in which we now live, and cuts us off permanently from the Edenic 'grove of our spring'.

'Spring Song' anticipates the fuller portrait of Theseus in *The Temptations of Oedipus*. Here, as in his other adaptations of Greek drama such as *The Bureaucrat* or *The Sore-footed Man*, Baxter works by questioning, subverting, or inverting the moral structures of his sources. In Sophocles' *Oedipus at Colonus* Theseus, though a subordinate character, is an entirely admirable one. He offers asylum and hospitality to the exile Oedipus, defies the overbearing Theban ruler Creon who demands his extradition, and throws the resources of Athens into the rescue of his daughters when Creon abducts them. For Sophocles, Theseus is the heroic embodiment of the qualities Athens prides itself on: justice ('Ours is a land / That lives by justice, knows no rule but law': 913–14), magnanimity,

30 The Everest connection was pointed out to us by Arthur Pomeroy. Compare the emphasis on the 'folly' of mountain-climbing in 'The Climber' (N28.9), discussed in chapter 3.

protection of the weak and oppressed, defiance of tyrants.

Baxter's play begins in the same vein. Oedipus describes Colonus as 'a place ruled by a just king' (*CPlays* 231); and a citizen effusively praises Theseus as 'the best of kings', a builder of aqueducts, 'a great lawgiver', 'our educator' (235–36). But the praise is undercut when the citizen admiringly illustrates Theseus's skills as lawgiver and educator by describing his conduct of a torture session. For Baxter, Theseus is the archetype of the politician, a compound of ancient despot and modern bureaucrat. The choice of the aqueduct as his defining achievement, here and in 'At the Tomb of Theseus', is significant. Providing clean water for the citizens ('Now the water flows between the olive trees and our women wash their linen where there was only dry rock before') is obviously the act of a benevolent and enlightened ruler. But the image is anachronistic: aqueducts are a Roman, not a Greek invention—indeed the aqueduct, its straight arches driving through the landscape, is a classic symbol of Rome's harshly efficient technocratic power. Through this Roman image Baxter defines Theseus as a type of 'Caesar', his primary symbol of worldly authority.

By his own lights Theseus is indeed 'a just king', genuinely concerned for the welfare of his subjects. He assures the people, like a modern democratic politician, that he is no tyrant but merely their servant, because 'the life of a king has to be devoted endlessly to the service of the public good'. But this service to the people (whom he frankly describes in private as 'half-witted cretins') consists of relieving them of the need to think: 'You are free to act because you have a ruler who takes responsibility for—because, to put it bluntly, you are obliged to obey' (242–43). In Theseus's Athens, as in Baxter's 'Wellington', the people are merely worker bees in the 'labyrinthine hive' of the state. The state takes precedence over any individual in it. Theseus identifies himself completely with 'the order of the State' (258–59); its preservation is his only value, and he is prepared to do anything required to safeguard it. As a result, Sophocles' 'just king' ultimately becomes in effect the villain of Baxter's play.

In his Introduction to the play, Baxter refers to 'Theseus

the Commissar' in conflict with 'Oedipus the yogi' (335). He is alluding to Arthur Koestler's 1945 essay 'The Yogi and the Commissar', in which Koestler defines two type-figures lying at the extreme ends of a spectrum of values. The Yogi is the mystic, purely inner-directed, focused on the 'invisible umbilical cord' which connects him to the universe, and believing 'that nothing can be improved by exterior organization and everything by the individual effort from within'. The Commissar is the purely outer-directed political man:

> The Commissar believes in change from Without. He believes that all the pests of humanity, including constipation and the Oedipus complex, can and will be cured by Revolution; [. . .] that this end justifies the use of all means, including violence, ruse, treachery and poison; that logical reasoning is an unfailing compass and the universe a kind of very large clockwork in which a very large number of electrons set into motion will for ever revolve in their predictable orbits; and that whosoever believes in anything else is an escapist. (Koestler 9)

Koestler suggests that 'the Commissar can be defined as the human type which has completely severed relations with the subconscious', a severance which may lead him to crack traumatically when the limitations of his world view are exposed (14–15).

Koestler's archetype closely matches Baxter's portrayal of Theseus, in *The Temptations of Oedipus* and elsewhere. The play's Theseus is a benevolent despot not a revolutionary, but like the Commissar he is a man who exists solely on the political plane. He uses the language of religion and spirituality for public consumption, uttering platitudes about 'the invisible order that joins the earth to the sky and each man to his fellows' (242; compare Koestler's 'invisible umbilical cord'), or manipulating the citizens by threatening or promising to placate the anger of the gods. But as Oedipus recognises, 'the master-bureaucrat' is only concerned that the proper public rituals be correctly carried out to keep the people happy (236). His true attitude is rational and scientific. He understands the plague that falls on Athens as a natural phenomenon rather than a sign of divine anger. Like a modern liberal politician he puts his faith in public health and educational reform. 'I need reasonable sanitation,' he tells Oedipus. 'In time I'll stamp out even the plague. But the people have to be educated . . ..' 'They might rather die,' replies Oedipus flatly (255–56). Theseus here resembles another of Baxter's important mythic figures, Prometheus, whose name is prominently invoked in the opening minutes of the play.[31] In the essay 'Choice of Belief in Modern Society', Baxter takes the Prometheus myth to symbolise

> the advent of modern science, and that popular belief which has accompanied it—that by biology, psychology, and science or -ism, man can master his remorse, banish his bad dreams, and to put it bluntly—be happy without being good.

This belief in progress through science and political change is the very twentieth-century 'abstract myth' that Theseus lives by.

Set against Theseus is 'Oedipus the yogi', the outcast, derelict and sinner who (as usual in Baxter) has a moral insight that the rich and comfortable lack. Oedipus's wisdom lies in his bleak recognition of the fallen nature of man and the impossibility of happiness or self-improvement in this world: he knows that man cannot be happy because he cannot be good. 'Man is a monster who does not know his own heart. Wherever he goes, the sun becomes an ulcer, bread becomes rotting flesh, water is turned to blood—because the weight man has to carry, and cannot, is his own weight. To be—that is the calamity' (233). The imagery, with its echoes of the Catholic Mass, hints at the Christian hope of salvation which for Baxter alleviates Oedipus's pagan pessimism. Oedipus's way is one of pure renunciation, to achieve the nothingness of death: 'I will become what I am—not Oedipus—no longer Oedipus. I will be what I am—the dead peaceful child who lies always at the breast of Queen Persephone' (233). Since the world cannot be changed, politics is merely a soul-destroying trap, 'the shirt of power that eats into the bones like acid' (252). Oedipus's plea to his son to renounce ambition echoes the imagery of 'At the Tomb of Theseus': 'The king cannot

31 The First Citizen boasts that the country round Colonus 'is full of that invisible fire that Prometheus gave to us' (234), and describes Theseus making a libation to 'Prometheus the Fire-Bringer'—significantly, as a prelude to using fire for torture (235). The first reference comes from Sophocles; the second is Baxter's invention.

possess the land; not even when his bones go down into the soil, with the fingers still clutched on an absent sceptre' (253).

For much of the play Baxter holds the balance apparently even between Oedipus the yogi and Theseus the commissar. Baxter's Oedipus is a more morally problematic figure than he is in Sophocles (as Lady Bracknell might have said, incest with one family member may be regarded as a misfortune; incest with two looks like carelessness). And Theseus is not an entirely unsympathetic figure, even a potentially tragic one as he confesses his past 'difficulties' and his sleepless suffering at the hands of the Furies (244–45). However, the scales are decisively tipped by Theseus's final act, when he sacrifices Oedipus's and Antigone's baby—an act of pure political expediency, justified by the sophistical (though technically correct) defence that he never explicitly promised to protect it. By the invention of this child-murder Baxter turns Theseus into a villain in the mould of Herod or Richard III.[32] Theseus' cool political rationalism, however sensible or admirable it may seem in some ways, is entirely ruthless and loveless. Oedipus, like the 'legless beggar at the gate' in 'At the Tomb of Theseus', represents a kind of flawed and ramshackle humanity that the enlightened ruler has lost.

Theseus redeemed

Baxter's final treatment of Theseus, in 'The Labyrinth' (1970, *CP* 488), takes a very different approach. For the first time Baxter speaks in the voice of Theseus and sympathetically identifies with him. This does not mean that he has changed his view of the values Theseus represents. It would be truer to describe the figure in this poem as an alternative or anti-Theseus, one who is yogi rather than commissar, seeking 'change from within'. He is an avatar of the ageing poet, making his way through a labyrinth which is on one level an image of life in the fallen world (as in 'Lost in the Labyrinth no Ariadne', more than two decades earlier), but

32 Theseus's excuse that the child was 'too young to be counted a guest' (259) echoes the sophistry of Richard's henchman Buckingham in taking the young Duke of York out of sanctuary to be killed: 'Oft have I heard of "sanctuary men", / But "sanctuary children" ne'er till now' (*Richard III* 3.1.55–56).

on another level an internal, spiritual quest for an ambiguously defined goal.

This quester has set out with a clear sense of his mission, 'mind on the Minotaur'. But now, after 'so many corridors,—so many lurches', he finds it hard to keep his mind on the object of the quest, continually distracted by tricks of the light or sudden noises, demoralised by the 'demons' of self-doubt and guilt.[33] 'I sit down like a little girl / To play with my dolls,—sword, wallet and the god's great amulet my father gave me.' The symbols of worldly power and authority, the royal inheritance which meant so much to Theseus in his earlier incarnations, are now seen as childish toys. It was 'easy / (Though heroic no doubt)' to show courage in the public arena in front of admiring eyes; it is much harder to show it in this solitary, private, internal quest, reduced to the status of a frightened child. Baxter, who elsewhere depicts himself as a child before God, knows how hard it is to go from being an admired public figure to a self-abnegating penitent. Nevertheless the quester holds to his essential lifeline:

> but I do not forget
> One thing, the thread, the invisible silk I hold
> And shall hold till I die.
> I tell you, brother,
> When I throw my arms around the Minotaur
> Our silence will be pure as gold.

The image here of Ariadne's thread is explicated by Baxter in a letter to McKay (3 December 1968, FM 22/4/11): 'Love is the clue in the labyrinth. Eros can be the arms and ears of Agape.' This comment throws a retrospective light on Baxter's entire treatment of Theseus and the labyrinth. Consistently Baxter has emphasised Theseus's lack and denial of love. It is that lovelessness which leads to his imprisonment in the worldly labyrinth. The 'clue' for which the labyrinth-dwellers were fumbling in 'Lost in the labyrinth' is, simply, love—in all its senses. *Eros*, sexual love, can lead (Platonically) to *agape*, *caritas*, *aroha*, the disinterested love of others, and in the end to the love of God.

33 Compare the demons who jeer at Baxter's self-flagellation in '[Letters to Frank McKay]' 3 (*CP* 481–82).

The poem's most radical reinvention of the myth is the revelation in the final lines that Theseus's quest is not to kill but to embrace the Minotaur. As the object of the quest, the Minotaur is a richly ambiguous symbol. At first glance it may suggest an image for God; O'Sullivan identifies it with death (*Baxter* 59), though, as he points out, in these poems 'Christ and death can coalesce' (58); Jensen sees it as a symbol of the unconscious (*Whole Men* 44), though it could also be read specifically as the Jungian shadow, the prisoner in the cellblock of one's mind. However interpreted (God, death, unconscious), the Minotaur represents something which appears terrible, but which must be willingly embraced if the individual is to achieve completion and peace.

By renouncing worldly power and 'turning inward his eyes', Theseus becomes a spiritual hero—like Hercules in 'The Tiredness of Me and Herakles', a role model for Baxter as he contemplates the end of his life. If Hercules represents the quest to regain childhood innocence, Theseus finally comes to represent the successful negotiation of the mazes of this world to achieve redemption in death.

CHAPTER 6

'THE MYTH OF OCEAN FREEDOM': ODYSSEUS

> He made Odysseus part of himself, as anyone can tell by reading his poetry. (M. Baxter 69)

Recalling her son's early delight in the stories of Greek and Norse mythology, Millicent Baxter singled out one character in particular as having a profound and lasting impact on him. Odysseus, or Ulysses (but Baxter prefers the Greek name), recurs throughout Baxter's work more often than any other mythological character, and always (as Millicent shrewdly noted) as a figure for the poet himself.[1] W. B. Stanford in his classic study *The Ulysses Theme* described a category of writer (his examples include Goethe and Tennyson) whose interest in the figure of Ulysses 'became a matter of self-identification, until for a while each saw himself as Ulysses and Ulysses as himself' in a relationship which was 'a means of self-discovery, self-encouragement, and self-realization' (Stanford 6).[2] This is clearly the category Baxter belongs in, though in his case 'self-criticism' is as important as 'self-encouragement'.

Baxter explains his fascination with the character in an Introduction to his 1967 play *The Sore-footed Man*:

> The character of Odysseus had [. . .] haunted me for many years, from the time I began to realise that neither conventional ethics nor the theology of Aquinas were much use in determining what choices a man should make who wishes to win a war, or court a woman, or even free himself from the chains of family conditioning. (*CPlays* 335)

1 Venus/Aphrodite is named more often, but Baxter's 'Venus' is more the label for a natural principle than a 'character'.

2 See also Davidson, 'Odysseus' 109.

This checklist of situations where Odysseus might be a role model is also a summary of the character's traditional roles: warrior, lover, exiled wanderer. Perhaps the key phrase here, however, is 'to *free* himself'. Pre-eminently, for Baxter, Odysseus represents the desire for freedom—freedom from marriage and domesticity, freedom from society and its constraints, freedom from 'conventional ethics'. Baxter identifies with Odysseus as an outsider and exile, a 'Man Alone', a man of clear vision who sees through conventional illusions and who defines his own identity and moral values. At the same time, he is aware of the limitations of what he calls 'the myth of ocean freedom' ('The Old Age of Odysseus', 1958–59, N19.89): that Odysseus's unfulfillable quest must end either in death or (as in the received story) in an anticlimactic surrender to Ithacan domesticity.[3] He is also aware that Odysseus as a pagan–existentialist hero of human freedom and self-creation, most triumphantly embodied in *The Sore-footed Man*, is hard to reconcile with Christianity and 'the theology of Aquinas'; and his very last allusion to the hero seems to imply a rejection of 'old Odysseus' in favour of the Christian Cross.

Baxter and the Romantic Odysseus

Baxter's Odysseus is very different from Homer's, though he shares aspects of that character: the ruthless military commander ('Homer's iron gunman'), the wily strategist, the lover, the much-enduring man.[4] But the hero of the *Odyssey* is no deracinated outsider, but a man as rooted in homeland and family as the

3 That Baxter's fascination with Odysseus did not reflect any particular sympathy with ocean voyaging is suggested by an anecdote told by his sister-in-law: when she tried to enlist Baxter's enthusiasm for the early European discoverers 'who took those incredible voyages into the utterly unknown', he infuriated her by responding that 'they would probably have been better off at home looking after their wives and children' (Lenore Baxter to Frank McKay, 7 July 1985; FM 19/7/32). Apart from its delightful irony, the story underlines that Baxter's 'myth of ocean freedom' must be interpreted as a psychological or spiritual metaphor, rather than literally.

4 Baxter wrote three poems simply titled 'Odysseus', which are here distinguished by number: 'Odysseus'-1 ('Blaze saw I once beyond a barren coast'), 1945–47, *CP* 42; 'Odysseus'-2 ('Coming into the middle years'), 1957, N19.22; 'Odysseus'-3 ('Remember, Odysseus'), 1957, N19.33. 'Homer's iron gunman' comes from 'Odysseus'-2.

living olive tree which forms the corner-post of his marriage bed. Throughout all his enforced wanderings, as a tough, wary, pragmatic survivor, his one goal is to make it home. He is, in Stanford's term, fundamentally 'centripetal'. Baxter's figure by contrast belongs to the Romantic tradition of the 'centrifugal' Odysseus, who travels not because he is forced to but because he longs for perpetual travel and discovery (Stanford 89 and passim).[5] Though post-Homeric classical writers had imagined further journeys for Odysseus after his homecoming, it was Dante in the fourteenth century who crucially shifted the meaning of the myth. In the flames of hell, Dante's Ulysses describes how he never in fact returned to Ithaca, because

> No tenderness to my son, nor piety
> To my old father, nor the wedded love
> That should have comforted Penelope
> Could conquer in me the restless itch to rove
> And rummage through the world exploring it,
> All human worth and wickedness to prove.
>
> (*Inferno* 26.91–96)[6]

Instead he led his followers out on a voyage into the unknown southern ocean, and was finally swallowed up by the sea as he was about to make landfall on the mountain of Purgatory—a punishment for what in Dante's eyes was the sin of curiosity, the misuse of his intelligence in a quest for forbidden knowledge.

This idea of the hero's wanderlust was given its classic expression in Tennyson's 'Ulysses' (1842), a source text which underlies all Baxter's versions of the story. This Ulysses, unlike Dante's, has come home, but is dissatisfied with his life as 'an idle king [. . .] Matched with an agèd wife' and ruling over a people who merely 'hoard, and sleep, and feed'. He resolves that he 'cannot rest from travel':

5 See also Auden, *The Enchafèd Flood* 21 (Ulysses as 'the typical Romantic Marine Hero'). Auden's 1951 discussion of the symbols of the sea, the desert, and the city seems to have influenced Baxter, especially his *Recent Trends in New Zealand Poetry* in the same year.

6 The translation by Dorothy L. Sayers is the one in which Baxter read the *Inferno* in 1950, and he pronounced Sayers 'either [. . .] a great poet or an excellent translator' (letter 26 June 1950; FM 11/6/9).

I am a part of all that I have met;
Yet all experience is an arch wherethrough
Gleams that untravelled world, whose margin fades
For ever and for ever when I move.
[. . .] and vile it were
For some three suns to store and hoard myself,
And this grey spirit yearning in desire
To follow knowledge like a sinking star,
Beyond the utmost bound of human thought.

So, abandoning the mundane work of government to his son Telemachus with a patronising commendation ('Most blameless is he, centered in the sphere / Of common duties'), he sets out on a more heroic course 'to sail beyond the sunset'—perhaps to be swallowed by the sea like his Dantean predecessor, perhaps to 'touch the Happy Isles' (Tennyson 138–45).

Tennyson's Romantic version, which turns Odysseus's travels into an endless spiritual quest and leaves him poised ambiguously somewhere between heroic visionary and egotistical dropout, was hugely influential. In New Zealand literature its influence can be clearly seen in A. R. D. Fairburn's 'Odysseus' (1930). Fairburn's hero, like Tennyson's, is discontented in the 'heavy idleness' of Ithaca, reflecting that 'It's only a fool who lets his dreams come true', and wishing he had died at sea or else remained 'out there in the cold and darkness' where 'dreams never came true . . . were always dreams / lovely and inviolable'. Like Tennyson's he sets off again to sea, but (unlike Tennyson's) fetches up on the pohutukawa-laden shores of Aotearoa (Fairburn 188–91; see also 186–87). Fairburn's poem is derivative and its ending (rather charmingly) kitschy, but it anticipates some of the themes of Baxter's more sophisticated work, as well as the persistent presence of Odysseus in later New Zealand poetry (Davidson, 'Odysseus' 117–18).

A sea-stranger: Odysseus as Man Alone

One of Baxter's earliest references to Odysseus strikes a keynote. In a passage from the 1944 poem 'At Balclutha' (*Spark* 358–59, later incorporated into 'Traveller's Litany', *CP* 140) he describes travelling by train through the Otago landscape:

> Passing, clothed in iron,
> Glass and raucous thunder, I saw only names—
> Platform-curve of names or hill-curve.
> A sea-stranger came I odyssean.

Odysseus, according to the opening lines of the *Odyssey*, 'saw the townlands / and learned the minds of many distant men' (Fitzgerald's translation). Baxter, travelling his own native land, sees the townlands but feels no connection with the minds. Odysseus as 'sea-stranger', the outside observer, becomes a symbol of Baxter's feeling of alienation in his own country, his sense of 'a gap [. . .] between [him]self and other people', which was increased by the years he spent overseas at the cusp of childhood and adolescence, and his return 'uncertain whether [he] was an Englishman or a New Zealander' ('Education', *MH* 124). The theme is taken up in 'Letter to Noel Ginn' (*CP* 27–29), in the same year:

> What land shall receive me save as a stranger?
> Sea-blown Ulysses said: and Ithaca
> More alien was than Troy.

It appears again in a powerful poem on his return from India in 1959, 'Return to Exile' (*SP* 82), where the Odyssean overtones are strong, though not explicit:

> Returning on shipboard from an older land,
> Amoeba in his bowels, one travelling man
> Sees with gratitude the home coast rise,
> *Lares et penates . . .*
> No trumpet on the mountain. From
> Exile into exile he goes home.

Odysseus the traveller is repeatedly a figure for Baxter's sense of himself as an alien and exile in his own country, an 'inner émigré' in Seamus Heaney's phrase ('Exposure', Heaney 136). He is perhaps Baxter's most important figure of the 'Man Alone', that 'dominant symbol [. . .] of New Zealand literature', which Baxter associates with the artist's necessary alienation from the everyday world ('Symbolism', *FA* 70).[7]

Odysseus's aloneness and alienation is at times seen as a matter for pity (or self-pity); for instance, in a 1954 verse letter 'To My Father' (*SP* 54–56) Baxter associates Archie with Laertes, happy at home in his fertile garden, and himself with the travelling Ulysses whose 'heart recalls / With grief, gone seasons'. On the other hand, Baxter often implies that it is something in Odysseus's nature (and in the side of his own nature which identifies with Odysseus) that makes him an outsider. This ambiguity is caught in the description of the hero in the opening line of 'What the Sirens Sang' (1951, N16.15) as 'cold Odysseus, strapped to the mast'. Odysseus is 'cold' literally—cold, wet, salt-water-soaked, on his endless voyage in exile—and pitiable for that. But 'cold' also implies that his nature is emotionally cold and detached from common humanity. He shares something of the quality of the ocean with which he is continually associated: cold, deep, inhuman and unknowable, a symbol of 'death and oblivion' ('Symbolism', *FA* 69). His heart 'like the sea / Becomes omnivorous, a sepulchre of storms' ('The Sirens'). His 'salt sperm' ('Odysseus'-2) suggest that his very blood and semen have been infiltrated by salt water.

His outsiderhood is often seen as a function of his superiority of intellect. This is perhaps his central characteristic in the classical sources. Homer's Odysseus is *polymetis* ('of many devices'), a great tactician, pre-eminent for cleverness and prudence; for Ovid (*Metamorphoses* book 13) Ulysses' victory over the beef-witted Ajax is the triumph of brains over brawn. Baxter is not so much interested in the figure of Odysseus the trickster (he never refers to the Trojan Horse, for instance, or the Cyclops story). His particular take on this tradition is a persistent link between Odysseus's intelligence and his disillusionment, his scepticism about the ideals and illusions that motivate other people. Like Shakespeare's Cassius, Odysseus 'is a great observer, and he looks / Quite through the deeds of men' (*Julius Caesar* 1.2.203–04). He has 'the wisdom of stratagem, the power / Learnt by looking at

7 As his review of John Mulgan's *Man Alone* in *Landfall* in 1949 makes clear, Baxter interpreted its title not in 'social' but in personal terms: the hero's 'personal isolation, his place on the outskirts of society, perpetually an outsider'.

[his] life's plague pit / With an unflinching eye' ('The Sirens').[8] In the 1946 sonnet 'Odysseus'-1 he recalls his exploits at Troy, how he

> wily rode the anarchic battle there,
> Tricked brutish heroes into fear beneath
> An iron thought, blunting the brazen spear.

Yet for himself 'ringing Troy was cold [. . .]. Troy died in me long ere her ashes died'. Baxter echoes Tennyson ('the ringing plains of windy Troy'), but there is no sense that this Odysseus has 'drunk delight of battle with [his] peers' (if he has any). While enjoying the exercise of his mind as a weapon (the cold iron of intellect defeating the softer bronze of mere courage), and the satisfaction of imposing intellectual order on the chaos of battle, he does not share his comrades' delight in war and military glory. In 'Odysseus'-3 he is depicted as the Machiavellian political fixer, taking delight in manipulating others:

> Some lizard in the under-mind
> Sprouted a tail with each crime,
> Ruling by stratagem the iron men;
> Your eloquence, the king's shadow,
> Your disrespect, adjusting laurels,
> An extra consolation in the brain.[9]

But this is immediately followed by the heavy reflection: 'War, love: habits you invented / And left like blackened oven stones.' Odysseus not only experiences war and love but in a sense invents them, as a culture hero who sets archetypal patterns of behaviour for later generations; yet these inventions are (for him) quickly burnt out and discarded as he moves on, searching for other kinds of satisfaction.[10]

8 Baxter puts some emphasis on Odysseus's eyes: he has the sharp and beady 'eyes of a gull' ('Odysseus'-2, 'Odysseus'-3), and in old age '[o]nly the eye remains' to show the man he once was ('Odysseus'-3).

9 In 'adjusting laurels' Baxter may have in mind the Ulysses of Shakespeare's *Troilus and Cressida*, cynically manipulating the reputations of Achilles and Ajax upwards and downwards for political ends.

10 This process of disenchantment is the subject of Baxter's very first Odysseus poem, 'Me Also' (1944, *Spark* 334), which takes the Ulysses/Circe story as a fable of disillusionment in love.

A discontent with contentment

This unsatisfied condition is also part of the Odysseus tradition. The defining quality of the Romantic Odysseus is his dissatisfaction with the actual: so Tennyson's Ulysses perpetually pursues an imagined goal which, like the horizon, 'fades / For ever and for ever when I move', and (more sentimentally) Fairburn's Odysseus mourns that he let his idealised dream of home be sullied by reality. But whereas Fairburn's hero wistfully regrets that he cannot be happy, Baxter's seems more fiercely to renounce the prospect of happiness. He is driven by a positive discontent with contentment, a refusal to settle for the conventional satisfactions of belonging, of love, family and home. In this respect he is the antithesis of Baxter's Hercules, whose quest is to return to the primal paradise associated with the maternal womb; Odysseus's driving force is the desire to escape from such confinement and passivity. If Baxter identifies on one level with Hercules' quest, he identifies equally strongly with that of Odysseus. As he wrote to Weir in 1967, 'What I have feared most in life is never some inward or outward pain, but the situation of being trapped in domesticity, in normality, in that segment of life which others no doubt quite properly find satisfying. I have feared it because it might choke up in me the double source of fantasy and truth' (19 April 1967, quoted McKay, *Life* 224).[11] Baxter's Odysseus—like Baxter himself?—can remain himself only while he remains an outsider, perpetually unsatisfied. He is like another great Romantic hero, Goethe's Faust, who will lose his soul if, and only if, he ever acknowledges that he is happy and calls for the fleeting moment to last (Goethe 787).

Odysseus's freedom, then, is unextricably tied up with isolation, estrangement and discontent. Even writing about *The Sore-footed Man*, the work which most celebrates the heroic quality

11 McKay uses the image of Odysseus in the final pages of his biography, confronting the question of whether Baxter was 'a happy man': 'Happiness suggests contentment with life and with what one makes of its possibilities. And the contentment is tempered by the realization that one must not expect too much from oneself, nor from the world. Baxter's was a questing spirit, he had too much restless vitality to be happy in the sense in which the word is generally understood. Like Odysseus, the Greek hero he so often referred to, he was eager to move on' (289).

of Odysseus's quest for freedom, Baxter acknowledged what is potentially 'the tragic nature of such a course in life' (*CPlays* 335). The early Odysseus poems make the dark side of the vision most explicit: that the only possible end for Odysseus's quest (in the sense both of 'termination' and 'goal') is death. The sonnet 'Odysseus'-1 surveys the hero's disillusionment—the dreams of love and heroic warfare which he once saw blaze are now ashes; his 'trusting' comrades are drowned—and concludes:

What though Calypso weep
Or blind Penelope, trees guessing not the snow—
Death is more deep than love; death is my spirit now.

In this 1946 poem the mood of despair seems to be a post-war one, close to that of the contemporary 'Returned Soldier' (*CP* 42), traumatised by war memories: 'The Cairo women, cobbers under sand, / A death too great for dolls to understand.'

The deeper implications of this death-wish are explored in the two poems on Odysseus and the Sirens. 'What the Sirens Sang' suggests that the almost irresistible lure offered to Odysseus by 'those snake-haired brazen-throated / Oracular women' was not lust, married love, martial glory or wisdom, but death.[12] Their temptation is developed further in 'The Sirens' (1952, *CP* 130–33), the poem Baxter later cited as defining 'the tragic nature' of Odysseus's course. Here they single out Odysseus from his crew, simple men who dream merely of food, drink, and sex, forgetting in their happily short memories that these pleasures have proved disappointing in the past. Odysseus, however, is immune to such 'fleshly allurements', having tried them all and ended up 'with a mind / Sharpened by excess, with a lust for oblivion keener'. These pleasures were 'a test at most to prove that you were human'. Now he claims that his sole desire is to return to Ithaca; but

12 The title picks up a famous question in Sir Thomas Browne's *Urn Burial*: 'What Song the *Syrens* sang, or what name *Achilles* assumed when he hid himself among women, though puzzling Questions are not beyond all conjecture' (ch. 5, Browne 307). The adjective 'snake-haired' (which has no classical warrant) links the Sirens with other female figures of terrifying power and knowledge in Baxter's poetry, such as 'the snake-haired Muse' or the Furies, the 'snake-haired daughters' who reveal to us the truth about ourselves ('The Eumenides', N23.67).

We must reply,
Since bound to truth: Ithaca is your remorse,
The home each sailor loves and runs away from,
And when you come there you will die of boredom.

Over six stanzas—pastoral, lyrical, not in the least mocking—they evoke the simple satisfactions of life on Ithaca: the '[b]enign, unchangeable' cycle of the constellations and the seasons, the homely rituals of birth, marriage and death, Laertes in his garden, Penelope at her loom. But this Edenic life is not for Odysseus; after all that he has experienced at war, how can he return to 'the joy of innocent men' and 'love concord and an old man's idleness'? The only possible satisfaction for him now is his 'longed-for bourne of oblivion': death and dissolution of identity in the cold, dark sea which is his natural element.

The dark dissolving tide can quench ambition;
And the indifferent rocks, whose weedy hair
Languishes serpentine, are undemanding lovers;
Within the whirlpool's virginal embrace
You shall become all things.

These resonant and mysterious images, echoing Eliot's drowned Phoenician sailor who 'passed the stages of his age and youth / Entering the whirlpool' (*Waste Land* part 4), and, behind that, Ariel's song in *The Tempest* (1.2.400–06), suggest that Odysseus's death by water may involve a 'sea change' which will finally end his isolation and estrangement.

The image of the death-directed Odysseus recurs in 'The Journey' (1945–47, *CP* 127). This is a fairly straightforward retelling of the Homeric account (at the start of *Odyssey* 11) of the journey of Odysseus and his men from Circe's island to the land of the dead.[13] The poem is built, however, around the contrast between life and death: Circe's island of Aeaea, 'the green isle summer-browed', rich in wine and apples and honey, and the bleak and barren beach 'where poplar and lamenting willow /

13 Its abrupt, in medias res opening ('Then, coming to the long ship [. . .]') suggests a passage torn directly from Homer, but also echoes the start of Ezra Pound's first *Canto*, which likewise tells the story of Odysseus's visit to the underworld: 'And then went down to the ship [. . .]' (Pound 3).

Let fall their vacant seed' and the dead gather like moths. At the centre of the poem is the image of all the crew looking back longingly towards Aeaea—'Only Odysseus, in the ship's prow standing, did not turn or speak.' With no context provided of Odysseus's reasons for visiting the underworld, the dominant impression is of his apartness from normal humanity, his obsessive drive away from the human world and towards death. The very dark vision of Odysseus in these early Baxter poems—the Romantic Tennysonian voyager turned into a kind of cursed Flying Dutchman figure—perhaps reflects Baxter's own dark sense of his alienated position in early 1950s New Zealand.

Returns to exile: Odysseus, Ithaca and women

In these early poems, Ithaca represents the simple satisfactions of home, family, a settled life—the 'rootedness' of the Homeric Odysseus—which Baxter's Odysseus cannot accept, partly because of his temperament (he would 'die of boredom') and partly because it is his calling to seek freedom and explore the darker, wilder reaches of human experience. But of course, according to the traditional, Homeric story, Odysseus *does* return to Ithaca. What happens to the perpetual wanderer, the hero of freedom and exile, when he returns home and settles down as a part of conventional society?

This is a motif to which Baxter repeatedly returns in the 1950s, in a series of poems on the return to Ithaca whose meaning has been debated. Doyle has argued that in the hero's journey 'the *return* seems as important as the outward movement', and that Odysseus's homecoming shows 'the self-making or self-sustaining ego [. . .] forced to encounter the world other than itself'; rather counterintuitively, he reads the hero's voyaging as a retreat into 'the cave of separateness' and his homecoming as a courageous emergence from the cave (Doyle 101–02). On the other hand, Davidson suggests that Baxter's Odysseus 'has [. . .] already travelled so far from his beginning that he has, in fact, broken away from it, and a return to it can only be an anti-climax' ('Odysseus' 114). And Rob Jackaman treats the hero's 'unsatisfactory return' as another of his various 'ways of failing', by which he retreats into a sterile and frustrated domesticity (338). Jackaman's reading seems more obviously persuasive, but the meaning of these poems is more complex than any single reading allows, especially if the unpublished notebook poems are taken into account. In these poems Baxter is using Odysseus to wrestle with issues—the poet's proper relationship with his own society, his position between bourgeois domesticity and Bohemian counter-culture—about which his feelings are extremely contradictory and divided, and the result of the wrestling shifts from poem to poem.

He is also wrestling with issues to do with women and sexuality. Taking his cue from the Homeric story, Baxter represents both Odysseus's travels and his homecoming largely in terms of his relationships with women: on Ithaca, his wife (or mother–wife) Penelope; on his travels, the beautiful women or demi-goddesses with whom he becomes involved, Circe and especially Calypso. Penelope—whom, as we have seen, Baxter once described as 'one of the most unattractive characters in fiction' (letter 20 October 1961, FM 27/1/11)—is almost always depicted unsympathetically, in the Tennysonian tradition: at best a tedious 'agèd wife'; at worst a suffocating and repressive presence. Calypso and Circe may be seen as a vital and life-enhancing part of Odysseus's quest for experience; or as distractions, entanglements, even destructive temptations. All the women, however, dwelling on their various islands, are consistently associated with earth—fertile earth and vegetation, or bare rock and stone. Penelope has 'the rock side of an island wife'; not only Calypso but also Circe (unlike her Homeric equivalent) lives in a cave ('Calypso's cavern, Circe's bed of stone'); Circe 'tempts [. . .] with eyes of rock', while Calypso has a 'mouth of broken clay'.[14] The women's element is dry (and fertile) land, whereas Odysseus is associated with the open (and barren) sea. The poems' treatment of Odysseus and his women thus reflects not only Baxter's anxieties about sexuality, promiscuity and chastity, but also the tension between freedom and confinement, settled stability and perpetual movement.

This tension can be seen in the first, most famous, and perhaps

14 Quotations from 'Odysseus'-2; 'What the Sirens Sang'; 'Odysseus'-3; 'To a Travelling Friend'.

the bleakest of the Ithaca poems. 'The Homecoming' (1952, *CP* 121) relocates the story in Baxter's native Otago landscape, with Odysseus as (presumably) a returned WW2 serviceman; its most striking change, however, is that Penelope is not the protagonist's wife but his mother. This change, which may owe something to Baxter's ambivalent relationship with his own strong-willed mother, is illuminated by a passage in *The Man on the Horse*, Baxter's explication of Burns' 'Tam o' Shanter'. He describes Tam's wife as a figure of 'the domestic Penelope', and her relationship with Tam as illustrating 'the melancholy dimension of distance between the independent male and his wife, who is also very much a mother figure, from whom his actual mode of being isolates him' (*MH* 100–01). 'The Homecoming' is built around this gender divide: the contrast and conflict, as bitter as the Trojan War, between the independent, adventuring male with 'a boy's / Dream of freedom' and the stay-at-home wife/mother who seeks to contain him at home. That Penelope here is mother rather than wife emphasises the regressive nature of her controlling love: she wishes to keep Odysseus permanently a child, symbolically to keep him shut in the womb, 'in the cage of beginning'. She refuses to acknowledge that he has changed and grown; refuses even to imagine the possibility of change. Against Odysseus's restless desire for change and movement the poem sets up a Miss Havisham-like sense of stasis: the house '[h]eavy with time's reliques', the browned photographs, the pendulum clock, the ghosts of the past. The image of 'the quiet maelstrom spinning / In the circle of their days' is a counterpart to 'the whirlpool's virginal embrace' towards which the Sirens invite Odysseus; but where the Sirens offered death and oblivion and the potential for a 'sea-change', the Penelope-mother has Odysseus trapped in a kind of living death, endlessly spinning, motion without change. At the end, instead of his heroic voyage, he is left with only the meagre day-to-day consolations of work, drink and male companionship, 'yet hears beyond sparse fields / On rock and cave the sea's hexameter beating.' As in Andrew Lang's famous line 'The surge and thunder of the *Odyssey*' ('The Odyssey', Lang 2: 63), the sound of the sea and the sound of Homeric verse merge in a reminder of the larger world of freedom and action (and art) from which the caged Odysseus is now excluded.

During the years 1957–59, around the time of his visit to India, the idea of Odysseus the traveller and his return to Ithaca seems to have been almost obsessively on Baxter's mind: he wrote five poems (only two of them subsequently published) on the theme. One might call them rather five versions of a single poem, since they overlap substantially, recycling passages, lines, and images; but they each take significantly different approaches to the material.[15]

The first (unpublished) poem, 'Odysseus'-2, presents Odysseus with some irony as a hero for those entering middle age (Baxter was thirty-one):

> Coming into the middle years
> When stone, leather, steel reward us
> For the lost movement of delight,
> Fettered at the ankle-bone,
> Remember Odysseus, that sly king [. . .]
>
> You who roast in the brass bull
> Of conscience, unload your pain
> On those much-travelled shoulders.

Those who have relinquished the freedom and idealism of youth for a middle age of material comfort, responsibilities and bad conscience can take the old Odysseus as a kind of patron saint. This is a very unheroic Odysseus: 'An old sea captain on his farm, / Sallow, small, with broken teeth', who spends his days drinking, quarrelling with his son and booming old war stories over dinner. His marriage suggests the diminishment of his land-bound state: 'Re-married to the frugal vine, / Burying his salt sperm / In the rock side of an island wife.' Penelope is earth—or, less invitingly, rock—to Odysseus's sea, and the 'salt sperm' which suggests his essential link to the open ocean is diverted to fertilise this barren

15 The poems are: 'Odysseus'-2 (N19.22); 'Green Figs at Table' (N19.23, *CP* 183); 'Odysseus'-3 (N19.33); 'The Old Age of Odysseus' (N19.89); 'The Tempter' (N20.25, *CP* 205). Also written around the same time were 'To One Travelling by Sea' (N19.16), and its published revision, 'To a Travelling Friend' (N19.18, *CP* 182–83); and 'Return to Exile' (N20.24, *SP* 82), which does not explicitly name Odysseus but clearly shares themes and images with the group.

land, bearing fruit presumably in 'his daughter the bent olive'. The other women in his past, Calypso and the rest, are dead memories, dust and ashes, or stowed in 'cupboards of the mind'. Only momentarily, watching the flight of a gull, does he recall the man he once was:

> Eyes of a gull follow a gull
> From a terrace by the sea,
> The thought flutters in his brain:
> 'I *was* Odysseus.'

But his only voyage now is 'into the darkest freedom' of death. In the final lines he watches a pair of young lovers kissing, and belatedly contemplates the simple positive values that (as in 'The Sirens') Ithaca represents and he has put behind him: 'Youth, abandoned for a labouring star, / Earth, the veined breasts of his mother, / Love, old and simple as a gourd.'

Though 'Odysseus'-2 is much less grim than 'The Homecoming', it presents an Odysseus sadly reduced to human scale. It also has a definite undertone of unease about sexuality. The image of roasting in the brass bull of conscience echoes Baxter's account of himself in 'Be Happy in Bed' (1958–59, *CP* 199–200): 'Sex taught him sadness, like St Lawrence / Roasting on the grid of conscience.'[16] While Odysseus is implied not to suffer such bad conscience, the grotesque and brutal image of 'rubber women ganched / In cupboards of the mind'—to ganch is literally 'to impale (a person) upon sharp hooks or stakes as a mode of execution' (*OED*)—again suggests repressed guilt, on Baxter's part if not Odysseus's. A mood of revulsion and renunciation towards sexuality can be felt in a number of Baxter's poems around this time, such as 'Be Happy in Bed', which rejects the advice of its ironic title, or the bitterly misogynistic 'A Clapper to Keep off Crows' (1959, *CP* 202–03).

The idea of sexuality as a temptation and threat is clearer in an earlier poem of the same year, 'To a Travelling Friend', where the temptress is Circe rather than Calypso. The poet warns his

16 The 'brass bull' image comes from the Sicilian tyrant Phalaris who, according to legend, used this nastily claustrophobic method of execution.

'Friend, other self' to 'think how Circe / Tempts, with song, then with eyes of rock. / We die with the birth-cord round the throat.' 'Sex destroys itself, / A scar whitened where the wound was.'[17] Sexuality as much as domesticity, in these dark and misogynistic poems, is a threat to the freedom and integrity of the Odysseus figure: the sexual temptress merges with the devouring mother, both (in very different ways) dragging the male hero back to the womb and leaving him strangled with the umbilical cord.[18]

It is the sexual aspect of 'Odysseus'-2 which Baxter develops in incorporating some of its lines and images into the published 'Green Figs at Table' (*CP* 183), which perhaps takes off from the vision of the young couple 'sharing pouched figs and kisses' in the earlier poem. In this rather Lawrentian seduction dialogue, however, the irony and unease of the earlier poem are largely lost, as Baxter takes a far more positive view of sexuality. The old sea captain Odysseus, stripped of his sad and ridiculous aspects, becomes a simpler figure of contentment in old age and freedom from sexual guilt, a state aspired to by the male speaker who still 'roast[s] in the brass bull' and dreams of sexual liberation: 'Oil boats rust, chained at darkened wharves. / One movement could shake // Us free, I think'.

The question of Odysseus's sexual adventures, and how they relate to his past quest for freedom and present domestic bondage, becomes central in the three Calypso poems ('Odysseus'-3, 'The Old Age of Odysseus', 'The Tempter'). Each poem is built around a contrast between the older Odysseus on Ithaca and the younger Odysseus making love to the nymph Calypso on her island; in each poem, however, the contrast takes on a different significance.[19]

'Odysseus'-3 begins by calling on the hero to remember his time with Calypso; it ends (after a transitional passage, quoted

17 'The Odyssean allusion is more explicit in an earlier draft, 'To One Travelling by Sea', N19.16: 'Remember, Odysseus, / How we drank from the same breast, before / You climb to her who smiles from stiff sheets / To die with the birth-cord knotted round the throat.' In this version the temptress is 'blonde Circe in her cave'.

18 Compare 'Green Figs at Table', where 'mothers' embody the repressive and life-denying power of 'Society as undertaker': 'Mothers admire the handsome corpse [. . .] They cover the rope mark on the throat.'

19 These poems are discussed in more detail in Miles, 'Three Calypsos'.

earlier, about the Trojan War and the hero's 'invention' of love and war) with a version of the lines from 'Odysseus'-2 about the 'old sea captain' on Ithaca watching a gull fly and remembering freedom. The description of Calypso and her island here is sensuous without being conventionally glamorous:

> Remember, Odysseus,
> How day climbed from the cave
> Of the summer nymph. Exhaustion
> Following the deep spondaic thrust;
> Honeysuckle, arbutus,
> Trailing down the rock of lust,
> A belly like a green gourd,
> Broad nostrils, mouth of broken clay
> Beside the talkative island wave.

Calypso, with her 'mouth of broken clay', is a mortal and earthy figure rather than an ethereal nymph; the cave, the 'rock of lust', the trailing vines, all associate her firmly with the earth and fertility, while the image of her 'belly like a green gourd' echoes 'Love, old and simple as a gourd' in the final line of 'Odysseus'-2. Though this image is much more appealing than that of Penelope, both women are associated with earth rather than sea and air (the gull's territory) which are Odysseus's elements. The time on Calypso's island is a pleasant interlude on his travels (and there is a mischievous humour in Baxter's depiction of their love-making in terms of the Homeric hexameter, 'the deep spondaic thrust'), but it might have been as much a cage as Ithaca if he had remained there.[20] At the end of the poem what he dreams of is not Calypso but 'the true bride, Freedom' and the 'voyage to no harbour'.

In 'The Old Age of Odysseus', however, the tone of the description of Calypso has shifted subtly:

> Old Odysseus on his farm
> Remembers still the summer nymph,
> The deep spondaic music playing
> From wave and cave when he rode
> That mare of days, that seashell bride.

20 As it is for the Homeric Odysseus, though for different reasons: he chafes in his seven-year confinement on Calypso's island because he longs to return home.

A belly like a green gourd,
Broad nostrils, mouth of broken clay,
Trouble his seadeep memory.

Now her earthy associations are countered by associations with water and the sea—and also with poetry and the imagination. 'Seashell bride' suggests the Botticelli Venus riding the waves. 'Mare of days', which may hint at the cliché of waves as white horses, also suggests a deliberate inversion of '*night*mare': Calypso is a beautiful waking dream. The comparison with Homeric verse is now applied not to copulation but (as in 'The Homecoming') to the sound of the sea echoing in the cave. The image evokes Baxter's primal poetic experience as a boy, listening for the first time to 'the unheard sound of which poems are translations' in a cave above the sea ('Education', *MH* 124). This Calypso is an anima figure, far more intimately connected than the last with Odysseus's sea quest and Baxter's poetic calling. Consequently in the second stanza,

It is not Calypso truly
Disturbs him at a good wife's side
Torturing old rheumatic blood,
But the myth of ocean freedom,
Ashes of the search for God.
Between the spasm and the sigh
He found and lost humility.

He mourns not for Calypso herself but for what she represents: his belief in 'ocean freedom' and his search for God, for something beyond the mundane world—a search which now, in Ithaca, seems like a delusion. The act of making love to Calypso was not just a pleasant diversion: it opened him up to a kind of epiphany. (Though perhaps a thwarted epiphany—we shall return to the implications of 'humility' in this passage.)

In 'The Old Age of Odysseus', then, Calypso is a very positive figure, offering Odysseus a kind of freedom and truth he is not quite capable of accepting. Her role in the final, published poem, 'The Tempter' (*CP* 205), is strikingly different. The opening lines of this poem quote almost verbatim the sensuous description of

Calypso and her island from 'Odysseus'-3.[21] But now it is no longer the poet in his own voice inviting Odysseus to 'Remember'; instead the quoted words are assigned to 'the Tempter':

> So the Tempter wheedles one
> Whose mind aches in dispossession,
> Whose limbs are fastened to the rock,
> One who has sailed beyond the reach
> Of hashish or a woman's touch,
> And now, uncertain of his gift, sets down
> For thefts of being words will never cure,
> As if on plates of tin or horn,
> A pedlar's maxim: *Thirst, obey, endure.*

The memory of Calypso is now a temptation which the hardened Odysseus must resist. She may not be a murderous trap like the rock-eyed Circe in 'To a Travelling Friend', but she is a drug, like hashish or the lotus of the Lotus-eaters, which will sap his resolution and distract him from his mission.

But 'The Tempter' raises other problems of interpretation. What exactly is Odysseus's imagined situation in the poem? The image of him 'in dispossession [. . .] fastened to the rock' may suggest at first that this is Odysseus at one of the low points of his voyage, shipwrecked and struggling for physical survival. But an alternative reading is suggested by comparison with the immediately preceding poem in Baxter's notebook: 'Return to Exile' (N20.24; *SP* 82), the poem on his return from India to New Zealand:

> No trumpet on the mountain. From
> Exile into exile he goes home.
> Secretly the glittering coast instructs him:
> 'Your lot is now intelligible pain.
> Ignore the whorish voice that whispers
> Of meekness, meekness among thieves.
> I am your angel. Rage against me.
> Older, so very little wiser,
> Set down your meaning with a shaking hand.'

21 Except that Calypso's belly is compared to 'a brown gourd' rather than a 'green' one.

Baxter sees himself returning to a home where he does not feel—or deliberately chooses not to feel—at home; where his task will be to suffer and to make that suffering 'intelligible' to others, and to find his poetic inspiration in rage against the injustices of his own society. The juxtaposition suggests that 'The Tempter' is also about Odysseus's homecoming to Ithaca: his 'dispossession' is his status as inner émigré; he is 'fastened to the rock' by his confinement to life on dry land. Like the traveller in 'Return to Exile' he must 'set down' his message shakily, no longer confident of his poetic or heroic gifts; the message is a simple one of endurance, self-denial, the attempt to retain his selfhood and integrity in a hostile society. Thus interpreted, 'The Tempter' suggests that Odysseus's homecoming is not a defeat or betrayal but a harsh duty he must accept, turning his back on the Romantic 'myth of ocean freedom', and on the temptation to retreat into pastoral dreams of love and sensual pleasure, in order to engage with the unattractive realities of the society Baxter called 'Pig Island'.

Baxter's final poem on this theme, 'Back to Ithaca' (*CP* 384), comes almost a decade later, in 1967. Bookending the sequence, it echoes the motifs and mood of the early 'The Homecoming'. (The poem vividly illustrates both the radical change in Baxter's poetic style—the early Baxter, with his high Romantic rhetoric, would never have perpetrated a phrase like 'chock-a-block in a Siren's vagina'—and at the same time the essential continuity of his themes.) Again, the setting is a New Zealand farm: the exile unwillingly returns to the 'fatherless clay acres' which 'have implored his duty', with their dank wells and 'old-maidish gloomy bluegums'. He will not be happy, but manages to feel 'a delusion of peace':

Given the setting, he will invent
destiny, nature,
a wife to brush his boots
and a soul as flat and hard as a bean.

In this bleak conclusion the homecoming is again seen in completely negative terms: the 'thefts of being' Baxter hoped to guard against in 'The Tempter' have taken place, and he now sees as a self-deluding invention the notion that to return home was his 'duty' or his 'destiny'. The poem seems to anticipate Baxter's decision, two years later, to drop out of conventional society and go to Jerusalem.

Bending Ulysses' bow

A very different and much more positive spin on the homecoming of Odysseus occurs in a small group of poems of 1956–60 which use the image of 'Ulysses' bow'. In these poems (written in traditional octosyllabic couplets or quatrains, like much of Baxter's lighter satiric verse, and calling the hero by his more traditional Roman name), Ulysses is a simple icon of heroism. Wielding his mighty bow, which no other man could bend, to shoot down the suitors who have taken over his palace, he embodies a dangerous heroic glamour which is set against the mediocrity and compromise of bourgeois New Zealand. In 'Threnos' (1956, N18.31, alternatively titled 'A Kiwi Wishes for Wings'), New Zealand's citizens are rabbits in 'the warrens of the State', in a land that is 'dully kind / And dully right and dully pure'—

And who will walk in Cressid's gown?
And who will bend Ulysses' bow?
Who'll pluck the golden apples down?
I do not know. I do not know.

Baxter answers the rhetorical question in the 'Letter to Bob Lowry' (1956, N18.39), a mock-Augustan epistle in the style of Swift which (as often with Baxter's light verse letters) cuts deeper than may at first appear. Wryly confessing an unaccountable dissatisfaction with his comfortable middle-class life—

A job, a young aquatic wife,
Could any man ask more of life?
But the Rack turns, the ageless Rack,
Blood spurts again *and* Sinews crack—

he imagines 'a Voice like a steel bell' proclaiming that his 'gift' is in danger of shrivelling away like a 'spider in a kauri stove'. In the final lines, he imagines himself taking on the role of Ulysses:

Penelope sings at her loom.
Drowned sailors in their seadark tomb

Cry luck to him who walks on Land.
On ruined Ithaca I stand.
The suitors clamour in the house,
Careless & cold then by carouse.
I see the lifted Aegis glow,
My task has come: To bend Ulysses' bow.

Free from the tragic complexities and doubts of many of the Odysseus poems, this is unequivocally the poet as hero. Armed with the bow and backed by the divine power of Athena, he prepares to challenge the corruption and misgovernment of his 'ruined' society.[22]

The bow is a recurring symbol in Baxter's poems, which (as discussed in chapter 2) he associates especially with his father, Archie the archer. With its Apollonian associations, it carries implications of 'straight-shooting' honesty and clarity of principle, of rational intellect and of poetry. Perhaps most powerfully it suggests the potential for effective action—as in 'To My Father' (1947, *CP* 65–66):

I shall compare you to the bended bow,
Myself the arrow launched upon the hollow
Resounding air. And I must go
In time, my friend, to where you cannot follow.
It is not love would hope to keep me young,
The arrow rusted and the bow unstrung.

In comparing himself to Ulysses bending the bow, Baxter suggests he is prepared to fulfil his potential at last.

A philosophical psychopath: *The Sore-footed Man*

The image of the bow is also central to *The Sore-footed Man* (1967), Baxter's most full-length and most positive and triumphant portrayal of Odysseus as hero. This is paradoxical, since in Sophocles' *Philoctetes*, of which Baxter's play is an adaptation,

22 The change in tone is marked by the last line's leap from satiric tetrameter to heroic iambic pentameter. In 'Footnote to *Antony and Cleopatra*' (1960, *CP* 212) Baxter applies the image to another poet-hero, Shakespeare, confessing that we can no longer understand how he achieved his greatness: 'Freud and Bradley cramp our thumbs / That try to bend Ulysses' bow.'

Odysseus is unambiguously the villain. As Sophocles presents the story, Odysseus had been primarily responsible for abandoning his comrade Philoctetes on the barren island of Lemnos, because the festering and incurable wound of a snakebite made him intolerable to be with. Now, nine years later, Odysseus returns, because an oracle has stated that Troy cannot be taken without the magical bow and arrows which Philoctetes inherited from the hero Heracles. To help him trick Philoctetes into giving up the bow, he has brought the young Neoptolemus, whom he coaches in his end-justifies-the-means philosophy:

> I know it goes against the grain with you
> To lie, or act deceitfully: but then,
> Success is worth an effort, make it now.
> We shall be justified in the end; for the present,
> Let honesty go hang, only for a day,
> I beg you; and then you can live for ever after
> A paragon of virtue. (Sophocles, *Philoctetes* 79–85; p.166)[23]

But Neoptolemus, moved by the nobility and suffering of Philoctetes, revolts against his dishonourable mission and finally turns to defend him against Odysseus. For his part Odysseus reveals himself as not only dishonourable but also cowardly by running away, not once but twice, from Neoptolemus's sword and Philoctetes' bow. He is thus absent from the conclusion of the play where Heracles appears, deus ex machina, to instruct Philoctetes to go after all to Troy and there be cured of his wound.

Baxter follows the basic outline of Sophocles' plot fairly closely, though he invents one new major character, Philoctetes' wife Eunoe, whom Odysseus seduces into stealing the bow from Philoctetes. However, Baxter shifts the moral bearings of the story dramatically: Odysseus becomes 'in a sense the main character' and the moral centre of the play (Introduction, *CPlays* 335). This can be seen most clearly in the ending: instead of Odysseus's ignominious escape and Heracles' divine intervention, the play ends with Odysseus confronting the vengeful Philoctetes and persuading him to accompany him to Troy.

23 The translation is the Penguin Classics one by E. F. Watling, which Baxter used (occasionally borrowing a line directly); line references are to the Loeb edition.

This change is the more striking because in some ways one might have expected Baxter to take Philoctetes as his hero and self-image. As Baxter notes in his Introduction, 'The situation of the main character in Sophocles' *Philoctetes*, cogitating in solitude on his island, mirrored so exactly the predicament of the modern intellectual' (335). Baxter himself would repudiate the label 'intellectual', a word he consistently uses with mocking disdain,[24] but as we have seen he is preoccupied with the isolation and estrangement of the artist. His reading of the myth may have been influenced by Edmund Wilson's 1941 essay 'Philoctetes: The Wound and the Bow', in which Philoctetes is taken as a symbol of the writer whose creative genius (the 'bow') is inseparable from the crippling psychological 'wound' which makes him intolerable to the conventional society which surrounds him. It seems very likely that Baxter also knew André Gide's play *Philoctète* (1898), at least from Wilson's account of it. Gide's Philoctète, alone on an island which appears to be somewhere in the arctic regions, has become an ascetic poet and philosopher, seeing himself as 'nature's voice' (Gide 144), and aspiring to a state of pure thought: 'I shall soon be, though still alive, quite abstract' (146). The coarsely pragmatic politician Ulysse, though he finally succeeds (by drugging him) in stealing the bow from Philoctète, admits that he is shamed by the beauty of his virtue (158), and the play ends with a kind of apotheosis of the exiled artist-hero, as '*birds from heaven come down to feed him*' (160).

Baxter's portrayal of Philoctetes is much less reverent. He calls Sophocles' protagonist 'an inveterate wailer and groaner' (*CPlays* 335), and his changes to the story seriously trivialise Philoctetes' tragic situation. Philoctetes' wound, in Sophocles a gangrenous horror which causes him at times to fall to the ground in paroxysms of agony, becomes something more like a touch of rheumatism which makes him limp and occasionally become grumpy; moreover, he is marooned not on a barren deserted rock

24 Note, at opposite ends of his career, his ruefulness at being lumped in with 'the academic crew' and 'other intellectual men' in 'Letter to Noel Ginn II' (1946–48, *CP* 70–72), and 'intellectual talk / Props up the Tower of Babel' in 'Two Songs for Lazarus' (1971, *CP* 520–21).

where he must struggle to survive, but on a civilised island where he lives quite comfortably (if rather discontentedly) with a wife and child. The invention of Eunoe—'Philoctetes needed a wife. I gave him one,' Baxter laconically explains (335)—turns him from an archetypal Man Alone into a semi-comic henpecked husband. Baxter's Philoctetes, like Gide's, sees himself as a philosopher and aspires to the beauty of abstract thought; but his 'philosophy' is a cranky autodidact's mixture of mysticism and pseudo-science which we are encouraged to take no more seriously than do Odysseus or Neoptolemus (who is bored almost to desperation by it). Baxter does show real empathy with Philoctetes' revulsion against 'the terrible boredom' of domestic life, 'the world of bandages and rheumatism and pots boiling over [. . .] All that personal domestic fug' (150). But Philoctetes' frustration is self-imposed, a product of his attempt to withdraw from the world into the safety of his private, abstract world; as Odysseus sees, he is 'caught in the burrow of his own mind, going round and round endlessly like a dog in the straw' (153). The sign of his impotence is his failure to use the bow and arrows that Hercules bequeathed him. Whereas Sophocles' Philoctetes vitally depends on them to kill the food he lives on, Baxter's Philoctetes keeps them as a museum piece, as Eunoe complains: 'What use are they? You've never even used them to shoot at a hedgehog!' (135). This is the sterile inactivity that Baxter condemned in 'To My Father'—'The arrow rusted and the bow unstrung'. Odysseus, then, becomes the hero of Baxter's play, 'since he alone has the power to liberate Philoctetes from his intellectual roundabout' (335). It is arguable, however, that the play's treatment of Philoctetes is its fatal dramatic weakness: his complete lack of heroic stature deprives Odysseus's mission of any sense of urgency and the play's moral debate of any tension.

In his Introduction Baxter defines the difference between Philoctetes and Odysseus in terms of a contrast between the 'beat' and the 'hip'.

> Philoctetes in my play is essentially a 'beat' type (as Norman Mailer expresses the distinction in his remarkable essay, *The White Negro*) where a universe of ideas rotates around his own

> navel, whereas Odysseus derives his sanction from the unknown fertilising power of action itself. (335)

Baxter is creatively misremembering Mailer's 1957 essay, which has nothing to say specifically about the 'beat' as a character type. It is rather a description and celebration of what it means to be 'hip', and of the hipster as 'American existentialist'. In the face of nuclear annihilation or slow death by conformity, the hipster understands that

> the only life-giving answer is to accept the terms of death, to live with death as immediate danger, to divorce oneself from society, to exist without roots, to set out on that uncharted journey with the rebellious imperatives of the self. In short, whether the life is criminal or not, the decision is to encourage the psychopath in oneself, to explore that domain of experience where security is boredom and therefore sickness, and one exists in the present [. . .]. (Mailer 271)

Hipster slang (*swing, groove, with it*, and so on), quaintly dated though it may sound today, seemed to Mailer in 1956 'a language of energy' (281) expressing 'a dark, romantic, and yet undeniably dramatic view of existence for it sees every man and woman as moving individually through each moment of life forward into growth or backward into death' (275). Through continual movement and action the hipster strives to be 'with it', 'to be closer to the secrets of that inner unconscious life which will nourish you if you can hear it, for you are then nearer to that God which every hipster believes is located in the senses of his body' (283). The hipster is 'a philosophical psychopath' (275): 'The only Hip morality [. . .] is to do what one feels whenever and wherever it is possible [. . .] to open the limits of the possible for oneself, for oneself alone, because that is one's need. Yet in widening the arena of the possible, one widens it reciprocally for others as well' (286).

Incongruous as the idea of 'Odysseus the hipster' may sound, Mailer's description obviously harmonised with Baxter's long-standing conception of the character; phrases like 'to live without roots' and 'uncharted journey' must have had particular resonance for him. It is in this same Introduction, within a few lines of the reference to Mailer, that he writes (in the passage quoted at the beginning of this chapter) of how he has long been 'haunted' by the character of Odysseus as an alternative to 'conventional ethics' and a model for successful action in the world.

The Odysseus of *The Sore-footed Man* is certainly liberated from conventional ethics; in fact, he shows many of the same qualities that make Sophocles' Odysseus a villain.[25] He is a smooth manipulator, an unscrupulous liar, a seducer (his seduction of Eunoe has some disconcerting echoes of Shakespeare's Richard III seducing Lady Anne).[26] This is the politician of 'Odysseus'-3 whose 'lizard in the under-mind / Sprouted a tail with every crime'—echoed here by the First Sailor's image of 'a little old snake moving very gently in the dark' inside Odysseus's head (*CPlays* 149). But the snake here evokes wisdom and power rather than Satanic evil. For Baxter, Odysseus's 'villainy' is a product of his clear-headed, free-thinking approach to life. He values intelligence and rationality, though he knows that 'A rational man among the irrational is like a leper' (132). Moving beyond the stiff 'honour' of Neoptolemus or the machismo of heroes like 'that brave, mutton-headed butcher Ajax', he is prepared to 'think like a woman' and lie to avoid unnecessary bloodshed (132–33); and he is able to argue, plausibly, that his manipulations of Eunoe and Philoctetes are for their own good as well as his.

Unlike his dramatic predecessors, his motives are not political. For Sophocles, Odysseus is the archetypal political man, justifying his actions by the Nuremberg defence (he was 'acting on the orders of our overlords', *Phil.* 6, p.163), and recognising no moral authority above the state. Gide's Ulysse cannot even conceive of any values that are not political: 'What other devotion, if not to one's country, is imaginable?' (Gide 153). But Baxter's Odysseus, though he deploys the rhetoric of patriotism and political necessity against Neoptolemus, finally acknowledges that he is entirely

25 Doyle (143) suggests that he *is* a Sophoclean villain, 'the apparently conscienceless man of action and expediency', who merely manipulates Philoctetes with his philosophy of risk-taking. This is a sustainable reading, but it guts the play of its most challenging content.

26 Like Richard (*R3* 1.2), Odysseus assures his victim that he committed his crime for love of her, and he finally wins her over by offering her the chance to kill him.

indifferent to the question of who wins the Trojan War: war is senseless, and 'Troy is nothing' (156–58).

Nor, however, is he motivated by self-interest in a conventional sense. The First Sailor—who serves not only as a shrewd commentator but also as a kind of low-comic shadow of Odysseus himself[27]—declares that

> King Odysseus doesn't like the nobs [. . .]. He only likes himself.
>
> SECOND SAILOR That's no—recommendation.
>
> FIRST SAILOR He doesn't like himself much either. He likes—space! (149).

Odysseus is not setting out to aggrandise himself, because he is not actually convinced that he *has* a self. 'What are you, Odysseus? A shadow of a shadow of a shadow. A man is a lie that Zeus created to amuse himself on a hot, stagnant afternoon' (134). To put it in other, existentialist terms: the existence of Odysseus precedes his essence. The hipster–existentialist Odysseus recognises no absolute truths—'I'd have to know the truth before I could tell it' (134)—and no essential self. His self is something he must create for himself, from moment to moment, out of the chaos of the world; and the main thing he desires is the 'space', the freedom of action, to do that—in Mailer's words, to 'open the limits of the possible' for himself.

Odysseus has an almost mystical sense of 'the unknown fertilising power of action itself'. 'To act is a great responsibility,' he tells Neoptolemus; 'to do the unpredictable, the new, the fully made thing.' The sources of action are mysterious, and symbolically located 'in a dark bundle' in the belly of a woman (Philoctetes' wife, the snake priestess); he confesses that he fears the 'terrible darkness [. . .] out of which action is born' (154). The darkness is perhaps the 'chaos'—the 'absurdity' in an existentialist

27 The First Sailor, like Odysseus, is a cheerful cynic, a liar and trickster (he is the only person in the play who deceives Odysseus—compare 129–30 and 136), and a braver of danger ('Of course it's dangerous! What isn't dangerous?', 138). His claim to have 'a god in my belly' (138) is echoed more seriously in Eunoe's words to Odysseus: 'There's a god inside you' (147). The analogy could be extended to associate the timorous, superstitious Third Sailor with Philoctetes, and the colourlessly in-between Second Sailor with Neoptolemus.

sense—of the world and of human nature; their lack of any inherent meaning. But to act is to bring some kind of order and meaning into existence. Symbolically, it is to cause something new to be 'born'; action is potency. Odysseus the man of action thus mirrors Baxter the playwright, whose task (as he explains in the play's Introduction) is 'to make a pattern out of the chaos of [. . .] experience' (334).

'I suspect,' Baxter wrote (with an interesting tentativeness in summing up the meaning of his own play), 'that *The Sore-footed Man* is mainly written around the enigma of human freedom' (335). The play's final confrontation between Odysseus and Philoctetes turns on a debate about the true meaning of freedom, or, as Odysseus sees it, a debate between 'the desire for freedom and the dread of freedom—the issues which will fight for ever in the heart and head' of every human being.[28]

Philoctetes has sought a negative kind of freedom in withdrawing from the world of public action into that of pure abstract thought—and aspires to go even further into absolute liberation from the 'soul-case' of the body (150). It is interesting that he fantasises about being reincarnated as a gull (144), the same bird which was associated in earlier poems with Odysseus's dream of absolute freedom.[29] For the Odysseus of the play, however, this is merely a sign of Philoctetes' fear of real freedom; he has retreated into the 'burrow' of his mind, into a sterile self-enclosure, unable to act, and increasingly trapped and frustrated. While the angry Philoctetes accuses Odysseus of entrapping him, 'trying to bind me with a web of words the way a spider binds a fly' (156), Odysseus claims that 'I think—I hope—I've set you free' (155).

Odysseus's concept of freedom is active, implying not withdrawal but total engagement with the world, the body, and human mortality. He accuses Philoctetes of seeking 'security', but 'Security is the demon I fled from, sailing to Troy—a wife's arms,

28 Odysseus says 'in the heart and head of their [Philoctetes' and Eunoe's] son', but the son clearly serves here as a representative of humankind.

29 In the prose poem 'Gulls' (N15.18) Baxter associates gulls with freedom and sees them as 'symbols of an undivided being'.

a quiet hearth, a dead soul!' (158). True freedom demands danger. Odysseus makes this point dramatically by handing the bow back to Philoctetes and walking away, risking a poisoned arrow in the back (a pointed reversal of the cowardice of his Sophoclean model). When Philoctetes calls him back, Odysseus explains the core of his philosophy.

> I couldn't tell whether you'd shoot or not. If I'd known you would shoot, I'd have been a madman—a suicide like poor Ajax. If I'd known you wouldn't, I'd have been a charlatan. But I didn't know, and that's the knife blade I walk on; darkness on each side of me and a blade of fear in the centre. Then my life obeys me; it shudders and obeys my will. If my fear of death were stronger than I am, I'd no longer be Odysseus. I carry my fear inside me like an unborn child.
>
> [. . .]
>
> What was Hercules? A man. A man whose soul came alive and gave strength to his body when he swallowed his fear and lived inside the jaws of death. And you are carrying his bow. Either throw it into the sea, or else use it. The bow of Hercules, carried by a man who wishes to be secure, is useless as a stalk of grass. You have to become Hercules—or rather, become Philoctetes. (158)

Like Mailer's hipster, Odysseus knows that 'security is boredom and therefore sickness', and 'the only life-giving answer is to accept the terms of death, to live with death as immediate danger'. In 'widening the area of the possible' for himself, he also 'widens it reciprocally for others', helping Philoctetes to gain his own freedom and become truly himself for the first time.

This moment is in a sense the apotheosis of Baxter's Odysseus-figure. It is the bright side of the dark vision of the early poems, with their sense of 'the tragic nature of [his] course in life' which could lead only towards death, or the bleak explorations of compromise and failure in the Ithaca poems. In *The Sore-footed Man*, Odysseus's desire for freedom and his perpetual awareness of death become a means of living life more intensely. The play leaves us with the gleeful words the sailor's song puts in Odysseus's mouth: 'I think it's one hell of a joke . . .' (159).

Odysseus and the mossgrown cross

Needless to say, this is not a final resolution of the issues Baxter has been exploring through Odysseus. The 'philosophical psychopath' of *The Sore-footed Man* is not, to put it mildly, an unproblematic role model. Baxter noted in his Introduction that 'I trust I have not made him a neo-Fascist' (335). It was a shrewd doubt: there is, potentially, something disturbingly fascist about Odysseus's Nietzschean glorification of action and will divorced from conventional morality, and his sense of action as something that arises instinctively from the gut. Moreover, the play's message is defiantly pagan: Baxter has edited out Sophocles' ending, in which Heracles declares that 'reverence for the gods [. . .] is the thing our Father holds most precious, / And piety does not perish when men die' (*Phil.* 1443–44, p. 211), to replace it with Odysseus's existentialist assertion of the power of human will to create meaning in a meaningless universe. It is virtually impossible to reconcile what Odysseus stands for with Baxter's Catholic Christianity and 'the theology of Aquinas'.

This tension between Odysseus and Christianity has been implicit in Baxter's poetry from the beginning. Like Dante, Baxter associates Odysseus with pride—a pagan virtue but a deadly sin for orthodox Christianity. 'Pride was his lodestar' in 'What the Sirens Sang'. In 'The Strait' (1962, *CP* 253) the passage between Scylla and Charybdis is allegorised as a choice between 'the rock of Pride, the whirlpool of Despair', in which Odysseus chooses to steer closer to Pride; the fact that he loses eight men but saves his ship perhaps suggests that Pride was the less destructive of the two options. The pride is also Baxter's own. In 'Letter to Noel Ginn', he appeals to Noel as 'confessor for my sin / Which is pride alone: yet pride alone will win / Niche of immortal marble despised and hungered for'; in the poem's final words, 'pride is the saviour' (*CP* 27–29). In the very poem in which he first identifies himself with Odysseus/Ulysses, he reveals an ambivalent identification with the hero's pagan pride and his yearning for worldly glory.[30]

30 'Pride' is a recurring motif in McKay's biography; see e.g. 146–47, where Baxter had difficulty with AA's demand that he admit powerlessness over his alcoholism: 'It demanded too much humility.'

For the agnostic teenage Baxter 'confession' was merely a poetic trope and 'saviour' a (perhaps defiantly) secular word. Even after his conversion to Catholicism, his Odysseus poems only guardedly hint at a Christian critique of the hero's values. The most striking example is the enigmatic ending of 'The Old Age of Odysseus', which associates his time on Calypso's island with 'the search for God': 'Between the spasm and the sigh / He found and lost humility.' Odysseus, perhaps, is so armoured in pagan pride and self-sufficiency that only for an instant, at the vulnerable moment of orgasm, can he open himself up to a sense of humility in the face of the divine.

But it is only in his very last Odysseus poem, 'Autumn Testament' 10 (1972, *CP* 545), that Baxter brings Odysseus into direct confrontation with Christianity:

> The mossgrown haloed cross that crowns this church
> Is too bleak for the mind of old Odysseus
>
> Coming home to his table of rock, surviving and not surviving
> Storms, words, axes, and the fingers of women,
>
> Or the mind of Maui, who climbed inside the body
> Of his ancestress and died there.

For the first time Baxter links Odysseus with a figure from Maori mythology: Maui, the great trickster and culture hero, who tried to end the power of death over humankind by killing the death goddess Hine-nui-te-po. And both are contrasted with a symbol of Christianity, 'the mossgrown haloed cross' on the church at Jerusalem. Both the Greek and Polynesian heroes are figures of pagan self-assertion, survivors and battlers against death, who find the Christian message of obedience to God's will and voluntary death, embodied in the Cross on which Christ was crucified, 'too bleak' to accept. In the poem's final lines, however, the poet himself accepts it:

> To the grass of the graveyard or a woman's breast
> We turn in our pain for absolution.

He turns to the earth, the feminine, the maternal womb and tomb—all the things Odysseus so determinedly fled from. As

Baxter wryly acknowledges in 'Autumn Testament' 29, Christ himself 'is incurably domestic' (*CP* 555), and to follow his path means to surrender the kind of Man Alone freedom that Odysseus stands for. So Baxter quietly turns his back on 'old Odysseus'. It is a very gentle and subtle rejection, however, appropriate for a figure who for so long had served as Baxter's vehicle for grappling with the issues most important to him.

CHAPTER 7

UNDER THE SIGN: BACCHUS/DIONYSUS

> On the curve of the wine jar Dionysus lying
> Naked and asleep in a black boat,
> With a beard like the waves of the sea—and out of his belly
> A vine growing [. . .] ('The Jar', *CP* 392–93)

> NARRATOR And the sweet, sly bottle talks turkey to [Jack] out of his swag. It sings in his ear like a wasp.
>
> BOTTLE [. . .] I'll be your Sunday wife. I'll make a bed of goose feathers, heavy as snow on the ground, and we'll creep in together. I'll kiss you to sleep like a bad, old mother. I'll hold you closer than your bones.
>
> (*Jack Winter's Dream*, *CPlays* 4–5)

One of the defining conditions of the first part of Baxter's career, and one which has become indelibly associated with it, is his alcoholism.[1] He clearly carried its scars long after he had gone 'dry'. Yet his vivid fictional recreation of his early Dunedin drinking days in the novel *Horse*, written two decades later, makes it clear that he looked back on that period with a kind of nostalgia—while at the same time seeing his escape from alcoholism through his experience in AA as a crucial and redemptive turning point.

> Baxter talked endlessly at this time about his alcoholism and how much he missed the camaraderie of the pub. It was clear to his listeners that entering A.A. had been a real, spiritual experience and was something of central importance in his life. (McKay, *Life* 215)

1 McKay refers to Baxter's alcoholism and the effect it had on those around him in a number of contexts (e.g. *Life* 104, 128–29, 143), and it features in the opening sections of Pat Lawlor's diary notes (9–15).

Although his life with respect to alcohol was to take a new direction, it is easy to see how the young Baxter could be seen as New Zealand's answer to Dylan Thomas. Baxter himself, referring to the play *Jack Winter's Dream*, conceded its similarities to Thomas's work, but argued that the similarity of their themes and experiences meant that they were 'bound to hack / The same Welsh jungle track' ('An Horatian Ode (to Frank Sargeson)', 1956, *NSP* 190–92). But, as well as the contemporary association with the drunken Welsh genius, Baxter could be seen as following a far more ancient Mediterranean track, associated with one of the most complex and ambiguous deities of the Greco-Roman pantheon.

Bacchus and Dionysus

Bacchus, the Roman god of wine, has in both classical antiquity and the modern period often been associated primarily with alcohol, and indeed has typically been portrayed as a genial figure, often somewhat overweight, deep in his cups, and surrounded by sensuous male and female followers. Keats captures this essence nicely:

> And as I sat, over the light blue hills
> There came a noise of revellers: the rills
> Into the wide stream came of purple hue—
> 'Twas Bacchus and his crew!
> [. . .]
> Like to a moving vintage down they came,
> Crown'd with green leaves, and faces all on flame
> [. . .]
> Within his car, aloft, young Bacchus stood,
> Trifling his ivy-dart, in dancing mood,
>   With sidelong laughing;
> And little rills of crimson wine imbrued
> His plump white arms, and shoulders, enough white
> For Venus' pearly bite [. . .].
>
> ('Endymion' 4.193–214)

In the juvenile poem 'The Gods of Greece' (N3.157) Baxter states that 'Bacchus must rise from drunken sleep'. The god clearly heeded the call, as can be seen from Baxter's revealing and often quoted comment about his academically unsuccessful time at Otago University: 'Aphrodite, Bacchus, and the Holy Spirit were my tutors, but the goddess of good manners and examination passes withheld her smile from me' ('Essay on the Higher Learning' 62).

Bacchus's forerunner, the Greek Dionysus, is rather different and carries with him a much wider range of connotations.[2] Although a wine god like Bacchus, Dionysus is generally pictured as slim and sinister, and whereas he too may be accompanied by a retinue of devotees—phallic satyrs and possessed maenads—there is a mystery and ambiguity about him which differentiates him from his Roman counterpart. He may be a liberator who brings blessings, but there is also an awesome power in him which may disturb human lives or even destroy them, and which may also shatter a community. He represents the enigmatic and intuitive, the elemental forces of burgeoning nature, and presides at the point where boundaries are crossed and paradoxes flourish. He has associations with death and the underworld too, as we shall explore later, and is seen as alien, intrusive and threatening, unable to be defined or controlled, of ambiguous gender even. Given all this complexity, it was the concept 'Dionysus' rather than 'Bacchus' that appealed more to Baxter.

In talking about his drinking, Baxter would sometimes focus on it not for itself but for its emotional effect on him, and for its lubricating function in the poetic process. In a letter to Lawrence Baigent on 4 March 1945 he reports how he composed a poem 'on commission' while fuelled by a continual supply of rum and gin (FM 19/3/19, quoted *Spark* 80). Dionysus has regularly been associated with creativity, as indeed has Bacchus, so that in a poem such as Horace, *Odes* 3.25 it is the factor of poetic inspiration which is predominant.[3] Baxter was well aware of this connection.

2 For a consideration of some appearances of Dionysus in the work of NZ poets, including Baxter, see Davidson, 'NZ Faces of Dionysus'.

3 'Quo me, Bacche, rapis tui / plenum?' (Where, Bacchus, are you snatching me away, full of yourself?)

Apollonian and Dionysiac

Along with other figures such as the Muses, the god Apollo has also been closely associated with poetic inspiration.[4] For Baxter, however, the Apollonian inspiration represented rationality and control; and given his own predilection for the bottle and his hostility to the establishment, it was to the Dionysiac aspect of the Nietzschean dichotomy that he was irresistibly drawn. Apollo does get a look in, however, from time to time. Thus, as 'the god of art' he becomes the favoured adversary of 'the kitchen god' who represents domesticity ('Virgin', *MH* 74), and in 'Letter to Robert Burns' his 'balls', along with the blood of Jesus, become the frozen victims of the 'old black frost' that is said to numb the 'dry, narrow-gutted town' of Dunedin (*CP* 290). Baxter's positive use of Apollo in this context, however, is related to Burns' own identification with Apollo in a poem discussed by Baxter ('Man', *MH* 108).

In general, Apollo represents a path antithetical to that taken by Baxter. In poem 2 of the early 'Songs of the Desert' sequence (*CP* 55), the god even becomes a symbol of not only the artificial but even the completely heartless: 'Let them tonight / sleep with no stone apollo / but the candelabra / of the innocent stars.' Weir comments: 'Once again the harshness of the world is mitigated by human love' (*Man Without a Mask* 163). It is, however, as a foil to Dionysus that Baxter generally employs Apollo. Two passages from *The Fire and the Anvil* best illustrate this.

In the first passage, Baxter writes: 'Where tradition is strong, an Apollonian role is most probable. The poet tries to remain unmoved and subjugate his images to a formal order [. . .]. Many poets, however, in the sterile order of modern civilization take on a Dionysia [*sic*] *persona* and submerge themselves in the flux of sensation and primitive mysticism.' He quotes Hart Crane 'who was accustomed to compose with a jug of wine on the table and a gramophone at full blast. He eventually stepped off the stern

4 Baxter makes an amusing link between the Muse and alcohol in a stanza of his 'Horatian Ode on the Banishment of Beer' (1944, *NSP* 173-75): 'And learned Greek authorities / Contended that Euripides / When most inspired paid toll / To the Muse of Alcohol.'

of a ship [. . .]. The fate of an Apollian [*sic*] poet is generally less spectacular: a job in the Army Intelligence Department' ('Mask', *FA* 49–50).[5]

In the second passage, Baxter is discussing A. R. D. Fairburn's poem 'The Voyage'. He refers to the ship's 'Master' who 'stands on the bridge', and comments: 'His role is Apollonian; and the sea over which he sails symbolizes the Dionysiac flux of experience' ('Symbolism', *FA* 76–77). A few years later, in commenting on the Burns Fellowship, Baxter presents the polarities with respect to himself:

> In a sense the Fellowship was awarded to the wrong man; my shadow, my enemy, my monster; the public person who would destroy if he could whatever gifts I possess. Art, the mainstay of culture, is not bred by culture but its opposite: that level of hardship or awareness of moral chaos where the soul is too destitute to be able to lie to itself. Thus the Fellowship should have been awarded, if at all, not to me—a family man, teetotal, moderately pious, not offensive to sight or smell, able to say the right thing in a drawing room—but to my collaborator, my schizophrenic twin, who has always provided me with poems.
> ('Conversation', *MH* 17)

The god Dionysus/Bacchus serves as one symbol, and an important and powerful one at that, of Baxter's 'schizophrenic twin', a being whose orbit includes poetic inspiration as well as alcohol and who is also commonly linked with Venus/Aphrodite as agent of sexual release. Given all this, it is no wonder that he became part of Baxter's mythical pantheon. The surprise perhaps consists in the fact that he does not feature even more than he does.

5 In the reprint of this in McKay's *James K. Baxter as Critic* 44–45, the erroneous words 'Dionysia' and 'Apollian' have been corrected to 'Dionysiac' and 'Apollonian' respectively. The passage as a whole can usefully be related to a sequence from *Horse* in which the protagonist attends a Literary Club lecture given by the visiting poet Grummet, who is blind drunk. The 'establishment' is at best embarrassed and at worst scandalised, but Horse is absolutely delighted, and even one of the 'respectable' members of the audience is moved to comment: 'I couldn't understand a word he said myself. But didn't you feel there was something—well, Dionysiac about it?' (88).

Bacchic rites

When we turn again to the published poetry, we find that the deity under his Roman name Bacchus is a rare animal. His shadow, however, hovers over the opening of 'Bar Room Elegy':

> Step in the swingdoor: here is the heart's cage
> Ornamented with wishes, drenched in tobacco fog.
> The public conjuring trick, the private rage
> Have each their place—but from the monologue
> Of man and ghost no Bacchic rite delivers
> Us, nor at length from the white tooth of the dog. (1951, *CP* 119)

This is a bleak poem which ends with the invocation of the bar room as a corrupted garden where 'The evergrowing brambles obliterate / Greenly the tablets of Mosaic law' and 'Anthropoid Adam mourns his lost estate'. The expression 'Bacchic rite' ironically confers a quasi-sacramental character upon a common drinking session, yet this rite, with its pagan connotations working in tension with the later biblical imagery,[6] can give no final answer or bring deliverance. Even so, the celebration of Bacchus is somehow elevated above the squalid surroundings in which this takes place.

It is the wine-god aspect of Dionysus that is most prominent in 'Crossing Cook Strait' (*CP* 159–60), first published in 1958 but apparently in the process of composition for about a decade before this. In this poem, the poet/narrator on the deck of the interisland ferry is faced by an apparition which describes itself as 'Seddon and Savage, the socialist father'—in other words the spirit of the country, or rather of the country's past and its sometimes idealised socialist legacy. The apparition tells him, 'You have known me only in my mask of Dionysus / Amputated in bar rooms, dismembered among wheels.' It goes on to lament the fact that anger and the passion of the poor for social justice have been replaced by self-interest and apathy. The poem ends with the ship

6 This tension continues in the third stanza, which begins: 'Out of Eden flow the twelve great rivers / (The Flaming and the Oblivious are best known)', the names of the two specified rivers being English versions of (Pyri)phlegethon and Lethe, two of the rivers of the classical underworld.

moving into rough seas, a striking contrast with the calm seas in which the voyage had begun—perhaps indicating a reawakened conscience in the poet/narrator. The Dionysus figure seems to represent a kind of deadened and benumbed socialism, suggesting a working class whose energy and vitality have been sapped by the alcoholic drug and whose essential nature has been transformed and deformed.

O'Sullivan takes Baxter to task for the sentiments expressed in this poem in which he belittles fellow New Zealand poets and laments the impoverishment of the country and the corruption of its people (*Baxter* 36–37). There is much truth in this criticism, though one would expect Baxter to exaggerate in order to give added impetus to his criticism of society. Indeed Weir, in a discussion of Baxter's social verse, notes that the poet has attempted to honour the position he once championed as necessary for an artist—'to remain as a cell of good living in a corrupt society, and in this situation by writing and example [to] attempt to change it' (Weir, *Poetry* 61, quoting *Trends* 18).

What is fascinating here, however, is to find the figure of Dionysus used as shorthand for the entire pub culture of this country, which, as in 'Bar Room Elegy', is presented as a kind of debased substitute for the imaginative life.[7] Moreover, in Greek culture Dionysus was, in a sense, lord of the mask, which was especially, though not exclusively, associated with the theatre. Thus when the apparition claims that he has been recognised 'only in my mask of Dionysus', there is also the underlying idea that drinking New Zealanders are playing an artificial role that does not, or at least should not, naturally belong to them.

Dancing with Euripides: *Mr O'Dwyer's Dancing Party*

Aspects of Dionysus that go well beyond the basic wine-god figure are apparent in Baxter's play *Mr O'Dwyer's Dancing Party*

7 The pub culture is also fingered by Baxter in the early poem 'Ode to the New Zealand Summer' (N14.906): 'Maoris have huddled from the island weather / in their bush caves—the homeless turn today / Crowding an empty bar', which is somewhat ironic, given that Baxter himself featured so prominently among this crowd.

(*CPlays* 261–91), written in 1967 and first produced in 1968.[8] Euripides' classic tragedy *The Bacchae*, on which Baxter's play is modelled, tells how Dionysus returns to his native city of Thebes in order to exact vengeance from its citizens, who have refused to recognise his divinity. He has already driven the women of the city out of their homes and away to the mountains in a frenzied state, and in the course of the play the god destroys the Theban king Pentheus by mesmerising him and persuading him to dress in female clothes and go to spy on the women who, led by his own mother, are induced to discover him and tear him to pieces. Despite his Theban origins, Dionysus is presented as an exotic, mysterious intruder.

For his version, Baxter updates the play's setting to a fashionable suburb of contemporary Auckland. His Pentheus equivalent is a builder, John Ennis, who ends up being humiliated by a group of women, including his wealthy wife. As happens with Pentheus, an inherent weakness in Ennis—in this case his liking for alcohol—is used as the means of bringing him to grief. At the same time, he is a hypocritical materialist who evaluates his own house as 'so many tons of cement—so many yards of reinforcing' and 'bolts and screws', and who offers a most cynical commentary on a new housing estate which he is developing: 'TV sets, hot and cold water, electric blankets, booze in the cupboard—that's civilization!' He is also driven to repress the freedom of others, refusing to acknowledge an alternative to his own narrow vision of life, and becomes an easy target for his polar opposite.

Baxter's choice for his Dionysus figure of the itinerant Irishman Tom O'Dwyer presumably owes something to his paternal Celtic ancestry and his idealisation of 'longbearded Gaelic-speaking giants distilling whisky among the flax from time immemorial' (*Trends* 7). O'Dwyer is an alien in 'polite' middle-class New Zealand society, and like Dionysus he turns the establishment on its head. What grants him right of entry is the fascination that he holds for women. In Euripides' play, the Theban women are driven away from their domestic environment and freed from

8 For earlier versions of some of the material included in this discussion, see Davidson, 'Euripides' *Bacchae*' and 'Greek Tragedy'.

social constraints. Baxter's somewhat watered-down version of this sees a number of housewives finding new self-expression in a free dance group overseen by O'Dwyer. The basic principle, however, remains the same, as Baxter uses the theatrical medium to propagate his ongoing message about what he saw as the sterility, rigidity and hypocrisy of the New Zealand society of the 1960s. Unlike the *Bacchae*, however, there is an important focus on the relationship between men and women, especially in the institution of marriage.

Alcohol is a constant factor in many of Baxter's plays, embodied in characters such as Concrete Grady in *The Band Rotunda* and Ben Hogan in *The Wide Open Cage*—characters in most cases based on individuals Baxter had known in real life but, as Howard McNaughton comments, 'absorbed into his private myths for so long that they had learned to speak his language and think with his own logic' (188). Most appropriately, too, Harold W. Smith singles out 'the cup of Dionysus' as one of the features that Baxter's plays share with those of Eugene O'Neill ('Poet as Playwright' 57).

Mr O'Dwyer's Dancing Party does not concentrate on the unrelieved alcoholism of some of the earlier plays; however, alcohol is a palpable undercurrent within it. Thus an opened wine bottle and partly filled glasses are a feature of the first scene of the play—a game of chess and conversation between Ennis and the blind Auschwitz survivor Ephraim Feingold. Implicit in the wine, Dionysus is also evoked by Feingold's opening words: 'The wind is blowing from the mountains' (263), a subtle reference to Mount Cithaeron in the Euripidean play, from where reports are brought to King Pentheus of the activities of the errant Theban women. The alcohol theme continues with references to Ennis's drinking and visits to the pub. The climax comes when O'Dwyer arrives for a second meeting with Ennis, supposedly to apologise for being 'half drunk' at their first encounter, but in fact to weaken Ennis's defences with a bottle of 'Irish bog water' and then to initiate the pub crawl that leads to his complete inebriation and subsequent humiliation (279–83). Thus the Dionysus figure deals with his 'enemy' wearing his wine-god hat, unlike the god himself in the

Euripidean play, who employs an altogether more subtle strategy.

Baxter, however, takes his Dionysus figure well beyond a simple personification of alcohol. We have already noted the appeal that O'Dwyer exercises over the housewives who, under his spell, are each in turn released from the shackles of their suburban morality to act out fantasies through dance. Moreover, from the moment he sets foot in Ennis's house, he takes charge of the situation, despite Ennis's protestation 'this is *my* house' (274). He then hypnotises him in a sense, as Dionysus does Pentheus, and gains the physical advantage as well. This creates the platform from which, at their second meeting, he can so easily convince Ennis to join him in drinking, using his innate yearning to do just this. Thus, like the Dionysus of Greek myth, he both liberates and enslaves.

Baxter's play, which has generally been panned by the critics, is low key. As an updating of the *Bacchae*, it falls well short of the excesses of Rodney Milgate's approximately contemporary *A Refined Look at Existence* (1966), with its climactic electrocution of the opponent of the Australian rock singer Dionysus figure. Likewise, it is tame in comparison with other contemporary refashionings of the *Bacchae*, such as the Performance Group's production of Richard Schechner's *Dionysus in 69*, whose opening performance was in June 1968 (see Zeitlin 49–75), or Wole Soyinka's work *The Bacchae of Euripides: a Communion Rite* (performed in London 1973). Despite this, however, it seems that Farrell Cleary somewhat underplays what is going on when he comments:

> In the Dunedin plays, Baxter moves from the absolutist reality of the Catholic universe to a more open universe where the Devil withdraws to re-emerge in Dionysian incarnations [. . .]. [*Mr O'Dwyer's Dancing Party*] attempts to transpose a Bacchic revel into a suburban Auckland context. Baxter portrays the proto-diabolical Dionysian figure of Dwyer [*sic*] sympathetically: he is very much the 'good companion', Rabelaisian kind of demon.
>
> (Cleary 130)

O'Dwyer embodies much more than that, having at least implicit points of contact with other dimensions of the wide-ranging Dionysus concept also addressed in Baxter's poetry.

Abandonment and liberation

One of these dimensions is, as we have seen, that of the liberator. In 'Songs of the Desert' 4 (*CP* 56), the poet/narrator senses that he is close to death even as he makes love to his woman. He sees 'upon her cheek the stone tear harden, / Inviolable mask.' There follows what appears to be an allusion to the abandonment of Ariadne by Theseus prior to her rescue by Dionysus:

> The alien lips
> Forsake me, seek in prayer
> Lost Dionysus[9] burning to her rape
> With wine and bread upon the traitorous air
>
> Of midnight festival. So am I drowned
> In grief at length, the final grave unfound.

What is striking here is the role reversal involved: 'Ariadne' is abandoning 'Theseus' and yearning for Dionysus who, for some reason 'lost', is 'burning to her rape'—a phrase that accurately reflects the passion of the mythical Dionysus for Ariadne, although he was to claim her as consort rather than as rape victim. The sequence raises significant questions of interpretation. Baxter's own association of sex with dissatisfaction and, more importantly, death itself is something of a leitmotif in his poetry. But what exactly does Dionysus symbolise here?

It appears almost certain that the poem, together with the other poems in the sequence—and others (most unpublished) from notebooks 14 and 15—reflects Baxter's relationship with Jane Aylward. A reading of the poem in this context, then, might well conclude that Dionysus simply represents another of the woman's lovers, perhaps even the man with whom she 'betrayed' Baxter and whom she left him to marry. In such a reading the only relevant aspect of Dionysus would be his role as Ariadne's lover. In fact, if the god's other aspects are taken into account, Dionysus would be a more appropriate disguise for Baxter the poet himself.

9 Baxter mistakenly spelled the name 'Dionysius' in the notebook version (N15.3), as he also did in N17.76 (he is not the first or last person to make this simple error!). The correct spelling already appears in the first published version, *The Night Shift* (1957) 12.

After all, his devotion to alcohol was clearly a complicating factor in the relationship, as can be seen from the last poem of the 'Songs of the Desert' sequence, written a decade after the others as a kind of nostalgic 'afterword': 'You cried once, "I am drifting, drifting." / Self-pitying, too often drunk, / I did not see your need of comforting' (*CP* 62).[10]

A further mythical complication is that Baxter calls the woman 'my undine'. This is an allusion to the water nymph of Germanic mythology who, according to some stories, cannot gain a soul unless she marries a mortal. On the other hand, if she does fall in love with a mortal and bears his child, she loses her immortality. This may be highly relevant to a situation in which marriage with Baxter was not a viable proposition, but it was with the other man in the triangle.[11]

Two other possible readings suggest themselves. The abandoned Ariadne's acceptance of Dionysus, in the Greek myth, has been demythologised as a descent into alcoholism. Alternatively, the reference to 'wine and bread' and 'festival' suggests the Christian mass or communion, in which case Dionysus could be taken as symbolising Christ, and the woman might be reaching out again to a religious faith that she had lost, turning her back on her lover in the process. However, these readings make little sense in the biographical context, since Jane Aylward was neither a problem drinker nor a religious believer. Perhaps all that can be said in the final analysis is that there is in this poem an enigmatic and open-ended use of the polyvalent Dionysus figure, and the expression 'inviolable mask' immediately before the section quoted could again be taken as a nod in the direction of theatre and role playing.[12]

10 The poem as a whole is reminiscent of Robert Graves' poem 'Theseus and Ariadne' (Graves 197), which begins: 'High on his figured couch beyond the waves / He dreams, in dream recalling her set walk / Down paths of oyster-shell bordered with flowers / And down the shadowy turf beneath the vine. / He sighs: "Deep sunk in my erroneous past / She haunts the ruins and the ravaged lawns."'

11 In another even earlier poem, 'undine' is a death figure ('Death I have ever seen: undine who / Globed in air's whirling cavern swam / And chilled the corridor into a cloister': *Spark* 359), so that we may also be dealing with Baxter's familiar association of sex with both the re-entry into Eden and death.

12 It is extremely tempting to link Baxter's choice of words in this poem with a

The story of Theseus and Ariadne is alluded to more explicitly in 'Spring Song' (1953, *SP* 50–51). The fourth stanza of this poem reads as follows:

> Turn inward then your eyes.
> From Naxos' angry beach
> Forgetful Theseus rows,
> Love's lucid power to teach
> Left in the Bacchic maze;
> Stony his breastplate gleaming,
> At his prow the black sail booming.

The symbolism of the Theseus figure, in the context of the poem as a whole, has been considered in chapter 5. Here, we are concerned with Dionysus, implicit in the expression 'Bacchic maze' which involves another touch of mythical transference. Baxter is hinting at the mating of Ariadne with the god after Theseus's departure. However, he locates this god by suggestion, along with Ariadne herself as the personification of love, not on the shore of Naxos but in the labyrinth or maze, the site of the preceding episode in the myth in which Theseus, aided by Ariadne's strategy, is able to slay the minotaur and find his way out again. The reader is thus presented with the felicitous association of 'love' and the liberating principle embodied in the adjective 'Bacchic', placed together in an environment whose logical disposition is difficult to unravel.

A similar environment is described by Baxter in one of his critical essays:

> It seems that the 'beach', which symbolises a no-man's-land between conscious and unconscious, plays a most important role in New Zealand poetry. Sinclair writes of the 'beach' which 'fends off the wild-tongued sea . . . from our bright crumbling enclosure'; almost every New Zealand poet uses the symbol at

sequence from Alistair Te Ariki Campbell's poem 'The Return': 'Face downward / And in a small creek mouth all unperceived, / The drowned Dionysus, sand in his eyes and mouth, / In the dim tide lolling—beautiful, and with the last harsh // Glare of divinity from lip and broad brow ebbing' (Campbell 30). The association of lips, drowning and Dionysus may be coincidental, but Baxter and Campbell were reading and critiquing each other's work at the time in question. 'Crossing Cook Strait' with its other Dionysus reference may also be relevant. Baxter had praised 'The Return' at a forum in Christchurch, and had then begun to write 'Crossing Cook Strait'.

> some time or other. One might infer from the evidence of our poetry that every erotic adventure which finds its way into print has its setting somewhere among the sandhills: a nonsensical conclusion. But the Sea symbolises the fruitful chaos which nourishes the sexual instinct; and the Beach the meeting-place of conscious and unconscious, the Dionysiac ground, the haunted playground of children and lovers, scattered with orange-peel but swept clean each day by the tide, the place where we can sleep without bad dreams and wake refreshed.
>
> ('Symbolism', *FA* 68)

In 'Spring Song', however, Theseus has left behind the possibility of cleansing.

The power of transformation

From Dionysus as liberator, we turn to another aspect—the god's awesome power as revealed in miraculous or catastrophic natural events. In Euripides' *Bacchae* he is manifested in the earthquake which destroys Pentheus's palace. In the Homeric *Hymn to Dionysus*, the young god is kidnapped by pirates who, with the exception of the helmsman, fail to recognise his divinity. The consequences for them are astonishing. Wine starts to ooze all over the ship, clusters of grapes drape down the sail and ivy twines itself around the mast. Dionysus then takes the form of a lion and devours the captain while the sinful crew jump overboard and are transformed into dolphins.

This incident is reflected in the famous painting by Exekias on the inside of a drinking cup of the sixth century BC. Baxter alludes to this in his poem 'The Jar' (1967, *CP* 392–93).[13] The poem is a 'reminiscence' of an occasion in the house of Bob Lowry who, as McKay records (*Life* 143–44), was a frequent drinking companion of Baxter in his visits to Auckland in the 1950s. Half-

13 D. H. Lawrence's poem 'They say the Sea is Loveless' is one of a number of other poems inspired by this same drinking cup: 'They say the sea is loveless, that in the sea / love cannot live, but only bare, salt splinters / of loveless life. // But from the sea / the dolphins leap round Dionysos' ship / whose masts have purple vines, / and up they come with the purple dark of rainbows / and flip! They go! With the nose-dive of sheer delight; / and the sea is making love to Dionysos / in the bouncing of these small and happy whales' (Lawrence ii.693).

gallon jars of red wine from the Henderson vineyards acted as the social lubricant. The poet has 'bought a peter of wine / From the owner of a Dalmatian vineyard', which becomes his constant companion. His imagination transposes onto it the scene from the Exekian cup:

> half drunk, I held it up,
> And saw what I had never even thought of—
>
> On the curve of the wine jar Dionysus lying
> Naked and asleep in a black boat,
> With a beard like the waves of the sea—and out of his belly
> A vine growing, vine of ether, vine of earth,
> Vine of water—growing towards the sky
> Blue as the veins on the inside of a woman's arm—

This is burgeoning, explosive nature, encompassing earth, sea and sky, with the Dionysus principle at the centre. But there is a sting in the tail, as the poem's conclusion illustrates: 'Black boat, white belly, curved blue sky / Holding us in its hands, as if Earth and Heaven / Were the friends of man, permanent friends—// A picture of what can't be, as I sat gripped by / The mad, heavy vine of sleep.'

It is a vision of the perfect harmony between humanity and nature which emanates from Dionysus. In Euripides' play, indeed, the female worshippers of the god are said to suckle wild animals and be able, at a touch, to draw wine and milk from the earth. In Baxter's poem, however, this integration of all parts of the world, this abolition of barriers, is the impossible dream of a state resembling that of Eden before the Fall, whose loss Baxter laments in so many contexts. Ironically, this dream can manifest itself only to one in the grip of the wine-god.

Other poems, too tread the ground where Dionysus explodes normal patterns and structures or arrives as the intrusive harbinger of change. In the unpublished poem 'Thoughts of a Headmistress in Spring' (c.1961, N22.40), the speaker is in bed with an open Victorian novel but contemplating the action, 'inappropriate' for her, of lighting a cigarette. The thought that 'The girls were restive' leads on to the conclusion that 'it must be spring, / when Dionysus hammers on the door / with Phrygian ivy. When I heard that thing, / that crayfish scrabbling on the kitchen floor, / You quoted Pliny.'[14] Dionysus is associated with spring, which resurrects the natural world; and his most famous festival at Athens was precisely the spring festival known as the Great Dionysia or City Dionysia. What is disturbing, however, is that this festival was most noted for the performance of tragedy. Moreover, the phrase 'Phrygian ivy' creates the sense of something alien and threatening. This feeling is developed in the last part of the poem where the speaker, still addressing her father, reminds him of a time when, without the knowledge of her mother, he put her on his shoulder and swam 'like a brown porpoise' out to a rock in the sea. The poem's final words are: 'I hate you! Why / Did you teach me so early how to die?'

Unexpected light is thrown on this poem in a letter of 30 October 1961 (FM 27/1/13) in which Baxter speaks of 'an unchanged Electra complex' being, in his opinion, commoner than 'an unchanged Oedipus one'. He also asks whether it is 'unsuitable to equate Dionysus and a crayfish'. It thus appears that in the poem we have what might be called an overdetermination of the Dionysus motif. The god is evoked not only as his most common plant symbol, which is external to, albeit threatening, the woman's domestic life, but also in the form of the incongruously flailing crustacean already inside as part of this life. This is the Dionysus who subverts, who overthrows certainties and undermines propriety.

This same Dionysus, in even more threatening guise, features in 'Fitz Drives Home the Spigot' (1966, *CP* 375). Fitz's action has the town dreading the possibility that drunkenness would reign, and

> That the meticulous sorrow
> Of widows and spinsters with small zip purses
> Would be disregarded by drunken coalmen
> Pissing against the hedge,

14 The reference to Pliny is somewhat obscure, but it may refer to the Elder Pliny's *Natural History* 9.95, where *locustae* (crayfish) are said, like *cancri* (crabs), to 'discard their old age at the beginning of Spring in the same way as snakes do, by renewing their skins'.

That daughters would go down singing in droves
To the oil tankers and open their white legs
To rough-handed rum-fed sailors, that well-bred sons
Would dive in your great barrel and happily drown,

That the black bones of Dionysus
Buried under the Fire Assurance Building
Had sprouted a million wild green vines
Cracking the pavements and the gravestones—

This is a dramatic and carnivalesque evocation of the Dionysus principle bursting through the most solid barriers and symbols of permanence. What is perhaps most striking is the idea of the bones of Dionysus being buried under a symbol of security, yet with the potential to explode and engulf the world it would secure. For a moment the possibility is held out of a major shake-up of what Baxter so often castigated as polite, soulless, puritanical middle-class New Zealand. But the possibility is only momentary, and the poem concludes: 'But fortunately you did not strike too hard! / The town shook once, and then regained its proper / Monotonous man-killing identity, / While you rubbed your belly and drank one pony beer.' In the end, there was clearly no permanent place for Dionysus in a society on which Baxter would soon finally turn his back.

Further evidence that Baxter was still carrying the idea of Dionysus with him during this period, the second half of the 1960s—the years which were also to see his 'Greek' plays, with their special connection with the god—is provided by 'The Fear of Change' (1967, *CP* 404). The name Dionysus is not used on this occasion, but the god's essence is captured by another symbol. The reader is asked to imagine a sudden, cataclysmic overthrow of normality such as a revolution or the appearance 'Upright and singing' of

a young bullfighter
With a skin of rough[15] wine, offering to each of us
Death, sex, hope—or even just an

15 Baxter's first choice of epithet for his wine in the notebook is 'red', after which a number of other options are listed; the final one, 'rough', was the one selected by Weir for its publication in 1974.

Earthquake, making the trees thrash, the roofs tumble,
Calling us loudly to consider God—

This could almost stand as a summary of all that Dionysus offers—youth, virility, the blessings and dangers of alcohol, the encounter with death itself. It also goes to the heart of aspects of the god featured in Euripides' *Bacchae*—the power to cause earthquakes; the demand for the recognition of divinity. The bullfighter too provides, perhaps quite unintentionally, another echo, albeit inverted, of Dionysiac lore in general and the *Bacchae* in particular. Dionysus was often manifested in animal form—with the bull a prominent aspect of this theriomorphism—and in Euripides' play the hallucinating King Pentheus at one point finds himself fighting unsuccessfully *against* a bull. The poem goes on to conclude, however, that 'We are not that kind of people' and that 'Our talent is for anger and monotony'. There is thus no place for the colourful, the innovative or the soul-changing. We will bury it and argue about 'whether the corpses were dressed in black / or red'.

Two further poems from this same period which make specific mention of Dionysus or the Dionysiac also merit attention. The first of these is 'Bacchante' (1968, *CP* 417–18). Stemming from Baxter's experience as Burns Fellow at Otago University, it records the poet/narrator's response to the entry into his office of 'one of the Bacchantes', presumably a female student, intruding on his peace and solitude. Her very presence, and her words categorised as 'the chant / That ends only when the hours of your life are ripped and broken / On the black earth', cause tumult.[16]

In Euripides' *Bacchae*, King Pentheus is cajoled by Dionysus into spying on the maenads or Bacchantes from the apparent safety of a pine tree. The god, however, reveals his presence to the women and pulls down the tree, enabling the women, including Pentheus's own mother, to tear him limb from limb in a frenzy, despite his piteous pleas. Pentheus thus pays dearly for his refusal to acknowledge Dionysus. The conclusion of Baxter's poem refers to this:

16 The expression 'the black earth' also has classical resonances, being most famously used by the poet Sappho in an erotic context (Sappho, Fr. 16 Campbell).

It was that shrill desire
For safety that won the attention of the Bacchantes,
Curling their lips, making their eyes glitter;
To wish for safety is the first drop of blood.

Dionysus, whether manifested in alcoholic or sexual terms, is a force that cannot be resisted without catastrophic consequences. The attempt to hide away from it is not an option. In 'Fitz Drives Home the Spigot' and 'The Fear of Change' the point was that New Zealand society cannot accommodate the unusual, the adventurous, the iconoclastic, the inspirational, the irrational, and solves the problem by ignoring or burying it. In 'Bacchante', however, the issue is sexuality, especially female erotic desire which exacts a tribute from the male—something which cannot be ignored or suppressed, especially by Baxter himself.

The other specifically 'Dionysus' poem from this period is 'The Bluegums (for Patric Carey)' (1967, *CP* 410).[17] The poem appears to be contrasting 'reality', as seen in the harsh natural environment of Otago, and the graves of those who have gone to rest in it, including Baxter's own Scottish forebears, with the trivia of people's everyday lives. Because 'reality' cannot be, or at least is generally not, directly confronted, the poet suggests a 'compromise' by which it can be filtered through in the silences, so that the voices of the dead speaking about what really matters can be heard.

Those who do hear and can give expression to these voices are the poets. The poem concludes: 'Those would be our poems: / Marks of the whip; a kind of punishment / For us who have drunk without hope the blood of Dionysus'. Dionysus seems to bear a heavy load of significance here. On one level, we are dealing with poetic inspiration in general. However, a poem addressed to Patric Carey in 1967 suggests inspiration for dramas specifically, an idea reinforced by the '[Dionysus]' of the original title in Baxter's

17 N28.22 where the title is actually given as '[Dionysus] The Bluegums (for Patric Carey)'. The '[Dionysus]' was omitted from the title in a list of poems made by Baxter in this same notebook for a collection which he wished to be published under the title of *Runes*. This collection duly appeared in 1973, but the poem was not included. Under the title 'The Bluegums (for Patric Carey)', it was first published in *CP*.

notebook. But there is a pessimism here, with poets being seen as condemned to suffer, for their awareness of 'reality'.

There are further complications. In one branch of Dionysus mythology, the god was torn to pieces and eaten by the Titans, who were then blasted to ash by Zeus's thunderbolt. The human race was then born from the ashes and thus inherited mortal, sinful nature from the Titans but also the spark of divinity from the god (who was subsequently resurrected or reconstituted). Then too, in mainstream Dionysus mythology, his followers were represented as consuming the flesh and blood of wild animals (which embodied the god's essence) and thus gaining access to his power.

Dionysus and Christ

The connections between this mode of thinking and Christian doctrines of the Mass or Eucharist have long been pointed out, and so it is a short step from 'the blood of Dionysus' to 'the blood of Christ'. One need look no further than 'The Flame' (1967, *CP* 400–01) to see the link between the two systems:

In forty years

I haven't found a cure
For being human. I can't get drunk
Now as I used to, dowsing the flame with whisky;
I have to live and burn

Thinking of Christ—Christ, who is all men
Yet has to be discovered
By each on his own—not this morning
His blood only, but his resurrection,

Like the voice of the wind blowing on troubled waves,
Like hard buds of japonica,
Christ who is ointment, and for whom I carry
The incurable wound of life, and stand in the black flame.

Both the human condition in general, as well as artistic composition, involve pain and suffering, and Baxter's writings testify to an awareness of this two-pronged assault. It is easy to see why, for Baxter, the figures of Christ and Dionysus, though in some respects clearly separate, touch at certain points of the spectrum. There is in Baxter in general a sense of the sacramental associated with alcohol, and as he put it himself in an interview held towards the end of his life when the question of his Roman Catholicism was being aired:

> Well, a man is a Catholic because he believes. He is a poet because he has a particular gift and function and also way of approaching things. If he says 'I am going to tell the world they should be Catholics', this would be absurd. But if he says 'I am a Catholic poet . . .' I think the practice of one's religion has a very subtle effect on the way one thinks. I think that Catholic art—Christian art I'd rather say—at its best is wounded art. There is blood in it; you know, the wounds of the person are present in it. It's close to the Crucifixion. It's not Apollonian: it's more Dionysiac. (Weir interview, 243–44)

This same connection between Dionysus and Christ is also manifest in the concept of the vine, naturally linked to Dionysus as god of wine and used by Baxter in Dionysus contexts, but also one of the images associated with Christ in the New Testament. Baxter picks this up in a poem such as 'Song to the Lord Jesus' (1972, *CP* 571), whose last stanza reads:

> Lord Jesus, you are the house and we are the timber,
> You are the vine and we are the branches.
> Send your Spirit so that the vine may flower,
> Heal in us whatever is at fault.

Dionysus, as we have seen, is often an outsider, an alien intruder, who overturns comfort and security and subverts 'normality'. In Baxter's view, New Zealand society could not cope with such a force, not understanding its potential to liberate and instead seeking to suppress and destroy it. Again, Dionysus is like Jesus, who is represented in the Gospels as predicting the persecutions and even intrafamilial discord that will result from his advent.[18] His own crucifixion was, of course, to follow.

Baxter used a variety of methods to stress the 'alien' nature of both Christ and Dionysus. One of these was to find the 'true'

18 See e.g. Matthew 10.16–21 and 34; Mark 13.9–13; Luke 12.51–53 and 21.12–17.

spirit which they represent in Maori people or Maori society, to whose values he increasingly turned in the last years of his life as providing what he saw as lacking in the Pakeha system. Thus we find a poem such as 'The Maori Jesus' (1966, *CP* 347–48), with its trenchant criticism of what, in Baxter's view, was the victimisation of Maori and the destruction of the only real source of light for the country. The poem begins: 'I saw the Maori Jesus / Walking on Wellington Harbour. / He wore blue dungarees. / His beard and hair were long.'

It is useful to compare this with a draft of the poem 'At Rakiura', written in 1966, the revised and shortened version of which was published posthumously in 1973 (*CP* 376–77).[19] The second section of the earlier version begins:

> One cannot expect the impossible. No childless matron
> Will row out in a dinghy and sit on the phallic rock
>
> At the centre of the harbour, nor is that Maori lad
> Unloading beer crates down at the jetty
>
> Another Dionysus.

Admittedly here the identification of the 'Maori lad' with Dionysus is explicitly denied. What is striking, however, is yet another example of the Dionysus concept surfacing in Baxter's thought in the second half of the 1960s, and it is clear that the Maori/Dionysus association becomes implicit in the very moment of its conscious rejection in this context.

The dark and the sinister

Dionysus, as we have seen, is an ambiguous figure at the best of times. On the one hand he may bring blessings and be the harbinger of positive change, even if this is denied and suppressed, while on the other he may cause strife even for those who welcome him. However, there is also a purely dark side of him which goes beyond the merely threatening and sinister and embodies the potential for sheer chaos and destruction. Among other symbols of this idea which attracted Baxter was the dragon. McKay (*Life*

19 N27.34 is the first draft; the revised, later to be published, version was N27.35.

167)[20] records his application of this to the situation of the Japanese as he found them during his Asian visit which began in September 1958:

> . . . like people in a bamboo boat on a rough sea—there are such boats in one of their paintings, with incredibly towering waves above them. The rough sea, or the dragon, symbolizes chaos: chaos is always close to them, held off by a bamboo fence, and not the least when they wake to hear pneumatic drills at work in the ashy Tokyo dawn. To them at heart our Western processes of thought seem to belong to that chaos. The most spectacular results of Western technology they have so far seen have been the giant bulldozer and the atom bomb. We will only win their confidence by learning to understand *their* ways of thought—not to change it or exploit it, but in order to meet them more than half-way with respect and even love.

The irony is that whereas the 'chaos' figure is often something threatening Western society, in this case it is Western society itself which is seen to embody their chaos and be threatening another culture.

Two short poems written in 1963 are worth quoting in full in this context. The first, 'The Dragon Mask', was first published in 1964 (*CP* 268).

Since my grandfather dreaming ignores his debts
With Green Island clay for a coverlet
I'll not remind him how the horses stamp
In the dawn stables. After twelve years or more
Without tobacco, he trimmed his miner's lamp
As if it were a pipe, and looking out of a door
One night at the star-crowded dragon sky,
Said, 'Man, it makes you think'. I,
Bellowing, ask what he would never ask:
'Come out, You there, from behind the dragon mask!'
Whisky that flung him out to sleep in ditches
Has all but killed me. A poet is
The sore thumb of the tribe. Old man, peel off your robe
Of earth and let me learn from the boil-scarred face of Job.

20 From a letter to Dr. C. E. Beeby, 7 October 1958. Reference in McKay 309 n.5.

Here the sky is the inscrutable mask of the dragon, concealing the answer to the mystery of divinity, defying the attempt to impose order on the chaos beyond the mythologising process of the poet. Although there are significant differences of emphasis, there are connections too with the smiling, inscrutable mask of Dionysus, that humans may be unable to penetrate.

The second poem, 'Dragon's Hour', was written in the same year but not published till 1976 (*CP* 269). 'Adam's desire to be a god' goes, according to Christian doctrine and thus in Baxter's view, to the heart of the problem of the human condition with the loss of Eden and consequent disruption of the universe:

> Pillars of fire!
> It is the lost temple
> in which that raging void, Adam's desire
> to be a god, grows ample
>
> and overshadows us. The calm sea
> quakes; the imponderable
> tears of apocalypse on field and city
> fall,
>
> on children's limbs, on veins of the breast,
> quenching the daystar
> with blood; as in their youths our fathers dreamt they saw
> the fire-drake rising from his cloudy nest.

This can be related to the Greek idea of the *theomachos* figure, the human who fights against the god despite overwhelming odds in favour of the adversary. As we have seen in poems such as 'The Fear of Change' and 'Fitz Drives Home the Spigot', the Dionysus figure appears to be defeated and suppressed by the forces of drab monotony and materialism. In the end, however, the consequences of the fight against the spiritual 'other', whether symbolised by Dionysus or seen in Christian terms, is unmitigated disaster.

Of all the figures used by Baxter to symbolise the forces of chaos and darkness, perhaps the most sinister is Baron Saturday. A short profile of him is offered, for example, in 'Auckland' (1956, *CP* 178):

> *Shield us from the dog-toothed night,*
> *Baron Saturday, baron of the cemeteries*
> *To whom the Haitian negress offers rum,*
> *Feathers, cakes and menstrual tokens:*
> *Protect us when the well of day runs dry.*

This Baron Saturday (or Baron Samedi) is an important figure in Haitian Voodoo. He is the 'Loa' of the dead, one of a range of menacing and deadly deities. In 'Auckland', Baxter appropriates him as god of alcoholics, because the poem is about his drinking sessions with Bob Lowry, already alluded to in connection with the later poem 'The Jar'. The expressions 'Dalmatian wine, black in a warm jar' and 'the vine of sleep' (from 'Auckland') are directly echoed in the later poem, which substitutes Dionysus for Baron Saturday, offering a far more positive image of 'deity'. The earlier poem is far bleaker, despite its warm closing tribute to Lowry himself, who is described as 'Opening his heart like a great door / To poets, lovers, and the houseless poor'. Baron Saturday, then, can be seen as the darkest end of the Dionysus spectrum. He is very much the enemy of those who wish to go on living, controlling and manipulating the dead and sending them out on assignments. In the poem 'Ballad of the Junkies and the Fuzz (for Hoani)'—written in 1969 and reflecting Baxter's experiences at Boyle Crescent—Auckland becomes his new home:

> Baron Saturday, baron of the cemeteries, for whom they cut the black rooster's throat, whose altar is always a grave at the crossroads,
> You have shifted, man, out of thin Haiti. Now you grow fat on the fears of five thousand junkies in Auckland. (*CP* 443)

When the police arrive to 'harass' the residents of Boyle Crescent, it is they who are seen as 'The servants of the Zombie King' and therefore the representatives of death, not the drug addicts who are, however, enslaved to Baron Saturday too.

Another embodiment of Baron Saturday features in the slightly earlier poem 'The Lion Skin' (1965, *CP* 329): 'The old man with a yellow flower on his coat / Came to my office, climbing twenty-eight steps, / With a strong smell of death about his person / From the caves of the underworld.' This old man, 'with a cigar in his teeth', is either the Baron himself or one of his possessed devotees or zombies, also known as 'horses', who typically tell dirty jokes, wear dark glasses, smoke cigarettes or cigars, eat voraciously, drink large amounts of alcohol and dress outrageously. The receptionist finds the old man disturbing but manages to suppress the relevance that he actually has for her. Meanwhile:

I welcomed him
And poured him a glass of cherry brandy,
Talked with him for half an hour or so,
Having need of his strength, the skin of a dead lion,
In the town whose ladders are made of coffin wood.
The flower on his coat blazed like a dark sun.

As an alcoholic, Baxter had known, welcomed and needed Baron Saturday, who was just, however, another face of Dionysus, heralding death.[21]

It seems appropriate to conclude with reference to Dionysus's own direct connections with death. As the transforming power in alcohol and drugs he carried death on his very breath, so to speak. In Greek mythology, he brought death to those who resisted him. Even those who acknowledged him were sometimes caught in a death trap. Thus, according to one well known story, the Athenian Ikarios, who received the god with kindness and was rewarded by being taught the culture of the vine, gave some of the new drink to shepherds, who became intoxicated and, believing themselves poisoned, beat Ikarios to death. In Greek religion, moreover, Dionysus had significant connections with the underworld through his mystery cult (Burkert 290–95); and the explicit identification of Dionysus with Hades was made by the pre-Socratic philosopher Heraclitus (Freeman 25, fragment 15).

Baxter brings Dionysus neatly into an association with Death in the short poem 'Inscription for Dylan Thomas' (*Listener* 1954):

Dionysus has met Charon on the bronze threshing-floor
And Charon conquered. In a foreign land, alas,
Died the God-bearer, nor did his songs help him.

21 'Lament for Barney Flanagan' (*CP* 136–37) begins: 'Flanagan got up on a Saturday morning.' Flanagan is an alcoholic and destined to die that day. It is no accident that his death takes place on a Saturday.

These three lines (out of five) could stand as an exercise in classical allusion. The death of the alcoholic poet Dylan Thomas is seen in terms of an encounter between Dionysus and the ferryman of the dead, a scenario reminiscent of Aristophanes' portrayal of the god's access to the underworld in his comic play *Frogs*. The failure of the poet's artistic gift to stave off death then recalls such purple passages as Horace, *Odes* 4.7.23–24, where Torquatus's *pietas* has proved similarly ineffective; or Virgil, *Aeneid* 2.429–30, where not even the fillet of Apollo in addition to *pietas* could save the Trojan Panthus.

The closest direct identification with death which Baxter bestows on Dionysus, however, is to be found in a poem written in 1960 which looks back at the time he spent in Christchurch as a young man. McKay (100–19) gives a detailed account of Baxter's often difficult living conditions and alcohol-fuelled life in this period and quotes (111) part of this poem, which is entitled 'Christchurch 1948' (*CP* 215–16). The relevant lines run as follows:

> Hunger for light sustained me there
> Under the sign of Dionysus-Hades,
> In a kennel with a torn gas mantle,
> Alive on milk and benzedrine,
> Haruspex, probing the flight of birds.
> Once came an old man with a rotting face,
> And more than once my girl, to squeeze
> Kisses out, cool whey from curds.

The human subject is depicted as living in conditions more appropriate for an animal, and the threatened disintegration of his environment and indeed his whole life is captured in the detail of the torn gas mantle. In this context, the expression 'Under the sign of Dionysus-Hades' works at several levels.[22] On the one hand, what could be evoked here is a kind of nightmarish quasi-pub where the patronage of Dionysus can lead to death. On the other hand, the 'sign' could be like a star sign, proclaiming the poet's inevitable destiny.

22 The Dionysus-Hades formula is also used in *Horse* (58); see ch. 8 for further discussion.

However the expression is to be taken, though, the animal associations of Dionysus, which include his power to dismember, are allied with his function as god of alcohol. Moreover, the entire Dionysus concept is juxtaposed with Hades, a juxtaposition which not only throws a sidelong glance at the specific identification of the two deities by Heraclitus, but evokes Dionysus's underworld cult connections (and which also, ironically, given the link between the underworld and ancient mystery religions with their emphasis on salvation and 'resurrection' for the initiated, points towards Christianity). Baxter apparently came close to suicide during the course of his Christchurch year, and his alcoholism would have pushed the staying power of his body to the limit. He was, of course, to conquer Dionysus later, although the effects of his drinking left a shadow over his health and at least contributed to his early death. It was, in the end, the Hades side of the equation with which he became increasingly preoccupied, as chapter 8 will illuminate in greater detail.

CHAPTER 8

'CHAOS AND THE GRAVE': BAXTER'S UNDERWORLDS

> Man is a walking grave,
> That is where I start from.
>
> ('Pig Island Letters' 1, *CP* 276–77)

> There goes Jim Baxter, carrying his grave with him and ready to leap into it by appointment.
>
> (Denis Glover, quoted in McKay, *Life* 178)

Baxter's solemn enunciation of first principles in 'Pig Island Letters' and Denis Glover's irreverent quip make the same point, which many succeeding critics have echoed: death is Baxter's most constant preoccupation. As the consequence and symbol of our fallen condition, death is the central defining fact of human life. As O'Sullivan comments, talking about Baxter's early poetry, 'There is not much, now or later, which puts the grave far from Baxter's thinking' (*Baxter* 17). The landscape of the early, Romantic poems is haunted by the omnipresence of death. The mature poetry is increasingly shaped by the tension between negative and positive values of death: fear of it as entropy and chaos; attraction to it as return to the maternal womb/tomb and reunion with the ancestral dead. In the late poems the positive value comes to dominate, as Baxter becomes increasingly focused on the ideal of kenosis, self-emptying, and union with 'the darkness I call God' ('The Ikons', *CP* 499).[1]

A general discussion of Baxter and death is beyond the scope of this book. In fact, in this key area of his thought, classical myth has a rather marginal presence. No classical figure embodies death

1 Harkiman's 1993 thesis 'The Poetry of Death' is a useful survey of Baxter's changing views, though it overstresses Catholic theology at the expense of Baxter's symbolic way of thinking. On *kenosis*, see Russell, and Millar, 'Hemi te Tutua'.

for Baxter in the way that Venus embodies sexuality (though Persephone, perhaps, comes closest). Imaginatively, he tends to represent death less through mythological symbolism than through images of the natural world: earth, sea and mountains all become powerful death symbols.[2] Intellectually, his view of death is shaped most obviously by his developing Christianity, modified in later years by elements of Eastern and Maori spirituality.

Nevertheless, Baxter does frequently return to images of what he once called 'the not-so-imaginary Greek underworld' ('Writers in New Zealand: A Questionnaire' 41)—Hades, the world of the dead and its inhabitants in Greek and Roman mythology. Sometimes Baxter's Hades literally represents death and the afterlife; much more often, it functions as a metaphor for aspects of life, related only obliquely to the literal fact of human mortality. It is Baxter's use of the image of Hades which will be the focus of this chapter.

'The not-so-imaginary Greek underworld'

In Christianity, our present life may be seen as essentially a brief preparation for the eternal life that is to follow after death. The Greek view of the afterlife was very different. What came after death was only a shadowy half-life in the dark 'house of Hades' or 'house of Persephone', ruled over by the grim death-god Hades (or Pluto, or Dis) and his reluctant bride Persephone.[3] This might be located beneath the earth (hence 'underworld'), or accessed at the edge of the world, beyond the stream of Ocean: Odysseus, in *Odyssey* 11, sails there and beaches on its dark and gloomy shore. Homer's description unforgettably conveys its dreariness: a featureless plain on which eternally wander the 'dimwitted dead [. . .] the after-images of used-up men' (*Od.* 11.476). Given this bleak conception of the afterlife, it is not surprising that both Greeks and Romans tended to focus their aspirations on the present world. As the ghost of Achilles tells Odysseus, 'Better, I say, to break sod as a farm hand / for some poor country man,

2 See 'Symbolism' (*FA* 69) and Jones' discussion in 'The Mythology of Place'.

3 See the Mythological Who's Who for more detailed discussion of these and other figures.

on iron rations, / than lord it over all the exhausted dead' (*Od.* 11.489–91).[4]

Post-classical writers tend to assimilate the underworld to the Christian hell and its ruler to the devil. But Pluto, though cold and implacable, was not evil, and Hades was not a place of punishment but a universal destination where 'Good and evil alike lead an equally cheerless existence' (Garland 60). Nevertheless, Homer does imply that some who committed abominable crimes against the gods (such as Tityus, Tantalus and Sisyphus) suffer imaginative forms of torment there (*Od.* 11.576–600), and also that heroes specially favoured by the gods may escape the common fate to spend eternity in paradisal Elysian Fields or Islands of the Blest (*Od.* 4.561–69). Philosophers and moralists (perhaps influenced by the doctrines of mystery religions) picked up these hints of extraordinary cases and generalised them: so Plato (*Gorgias* 523–27) describes the souls of the newly dead coming before the judges Minos, Aeacus and Rhadamanthus, who dispatch them either to punishment in Tartarus or happiness in Elysium. This moralised version of Hades informs the most famous classical depiction of the underworld, in Virgil's *Aeneid* 6 (and more briefly in *Georgics* 4).[5] Virgil provides the most complex account of the infernal geography and inhabitants, with vivid images of the surly ferryman Charon and the three-headed hellhound Cerberus, of the dark descent into the underworld, the sorrowful Plains of Mourning, the torments of Tartarus, and the green pastures and lilies of Elysium. The Platonic/Virgilian version of the afterlife is more compatible with Christianity than the older Homeric conception, and Baxter draws freely on it, but it is clearly Homer's version which impressed his imagination most profoundly.

The mythological underworld features in some of the most famous classical legends: Hercules, Theseus, Orpheus, Odysseus and Aeneas all venture down there to test their heroism literally

4 See e.g. Mikalson 82: 'Clearly what mattered to the average Athenian was this life, and in the fourth century he took little interest in the bleak and uncertain prospect of the afterlife.' The generalisation applies with some qualifications to later Greek and Roman culture.

5 *Aeneid* 6 was one of the texts Baxter studied in his Latin paper at Otago University (McKay, *Life* 72).

in the face of death. It is debatable, however, how far ordinary Greeks and Romans actually believed in it. For Romans, at least, it seems to have been largely 'a literary convention' unrelated to actual funerary beliefs or practices, which focused more on the veneration and propitiation of ancestral ghosts at their tombs (Toynbee 37). Educated Roman writers mock the myths of Hades: the satirist Juvenal declares that 'Today not even children [. . .] believe all that stuff about ghosts, / Or underground kingdoms and rivers, or black frogs croaking / In the waters of Styx' (2.149–52), while Lucian's *Dialogues of the Dead* use the traditional underworld for the purposes of deadpan humour. For post-classical writers in a Christian world, for whom belief is no longer a question, the traditional furniture of Hades is even more problematic; it risks becoming a melodramatic cliché or a joke, as kitschy as the cloud-riding cherubs or pitchfork-wielding devils of naïve Christian iconography. This danger of bathos is probably the reason that Baxter tends to avoid bringing the mythological underworld into too close contact with the monumental seriousness of death.

In Baxter's juvenilia, Hades sometimes appears as a literal image of death, in the Romantic convention of poetical paganism. For instance, he prays to Hermes as psychopomp ('To Hermes', N4.175):

> Conductor of all souls, be merciful
> And lead me not to Hades where
> The bright sun shines not and no bird may sing,
> But guide me to the regions beautiful!

But in 'The Gods of Greece' (N3.157, also written when Baxter was fifteen), Hades is already a vanished myth: 'Even stern Pluto long has fled [. . .] The tortured Tantalus no more / Doth thirst upon the Stygian shore.'

References to the classical underworld as the place of the dead appear occasionally in Baxter's mature poetry, for instance in his epitaph on Dylan Thomas—'Dionysus has met Charon on the bronze threshing-floor / And Charon conquered' ('On Dylan Thomas', *Listener* 1954)—where he is imitating the epitaphs of the *Greek Anthology*. Mostly, he confines such literal imagery to explicitly classical contexts. It is appropriate that Oedipus in *The Temptations of Oedipus* should think of death as 'the ice-cold region of Persephone' (*CPlays* 232). In the Odysseus poems it is appropriate for the Sirens to speak of the hero's dead comrades as 'twittering ghosts in Hades', and praise him as one who 'even in Hades would walk with a heavier tread / From the wisdom of stratagem' ('The Sirens', *CP* 130–33)—the weightlessness and birdlike voices of the dead are Homeric images. 'The Journey' (*CP* 127) closely follows Homer's account of Odysseus's voyage from Circe's island to the world of the dead, recalling a number of evocative Homeric details: the location of the world of the dead near to 'Cimmeria the sunless', a land wrapped in 'clammy nightfogs' (cf. *Od.* 11.14–19); the beach 'where poplar and lamenting willow / Let fall their vacant seed' (cf. 10.509–10); the spirits of the dead gathering 'with wrath and ululation' (cf. 11.42–43). 'Traveller's Litany' (*CP* 144) recalls Odysseus's encounter there with the ghost of Elpenor, a young crewman who died in a drunken accident and who appears to him 'among the drowsy shades' to beg for a proper burial (*Od.* 11.51–83).[6] These allusions are primarily fitted to their literal, classical contexts, though they also have symbolic resonances: 'The Journey' irresistibly suggests the larger human journey from life to death; Baxter spells out in his notes to 'Traveller's Litany' (*CP* 626) the secular and sacramental associations of the Elpenor image, and later reuses the lines, shorn of some of their classical detail, as personal memory in 'The Watch' (*CP* 273).

Much more often, however, the symbolic level predominates: Baxter's Hades functions not as a literal representation of death but as a symbol for an aspect of human life. The Greek underworld is 'not-so-imaginary', not because there really is a kingdom of

6 It is interesting that Baxter uses Elpenor here rather than the corresponding Virgilian figure of Palinurus (*Aen.* 5.827–72; 6.337–83). Palinurus, Aeneas's helmsman, who was enticed by the god Somnus (Sleep) into falling asleep at the wheel and so drowned, would have been a closer parallel than Elpenor to Baxter's sailor who is fatally visited by Mother Carey. If Baxter at some level had Palinurus in his mind, he nevertheless typically prefers to draw on Homer than on Virgil (and more generally to draw on Greek rather than Latin literature). He may also have been attracted to the name 'Elpenor' because that was the pseudonym of Brian Dalton, one of the major contributors to *Canta* when Baxter was its literary editor in 1948 (Millar, *No Fretful Sleeper* 153).

the dead under the earth, but because it embodies permanent psychological and spiritual realities. Hades, as one Baxter character puts it, is a state of mind (*RW* 9).

Chaos

But the interpretation of the symbolism is complicated by Baxter's characteristic doubleness. Like so many motifs and characters in Baxter's personal mythology—and most strikingly like that other sinister subterranean realm, the Labyrinth—Hades has both a negative and a positive value. On the one hand, it is a symbol of spiritual death, alienation and despair. On the other, it is a figure for the unconscious mind, a dark and fearful place but also the source of wisdom and creativity.

Perhaps the clue to reconciling this contradiction is the association of the underworld with 'chaos'. Chaos is a key concept for Baxter throughout his life. In a poem written at the age of fifteen he described how the 'thought of God' can 'chaos to cosmos turn' ('Truth', N2.128); near the end of his life, in his 1971 interview with Weir, he makes the ordering of chaos central to the poet's role. Chaos is the universe perceived as alien, meaningless or incomprehensible. Its most obvious manifestation is death, the great unknown in the face of which all our human constructions of meaning seem fragile and trivial. 'When you are dealing with the world you tend to see it as Chaos,' Baxter told Weir. 'Perhaps to the eye of God it is not Chaos at all but to us it looks like Chaos.' The artist, like the scientist—or like God—must try to turn chaos to cosmos by finding order and meaning in it (Weir 'Interview' 242–43).

On one level chaos is a profoundly negative image. It embodies the sense of the meaninglessness and futility of life—a tale told by an idiot, signifying nothing—which, for Baxter, is how most people at least in the modern world experience it. Without some kind of external role to give it structure, he suggests in his introduction to *The Sore-footed Man* and *The Temptations of Oedipus*, 'life tends to be experienced as chaos. The unveiling of this chaos is perhaps the theme of all my plays' (*CPlays* 336). This vision of life's emptiness is fittingly symbolised by the bleak pointlessness of the Homeric underworld—Pluto's 'world / of chaos and the grave' ('Thoughts of a Remuera Housewife', *CP* 314). Its most 'aboriginal' and terrifying forms are the Furies (*CPlays* 336), or Medusa, 'child of derisive Chaos / And hateful Night' ('Perseus', *CP* 129), monsters of the underworld which represent 'the horror' at Baxter's heart of darkness.[7]

But chaos can also have creative potential. '[I]n all good mythologies,' as Baxter famously wrote, 'first there was the gap, the void' ('Education', *MH* 122). In Greek myth the world emerged out of chaos. This chaos may be conceived as vacancy and absence: according to Hesiod, 'In the beginning there was only Chaos, the Abyss,' after which were born Earth and Eros (*Theogony* 116). Or it may be conceived as substance in disorder: for Ovid chaos is the raw material, 'all heaped / together in anarchic disarray', out of which some artist-god fashioned the universe (*Met.* 1.7–9). The biblical account of creation similarly begins with chaos: Baxter refers to the '*tohu* and *bohu*'—the Hebrew words translated in the King James Bible as 'without form, and void' (Genesis 1:2)—out of which God created the world, turning chaos into cosmos (Weir interview 248). Maori myth offers yet another parallel: traditional creation chants begin with Te Kore, nothingness, out of which came first Darkness and then Sky and Earth (Alpers 15). This nothing which is the origin of everything is obviously related to 'Wahi Ngaro, the void from which all life comes' ('Autumn Testament' 2, *CP* 541), a concept which becomes very important to Baxter in his late poetry. He identifies wahi ngaro both with God and with death, and wishes to embrace it, leaping into 'the darkness I call God' ('The Ikons', *CP* 499). As the chaos and emptiness of death comes to be seen by Baxter as a liberation from the constraints of selfhood and rationality, so the image of the underworld, despite its bleak associations, can also be a positive symbol, associated especially with the creative potential of the unconscious from whose

7 The Furies, of course, are creatures of the underworld. Baxter does not explicitly connect Medusa with the underworld, but compare *Od.* 11.633–35, where Odysseus flees from the world of the dead because of fear 'that august Persephone might send upon me out of the house of Hades the head of the Gorgon, that terrible monster' (Loeb translation).

'anarchic disarray' his poetry springs. It can be—to borrow a phrase used by Baxter in a different context—a 'fruitful chaos'.[8]

The rafters of Hades: acedia

It is the negative associations of Hades which are more immediately obvious in Baxter's work. The dismal half-life of the 'after-images of used-up men' in the Homeric house of Hades represents a state of spiritual death-in-life. Baxter likes to call this state 'acedia', the medieval theologians' term for the sin of sloth or spiritual torpor in which the soul turns listlessly away from God.[9] This state of alienation, boredom, numbness and despair is particularly the product of modern industrial society and its 'great swamp of economic liberalism': 'the devil of acedia [. . .] rises from that swamp and inhabits, like an honoured guest, our Government Departments, our business offices, our schools, our places of entertainment, our art galleries and our homes' ('Conversation', *MH* 14). In a more extreme form, it may be the listless despair of someone trapped in a state of sin or in an addiction such as alcoholism, from which it seems an impossible effort to escape. Under the power of acedia, ordinary life becomes an 'other death', as Baxter calls it in 'Epilogue for Ian' (1968, *CP* 425–26), where he sees 'my friends the suicides / Stabbing like needles through the cloth of life / To find the space behind it,' because 'They did not want to share the fug with us in / This other death.'[10]

Two powerful poems of the early 1960s depict the modern city as an outcrop of Hades. 'The Eyes of Dis' (1962, *CP* 259–

8 'Symbolism', *FA* 68: 'the Sea symbolises the fruitful chaos which nourishes the sexual instinct'. The context is not so different: in the next paragraph Baxter identifies the sea as 'a symbol of death and oblivion' and as 'a symbol of regeneration'. Once again chaos is associated with death, and is seen as both destructive and creative.

9 The *New Catholic Encyclopedia* defines it as 'a disgust with the spiritual because of the physical effort involved' (s.v. *acedia*). It was sometimes referred to as 'the noonday demon', a phrase Baxter also uses (e.g. 'Words and Money', *CP* 236; 'Jerusalem Sonnets' 28, *CP* 468). In Catholic tradition it is identified as the besetting sin of solitary monks; Baxter's association of it with the social life of modern cities is a striking reappropriation.

10 Cleary has a good discussion of the idea of spiritual death in Baxter, distinguishing 'death as the grim reaper ready to cut off the physical existence' from 'the death of the soul which could undermine people's lives long before their physical death' (123).

60) represents a wintry, rain-lashed Wellington as 'Cimmeria', the country of perpetual darkness which lies at the border of the underworld in Homer (and in 'The Journey'). It is a place 'where the blood grows dull' and where 'The white-hot coal / That touched Isaiah's lips / Is quenched'. Instead of the white-hot coal of prophetic inspiration (see Isaiah 6:5–7), the 'image for Cimmeria' is 'A square black stone, an armless Niobe / Whose surface sweats, a weeping stone in the mind'—an image of silent, self-enclosed, numb despair, like Niobe or the petrified victims of the Gorgon. The poem's central lines make explicit the association of 'Cimmeria' with Hades:

> The eyes of the abyss
> Examine us; the eyes of Dis
> Have understood our case. They cut the soul
> Out by the roots.

'Dis', like 'Hades', is the name of both the god and his realm; it is probably the collective, sinisterly unspecific eyes of the underworld itself which are watching here, as Baxter echoes Nietzsche's famous aphorism: 'If you gaze for long into an abyss, the abyss gazes also into you' (*Beyond Good and Evil*, aphorism 145).[11] The inhabitants of 'Cimmeria' have contemplated chaos for too long and it has entered their souls.

In 'Morning Train' (1963, *CP* 272–73) the poet travels to work under heavy clouds that seem to him like 'the rafters of Hades'. As Eliot saw the office workers streaming across London Bridge as figures in Dante's Limbo—'I had not thought death had undone so many' (*Waste Land* 1.63, quoting *Inferno* 3.55–57)—Baxter sees his fellow-commuters as dead souls in 'the den of shadows': 'They do not need a book / To tell them where they are, in the burrows of the grave.' Images of stone—'faces of tired rock', 'like mountains walking'—again suggest the emotional petrification and dull indifference of acedia. They are the victims of what Baxter elsewhere calls 'the Medusa's head which present-day urban civilisation turns towards them: depersonalisation,

11 There may also be a Dantean allusion: in the *Inferno* the city of Dis encloses the lower levels of hell, and its entrance is guarded by the Furies and Medusa (canto 9).

centralisation, desacralisation' (Westra 8).

The metaphor of Hades as spiritual death is developed at greater length in the unpublished play *The Runaway Wife*.[12] Here Baxter turns the tragic legend of Orpheus and Eurydice into a black comedy which he describes as 'near to vaudeville' (2). It looks in fact like an attempt at an Aristophanic comedy, built on the model of *The Frogs* (the hero's rescue mission to Hades; the culminating 'trial') and complete with infernal chorus, central *parabasis*, and the slapstick use of a gigantic phallus. McNaughton dismisses *The Runaway Wife* as a failure, with an ending that is 'about as stylistically inept as can be imagined' (192), but it is at least an interesting failure. As Baxter's most extended treatment of the classical underworld it claims an important place in this chapter, and since it is little known a fairly full summary may be useful.

The play opens with a typically fraught Baxterian marriage: the poet Orpheus, feeling stifled by domesticity, has taken refuge in Bohemian drinking and womanising, while the resentful Eurydice sinks into depression and neurotic nagging. Their quarrel climaxes when Orpheus tells Eurydice to 'go to Hades!' (5)—and she does. What this means becomes clearer in the next scene. The remorseful Orpheus comes to a bureaucratic office (a dreamlike blend of Missing Persons and Immigration) where a clerk is explaining to an enquirer in search of her missing husband that Hades is not, as she surmises, in Australia: 'Not in any particular country. Hades is—well, I suppose it's really a state of mind—absence, death, separation' (9). People go there of their own free will:

> You see—all over the world people are sighing out for oblivion—for a state where things no longer matter. Business men—housewives—parsons—bureaucrats—murderers—schoolteachers—thieves—soldiers—prostitutes—wharf workers—children even—there comes a time when reality—

12 *The Runaway Wife* was produced by a student group in Dunedin in 1968. Quotations are taken from Baxter's corrected typescript in the Hocken Library (MS-0975/069), though we have also consulted the original manuscript (MS-0975/051). There are useful brief discussions in Cleary, 128, and McNaughton, 'Baxter as Dramatist', 191–92.

the usual kind of reality—just can't be carried any longer. They snap. They may blame themselves—but still, they snap. And then they come to us for a ticket to Hades. (10–11)

The bureaucrat in charge of the department, Mr Rhadamanthus, tells Orpheus, 'Hades is the condition of endless waiting. Why quarrel with Hades? It's the normal state of the human race—endless waiting for a reality that never arrives. Life is temporary. Hades is eternal' (12). Hades is an image not of the modern world itself, but of the state of withdrawal and alienation into which that world drives us.

Orpheus's persistence at last forces Rhadamanthus to give him a ticket for admission to 'an all-night sitting at the Hades coffee bar', run by Mr Pluto, where Eurydice is now working. It is, he warns, 'a rough place' (12). The Hades coffee bar proves to be a kind of beatnik-Bohemian limbo where a Godotian crowd hang out drinking, gambling, flirting, listening to poetry readings by trendy 'protest' poets such as Tantalus and Sisyphus, and heckling the politician Mouldybroke's reactionary harangues.[13] Eurydice is serving as a waitress, wearing (in another image of the underworld as transformation to stone) a Gorgon mask. The same imagery appears in the contemporary poem 'Seances (for Colin Durning)' (*CP* 426), where, on one of 'these mornings when the dead harass our lives', Baxter suggests that he and his friend should

sit as usual in that café
Underground, a not too hard to bear
Grotto of the mind—talk, drink—where one can see
On certain days the stone-white face of Eurydice
Carrying in scorn her great gold helm of hair.

The underground café suggests Bohemia, a way of 'dropping out' of the conventional society represented in its ugliest form by Mouldybroke. When the modern world is intolerable it can be a relief to drop out and simply stop caring. The Hades coffee bar is an apparently 'not too hard to bear' version of chaos, but

13 Mr Mouldybroke—a satiric compound of Prime Minister Keith Holyoake and Finance Minister Rob Muldoon—is a recurring figure in Baxter's poems, e.g. 'a death song for mr mouldybroke' (*CP* 411–12). His long speech, which disastrously stalls the play's dramatic momentum, is heavily cut in Baxter's revised typescript.

ultimately a place of deadly boredom and sterility. The young women hanging around the bar complain that 'the trouble with Hades is, there's never really anywhere to go': you get sick of copulation and going to watch the tortures, though there's always drink and pills for solace (21–22).

Vaudeville turns to drama when Orpheus attempts to drag Eurydice away. Suddenly the old drunk Calico Jack unmasks to reveal himself as Mr Rhadamanthus, the women assume the masks of the Furies, and Orpheus finds himself on trial. Defending himself, he describes how he was torn between domesticity and Bohemia:

> I seemed to be cut in half—half belonged to [Eurydice]—half belonged to—
>
> RHADAMANTHUS To Hades.
>
> ORPHEUS Yes—now you mention it, that half of my life did resemble Hades—nothing quite made sense—
>
> RHADAMANTHUS The problem's quite simple. You'd both fallen into the grip of Hades. It's not at all unusual. Ninety nine per cent of the human race lives in Hades all the time. Those ones out there—*[he gestures to the audience]*—they live in Hades all the time—but nearly all of them don't know it. (27)

Rhadamanthus's image for this universal condition is startlingly grim amid the satiric comedy: the story of an African villager during the Congo civil war who was impaled on a wooden stake, and who tells the well-meaning missionary who attempts to comfort him to 'bugger off' because from his point of view 'nothing exists except twelve inches of fire-hardened wood' (27–28). In this passage (a late addition to Baxter's original manuscript) Hades becomes not merely the tedious emptiness of escape from reality but the pain of reality itself: not boredom but torture.

'But there are exceptions,' Rhadamanthus goes on. 'Once in a while, some people get free of the smell of Hades—it's hard to say how—by luck—by sexual love—by art—even by religion' (28). Orpheus, the artist and lover, has the chance to get free, but to do so he must 'make a sacrifice'. He is given the choice of what to sacrifice: his eyes, his tongue or his private parts. He chooses castration, and after undergoing this ordeal at the hands of the Furies he is allowed to leave with Eurydice. Farrell Cleary's comment that 'Orpheus the young poet [. . .] has escaped from the land of the living dead' (128) perhaps makes this ending sound too ringingly optimistic. The play ends in grotesque slapstick: the Furies emerge from their attack on Orpheus carrying *'a large artificial phallus'*, Orpheus declares in a *'shrill'* voice that 'I don't feel much different' ('No, you're just like any ordinary Civil Servant now,' responds Rhadamanthus), and he is finally driven off stage by the disgruntled Eurydice (who deeply resents his choice of sacrifice) *'whacking him on the head and shoulders with the phallus'* (29–30). It is hardly a triumphant picture of art overcoming spiritual death. *The Runaway Wife* is much more convincing in its representation of the power of Hades than of the forces which can liberate us from it.

Prisoners of Hades: addiction and despair

So far we have seen the Hades of acedia treated as a universal condition; but Baxter also uses it more specifically to depict the inner landscape of an individual trapped in a state of sin or despair. The speaker in 'Thoughts of a Remuera Housewife' (*CP* 314), an adulterous upper-middle-class woman whose lover has abandoned her to her loveless marriage, sees herself in fantasy as Persephone carried off to be Pluto's bride in the underworld. Her tranquillisers, compared to the pomegranate seeds which trapped Persephone, will carry her 'quietly through // the dark mirror to his world / of chaos and the grave'. On one level Baxter is playing with the sexual overtones of the myth: as he noted in a talk on Edith Sitwell's poetry, Persephone can be read punningly as a 'fallen woman', and the underworld as a sexual demi-monde, 'that sealed-off, terrible underworld which waits for anyone who falls from the tight-rope of fidelity' ('The Pythoness').[14] On a profounder level, the underworld represents the housewife's inner state of alienation and quiet desperation. In the eyes of her mother

14 The Sitwell poem is 'Sir Beelzebub': 'When / Sir / Beelzebub / Called for his syllabub in the hotel in hell / Where Proserpine first fell' (Sitwell 158). Baxter's amused appreciation of the 'hotel in hell' image may have contributed to his creation of the Hades coffee bar, a more modern kind of infernal demi-monde.

and husband she may be going normally about her daily routine; but in emotional reality she exists in a world of frozen cold and silence, 'in Pluto's cave' among the dead souls, or—in a striking fusion of mythological and astronomical imagery—on 'Pluto's / iron-black star, the quiet / planet furthest from the sun'. The poem conveys a surprising empathy with its subject—surprising from Baxter, who is not noted for his sympathy with the *haute bourgeoisie* and who (as we have noted) tends to present women more as Jungian archetypes than as fully realised human beings. Here the mythic approach, instead of stereotyping, helps to give the Remuera housewife a sense of complex interiority.

The moral emphasis is stronger in another dramatic monologue from the same period, 'Henley Pub' (*CP* 324–25). The speaker, a Catholic commercial traveller wracked by guilt and self-disgust over an adulterous affair, churns together Christian and pagan images as he drunkenly broods on suicide:

> The Taeri flood, Jehovah's book,
> Ruffles its page, does not untwist our sin
> Which is itself, the triple snarling grin
> Of Cerberus.

Baxter's own explication of the poem in 'The Virgin and the Temptress' (*MH* 64–89) reads this image in a way more precise than any reader could be expected to grasp:

> He is, after all, a Christian who has strayed into the pagan underworld. [. . .] His sin—or rather, *our sin*, for he recognises that he and his mistress are linked in the same calamity—belongs to the pagan underworld, since it involves a rebellion of the natural powers. It appears to him in the shape of Cerberus, the three-headed dog at the gate of the Greek Hades: the three heads being remorse for past evil, attachment to present evil, and dread of future evil. (76)

The underworld is here being assimilated to hell, and its figures complexly moralised and allegorised in the spirit of medieval interpretations of scripture and myth. Baxter also suggests that the poem's Taieri River 'is the river of death [. . ..] On the pagan level it is the river Styx which encircles the underworld' (77). He does not suggest a connexion between the poem's Leith Stream and the underworld river of Lethe, but that echo is hard to ignore in the context. As the souls in Virgil's underworld are confined where 'the Styx coiling nine times around corralled them there' (*Georgics* 4.480), the traveller is entrapped by sin and guilt, and 'the waters of the grave have extinguished [his] spiritual life' (*MH* 78).

It is striking how often Baxter associates the underworld, and in particular the infernal rivers, with alcohol and drugs. The alcoholic travelling salesman soliloquises at the Henley pub; the Remuera housewife has her tranquillisers to transport her into Pluto's realm. The Hades coffee bar of *The Runaway Wife*, despite its name, deals in stronger stimulants than coffee: Pluto and Rhadamanthus drink brandy, Arethusa recommends 'some marvellous new pills' that make everything look greenish-blue (22), and Calico Jack supplies the recipe for a 'Glasgow cocktail'—gas bubbled through milk (17). In 'Night in Tarras' (*CP* 81) the country pub becomes 'Lethaean night's abode', a place for forgetfulness, and the walkers drinking at the bar, like Odysseus in Hades, find ghosts flocking around them 'lapping their honey mead and blood'. And in 'Portrait of a Fellow-Alcoholic' (N23.36) Baxter uses Phlegethon, the river of fire, as an image for the alcoholic's condition:

Mother, have mercy on
Two idiot burnt brothers walking by
That cindered Phlegethon
Whose waves of fire and blackness I
Know better than the Mass.

The *Flowering Cross* essay 'The Church and the Alcoholic' similarly images alcoholism as an underworld: recovering alcoholics have 'a spiritual landscape of rock and water' (*FC* 36) and live in perpetual terror of 'descent to the half-world that seems to be their natural habitat' (34). Drink and drugs, like the condition of acedia itself, offer a means of escape from reality into comfortable numbness, but can become in themselves (for the addict) an imprisonment and a torture.

The futility that Hades embodies is seen most clearly in the figures of the great sinners punished there. Some, as in the Christian hell, suffer physical torture (like Ixion on his wheel of fire); but others are tormented primarily by endless frustrated effort—Sisyphus perpetually trying to roll a huge stone uphill; Tantalus tantalised by food and drink which he cannot reach; the Danaids trying to fill a pot with water using a sieve. As a familiar part of the literary furniture of Hades, these figures make a number of appearances in Baxter. We get sketches of several of them in 'The Descent of Orpheus' (*Landfall* 1957). Tantalus and Sisyphus appear in *The Runaway Wife* as ineffectual protest poets: Sisyphus the young Maori radical, Tantalus the existentialist interminably analysing 'the experience of the void in modern life' (14–15)—a sly piece of Baxterian self-parody. Tantalus is the vehicle for a much more painful self-exposure in the unpublished 'Tantalus' (c.1951, N16.41), which makes his predicament an image for the alcoholic's unassuageable thirst and moral paralysis:

> Again and again, waking up, he has lain
> Stonefast in the lock of despair. No protestation
> Of will, love, quiet living, can make sense
> After the nth betrayal.

Unsparingly realistic despite its mythological title, this poem grants the drunk none of his usual Baxterian privilege as saintly reprobate or holy fool; Tantalus is a 'moral bankrupt', bitterly aware that his fate is to 'mourn / At his own funeral, pissing against the headstone'. It is a particularly brutal image of spiritual death.

Sisyphus is a more significant figure. Albert Camus made him one of the central mythological figures for the twentieth century. For Camus he is an emblem of the 'absurdity' of human existence. The utter pointlessness of his endless labour is universal—'The workman of today works every day of his life at the same tasks, and this fate is no less absurd' (121)—but Sisyphus gains a tragic and ironic dignity in his recognition of that pointlessness, and hence, unexpectedly, 'One must imagine Sisyphus happy' (123). Baxter's treatment of Sisyphus is almost certainly influenced by Camus' famous essay, but he generally does not embrace the French writer's paradoxically positive spin. For him Sisyphus and his stone is one of the most powerful images for the soul-destroying quality of the modern world. In 'Air Flight to Delhi'

(1958, *CP* 193) Baxter's first appalled response to the poverty, suffering and injustice of India culminates in the image of 'The stone of Sisyphus rolled on the heart'. In 'Pigeon Park' (c.1964, N25.45), 'Like the stone of Sisyphus / the sun rolls on the hills' edge' as the poet walks among the meths-drinkers brooding on the ruined state of 'the glib / scarred whore, our mother planet'.[15]

Sisyphus's task is always an image of monotonous futility, but the specific meaning of the stone varies. In 'The Descent of Orpheus', 'Grum Sisyphus, who takes to heart / All that ever happened' is pushing 'the stone of conscience'. In 'Sisyphus' (1959, *CP* 202) the stone is simply 'the hour', the unbearably tedious succession of tomorrow and tomorrow and tomorrow. Sisyphus, a rich businessman, 'king of the silver mountain', nevertheless feels his daily life as a cage and a treadmill; despite his external wealth, the emptiness he finds inside himself—'The deepest tunnel leads you down / To a torn and blinded mirror / And the angers of the tomb'—leads him to suicide.[16] For the old 'bummer'[17] in 'Dunedin Revisited' (1961, *CP* 235) the stone is a sexual compulsion:

> like glum Sisyphus rolling his boulder
> The old museum bummer sighs
> For bouncing boys with football-blackened knees
> Who do not care for him at all.

Baxter views the pederast with compassion: like Baxter's alcoholics and drug addicts he is trapped on a treadmill of habit that can deliver only frustration. In 'Ballad to the Dunedin City Mothers' (1964, N24.76) the same character is ironically described as 'your patron saint, the town bummer', his pathetic entrapment mirroring the acedia of the city and society he inhabits.

In other contexts Sisyphus becomes one of Baxter's 'figures of

15 This is the last of three versions of a poem which never reached publication; the earlier drafts were 'Noises from Jupiter' (N24.44) and 'Pigeon Park' (N25.8): the Sisyphus image appears in all three. Goulter (75) sees a similar Sisyphean allusion in 'The Sailor' (1967, *CP* 406), where Auckland is the place 'Where one must lift and carry the great boulders', and, less persuasively, in 'Bonfire' (1967, *CP* 390).

16 The 'pearl-handled revolver' with which Sisyphus kills himself may carry an ironic allusion to the biblical 'pearl of great price' (Matthew 13:46).

17 'Bummer' clearly means 'homosexual' or more specifically 'pederast', though neither *OED* nor the *Dictionary of New Zealand English* recognises this sense.

self'. This is most explicit in a touching poem addressed in 1968 to his infant granddaughter, 'Stephanie' (*SP* 181–82), in which he calls himself 'your grandfather Sisyphus', and confesses that 'you have betrayed me into / Uncalled-for tremors of joy in the rock of the heart / It is my business to shove uphill each day— / O what if it should split!' Here his rock is a personal one, implicitly a burden of pain or guilt or discouragement. More often, Baxter relates the image to himself in a social context, reading the rock as the burden of working for a living in New Zealand's bourgeois-Calvinistic society. His view of this burden was equivocal. In his first year as Burns Fellow, for instance, he confessed in a letter that he rather missed working under a boss—'Sisyphus feeling lost without his boulder' (11 March 1966, FM 11/6/55).

The most striking example of this is a passage quoted at the very start of this book: Baxter's response to the 1960 *Landfall* questionnaire about the predicament of New Zealand writers, in which 'that remarkable boulder which Sisyphus, streaming with sweat, shoves uphill every day and night in the not-so-imaginary Greek underworld' symbolises his own condition as a wage-slave. He concludes that he would not wish to be parted from his boulder: its weight and roughness are 'the strongest intimations of reality which I possess, and the source of whatever strength exists in my sporadic literary productions.' Like Camus, Baxter finds something unexpectedly positive in the nightmare image of Sisyphus. But whereas Camus' philosopher rises above the masses by recognising the essential meaninglessness of life, Baxter creates meaning by his own participation in the common human condition. In this passage the living death of Hades becomes for once life-enhancing and potentially redemptive, and so it leads appropriately into Baxter's more positive uses of the not-so-imaginary underworld.

The waters of the underworld: the unconscious

The interpretation of the underworld as a symbol of the unconscious mind is a familiar Jungian one. According to Jung,

> 'Beyond the grave' or 'on the other side of death' means, psychologically, 'beyond consciousness'. There is positively

> nothing else it could mean, since statements about immortality can only be made by the living. ('The Relations between the Ego and the Unconscious', *CW* 7: 189)

Though the Catholic Baxter would not have subscribed to this offhand dismissal of the afterlife, his uses of the classical Hades often invite such a Jungian reading. By paradoxical contrast with the image of Hades as spiritual death, this Hades often appears as the source of spiritual life. It is a place of chaos, dark and fearful, haunted by monsters and the terror of death, but it also holds the wellsprings of imagination and creativity. This is the 'abyss of his own soul' that the creative writer must descend into in a quest 'to find [. . .] the source of holiness and the meaning of the creation' (*MH* 11).

The idea of the descent to Hades as a psychological journey is perhaps first broached in 'The Cave' (*CP* 69), where a rock crevice discovered in the fields is imagined as leading 'to the sunless kingdom / Where souls endure the ache of Proserpine'. In this early (1948) poem, which Vincent O'Sullivan has seen as embodying Baxter's central mythic paradigm of 'separation, death, and rebirth', an utterly 'commonplace experience'—man enters a cave, stands a moment, comes out again—takes on overtones of the heroic underworld descent of a Hercules or Orpheus (*Baxter* 8–9). The poem's mythic power comes partly from the ambiguity of what the cave and its 'sunless kingdom' represents. It can be taken on a fairly simple level as an emblem of death: the animal bones and the smell of earth serve as a memento mori, the poet being vividly confronted with the reality that in the end we all return to a hole in the ground. On another level, the poet's descent into the cave may be read as a Jungian descent into the heart of the self or of the collective unconscious, where he can discover the 'secret language / That dead men speak and we have long forgotten', and emerge to 'dazzling daylight' with new self-knowledge. This blurring of the line between the literal realm of death and the psychological realm of the unconscious is characteristic of Baxter.

The image of the underground river, 'a rivulet [. . .] running in the dark', will also recur. Whereas the traditional rivers of the underworld (Styx and the rest) are associated for Baxter with entrapment and stagnation, these unnamed, mysterious running waters suggest a more positive force, a kind of buried life running beneath the surface of everyday existence. In 'Was It As Children?' (1945, N14.871), which echoes the imagery of 'The Cave', it is 'the cold river / Of underground regret'. But in 'The Buried Stream' (1962, *CP* 260–61), regret for lost chances is replaced by a tentative hope of renewal:

> I hear the voice
> Of the buried stream that flows deep, deep,
> Through caves I cannot enter, whose watery rope
> Tugs my divining rod with the habit some call hope.

Most hopeful is the image of the 'springs of the underworld', in which the waters are no longer confined in inaccessible caves but actively well up to irrigate the desert of modern civilisation. This image recurs in Baxter's poems of the early sixties. In 'To a Samoan Friend' (1961, *SP* 97) he addresses Albert Wendt:

> As those cold waters rise at Rainbow Springs
> Endlessly from the underworld
> [. . .]
> So the creative current of your mind
> Rises and flows in this dry land
> Bringing to one or two the taste of peace.

'Then' (1963, N24.26) recalls a drunken, joyous dance in a bar at New Year, in which 'we were made / Free of the springs of the underworld'. Closely linked is the image of the spring of fresh water rising up beneath the sea at Waimarama, which in 'Pig Island Letters' 13 (*CP* 285) is associated with divine grace, and in 'Inscription (for Te Kare Jack)' (N24.22) with his love for Jacquie. Love, joy, creativity—all spring up from underground sources, from the unconscious.

A darker version of this image appears in an unpublished and untitled late poem from the Jerusalem period (FM 18/1/26, pp. 21–23):

> Now in the darkness of the moon
> The wind blows this way from the graveyard

And my heart is failing—so long a journey
I have to undertake [. . .].
        To be no longer man
Is what I fear, bending my head
In the darkness of this cave. The face I see
Is not the face of love but the face of night.
I am drinking the waters of the underworld.

Obviously Baxter is contemplating his own imminent journey into death; to drink the waters of the underworld is to experience the fear of mortality. But the context suggests other meanings. The poem is embedded in a Jungian essay, 'Things and Idols', which criticises Western civilisation's exclusive emphasis on the rational mind, Jung's animus; to discover God we must undertake 'a contemplative journey' first into the anima, 'the hidden self, passive and feminine' (21), and then into the spiritus, the site of spiritual awareness. The first effect of opening up the anima, Baxter suggests, 'is the experience of the preternatural—not experience of God, who alone is supernatural, but experience of elements in nature and elements in one's own soul—perhaps even an obscure experience of angels, demons, and the spirits of the living and the dead' (23). These are the horrors—'ghosts, werewolves, hags, demons, and the various zoo of the living dead'—whom Jung, many years earlier, had taught the adolescent Baxter to see as inextricably associated with the 'sources of peace and wisdom' to be found in the subconscious ('Education', *MH* 127). As in 'The Cave', the underworld represents not only the literal fact of death, but also and more importantly the subconscious levels of 'one's own soul', and the knowledge and creativity (as well as terror) that come from exploring them.

Baxter's most striking embodiment of the link between underworld and unconscious is the figure of 'Dionysus-Hades'. This mysterious compound deity from the ancient mystery religions (discussed in chapter 7) fuses the god of wine and poetry with the god of death and the underworld. We have already seen Baxter associating alcoholism and drug addiction with entrapment in the living death of the underworld, and Dionysus-Hades can suggest this dark connection. But he also carries positive connotations—the power of intoxication to open the doors to the vital creative power of the unconscious. In 'Christchurch 1948' (1960, *CP* 215–16), Baxter describes his younger self as living 'under the sign of Dionysus-Hades'—in squalour, isolation, and 'wanhope', but 'alive on milk and benzedrine' (the milk, perhaps, that is offered along with wine and honey in Greek libations to the dead), and seeing visions like a Roman *haruspex* reading the future from omens. It is a state which could be seen as a death-in-life, but also as an initiatory ordeal, Dionysus-Hades presiding over his painful transformation into a true poet. Horse, another version of the young Baxter, invokes the same god to contact his ancestral dead, tapping into the collective unconscious of his people: 'With these green-boned ancestors Horse communed when he was on the grog, sheltered by the black vine of Dionysus-Hades' (*Horse* 52). Baxter makes the complex of ideas explicit when he attributes it to Burns, in his Jungian reading of 'Tam o' Shanter'. Tam's drinking of whisky as he prepares to 'face the deevil' is not merely a Scots version of Dutch courage:

> In the folk image of John Barleycorn an earth god is concealed—Dionysus the god of wine—and it is suitable that he should stand beside Tam and give him courage at the gates of the underworld. [. . .] Without the help of this principle, Tam would not be bold enough to break into the area of the unconscious mind.
> ('Man', *MH* 110–11).

Dionysus-Hades also appears in more disguised forms. One is Baron Saturday in 'The Lion Skin' (1965, *CP* 329), a fearful figure of death and madness, but one whom the poet embraces, because he brings with him a creative vitality lacking in the 'town whose ladders are made of coffin wood'—once again, spiritual death-in-life contrasted with the reinvigorating power of the underworld/unconscious. Another avatar, perhaps, is Mr Rhadamanthus in *The Runaway Wife*. The enigmatic Rhadamanthus, the bureaucratic director of Hades, also appears behind the mask of Calico Jack, the drunken old derelict whose songs about death ('There's a man with an axe waiting just round the corner, / One bang from his axe and you'll know who you are!') lead Orpheus to describe him as being 'at the centre. The dead centre' (*RW*

21). Baxter's introductory notes in the manuscript version identify this character as 'Death'; they also characterise him as a 'drunk Silenus', the follower of Dionysus who is famously described by Plato (*Symposium* 215) as concealing the figure of a god within the shell of a fat, drunken old man. There are hints, indeed, that Calico Jack/Rhadamanthus may be a mask of God himself.[18] It is he who explains to Orpheus how and why the gods create poets, taking ordinary human beings with potential and making them do extraordinary things: 'some go mad, of course—but the ones who survive the experience—they become artists and suchlike' (*RW* 24)—though at the inevitable cost of being pursued by the Furies, those 'aboriginal' embodiments of chaos.

The metaphor of the unconscious as an underworld makes intuitive symbolic sense: it lies beneath the surface of ordinary conscious life, it is primitive, secret, accessible only to those who are willing to descend from the daylight of reason into the darkness of a dream-world. The association of the unconscious with death is less intuitively obvious. But they are connected in Baxter's mind, on at least two levels.

The first connection is that, for Baxter, to confront one's deepest self is also necessarily to confront death. We have seen this association in a series of Baxter's poems, from the early 'The Cave', with its seamless conflation of the two kinds of descent, to the late 'Now in the darkness of the moon'. For Baxter, true self-knowledge is inextricably tied to an awareness of mortality. Both at the macrocosmic level of the universe and at the microcosmic level of the individual soul, the heart of things is an area of chaos, darkness and emptiness—what Baxter variously calls the 'gap', the 'void', 'Wahi Ngaro'. Hence Baxter's later thought increasingly gravitates towards the ideal of kenosis. In 'Conversation with an Ancestor' he quotes Teilhard de Chardin:

> God must, in some way or other, make room for himself, hollowing us out and emptying us, if he is finally to penetrate into us. And in order to assimilate us in him, he must break the molecules of our being so as to re-cast and re-model us. The

18 When Pluto rebukes him for singing about Jesus ('We don't really mention God in these parts'), Calico Jack replies, 'I've got a special licence' (*RW* 21).

> function of death is to provide the necessary entrance into our inner selves. (*MH* 27)

To see Baxter's Hades as an aspect of 'the gap', both on microcosmic and macrocosmic levels, provides a clue to its paradoxical doubleness. The emptiness and acedia of spiritual death, the negative side of the underworld, can become a productive self-emptying, a stripping away of layers of social convention and individual selfhood to arrive at the essential human soul in relation to God.

Immediately after quoting Teilhard in 'Conversation with an Ancestor', Baxter goes on to express his sense of kinship with the dead: 'In the light of these words [. . .] one comes to see the dead as one's destitute brothers and sisters, hidden in the silence of God, to whom one may speak and receive an imperceptible reply' (*MH* 27). To strip away individual selfhood to arrive at the core of common humanity is to acknowledge oneself as part of a collective or 'tribe' rather than an individual identity. Knowledge of death, Baxter says, makes him 'reach out to the tribe which no longer exists', for modern Western society has lost its sense of the 'tribal matrix' and hence lost the collective strength to cope with death (*MH* 28). In a letter to Weir, Baxter identifies this as a Greek idea. He explains that his relation to death has

> become more a relation to the Dead—the lost friends, the Holy Souls, what have you [. . .]. The Dead as ancestors; then by degrees the Dead as the Greeks saw them, the ghosts, the creatures of silence and memory—a bit of an echo chamber, maybe, but resonant. (25 October 1967; FM 20/4/11)[19]

This is the second level on which Baxter's Hades links death and the unconscious. Jensen ('Drunkard' 219) puts his finger on the logic of the connexion when he refers to 'the land of the dead (that is, the collective unconscious, where the dead remain alive)'. The collective unconscious is the level, beneath the superficial shell of individuality and modernity, on which we can get

19 Baxter adds, 'I enclose a poem along these lines.' The enclosure has not survived, but the poem was probably 'The Titan' (1963–66, *CP* 372), with its description of the 'others', faceless and inaudible, who 'gather / To share the Titan's blood with us'.

in touch with our ancestors and with common humanity as a whole. These are the 'green-boned ancestors' with whom Horse communes while under the influence of Dionysus-Hades. To communicate with them on the unconscious level is to relearn the 'secret language / That dead men speak and we have long forgotten' ('The Cave'). Baxter's poetic faith in the creative power of the unconscious mind thus becomes allied to his kenotic longing to submerge his individual self in a collective and tribal one, becoming part of 'that community of the living and the dead which I have looked for all my life' ('Education', *MH* 154). It is this longing for community which draws him, towards the end of his life, towards the Maori world, which (as he says in 'Tangi', 1967, *CP* 400) has the understanding and peace which can only come when 'death is accepted // As the centre of life'.

Mother Persephone

When Baxter uses the classical underworld as a way of talking directly about death (rather than as a metaphor for life), the figure he gravitates towards is the death goddess, Persephone or Proserpina, rather than her husband, Hades/Pluto. Baxter's Pluto—like the classical god himself, whose most iconic attribute was a helmet of invisibility—is a shadowy figure. He makes only a few memorable appearances: as a darkly threatening presence in 'Thoughts of a Remuera Housewife'—the 'rough king' ruling over his 'iron-black star'; as an undignified comic butt in the carnivalesque *Runaway Wife*; as the embodiment of Thanatos, in a striking sentence from 'Notes on the Education of a New Zealand Poet': 'When Venus leaves us to ourselves, her uncle Hades enters the door of the heart' (*MH* 154). But it is the feminine figure who has the greater imaginative appeal for Baxter: he thinks of the pagan land of death as 'the dark house of Persephone' (letter 22 April 1964, FM 22/4/4).

This is partly perhaps because Persephone has the doubleness characteristic of Baxter's mythological images. It is captured in an ambiguous phrase in 'The Cave': 'the sunless kingdom / Where souls endure the ache of Proserpine'. Is 'the ache of Proserpine' something which she actively inflicts on the souls of the dead, or something which she suffers along with them? Persephone may be seen either as a grim and terrible embodiment of death, or as a sympathetic victim of it. The story of the rape or abduction of the young spring goddess by Pluto and her confinement in the underworld makes her a mythic counterpart to our human experience of death, though her partial escape and her seasonal passage between the lower and upper worlds may set her apart from us. O'Sullivan, as we have seen, identifies the Persephone myth, with its pattern of 'separation, death and return', as Baxter's central mythic archetype and the point where his classical myth most obviously fuses with his Christianity (*Baxter* 9–10). Certainly Baxter repeatedly returns to Persephone's story, though the thematic focus, and in particular the importance of the 'return' motif, varies greatly from poem to poem.

'Persephone' (N14.932), written around 1945–47, treats the myth quite conventionally: 'Lament then for the young Persephone / Borne down in darkness and captivity.' The young Baxter associates the winter that follows the goddess's departure with the wartime world of 'pain and anger', and offers no hope of return: 'Nor shall we see her like on earth again.' The contemporary 'Resurrection' (*CS* 32–35), on the other hand, explicitly associates Persephone's resurrection with Christ's:

> O Christ, as from the crucificial tomb
> Come thou; with pale Persephone come
> The bread of blessing in thy healing hand.
> Make new with leaf and fruit
> A green land.

Christ's bread of life resonates with Persephone's role as daughter of the corn goddess Demeter, and both are seen as bringers of new life to a blighted world.

The same dichotomy between despair and hope appears in two poems of the 1960s which draw on the image of Persephone as 'fallen woman'. In 'Thoughts of a Remuera Housewife', as we have seen, the underworld is associated with the paralysis of despair, and there is no hint of escape, though there is a certain tragic dignity in the speaker's acceptance of her world of 'chaos and the grave'. But the unpublished poem 'The Red-Haired Girl' (c.1962,

N23.45), again associating Persephone with Christ, unexpectedly turns the fallen woman into a potentially redemptive figure. The red-haired girl is a prostitute, admired for her grace and courage: 'that wheat-red, urn-bright beauty tossed / On the wild bull's horns, is lost / Like Demeter's child among the dead.' She is urged to turn to Christ ('fly to the font'); but at the same time is herself compared to Christ:

> The bouncer and the cop,
> Blind undertakers, soldiers at the tomb,
> Did not bring sponges for her thirst; to be
> Our tree of life, a walking Christmas tree
> With lights and bells.

The echo of the derisive catch-phrase 'all dressed up like a Christmas tree' does not entirely counteract the positive implications of 'our tree of life'. Prostitution is to true love as the commercial Christmas tree is to the Cross, but the allusion to Persephone suggests that the prostitute's likeness to the suffering and resurrected Christ is not merely parodic.[20]

Baxter's interest in Persephone as a death goddess, however, is not primarily in her seasonal descent and return, nor in her role as the fallen virgin-turned-whore. More fundamentally, she is tied in to a complex of associations linking the female, motherhood, nature and death. She is one of many goddess-figures in his work who embody both earth and death—images of the universal earth mother who is the womb and tomb of all. Inevitably, this mother goddess is regarded both with desire and with dread. The primordial earth goddess Gea is almost always, for Baxter, a benign Mother Nature, offering support and comfort to humans alienated from modern culture. He imagines himself lying on her breast, 'the broad nurse / who bears with me' ('At Day's Bay', *CP* 308–09), and finding truth, rest and peace in her

20 Goulter (91) also plausibly identifies 'The Girl in the Bookshop' (1967, *CP* 386) as a version of the Persephone/Hades myth. In this bleaker version the girl, again potentially a figure of life and creative destruction ('she has need of / A lover made of bread and gelignite'), is condemned by society to a sterile half-life—'We have given her over to Winter, / Riding her way on a horse of wind and ice', who will 'carry her into the deep caves / Of that security we also die in'.

'changing and austere / testament of sand' ('At Aramoana', *CP* 336–37). The latter poem, as Baxter points out in his explication in 'Conversation with an Ancestor' (*MH* 25), identifies Gea as a life figure ('the symbolic ground of existence'), and contrasts her with the death and transfiguration symbolised by the ocean and associated with God the Father. Other versions of the mother goddess are darker and deadlier: for instance, Cybele, with her 'cancered breast' ('Letter to Australia', *CP* 151), '[w]hose gate of love is an open grave' ('Reflections at Khandallah Baths', *CP* 288), or 'the ferocious Earth our mother whose vulvae are a million graves' ('Kiwi Habits'). These are devouring mothers closely akin to the demonic female figures discussed in chapter 4. Persephone's mother Demeter partakes of both benign and terrible aspects: in 'The Matriarch' (*CP* 217) she is an 'elemental, ancient power' wielding 'uprooted pines'; but in 'Skull Hill' (*CP* 275), which draws on the imagery of the ancient mysteries of Eleusis, she is a figure of archaic female wisdom whose 'laws' teach us 'how to die'.

Chthonic goddesses from non-classical mythologies fulfil similar roles for Baxter. In 'Ballad of One Tree Hill' (1963–64, *CP* 293–96), death is not the house of Persephone but 'the house of Hella', the Norse goddess of the underworld. The Maori Hine-nui-te-po is an even closer analogue to Persephone, a beautiful maiden who became a dark underworld goddess after a sexual violation (unknowing incest with her father Tane). Mr Grummet in *Horse* associates female sexuality with Hine-nui-te-po: 'The death goddess. The sacred earth. Maui entered her gate. It closed upon him' (93); and 'East Coast Journey' (1962–63, *CP* 273) restates Baxter's aphorism about Venus and her uncle Hades in terms of Maori myth (and in death-imagery of the sea rather than the earth):

> As a man
> Grows older he does not want beer, bread, or the prancing flesh,
> But the arms of the eater of life, Hine-nui-te-po,
> With teeth of obsidian and hair like kelp
> Flashing and glimmering at the edge of the horizon.

In the 1970s the role (shorn of its sexualised aspects) comes to be filled by Te Whaea, the Maori version of the Virgin Mary. Baxter's punning line about Gea in 'At Day's Bay' is reworked in the 1971 'Night Clouds' (*CP* 505):

> Night, cold and memory
> Are his instructors, teaching him how to let go of life,
> Accepting the dark unknowable breast
> Of Te Whaea, the One who bears us and bears with us.

We can trace in Baxter an unbroken continuum of mother earth/ death figures, cruel or benign, stretching from Gea and Persephone to Hine-nui-te-po and Te Whaea.

Persephone as death goddess appears most strikingly in *The Temptations of Oedipus.* When the director Patric Carey first suggested to Baxter that he adapt Sophocles' *Oedipus at Colonus,* Baxter refused: 'I'm not going to touch that one. Sophocles was ninety when he wrote it, and he was dying. [. . .] I'll come back to it when I'm old.' He took the proposal up in 1968, just before leaving for Jerusalem, announcing, 'I'm ready to do it now because it's my last play' (Carey quoted in Harcourt 130). Written not when he was dying but at a moment when he was about to renounce the world, *The Temptations of Oedipus* feels very like Baxter's final summing-up, in the form of a classical myth, of the human relationship with death.

The action of the play is Oedipus's movement towards death, which he imagines in the opening speeches as 'the ice-cold region of Persephone' (*CPlays* 232). Unattractive as this image initially sounds, Persephone soon emerges as a benign embodiment of death, which is seen as return to the womb of the earth mother. Oedipus looks forward to it as a kenotic loss of individual identity: 'I will become what I am—not Oedipus—no longer Oedipus. I will be what I am—the dead peaceful child who lies always at the breast of Queen Persephone' (233). Echoing Sophocles' famously bleak choric lines—'the greatest boon is not to be; / But, life begun, soonest to end is best' (*OC* lines 1224–25)—he argues that it is a consummation devoutly to be wished: 'To be—that is the calamity. Your dreams tell you this, but you ignore your dreams. In your dreams you desire death—you desire not to be' (233).

Oedipus again invokes Persephone as loving earth mother

when he promises Theseus that his buried body will be Athens' secret weapon, drawing invading soldiers to death:

> my bones under the soil of Athens will attract each corpuscle in their veins; they will want to sleep—they will let their shields drop—they will want to be united with the roots of corn in the fields they march over. They will hear the voice of Persephone calling, 'Little children, it is time to sleep!' (246)

The passage is harsher in Sophocles' play, where Oedipus exults that 'my cold body in its secret sleep / Shall drink hot blood' (*OC* lines 622–23); Baxter's Oedipus, after using the same image, disclaims its cruelty ('Not as a vampire, no') and adds the comforting image of a mother calling children home to bed. A curse becomes an image of peaceful return to the ancestral earth. Similarly, where Sophocles' Oedipus cursed his son Polyneices to 'the Father of Darkness and the bottomless pit' (*OC* lines 1389–90),[21] Baxter's Oedipus prays to 'Mother Persephone' to 'grant [him] whatever peace you can give' (254).

Set against Mother Persephone are the Furies. Oedipus invokes them together at the start of the play, linking 'the ice-cold region of Persephone' and 'the power of the Furies' as elements of the human condition from which he—or any man—cannot be delivered (232). Given the close association of the Furies with the underworld, we might read these simply as two different images for death. In fact Baxter's symbolism, though hard to interpret, appears to work differently.[22] The Furies are, as Oedipus calls them, 'daughters of Chaos' (260); and the chaos that they emerge from and embody is, as usual in Baxter, not literally an aspect of death but of life. Here they represent the pain, fear, guilt and misery which are intrinsic to human life in this world, which in fact define human existence and human nature: man is '[a] creature made of chaos' (232). The Furies could thus be seen as a pagan image of

21 More literally, 'the hateful paternal darkness of Tartarus' (Loeb translation).

22 The problem of interpretation is not helped by Baxter's rather irritating trick in this play of allowing statements to trail off in ellipsis, leaving the key word unspoken—e.g. 'The pure light that blazes on [the Furies'] foreheads is our deliverance from . . .' [meaninglessness? futility?]; 'The fire that eats at my soul is inextinguishable except by . . .' [death?] (237).

the Christian concept of original sin. The suffering they inflict does serve the purpose of confirming in us a sense of our own personal identity: 'To be punished is to be confirmed in existence' (237). They can only torment us, however, so long as we are tied to this world.[23] Oedipus, contemplating his self-abnegating retreat to the breast of Persephone, is able to dismiss at once selfhood, world and chaos: 'If chaos came out of nothing, and the world out of chaos—it does not matter. I am no longer Oedipus' (233). His struggle throughout the play is to maintain this absoluteness for death, to overcome the ties—the 'temptations' of the title—which bind him to life, of which the most important is his and Antigone's child. Theseus's ruthless killing of the child, sending it as a messenger to 'Persephone, Queen of the Underworld', breaks that last tie, prompting Oedipus's furious renunciation of life and of 'the power of the Furies' (already quoted in chapter 4):

> Old, foul nurses—daughters of Chaos—now I feel the grip of your teeth! [. . .] Old hags! I deny you. I give you no more worship. Feed on the living. All men belong to you. What is there left in me for you to take? Now the parricide will die—the incestuous son—incestuous father—he will marry the Earth. You have lost your power. (260)

In the end Oedipus 'marries the Earth' in a very literal sense, physically descending into a chasm in the ground to be absorbed into Persephone's sunless kingdom.[24]

There is a risk of making the treatment of death in *The Temptations of Oedipus* sound too cosy, playing down the intense bitterness of many of Oedipus's speeches and the despair of his final exit (very different from the uncanny serenity of Sophocles' hero). Nevertheless, Oedipus's bitterness is primarily directed towards the horrors of life; death is consistently imagined as peaceful sleep in the quiet earth.

The idea of death as a return to mother earth and an absorption into the seasonal processes of nature recurs throughout Baxter's work: for instance, in 'Poem in Naseby Graveyard' (1946, *CP*

23 Compare the Buddhist concept in 'Pig Island Letters' 12 (*CP* 283–84): 'Our loves have tied us to the wheel / From which it is death to be unbound.'

24 Jane Kruz's MA thesis was helpful in developing this reading of the play.

48–49)—'Within this green enclosure lie / The seed of earth's tranquillity'; or in 'The Hollow Place' (1962, *CP* 251–52), with its vision of the aged poet knocking on the ground and crying 'Open, mother. Open. Let me in.'[25] It harmonises with Baxter's sympathy for the Greek or Maori 'tribal' vision of death as return to the ancestors; and the idea of individual identity merging into the collective identity of the tribe, of common humanity. The classical and mythological images of death in the earlier poems are entirely in tune with the Maori imagery of a late poem like 'He Waiata mo taku Tangi' (1971, *CP* 505–13), where the house of Persephone has become 'Te Whiro's hut / whose doors are made of stone', and he hopes that his soul will rest in 'the place / where the Maori corn grows green'.

This view of death is not (explicitly) Christian. Though it would be foolish to deny the profound seriousness of Baxter's Catholic faith, his imaginative vision of what comes after death tends to be expressed in pagan rather than Christian terms. It is striking how seldom he refers to the traditional Christian visions of the afterlife. The word 'heaven', in Baxter, almost always refers either to the physical sky, or to the imagined abode of God, the Virgin and the saints, rather than to the destination of the souls of the blessed after death. When he does talk about a heavenly afterlife, he tends to be ventriloquising the views of traditional Christians like the 'Dying Calvinist' (1950, *CP* 94–95); or imagining it in Maori imagery, as in 'the hot springs of Heaven' in 'Winter Monologue' (1971, *CP* 495–96); or both, as in the delightful vision of Mother Mary Aubert playing scrabble with the Pope in 'the Maori Heaven' ('Letter to Eugene O'Sullivan', 1970, *CP* 489–91). The earth, the sea and the tribe are much more real to Baxter than the church's heaven. Despite his Christian faith, he, like the ancient Greeks and Romans, ultimately treats death as something that happens and matters in *this* world.

25 An echo of the old man in Chaucer's 'Pardoner's Tale': 'And on the ground, which is my moodres gate, / I knokke with my staf, both erly and late, / And seye "Leeve mooder, leet me in!"' (729–31).

CHAPTER 9

CONCLUSION

> And who will walk in Cressid's gown?
> And who will bend Ulysses' bow?
> Who'll pluck the golden apples down?
> I do not know. I do not know.
>
> ('Threnos', 1956)

This book was modestly conceived, on the basis of our reading of Baxter's published work, as a general guide to the strand of classical myth that snakes in and around his poetry, and an opportunity to illuminate some of his more obscure and unusual usage. These unassuming origins reflected our sense that we were producing a work of specialist criticism, its utility limited to a sprinkling of classicists and literature scholars. Later, as our findings grew, we came to believe that there would also be appeal in such a study for students of Baxter and for informed general readers. However, we were well aware from the beginning of the project of the general critical ambivalence towards Baxter's myth-themed poems, which we outline in chapter 1. While *we* found such poems fascinating, our initially modest approach to studying them was influenced by such sceptical criticism. The general view that Baxter's early myth-inspired poetry was an affectation, which evolved into something more essential and original, is vividly summed up by Gregory O'Brien:

> the Western literary canon was the young Baxter's 'Hollywood', with its studio/workshop crammed full of devices, special effects and virtuosic techniques. The difference is that this phantasmagoria of beasts and mythical figures, arcane symbols and heightened language—Baxter's 'special effects'—only serve to *remove* the production from its audience (or so it feels in the

> present era). [. . .] However, as any reading through the *Collected Poems* makes clear, the quarter century of poetic output that followed [. . .] could be considered a triumphant exercise in the removal of such effects, a reduction to essence.
>
> (O'Brien, 'No Dream But Life' 108)

Our expectation was that the substantial strand of early classical myth poems would thin, at times break, and eventually interweave with Christian belief and Maori tikanga to produce a more twentieth-century, New Zealand-sourced kit of mythic themes. However, as the preceding chapters and the following Who's Who demonstrate, this isn't what we discovered. Baxter's resort to classical myth remained strong and complex to the end of his life. The thing we least expected was that this study would suggest a new way of thinking about his place in New Zealand literature. But looking back at what we have learned, we now contend that a developed understanding of Baxter's relationship to classical myth accounts in important and positive ways for his youthful Romanticism and also its various adult manifestations and permutations. Lawrence Jones anticipated this argument in 2002, in a review of *Spark to a Waiting Fuse*, when he observed that:

> The importance of this volume is that it gives us the early Baxter very fully and makes us see that he was not a 'New Zealand' poet who had unfortunate rhetorical tendencies he could not curb, not Curnow's man at all, but his own, consistent in his own terms, even maddeningly so, as he was to be for the rest of his life. The book helps us to see that he was not a poet who started well, deviated badly, and then miraculously returned to the true path (but a Modernist version of it) late in his life. Rather, by showing us that the boy was father of the middle-aged man, these letters and poems help us to see that he was all of a piece, for better or worse cut from a Romantic cloth. (Jones 28)

Baxter's problem—his cross, let's say—is that twentieth-century New Zealand literature harboured a deep suspicion of writers with Romantic 'pretensions'. As O'Brien had observed in 1993, 'Baxter's Romanticism, in all its permutations, is probably one of the reasons he isn't such a useful cog in the wheel of current literary discourse and as a result has fallen from critical favour' ('After Bathing at Baxter's' 125). Even Jones, though perceptively arguing for the fundamentally Romantic and mythic nature of Baxter's poetry, has Curnovian reservations about his 'mythological reference, [. . .] plethora of metaphor, and other rhetorical inflation' (26–27).

However, in a review of Baxter's early, myth-infused collection *Cold Spring*, John Newton set the stage for a more positive, intercessory approach to the Romantic Baxter by arguing that 'a critical intervention in favour of Baxter's youthful romanticism would promise to be a radical and unsettling event. By definition, it would have to entail a challenge to a hegemonic regime of value' (150). The present book can be read as the beginning of such an intervention: a sympathetic argument for Baxter's essential Romanticism and the central role of myth in his work. It is an intervention which hinges on recognising that Baxter's Romanticism endures beyond youthfulness, drawing its strength from Dylan Thomas and the post-WW2 Neo-Romantics, but never severing its associations with his iconic mythical poet forefathers (Blake, Byron, Shelley, Burns et al) or with classical myth itself.

One positive outcome of Baxter's Romantic and mythic cast of mind is that, unlike many of his fellow mid twentieth-century New Zealand poets, he never had to contend seriously with deracination. Where other poets searched for some outgrowth of realism to graft onto, Baxter was already deeply rooted in a rich tradition through his Romantic engagement with classical myth, bedded in youthful experience, which set him apart from the debates defining New Zealand's twentieth-century literary culture. In 1945—a year central to the Baxter myth—Allen Curnow made his eleventh-hour selection of six poems from *Beyond the Palisade* for inclusion in the landmark anthology *A Book of New Zealand Verse: 1923–45*, delivering the verdict that 'since Mason in 1923, no New Zealand poet has proved so early his power to say and his right to speak' (56). But rather than take his future direction from Curnow's criteria for New Zealand poetic success, Baxter in the same year assembled a highly Romantic, densely symbolic and mythic collection of verse, *Cold Spring*, which he considered better than his first collection but which no New Zealand publisher would contemplate. In the foreword to *Cold Spring*, he was at pains to counter the local objections to his approach by arguing that while it may seem strange to some 'that verse assumedly modern, should be rhetorical or bear any resemblance to that of the Romantic era', the collection embodied his belief 'that the root of poetry must always lie in personal emotion, and that rhetorical gestures may be a truthful and natural mode of expression for this emotion' (CS xxi). Thus he could exhort his friend Noel Ginn, around the same time, to '[r]emember WE two hold in our hands the future of N.Z. poetry, which has really not yet pierced ground' (*Spark* 277), and advance the opinion that Frank Sargeson's early stories are 'able but of a style and plotting too cut-down for this N.Z. society: Europeans have to prune their material; we have to build it up' (*Spark* 358). While neither Curnow's acolytes nor his opponents had much time for Romanticism when New Zealand poetry was being mapped by degrees of settler modernism, it was Romanticism, not classicism, which impelled the youthful Baxter towards myth, and it was Romanticism *and* myth which kept Baxter outside New Zealand literature's main camps. He never felt part of the internecine struggles dominating the local literary scene; and his ability to turn on compatriot writers, leaving a wake of aggrieved 'friends', was legend. Indeed, when the cliques and quarrels became too much, he satirically abandoned his fellow authors to their own dance:

> I couldn't stand the strain,
> So I clambered out the window and I staggered home again
> And I fell asleep a-listening to the rattle of the rain
> Not caring that our writers have water on the brain
> Or whether we've a culture to fiddle down the drain
> With a fol de rol de rolly O.
> ('The Boathouse by the Sea,' 1960, *NSP* 195–97)

There is always the risk that an 'intervention in favour of Baxter's youthful Romanticism' could be perceived as a call to shoehorn him into an acceptable narrative of New Zealand literary history. We are aware of an impulse among critics to account for Baxter, apologise for Baxter or indeed castigate Baxter for failing to cleave to some collective norm. The harder task seems to be to accept Baxter on his terms—unapologetically mythic, enduringly Romantic, and idiosyncratically religious. There is some substance to O'Brien's argument above that Baxter's final published poems 'could be considered a triumphant exercise in the removal of such effects, a reduction to essence', but let's not forget that it was in the final month of his life, when he was in poor health and living itinerantly in Auckland, that he produced his penultimate long poem, 'The Tiredness of Me and Herakles', which, with its deeply personal reflections on decades of toil, endows classical myth with an authority both autobiographical and testamentary.

In his religious practice, even more so than his unfashionable stance of Romanticism, Baxter revealed a capacity to affront believing and unbelieving friends alike. Catholic Pat Lawlor, for example, printed a small book, *The Two Baxters*, to memorialise his ambivalence, while atheist Denis Glover trenchantly refused to 'share in the beatification of Baxter' at his tangi (Taylor 125), and used the poem 'Up the River at James Baxter's Funeral' to expand his scepticism concerning the Jerusalem aims of his 'guided misguided friend' into a general critique of Baxter's inconstancy (127). In the same poem, Glover stretched back in time to finger 'The Unicorn'—a poem he knew well because his Caxton Press published it first in 1944—and by deft association to question not simply Baxter's Catholicism, but also the idealised Romanticism represented by such an important early mythic figure of the self. Glover evidently doubted Baxter's 'sea-blown wood' through which the youthful unicorn/self walks 'steadfast and alone', because in his estimation neither religion nor Romanticism 'did [Baxter] good. You saw / One at a time the sick trees. / No one can enter the whole wood' (128).

Interestingly, one of Glover's closest friends, Allen Curnow, seems to have understood Baxter's essential motivations better than many who assumed they knew him better. In March 1973, five months after Baxter's death, Curnow was also prompted by events to write a poem, 'A Refusal to Read Poems of James K. Baxter at a Performance to Honour His Memory in Cranmer Square, Christchurch'. The poem is a brilliantly balanced combination of attitudes, half-critical and half-admiring, both a tribute and a dismissal. Curnow writes:

Jim, you won't mind, will you,
if I don't come to your party?
One death is enough, I won't kill you
over again, ritually,
being only one other poet
who knew you younger and never better,
I would hardly know under which hat or which crown
to salute you now—
bays, or myrtles, or thorns,
or which of them best adorns
that grave ambiguous brow.
The quandary's mine, yours too,
Jim, isn't there always too much
we don't understand, too much that we do?
Winged words need no crutch,
and I've none for you. (*Early Days Yet* 142)

The poem may appear at first to be a gesture of residual animosity on Curnow's part for the tensions that had existed between himself and Baxter in life, but read closer, a homage of sorts emerges, seemingly based on a sophisticated understanding of Baxter's work and motivations. Despite the poem's colloquial tone it is full of classical reference. While the triple crowns sardonically suggest Baxter's self-glorifying identities, his 'grave ambiguous brow' accommodates both gravitas and intellect, indicating that although Curnow is not in any sense buying into the Baxter myth, he allows and recognises it. The most significant nod to classical myth occurs at line nine, the poem's swelling midpoint, where Curnow questions which crown—'bays, or myrtles, or thorns'—Baxter most deserves to be saluted under. This is also a question about which version of Baxter will ultimately be honoured—the prolific young poet seeking to soar near the sun, the conflicted, appetite-driven poet of middle years, or the prophet-poet striving to emulate the poverty and sacrifice of Christ. The first crown of bay laurel, with its symbolism of the pursuit of the Muse bound up in Apollo's pursuit of the nymph Daphne, has association as a prize both with games in honour of Apollo and also with poet laureates. It is the crown that would most appropriately have decorated the head of the youthful, myth-infused Baxter who, as a marvellous boy, was welcomed to the ranks of New Zealand poetry by Curnow himself. Similarly appropriate is the second crown, crafted from myrtle, which signifies the adult phase of Baxter's life through association with Venus/Aphrodite and Baxter's pursuit of carnal satisfaction. The final crown, of thorns, identifies the Jerusalem era by associating Baxter, as a type of prophet or Christ figure, with Christ's own passion and sacrifice. While Curnow views each incarnation of 'Jim' with an ironic eye, there seem to be various levels of mythical insight in his final assertion that 'Winged words need no crutch', for it might be read as an Apollonian homage to the best of Baxter via deliberate use of Homeric poetic formulae and a subtle reference to Baxter's play *The Sore-footed Man*. Then again, Curnow holds his own in any contest of ambiguity, and 'Winged words need no crutch' might equally be construed as a curt reminder of the value of quality writing in response to this couplet from 'Jerusalem Sonnets' 37:

> Colin, you can tell my words are crippled now;
> The bright coat of art He has taken away from me. (*CP* 473)

There is evidence that Baxter had some similar reservations to Curnow when it came to his poetic practice and legacy. In a letter written in June 1972, just months before his death, Baxter underscores his awareness that to invoke Arcadia is to engage with an ideal that has the dangerous allure of Siren song. His letter is a reply to a schoolgirl, Catherine Hickey, who had written to him at Jerusalem asking if he would explain to her the following lines from his 1946 poem 'The Bay':

> A thousand times an hour is torn across
> And burned for the sake of going on living.
> But I remember the bay that never was
> And stand like stone, and cannot turn away. (*CP* 45)

In June 1972 Baxter was approaching the low point of his life: his health was failing, his relationships were sundered, he doubted his spiritual and social mission, and he would soon leave the Jerusalem commune for good, moving towards Auckland and his abrupt death in October. But for a moment he put these troubles aside, and replied with a lucid explication of this well known quatrain. His explanation, while pitched at the level of a student, is sufficiently complex to substantiate arguments for the centrality of that essential tension between 'the mutable and the ideal' in his work (Weir, *Poetry* 63), and to emphasise the permanent link between Baxter's Romanticism and his mythic mode of thought. The letter has never before been published.[1]

Private Bag,
Jerusalem,
Wanganui River
16/6/72

Dear Catherine Hickey,

Thank you for your letter. I will try to help.

'A thousand times an hour is torn across
And burned for the sake of going on living . . .'

Imagine somebody tearing up a love letter or a letter from a friend and throwing it on the fire.

Meaning—these hypnotic memories of childhood joys hinder our growth and may lead us to despair, because the joys cannot be re-animated. One has to 'rip them up' and get rid of them. And one has to do this a thousand times in a lifetime.

'And I remember the bay that never was
And stand like stone and cannot turn away'—

The actual bay is water, sand etc. The 'bay that never was' is the Garden of Eden, an early paradise. It happens that the second bay is mythical.

Imagine a married woman remembering a relationship with another man (not her husband) before marriage, as something quite perfect, quite paradisal.

This image would be in her mind. She is real. The man is real. But the memory is a mythical idealisation. You see this could be a danger? She might reject a present, difficult relationship (her marriage) in favour of an imagined past, though the source of the idealisation was a real event.

1 Courtesy of Catherine Kelway, copy in possession of the authors.

> I am hypnotised by 'the bay that never was', the Earthly Paradise I never actually entered and can never actually enter. This 'backward-looking' is present in many of my poems. I think others must share it, or else they wouldn't like the poems.
>
> All good wishes,
>
> Yours,
>
> James K. Baxter

Like Curnow's poem, this letter is ambivalently balanced. Baxter explains his mythic world view without entirely endorsing it, as if backward-looking idealisation can be a danger capable of hypnotising one into disregarding present reality. His recognition of the danger of mythic idealisation was not a recent phenomenon; as far back as November 1944 he had declaimed as much in the poem 'Under the Dank Leaves' (*Spark* 501):

> I will turn from the rooks of an imagined England
> (Unrest alone she lent me); turn to the strange
> And snarling abyss of this lank land of my birth [. . .]

But given Baxter's personal situation in 1972 of loneliness and illness, his impending departure from the Jerusalem commune, the final turn of the back on his Kiwi Arcadia, it isn't hard to discover in the Catherine Hickey letter a deep undercurrent of poignancy. Perhaps he is by then more acutely conscious than ever of the dangers of his mythic method if it renders him incapable of dealing with the imperfect realities of life. The letter echoes Baxter's wry caveat in the passage in 'Notes on the Education of a New Zealand Poet' about mythologising his life: 'The trouble is, I can't demythologise it.' What his letter does is bring out the force in that word 'trouble'.

The critical disfavour that Baxter received for his Romanticism, it is worth noting, appears to have been reserved for Pakeha writers. Around the time he renamed himself 'Hemi' and headed to Hiruharama, Maori writers like Hone Tuwhare, Witi Ihimaera and Patricia Grace were beginning to produce work contrasting the urban materialism of settler society with Maori cultural and spiritual values associated with family and tribal land. Narratives like Ihimaera's *Whanau* (1974), tales of embattled Maori nurturing the embers of a customary, rural existence while the iwi unravels at the fringes through urban drift, evoke a dynamic that in traditional English literature would be inescapably Romantic—particularly if one recalls how Baxter's favourite Romantic, William Blake, juxtaposed to great rhetorical effect a pastoral ideal of 'green and pleasant lands' with contemporary England's 'dark satanic mills' to invoke a mythical Arcadia. Baxter's Arcadia, as we have seen, is usually some form of an Edenic childhood, although as he himself conceded it is no simple paradise.

What, then, is the difference between the Romanticism of a Pakeha writer like Baxter, and that of a Maori writer like Ihimaera? Authenticity is the foremost issue: unlike Maori, whose referents are foundational, pre-contact and indigenous, Baxter's Romantic and classical referents breach the historical, cultural and geographical boundaries that in mid twentieth-century New Zealand define and authenticate the settler nation. New Zealand literature of the nineteenth and early twentieth centuries accommodated a healthy vein of Romantic and mythic poetry, which the literary arbiters of settler modernity effectively silenced (in the process turning *Kowhai Gold* into a byword for the failure of authenticity). Perhaps what is most remarkable is that Baxter successfully transgresses all the embedded strictures against Romanticism and myth more thoroughly than any dozen of New Zealand's neglected Georgian poets, yet still dominates the nation's literature—a testament to uniqueness beyond mainstream reproof, and a singular kind of authenticity.

Questions of 'authenticity' inevitably arise when Baxter, in his later poetry, starts to draw on Maori mythology and symbolism. It is not in the least surprising that he should do so. One of his enduring traits was his magpie-like habit of appropriating elements from any mythology or cultural tradition that appealed to him. So his juvenilia traverses not only classical but also Norse, Egytian, Celtic, Aztec and other traditions; and thirty years on he is doing the same thing, in an almost self-mockingly offhand manner, in the eclectic multiculturalism of a late poem like 'Autumn Testament' 48, which hails a spider in a mixture of classical, Polynesian, prehistoric and European folkloric imagery. Typically, however, he borrows from any system of belief or philosophy only those elements which fit into his existing personal structures of thought, belief and literary practice. He extracts images corresponding to his own patterns, much as the Romans picked out gods from other religions that corresponded to their own deities.

Thus it was inevitable that when Baxter travelled to India in the late 1950s Hindu deities would appear in his work—but equally inevitable that the treatment would be recognisably idiosyncratic. For example, the association of 'Vishnu in his square sea chamber', from the poem 'The Carvers' (*CP* 195), with the 'flutes of love in the sea's anger' is characteristically Baxterian in its evocation of both the oceanic unconscious and the sea as the source of poetic inspiration. Similarly, the poem 'The Flame', which describes his son's room smelling 'of the incense he burns / Before the Buddha', refers back to Baxter's own adolescent fall, through an observation that this activity is 'as good a way as any / Of yoking the demons that rise at puberty, // Not demons, other selves' (*CP* 400). Nevertheless, no alternative set of gods and goddesses came close to offering Baxter the sheer range and depth of what he could draw from classical mythology. Through childhood immersion it was the system he knew by far the best, and the closest thing he had to a universal mythic language. To quote O'Sullivan again, it was the system best able to afford him an artistic relationship 'with the more permanent figures in human imagination'.

We would expect Baxter to make use of Maori mythology in the same way. In his 1952 response to Noel Hilliard (quoted in chapter 1), while defensively insisting that there was no reason why a New Zealand poet should draw on the myth of Maui rather than that of Odysseus, he also argued that Polynesian and Greek symbolism could sit side by side. And to some extent in the later poetry we can see Baxter mapping familiar figures onto Maori ones. So in 'East Coast Journey' (*CP* 273) there are echoes of Medusa and Kali in 'the eater of life, Hine-nui-te-po, // With teeth of obsidian and hair like kelp / Flashing and glimmering at the edge of the horizon'; and the image in 'Autumn Testament' 9 of the poet 'carried as a foetus / On the breast of Tangaroa' (*CP* 545) echoes 'The Rock' where he 'cannot forget / The shielding arms of a father, / Maybe Poseidon' (*CP* 362).

But such translations are used less than we might expect. It is partly just that Baxter here lacks the bone-deep familiarity that he has with classical myth; his range of Maori myth and tribal lore is comparatively shallow. A revealing manuscript poem around 1962–63, 'The Maori Education Foundation Trust' (N23.58), shows Baxter writing 'Kupe's children', then crossing out 'Kupe' to replace him with 'Tane' and then with 'Maui'—clearly, to some extent, one Maori culture hero was interchangeable with another.

There is a more crucial distinction, however: Maori mythic figures are cast as real and present, as if Baxter sees Maori mythology as a living system bedded in the now, unlike classical myth's layered traditions which can be bent and shaped to his own ends. The later Baxter employed Maori mythological figures and symbols in cautious awareness that his relationship with them was both real and symbolic. He knew his wife's close connection through whakapapapa to Parihaka, for example, and recognised the history of the passive resistance by Te Whiti o Rongomai and Parihaka's people as an account at once real and mythical, with striking similarities to his own father's narrative of pacifist tribulation. Similarly, in the Jerusalem poetry the local taniwha inhabits the world as literally as any of Hiruharama's human inhabitants: 'the dark one rises to the light, / The taniwha who guards the tribal paddock // And saves men from drowning' ('Sestina of the River Road', *CP* 590). In this poetry there is a recognition that for Maori, myth belongs to a cultural present, and that Baxter's position is that of an outsider looking in, necessarily circumspect, acutely aware of the boundaries of his knowledge, and never as comfortable with Maori myth as he is with his classical referents. Ultimately, it is Maori themselves who move Baxter's imagination; as if through the experience of the tangi and relationships with tangata whenua he is being led to an understanding of the mythic that isn't Romantic or classically distanced:

And I knew for the first time the meaning of
The yellow woven tukutuku panels,
The shark's tooth, the flounder, the tears of the albatross,
Understandable only when death is accepted

As the centre of life—The opening of a million doors!
The rush of canoes that carry through breaking waves
The dead and the living! ('Tangi', *CP* 400)

In important respects, Baxter's relation to Christian symbolism is similar to his relationship to Maori mythic symbolism. The surprising thing about Baxter's Christianity is the extent to which it is immune from mythologising. The central figures of his Christian faith—God the Father, Christ, Mary—are not symbols but real presences who cannot be made to stand for anything other than themselves. If anything, they are treated more like family members; and just as Baxter has ambivalent relationships with the real people in his own life—his wife, his mother, his children and friends—so he has ambivalent relationships with God and Christ; accepting, for example, 'God's bribe, / To be content with not being dead, / His singing eunuch' (*CP* 421), and striving to love a Christ who is 'my peace, my terror, my joy, my sorrow, my life, my death, but not my security' (*JD* 15). Where he identifies most closely with the central figures of Christianity, it is almost on a literal level, as when he compares himself with Jesus: 'A family man who never lifted a sword, / An only son with a difficult mother' (*CP* 555). Baxter's associations between Christian and classical 'myth' are thus much more circumscribed than one might expect. When he portrays Prometheus or Hercules as Christ figures, he is drawing on very traditional Christian associations rather than evolving such connections out of his personal mythology. The Christian figure who comes closest to being treated as a mythic archetype is Mary, who as the positive side of the feminine takes a slightly uneasy place on his continuum of female mythic figures. Thus in 'Traveller's Litany' and 'In Fires of No Return' she is linked to Venus (CP 139, 165) and to Isis and Semele, the mother of Dionysus (*CP* 143); and in the Maori form of Te Whaea she becomes a new and more benevolent version of Diana the moon goddesss ('The Moon and the Chestnut Tree', *CP* 496–98).

One poem which suggests what might have been possible had Baxter wished to deal equivalently with Christian, Maori and classical figures is 'Autumn Testament' 10, which is a rare linking of Christ, through the symbolism of his passion faded and eroded by time, with Odysseus declining into domesticity and Maui dying in an inversion of birth, a startling example of being consumed by 'our mother the grave':

The mossgrown haloed cross that crowns this church
Is too bleak for the mind of old Odysseus

Coming home to his table of rock, surviving and not surviving
Storms, words, axes, and the fingers of women,

Or the mind of Maui, who climbed inside the body
Of his ancestress and died there.

But the poem doesn't end here, for when those 'who ride up river /In cars or the jetboat, see that high cross lifted / Above the low roofs of Jerusalem', they relate what they see to the first mythic figure of Jerusalem, 'And speak of Mother Aubert and the Catholic Mission'.

The Jerusalem myth of Mother Aubert links inevitably to the Jerusalem myth of Baxter. In the end it seems that identification as a mythic figure was something Baxter both sought and recoiled from, much as his adolescent self desired and rejected 'the empty lion-skin' of popular success as a poet (*CP* 27). Our focus on Baxter's use of classical myth places the exploration of the complex subject of his own self-mythologisation beyond the scope of this book. Nor have we the space to examine his extensive mythologisation (and demythologisation) by others. But Baxter's sense of himself as a mythic figure has its roots in his tendency to mythologise others in his life, first and most notably his father Archie. It is in this relationship that the full poignancy of Baxter's idealising tendencies are realised, because of the implication that the man he mythologised and venerated might be a figure from an imagined past, though the source of the idealisation was a real childhood.

Baxter's childhood veneration of Archie is reflected many years later in his description in 'Autumn Testament' 14 of his father's portrait as 'an ikon' (*CP* 547). But in Baxter's poetry 'ikon' is a word with dangerous connotations. In 'Before the Battle' he describes the loss of 'those early ikons, / The selves we wore when young' as a sort of secular kenosis, an emptying of the individual's humanity (*CP* 402). He elaborates on this in 'The Ikons' (*CP* 499), describing 'the fist of longing [which] / Punches my heart':

> Since the great ikons fell down,
> God, Mary, home, sex, poetry,
>
> Whatever one uses as a bridge
> To cross the river that only has one beach,
>
> And even one's name is a way of saying—
> 'This gap inside a coat' [. . .]

Baxter's attitude to icons hasn't always been picked up in Baxter iconography. One example of this, which gestures to the complexity of the Baxter myth in New Zealand culture, would be Nigel Brown's triptych *Poet 3 Times*—almost literally an icon, with Baxter placed in the central position where one would expect to find Christ or the Virgin (Miles, 'Baxter as Icon'). Brown's iconography challenges us to decide where we each locate Baxter on the spectrum running from the prophet, guru and saint through to the 'gap inside the coat'.

Such a decision is not for this book to make. It is down to the individual to decide whether Baxter is prophet or poseur, a marvellous poetic talent or as relevant to the history of New Zealand literature as the moa. What is not in doubt—and what we believe this book has established—is the centrality of mythology, in particular classical mythology, to his work. Baxter employs characteristically mythic terms when he sums up his peculiar position in New Zealand literature in the unpublished poem 'Threnos' (1956, N18.31), wondering in Seussian rhyme who in New Zealand's future might be capable of donning his distinctive mythic mantle.

> Reached, after Heraklean search,
> The serpent-kept Hesperides . . .
> We found a swamp, a wooden church
> And Maori women felling trees.
>
> I do not want to live in Nice;
> I do not love the London smog.
> I'll take a tram, and die at peace
> And fertilize a Southland bog.

But in the warrens of the State
My ferret soul will live and lurk
To snicker and intimidate
Good rabbits pattering plump to work.

Because this land is dully kind
And dully right and dully pure;
Because fat rabbits do not mind
The dull stench of their own manure.

And who will walk in Cressid's gown?
And who will bend Ulysses' bow?
Who'll pluck the golden apples down?
I do not know. I do not know.

FLIGHT OF LAMENTATION

A MYTHOLOGICAL WHO'S WHO IN BAXTER

This final section is an encyclopedic catalogue of every character or story from classical myth mentioned in Baxter's work. It thus extends the book's coverage to a number of myths which have so far been only briefly discussed or entirely passed over, some of which are potentially just as interesting as our major case studies (see, for instance, DIANA, EROS, JASON, ORPHEUS and TROY). It also contains some entries which fall only marginally into the category of 'classical mythology' (e.g. ATLANTIS, CAESAR), and one or two which are interesting simply for the fact that Baxter does *not* refer to them (e.g. ACHILLES). Each entry includes a brief summary of the 'facts' of the story, a complete list of Baxter's references to it (at least that is our intention, though inevitably some allusions will have slipped through our net), and some succinct interpretive comment. Entries are alphabetised under whichever version of the character's name, Greek or Latin, Baxter most often uses—hence VENUS (not Aphrodite), DIONYSUS (not Bacchus); alternative names are cross-referenced.

Our summaries of the myths are brief, and focused on the story as Baxter knows it and the aspects he is most interested in. For more detailed accounts of the myths as the Greeks and Romans knew them, readers should consult a dictionary of classical mythology such as those of Grimal or March; for explorations of their original Greek contexts and meanings, see Kirk, Kerényi, Burkert, Gantz or Buxton; for post-classical traditions of interpretation, see Brumble.

Absyrtus Younger brother of MEDEA, killed by her when she and JASON were fleeing from Colchis. According to the more spectacular account, she threw his dismembered body from the

Argo to delay her father's pursuing ships. Baxter refers to the story in 'For those who lie with crooked limbs in the straight grave' (1944, *Spark* 368–70): 'Young Absyrtus dead / In the blue seaway, drowned and floating head: / With him the Spring rots livid, unfulfilled.' See also MEDEA.

Acheron A river or lake in the underworld (see HADES), sometimes seen as marking the border between the worlds of life and death (though the river STYX more usually has this function). Baxter uses it as a signifier of death in 'Her Dream' ('Cressida' 14, 1951, *CP* 109–10): '*This doom he bears who passes Acheron.*'

Achilles The greatest Greek hero of the Trojan War, protagonist of Homer's *Iliad*; the archetype of the brilliant, glory-seeking, doomed warrior hero. Baxter's lack of interest in such figures is suggested by the fact that he never refers to Achilles except for a casual use of the cliché 'Achilles heel' (*FC* 30).

Actaeon A young hunter who stumbled on DIANA (Artemis) bathing naked with her nymphs in a forest spring; the angry goddess turned him into a stag, and he was hunted to death by his own hounds. (See Ovid's *Metamorphoses*, book 3.) In his reading of Robert Burns' 'Tam o' Shanter' in 'The Man on the Horse' (*MH* 118), Baxter uses this as an analogy for Tam's encounter with the young witch; both Diana and the witch are figures of the anima, a figure vital to the poet's imaginative life but terrifyingly destructive if approached in the wrong way.

Adonis A handsome youth who became the lover of VENUS (Aphrodite); a byword for male beauty (as in Odysseus's conventional disclaimer, 'I'm no Adonis': *CPlays* 153). After going hunting against Venus's urging he was fatally gored in the groin by a wild boar. In 'A Poem to Read Before Sleep' (c.1961, N22.57) he embodies the irresistible power of sexual desire: 'Yet since no man can set aside / The Adonis-yoke of lust and pride, / My randy spirit at your bedside / Will rise up just the same.' Immediately after this Baxter travesties the myth in the bawdy 'Ballad of the Venus Man-o'-War' (N22.59), where the young lover Willy has an unfortunate encounter not with a boar but with a stinging jellyfish: 'Like young Adonis, strong, devout, /

He sported with his Venus— / Then suddenly he staggered out / Gripping his naked penis.' Baxter's most striking use of the myth is in 'Kiwi Habits (II)' where he uses it to characterise Rex (A.R.D.) Fairburn, suggesting that he 'was when young the doomed Adonis who courted the goddess Venus and was wounded by the wild boar Reality, and [. . .] his poems were the blood that fell from the wound and turned into flowers'.

Aeneas Trojan hero, son of the goddess VENUS and ANCHISES; a minor character in Homer's *Iliad* but the protagonist of Virgil's Roman sequel epic, *Aeneid*. After the Greek destruction of TROY, he is charged by the gods to lead the survivors to Italy and found a city which will be the ancestor of Rome. Characterised by Virgil as *pius*, 'dutiful', Aeneas carries out his duty to gods, nation, family and descendants, renouncing his personal desires which include a tragically aborted love affair with DIDO queen of Carthage. Baxter's 'Aeneas' (1943, *CS* 3; revised version, N15.46), presents him as a kind of anti-ODYSSEUS, a reluctant voyager who yearns for domesticity: 'Aeneas, the astute and priggish, driven / By half-loved duty on the seas of fame / Longed to forsake that fate but faltered, craven, / Fearing the wrath of gods or the after-fame.' Baxter has, as he notes in a letter to Ginn (25 Feb. 1944, *Spark* 332–33), 'humanized or de-humanized [the picture] a bit as I always do'—in this case by tracing Aeneas's problem to an unresolved Oedipal relationship with his eternally beautiful goddess mother.

Aeolus God of the winds, who keeps them imprisoned in a mountain cave on his island of Aeolia, and releases them as required; hence 'Aeolian' as an adjective for wind, as in the 'Aeolian harp' beloved of the Romantic poets. Baxter describes 'pale Aeolus' smiting the mountain to release the winds in an early poem, 'In Flames Politic' (c.1943, N10.603). In the misogynistic 'A Clapper to Keep off Crows' (1959, *CP* 202–03), to attempt to understand women is as futile as to 'cage the wind / In strong Aeolian mountain'. The image is used mock-heroically in 'The Old Earth Closet' (1954–65, *CP* 322–23), where Baxter describes how as a boy he would come to 'that seat of refuge' to meditate and 'hear / Aeolian voices hum / In the cave of the Delphic oracle, / Till my backside was numb'.

Ajax The biggest and strongest of the Greek heroes in the Trojan War, noted for his huge shield made from seven oxhides. His death is dramatised in Sophocles' *Ajax*: after losing to ODYSSEUS in a contest for the arms of the dead Achilles, he went mad with rage and slaughtered a flock of sheep, thinking they were the Greek generals, then killed himself in shame. In *The Sore-footed Man* Odysseus calls him 'that brave, mutton-headed butcher', and cites his fate as a warning to Neoptolemus against the dangers of being 'absolutely candid' (*CPlays* 132–33).

Amazons A legendary tribe of matriarchal warrior women dwelling somewhere in the wild regions to the north of Greece. Their name is said to come from the Greek for 'breastless'; as Baxter puts it in 'The Tiredness of Me and Herakles', (1972, *CP* 595–97), stanza 4, 'They cut one breast off to draw back the bowstring, / The other breast they keep to feed their children' (only female children—male ones were disposed of). Heroes, including HERCULES and THESEUS, were said to have fought and defeated these women, who are the embodiment of Greco-Roman fears of unconstrained female power. One of Hercules' Twelve Labours was to capture the girdle or belt of the Amazon queen HIPPOLYTA.

Baxter's references to Amazons reflect his response to the feminism of the late 1960s and early 1970s. In 'The Tiredness of Me and Herakles' the Amazons are outspoken women's liberationists who denounce Herakles/Baxter as 'Pornographer!'; but Hippolyta 'grew amorous / After defeat. I did not like her. / She smelt of dexedrine and cabbage water.' Baxter describes how the 'breast' lines quoted above came to him in sleep: 'my subconscious mind had delivered me a code message about Women's Lib' ('Some Comments on Women's Liberation'). In an undated letter to Weir (FM 20/4/17) Baxter suggests that, after emancipation, women 'feel obliged to become Hippolytas or Venuses instead of Marys—and may end by being neither.'

Amphitrite A sea goddess, wife of POSEIDON (Neptune). In

'Kelp' (1966, *CP* 343) Baxter associates floating seaweed with 'the unplaited / Hair of Amphitrite', as well as (more sinisterly and characteristically) with 'The dark locks of the dread Medusa' (see GORGON).

Anchises Father of AENEAS by the goddess VENUS (Aphrodite). The Homeric *Hymn to Aphrodite* relates how the goddess fell in love with the handsome young Trojan, came to him in the farmhouse in the fields where he grazed his cattle, made love with him, and then revealed her true identity—to Anchises' dismay, 'for the man who lies / with immortal goddesses is not left unharmed' (lines 189–90, trans. Athanassakis). Aphrodite tells him that she cannot make him immortal, citing the cautionary tale of TITHONUS, but she promises him the fame of their son Aeneas, and warns him never to speak of their encounter. Other versions suggest that Anchises broke his promise and was crippled as a punishment. Virgil's *Aeneid* describes how Aeneas carried the old Anchises out of burning Troy on his shoulders (book 2), and after his death visited the underworld to seek advice from his ghost (book 6).

In 'Aeneas' (1943, *CS* 3) Baxter describes 'Aged Anchises on his shoulder borne / From the red ashes of a broken city . . . / "The shrunken child; his godhead cannot return." / No reins but those of pity and self-pity.' A later version (N15.46) revises and clarifies the latter two lines: '(Mate of a goddess once—that hour cannot return / But leaves the rack of pity and self-pity.)'

The Anchises–Venus story becomes a recurring, bitter-sweet erotic image in Baxter's later work. In a semi-autobiographical story in 'Education' *(MH* 144) the protagonist, jilted by his girlfriend after a dance, imagines how 'To the hut of Anchises [Venus] came, entering to the fume of woodsmoke, and lay that night in his arms on a rough sheepskin.' In this version Anchises does suffer the fate of Tithonus: 'the Trojan shepherd drank from her embracing limbs the medicine of immortality, bitter to men. For he grew old, chewing the cud of knowledge, and when he wished for death the earth barred its gates against him. But she lived on, without remorse, for her nature was not subject to decay.' In the unpublished sestina 'The Climber' (1967, N28.9) a mountain climber in his hut experiences the 'darkly recurrent and improbable dream' that 'the earth could take the shape of a woman [. . .] / And Venus enter dull Anchises' hut, / He in the sweat and stink of selfhood lying.' Again, the encounter is fatal; the climber soon after falls to his death. The motif appears in other poems without explicit mention of Anchises, for instance 'Near Kapiti' (*CP* 302–03) or 'Ballad of John Macfarlane and the Water Woman' (*CP* 309–11)—a subverted version in which it is the supernatural temptress who dies. Ultimately, for Baxter, Anchises is a more resonant figure than Aeneas, associated with the allure and danger of the anima figure.

Andromeda An Ethiopian princess, condemned to be devoured by a sea monster after her mother had offended POSEIDON by boasting of her beauty. PERSEUS, returning from his defeat of MEDUSA, killed the monster and rescued and married the princess (see Ovid's *Metamorphoses*, book 4). In 'Perseus' (1952, *CP* 129–30), Baxter considerably muffles the drama of this story, briefly summarising Perseus's return 'To earth, Andromeda, the palace garden / Her parents bickered in' as part of his anticlimactic descent to everyday life. Later, in 'Jerusalem Journal' 3 (33) Baxter allegorises Andromeda as 'the soul of my country' threatened by 'the dragon of materialism' and defended by Baxter/Perseus (see PERSEUS for the full passage).

Antaeus A Libyan giant and a murderously invincible wrestler. The son of GEA the earth mother, he drew strength from the earth and so became stronger whenever he was thrown down; HERCULES finally defeated him by hoisting him up into the air and there crushing him to death. For Baxter he is a positive figure of closeness to nature, associated with the innocence of the garden of Eden. In 'The Giant's Grave' (1951–55, *CP* 153), the 'narrow tumulus' imagined as containing 'Antaeus' bones in the grave-mound bedded deep' is the central feature in the childhood paradise inhabited by the poet and his brother. In the unpublished prose poem 'The Dead House' (c.1947, N15.17) love-making is a way back to that paradise: 'Burying one's face in her golden hair, or caressing her childish breasts and responsive thighs, one is Antaeus, comforted by the soothing voice of Nature whose maternal arms still embrace the children she cannot save.' The idea of Antaeus's regeneration through sex is more cynically treated in a couplet bizarrely spelt backwards at the end of 'What Cannot Be Destroyed' (N14.1008); in normal order it reads, 'I win hte [*sic*] deal: you have my basdart [*sic*] maybe, / New-born Antaeus I, a bonnier baby.' In 'Pig Island Letters' 8 (1963, *CP* 281) the lost paradise is political: Antaeus is associated with the poet's father and the tradition of practical left-wing idealism that he represented, which has given way to bureaucratic state socialism: 'But he is old now in his apple garden, / And we have seen our strong Antaeus die / In the glass castle of the bureaucracies.' Other reference: 'Education', *MH* 139 ('in the morning I climbed from the grave like Antaeus').

Antigone Daughter (and half-sister) of OEDIPUS by his incestuous marriage with his mother Jocasta. In Sophocles' *Oedipus at Colonus* she is the faithful companion of her old blind father in his wanderings. In his *Antigone* she takes the protagonist role: placing family loyalty and piety before the power of the state, she defies her uncle CREON to give a proper burial to her dead brother POLYNEICES, and is put to death for it.

In *The Temptations of Oedipus* (1968), Baxter's adaptation of *Oedipus at Colonus*, Antigone is the same loving and self-denying figure as in Sophocles, but Baxter also gives her a child, conceived by incestuous union with her father in a night-time temple ceremony. It is unclear whether Antigone is genuinely unaware of the child's paternity or merely repressing her knowledge; her defensive reaction to Ismene's statement that 'You love father' (*CPlays* 248) suggests the latter. 'Antigone' (1967, *CP* 413) presents the heroine's burial of her brother as an act of self-sacrifice whose motives she does not fully understand: 'When I wake my hands grow tired of heaping up / Stones on top of stones. For whom do I make this cairn?'

Aphrodite *see* VENUS

Apollo God of light, music and poetry, prophecy (master of the DELPHIC ORACLE), healing, archery, and (in later times) of the sun (as his twin sister DIANA is of the moon). Sometimes known as Phoebus ('bright'). Depicted as a handsome, beardless young man armed with bow and arrow or with lyre, he embodies the 'classical' qualities of beauty, reason, harmonious order, and self-control.

Apollo as god of poetry is a strong presence in Baxter's juvenilia, such as the paired poems on the state of poetry in New Zealand, 'Apollo is Dead' (N3.144) and 'Apollo but Sleeps' (N4.203). In 'Song of Morning' (N2.84) he is the 'archer of song', linking sunlight and poetry. In 'I from high windows' (N5.304) 'bright Apollo glows above the clouds / Wherewith a mourning world is clad / To pierce the heart of the dragon of Truth'; the image links Apollo with Baxter's recurring symbol of the archer (e.g. in 'Rain-ploughs', *Spark* 363–64), a figure associated with Baxter's father Archie who embodies 'the power of rational life' (letter to Ginn, 3 June 1944, *Spark* 362).

The mature Baxter still occasionally pays his respects to Apollo as 'the god of art', for instance noting the 'absolute war' between Apollo and the 'kitchen god' who is the embodiment of philistine bourgeois respectability ('Virgin', *MH* 74). He invokes Apollo especially when using the satiric voice of Robert Burns: in 'A Small Ode on Mixed Flatting' (1967, *CP* 396–99), Burns swears 'Apollo! Venus! Bless my ballocks!'; and in 'Letter to Robert Burns' (1963, *CP* 289–91), Dunedin has 'an old black frost that freezes / Apollo's balls and the blood of Jesus'. Here Apollo simply represents poetry as a life-enhancing force, arrayed alongside sex (Venus) and true religion (Jesus) against grey puritanism.

More often, however, Baxter's later references to Apollo relate to Nietzsche's distinction between 'Apollonian' and 'Dionysiac' art. In 'Mask', *FA* 49, he distinguishes between the Apollonian poet who 'tries to remain unmoved and subjugate his images to a formal order', and those who 'take on a Dionysia [*sic*] persona and submerge themselves in the flux of sensation and primitive mysticism'. Baxter clearly puts himself on the Dionysiac side of this divide, against more Apollonian poets like Allen Curnow ('Symbolism', *FA* 59) or Charles Brasch (Weir interview 244). In the latter interview he argues that Catholic or Christian art is not Apollonian but Dionysiac because 'There's blood in it; you know, the wounds of the person are present in it. It's close to the Crucifixion.'

Baxter's final reference to Apollo is in 'Song for Sakyamuni' (1971, *CP* 500–02): 'My words are no longer the words of Apollo / But the river in its high gorges, life and death together, // Or the river in its shallows, mud and broken timber—'. This may be a rejection of poetry altogether; it is certainly a rejection of the Apollonian ideal of highly crafted, rationally controlled poetry.

In 'The Rubber Monkey' (1961, *CP* 237), 'Operation Phoebus' is the atomic bomb, with ironic reference to its light 'brighter than a thousand suns'.

Other references: 'The Gods of Greece' (c.1941, N3.157); 'To Hermes' (c.1941, N4.175); 'Bracchiae' (1944, *Spark* 473–74); 'Songs of the Desert', 2 (1947, *CP* 54–55); *The Temptations of Oedipus* (*CPlays* 242, 245).

Arachne A talented weaver who challenged ATHENE (Minerva) to a weaving contest and, when she lost, was turned into a spider for her presumption (see Ovid's *Metamorphoses*, book 6). Baxter, who normally finds spiders sinister, makes peace with her in 'Autumn Testament' 48 (1972, *CP* 564): 'The spider crouching on the ledge above the sink / Resembles the tantric goddess [. . .] Kehua, vampire, eight-eyed watcher / At the gate of the dead, little Arachne, I love you [. . .]'.

Ares *see* MARS

Arethusa A nymph who was pursued by the river god Alpheus, and was transformed into a spring to escape him. According to Ovid (*Metamorphoses*, book 5), Alpheus then attempted to mingle his waters with hers, but Arethusa escaped by plunging underground and re-emerging on the island of Ortygia (near Sicily). According to the second century AD travel writer Pausanias (*Description of Greece* 5.7), the river god actually flowed under the sea to reach Ortygia and mingle with Arethusa. Baxter creatively misremembers the details of the story ('Arethusa, the Greek fountain who plunged under the waves to escape or meet her lover—I forget which': 'Further Notes on New Zealand Poetry' 23), and applies it to a freshwater river which rises from the bottom of the sea at Waimarama. In an unpublished poem to his wife, 'Inscription (for Te Kare Jack)' (N24.22), this undersea river is 'A mounded water breast, a fountain, / An invisible tree whose roots cannot be found, / Younger than Arethusa [. . .] / As that wild nymph of water rises / So does your life flow into mine.' In 'Pig Island Letters' 13 (1963, *CP* 284–85) the same lines, without the explicit reference to Arethusa, are used to represent the upwelling of divine grace in man.

Argus A monster with a hundred eyes who was set by Hera to watch over IO when she was transformed into a heifer; he was lulled to sleep and killed by HERMES and his eyes were transferred to the tail of the peacock. (See Ovid, *Metamorphosis*, book 1.) The image of an 'Argus-eyed landlady' spying on young lovers occurs both in *Horse* (58) and in 'Metamorphoses' (1951, N16.36).

Ariadne A Cretan princess, daughter of King Minos, who fell in love with the captive THESEUS and gave him a ball of thread to enable him to penetrate the LABYRINTH and kill the MINOTAUR. Theseus took her with him in his escape, but abandoned her on the island of Naxos, where DIONYSUS found her and made her his immortal consort. Baxter refers to her in two unpublished poems: 'Lost in the Labyrinth no Ariadne' (c.1947, N14.1013); and 'Spring Song' (1953, *SP* 50–51), which refers to Theseus's desertion of her. Theseus regretfully recalls this past crime, or 'difficulty', in *The Temptations of Oedipus* (*CPlays* 244). For more discussion see LABYRINTH and THESEUS.

Artemis *see* DIANA

Asclepius God of healing, son of Apollo, more commonly known by his Latin name Aesculapius. Sick people would come to sleep overnight at his temple in the hope of a cure. In *The Sore-footed Man* (*CPlays* 134, 157) his sons will cure Philoctetes of his wound. More interestingly, in *The Temptations of Oedipus* (*CPlays* 247) Baxter uses his cult as an analogue for psychoanalysis:

ANTIGONE Maybe if you were psychoanalyzed. . . .
ISMENE That rubbish! The priest of Asclepius leaves you in the shrine—and then you dream a little dream, and

> you're 'all better now'—all the bad thoughts driven out. But after a day or two, when you come out, it's the same world outside the temple door—thunder, lightning, people, death—if you were actually cured you'd be a misfit.

Athene [Greek] or **Minerva** [Latin] Goddess of war, handicrafts and practical wisdom, a figure of militant intelligence, who sprang directly from the brain of ZEUS. She is depicted as a warrior goddess, with helmet and spear, and often with the *aegis*, a goatskin cape (or in some later depictions a shield) bearing the petrifying head of the GORGON. She is not a major figure in Baxter's personal mythology. Despite the prominence of Athene in the *Odyssey* as the hero's divine patroness and friend, she plays a minimal role in Baxter's many poems about ODYSSEUS, being named only to be dismissed in 'Letter to Noel Ginn' (*CP* 28): 'Nor could Minerva / Content him long'—Minerva here perhaps representing the pursuit of wisdom. Her support for him in the battle with the suitors is implied in 'Letter to Bob Lowry' (N18.39) in the line 'I see the lifted aegis glow.' In 'Perseus' (*CP* 129–30) 'the shield of art' (perhaps the aegis) is 'Athene's lovegift' to PERSEUS, returned to her at the end of the poem. Baxter's unsympathetic view of Athene comes out in a mocking reference in *Horse*: Fern, dressed for university with hair in a bun and sensible shoes, resembles no goddess but 'Pallas Athene, patroness of schoolteachers' (64).

In 'Ode MCMXLIV' (1944, *Spark* 335–38 (336)) Baxter refers to an enigmatic compound figure, 'Venus-Minerva', who seems to symbolise the quest for wisdom through sexual experience. Other reference: 'The Gods of Greece' (N3.157).

Atlantis Not exactly a part of 'classical mythology', Atlantis is first described in Plato's dialogues *Timaeus* (23–25) and *Critias*. It was supposedly a large island in the Atlantic Ocean, the site of an ancient civilisation which ruled over much of western Europe and Africa, but which was swallowed up overnight in a great cataclysm. The proportions of myth, fiction and historical fact in Plato's story have been much debated ever since. Atlantis has been connected with the paradisal Garden of the HESPERIDES, also supposed to be in the far west. The connection is made more plausible by Plato's statement that the founder-king of Atlantis was named ATLAS (though not apparently the same person as the mythical Titan).

Baxter draws on these traditional links in associating Atlantis, in several early poems, with the lost paradise of childhood. In 'Poem by the Clock Tower, Sumner' (1948, *CP* 73) the 'wild children' who still live in that lost garden are described as 'stranger than Atlanteans'. In the first version of 'Letter to Noel Ginn II' (1945, *Spark* 118–20), he identifies with those who 'remember / How first Atlantis undersea was drowned' and who know that 'the young heart is not found / Again, sea-fallen beyond sight and sound'. In the later published version (1946–48, *CP* 70–72) the Atlantis allusion is dropped, but Baxter refers to his childhood dream that he 'heard from the green water shade / The pealing of sea drowned cathedral bells'—an image which recurs in poems such as 'The Town under the Sea' (1962, *CP* 252–53), as a symbol again of the lost paradise.

In a more satiric version of the lost paradise image, in 'Notes on Being a New Zealander', Baxter compares the behaviour of New Zealanders going on pilgrimage to Britain in search of 'their mythical Victorian mother' to that of migratory birds, 'misled by an ancestral instinct', circling over the spot in mid-Atlantic where Atlantis once existed.

Other reference: 'Resurrection' (age 17, *CS* 32–35).

Atlas A TITAN, brother of PROMETHEUS. Of gigantic stature and strength (his name means 'enduring'), Atlas was condemned perpetually to hold up the sky on his shoulders. His standing-place was somewhere in the far west, near the Garden of the HESPERIDES; Ovid (*Metamorphoses* book 4) describes him as king of the western lands and owner of the golden apples (and see also ATLANTIS). He received a spell of relief when HERCULES took the sky on his shoulders while Atlas went to fetch the golden apples for him.

Atlas is an important recurring figure in Baxter's early poetry, often associated with the Garden of the Hesperides or its Christian equivalent, Eden. The association with Eden is clearest in 'The

Giant's Grave' (1951–55, *CP* 153): 'Some heavens ago, when the wind blew from a calmer / Airt [direction], and stood yet Atlas, benignant Titan, / At the winged horizon's gate, his locks of cloud unshorn, / Heaving the sky on his shoulders [. . .]'. The early and obscure 'Atlas' (c.1942, *Spark* 447–48) more darkly assoociates Atlas with the Fall of Man: 'In that same orchard steel and oaken still / Where Time's first dream dissolved to adamant rhyme / Atlas lost heart and will.' A note beneath the poem explains 'Atlas—Man bearing human destiny on his shoulders'. The image of Atlas as humankind recurs in other early poems, often with a sense of human hubris in assuming the sole burden of sustaining a godless mechanical universe: 'though power exalt us, though the stars / irk not our Atlas-shoulders; still / Klaxon and combat for our bread is given' ('Phantasmagoria of Silence', c.1942, N9.561); 'The world that we like Atlas / Upon our shoulders load / A lawful-lawless cosmos / And irredeemably dead' ('The Closed Picture', c.1943, N13.788). A syntactically cryptic sentence in the foreword to *Cold Spring* (xxii) applies the image to the contemporary poet: 'The weight of interpretation of environment [. . .] becomes a personal burden of death of the Atlas of traditional pose.'

Atlas as an Edenic figure returns in two late poems. In 'Getting Stoned on the Night Air' (1971, *CP* 519), a euphoric Auckland night prompts the reflection 'that's one way // To carry the world and its colours, to balance it / On shoulders that are immortal only because they love.' And 'The Tiredness of Me and Herakles' (1972, *CP* 595–97), stanza 3, implicitly casts Atlas as Adam/Mankind ('"Apples," he grumbled, "too many apples, / My troubles began with an apple"'), and Baxter/Herakles, taking the weight of the firmament 'on the strap-hardened shoulder / I got as a city postman long ago', as a possible analogy for Christ. For more discussion see chapter 5.

Atreus The 'house of Atreus', the ruling family of Mycenae, was one of the most bloodily ill-starred in Greek mythology, featuring in tragedies by Aeschylus, Sophocles, Euripides and Seneca. The power struggle between Atreus and his brother Thyestes culminated when Atreus killed Thyestes' children and served their flesh to him at a feast. Atreus's son Agamemnon was murdered by his wife CLYTEMNESTRA and her lover Aegisthus (Thyestes' surviving son); Agamemnon's son ORESTES avenged his father by killing his mother, and was pursued by the FURIES for that crime. Baxter several times alludes to the house of Atreus as an image of doom haunting a family or (literally) a house. In 'The Fallen House' (1950, *CP* 97–98) the melancholy surrounding his ancestors' ruined farmhouse is caused not by 'an Atridean doom that daunted / The heart with a lidness gorgon stare', but rather by the memory of 'dead joy'. In 'Martyrdom' (1961–62, *CP* 260) a peaceful but vaguely uneasy description of the poet and his family about their daily routine ends omimously with 'The house / Of Atreus glitters in the midday sun.' In 'Ancestors (I)' (1963, N24.7) the FURIES aim 'to divert / Us from knowledge of the Atridean pain / They battened on, like fleas in an old shirt, / Our fathers and their houses.'

Attis The young lover of the mother goddess CYBELE, who castrated himself (for reasons variously explained), a precedent followed in real life by the goddess's priests. Catullus's poem 63 vividly describes Attis's ecstatic madness, his bitter regret on recovering his senses, and his panicky flight when the goddess sends her sacred lion against him. Baxter imitates this in 'The Wound', poem 8 of the Catullan cycle 'Words to Lay a Strong Ghost' (1966, *CP* 360). Unlike Catullus, he relates the story explicitly to the love affair with 'PYRRHA' which is the central subject of the cycle, making Attis's suffering a metaphor for being unmanned by love: 'It is not women only / Who lose themselves in the wound of love— / When Attis ruled by Cybele / Tore out his sex with a flint knife // He became a girl. Blood fell / In flecks on the black forest soil— / So it was for me, Pyrrha, / And the wound will ache, aches now [. . .]'.

Bacchantes *or* **Maenads** Female followers of DIONYSUS (Bacchus), who would (at least in legend) take to the hills and forests to wander in ecstatic frenzy, clad in animal skins and wreathed with ivy; when enraged they would uproot trees and tear apart animals—or men, as they did to ORPHEUS and to Pentheus (in Euripides' *Bacchae*). In Baxter's 'Bacchante' (1968,

CP 417–18) the Bacchante (a female student, perhaps) entering the poet's university office embodies danger and self-abandonment breaking into a safe bourgeois life. In 'To a Spider Building in an Outdoor Lavatory' (N25.60) the spider who devours her mate is a 'Venerable Maenad'.

Bacchus *see* DIONYSUS

Bellerophon see CHIMAERA

Boreas Personification of the north wind, mentioned in 'The Dark Sun' (age 15, N4.198): 'the air / Is cold with Boreas' breath'.

Caesar Originally the family name of the Roman dictator Julius Caesar, his adopted son Augustus the first emperor, and their immediate heirs, 'Caesar' came to be the title held by all Roman emperors. Caesar is only in the most borderline sense a mythological character (Roman emperors were routinely deified, and the apotheoses of Julius and Augustus form the climax of Ovid's *Metamorphoses*), but Baxter does use the name in a quasi-mythic way. Echoing the terms of the biblical command 'Render to Caesar the things that are Caesar's, and to God the things that are God's' (Mark 12:17), he repeatedly uses 'Caesar' as a symbol of secular, state authority. Caesar is the ruler of the 'City of Man' (in Augustinian terms), and at least potentially an enemy of God: 'When Caesar claims to be a god, and establishes his power, he demands from his subordinates an absolute obedience' ('The Advantages of Not Being Educated', *Listener* 1959); but 'the final authority for a Christian is not Caesar' ('Thoughts of an Old Alligator'). Baxter's Caesar is consistently represented in the darkest terms, as tyrannical ('the whack of Caesar's whip'—'The Eccentrics', *CP* 434), warmongering ('From the black box of Caesar's heart / Rages, proclamations rise'—'Cotton Trousers', *CP* 231–32), insanely hubristic ('Caesar's mad black eye / That imitates Zeus'—'At the Grave of a War Hero', *CP* 363–64); with his 'iron crown' ('He Waiata mo taku Tangi' 3, *CP* 511–12) and 'throne of ice' ('The Benefits of a Secular Education', N20.88) he takes on satanic overtones. Baxter especially associates Caesar with the morally vacant pragmatism of bureaucracy—'Any kind of murder, / The nailing up of a Jew or desecration / Of strong maraes, to the man in Caesar's gut / Is valid because signed' ('The Bureaucrats', 1962, unpublished draft version, N22.110)—and much of his animus seems to stem from his own soul-crushing stint at School Publications in 1956–58, when 'In Wellington I did it hard / Carving stones in Caesar's graveyard' ('Ballad of Nine Jobs', 1965, *CP* 319). THESEUS in *The Temptations of Oedipus* is Baxter's most developed treatment of a Caesar-figure.

This symbolic 'Caesar' should be distinguished from Baxter's occasional, not unsympathetic references to the historical Julius Caesar: for instance, the description of an ancestor in 'The Immortals' (1959, *CP* 99) as 'that baldheaded Caesar / Playboy and general'; or an image of Caesar's assassination in 'Nocturnal on a Friday' (N20.65), 'like Caesar's ghost / Unanimously elected dead, // In the mad forum of a winter midnight'.

Calypso A beautiful nymph or minor goddess living on the paradisal island of Ogygia. (She is the daughter of ATLAS, though Baxter never makes the connection.) In Homer's *Odyssey* she keeps the shipwrecked ODYSSEUS for seven years as her lover, but her promises of immortality cannot shake his desire to return home to Ithaca, and she is finally ordered by the gods to release him. Calypso recurs in Baxter's Odysseus poems as an archetypal figure of the feminine whom the male hero must deal with. In the sonnet 'Odysseus'-1 (c.1946, *CP* 42) she and PENELOPE are the womenfolk who can never understand the hero's war-induced despair: 'What though Calypso weep / Or blind Penelope, trees guessing not the snow— / Death is more deep than love: death is my spirit now.' In 'What the Sirens Sang' (1951, N16.15), she and CIRCE are objects of 'lust' that he has outgrown: 'he had known / Calypso's cavern, Circe's bed of stone, / And wearied soon.' More complexly, a series of poems of 1957–59 ('Odysseus'-2, N19.22; 'Odysseus'-3, N19.33; 'The Old Age of Odysseus', N19.89; 'The Tempter', *CP* 205) explore the old Odysseus's memories of his time with Calypso, 'the summer nymph', and her ambiguous role as anima figure, temptress and inspiration; see chapter 6 (and Miles, 'Three Calypsos') for more detailed discussion.

Caucasus The mountain range where Prometheus was tortured; for Baxter's references, see PROMETHEUS.

Centaurs A race of creatures half-human, half-horse. (For their origin, see IXION.) They were generally seen as embodying the bestial and uncivilised tendencies in human nature, prone to drunkenness, lust and rage; heroes such as HERCULES and THESEUS fought famous battles against riotous centaurs. However, there were exceptions, notably the wise centaur Chiron, who tutored a number of the Greek heroes in their youth.

In Baxter's juvenilia the centaur is a romantically decorative image: 'silk-maned centaurs' in the clouds in 'Moonlight' (c.1941, N3.161), 'wind-centaurs' on the sea in 'Love-Lyric V' (1944, *CP* 25). In the mature poetry centaurs often connote the destructive effects of sexuality. In 'Be Happy in Bed' (1958–59, *CP* 199–200) 'The age of sex, the age of centaurs / Returns to punish after-dinner sleep.' 'An Old Man Walking' (1956, N18.48) refers to 'centaur pride, / [. . .] ass's / Hoof and whinny, lewd caresses / In the carnivorous, doomed bed'. In 'Traveller's Litany' (1954, *CP* 139–45 (140)) 'Love is indeed the centaur shirt / That burns, burns to the bone'—a reference to the shirt soaked in the blood of the centaur Nessus which caused the death of HERCULES. However, paradoxically, the centaur has quite an opposite significance in 'The Pass' (1967, *CP* 390–91), where it suggests the ideal union of horse and rider and the withering away of (hetero)sexual desire in the masculine camaraderie of a cattle drive: 'It seemed as if by the long riding, / By the dust, by the heat, the seed in our bodies had dried up / And we were turned into centaurs. No more dreams.' Other references: 'To the City of Corinth' (c.1952, N17.23); 'To My Father, Forbidding Grief' (c.1955, N17.112); 'Mask', *FA* 35—see under IXION.

Cerberus The fearsome three-headed dog which guards the entrance to HADES. In 'Henley Pub' (1961–65, *CP* 324), the adulterous traveller compares 'our sin' to 'the triple snarling grin / Of Cerberus'. Baxter explicates the allusion in 'Virgin' (*MH* 76): 'His sin [. . .] belongs to the pagan underworld, since it involves a rebellion of the natural powers. It appears to him in the shape of

Cerberus, the three-headed dog at the gate of the Greek Hades: the three heads being remorse for past evil, attachment to present evil, and dread of future evil.' 'The Descent of Orpheus' (*Landfall* 1954) gives a less serious account of the bard's encounter with the hellhound: 'Bulgy Cerberus, opening / His six jaws, begins to whine. / Rub your knuckles on his spine. / Your story, loosed from the bowstring, / Whistles in his dog's brain:— / "Meat, boy, bones and gravy!"' Other references: 'Letter from India' (c.1958, N19.101); 'Invocation at Midnight to the Blessed Virgin' (c.1962, N23.22).

Charon The ancient boatman of HADES who ferries the souls of the dead across the river STYX. Virgil gives a memorable description of him in *Aeneid* book 6 (Dryden's translation): 'A sordid god: down from his hoary chin / A length of beard descends, uncombed, unclean; / His eyes, like hollow furnances on fire; / A girdle, foul with grease, binds his obscene attire.'

Baxter has three explicit references to Charon, each interpreting the character in a distinctly different way. In 'On Dylan Thomas' (*Listener* 1954) he simply personifies death: 'Dionysus has met Charon on the bronze threshing-floor / And Charon conquered.' 'The Lady and the Boatman' (N17.88; *Meanjin* 1955) is, Baxter notes, 'an allegory of the flesh & spirit'. A boatman, described in terms similar to Virgil's Charon—'crustacean, hairy-armed, / Lobster-eyed, with a beard of verdigris'—demands that a holy nun pay him her virtue as fare to cross the river; 'meekly she pays the necessary debt / To lustful Charon,' and passes on serenely, leaving him in 'simian rage'; the moral seems to be that soul can submit to body's demands without being essentially corrupted. The most complex reference is in 'A Family Photograph 1939' (1961, *CP* 237–38): 'My brother shoots / The gap alone / Like Charon sculling in his boat / Above the squids and flounders.' Terence is negotiating the 'gap' between life and death, and his identification with Charon hints at his future entrapment in the living death of internment.

'Reflections at Lowburn Ferry' (1967, *CP* 391), without naming Charon, plays with the image of the ferry over the Styx and the custom of placing a coin under the corpse's tongue to pay the ferryman, in a wry riff on the tension between Catholicism and classical myth: 'Very likely they won't have heard / Of Good Pope John. They will ask me why / I have no obol under my tongue, / Or a cent, or a penny—unless the price has risen— / And I will float in the mud like an old sad turd.'

Charybdis *see* SCYLLA AND CHARYBDIS

Chimaera A grotesque, fire-breathing monster which was a compound of lion, goat and snake; it was killed by the hero Bellerophon (whom Baxter refers to only in passing in 'The Gods of Greece', N3.157). Its name has entered the English language to mean an imaginary fear or bogey, or simply a wild and impossible fancy. For Baxter it is a stereotypical imaginary monster: 'griffin and chimarea haunt their air' in 'The Salamander' (1943, *Spark* 240–41); in the rarefied world of the university, in 'Envoi [to "University Song"]' (1946, *CP* 52), 'oft on that enchanted green / Chimarea mates with hippogriff'. Other references: 'To a Poetry School Audience' (c.1960, N21.27); 'The World of the Creative Artist' 23.

Chryse The nymph or minor goddess of a small island of the same name, off the coast of Troy; according to Sophocles' *Philoctetes*, it was the guardian serpent of her shrine which bit PHILOCTETES when he stumbled onto her sacred ground, and so led to his being marooned on Lemnos. Baxter in *The Sore-footed Man* gives her more importance than Sophocles did: he relocates the play's action on Chryse itself rather than Lemnos, marries Philoctetes to the priestess of Chryse's shrine, and dwells on the fearful chthonic power of the goddess, which is allegorised in the final exchanges of the play: 'The serpent of the mother goddess is fear' (*CPlays* 158).

Cimmeria A legendary region of perpetual darkness, bordering on the underworld (see HADES). According to Homer it is 'the realm and region of the Men of Winter, / hidden in mist and cloud. Never the flaming / eye of Hêlios lights on those men' (*Odyssey* 11.14–16, Fitzgerald's translation). In 'The Eyes of Dis' (1962, *CP* 259–60) 'Cimmeria where the blood / Grows dull' is an image of Wellington (literally) and of the acedia of New Zealand society.

Circe A minor goddess (daughter of the sun god Helios) and a powerful enchantress, with the power to transform human beings into animals. When ODYSSEUS, in the *Odyssey*, came to her island of Aeaea, she turned his crew into pigs; but Odysseus, with divine aid, resisted her magical drugs, forced her to restore his men, and subsequently stayed for a year as her lover. The story has traditionally been moralised as an image of the power of sexual infatuation or self-indulgence to degrade men into beasts, or of the ability of wisdom and prudence to resist such degradation (Brumble 73–75).

Circe is one of Baxter's key anima figures, at once a Venus-like temptress and a devouring Gorgon-mother. In 'The Homecoming' (1952, *CP* 121) she is equated with the hero's suffocating mother PENELOPE: the mother's 'love demanding all' is what 'in Circe's hall / Drugged him'. She is associated with rock and stone, suggesting the fundamentally unforgiving nature of sexual desire: in 'What the Sirens Sang' (1951, N16.15) 'Circe's bed of stone' is one of the temptations of 'lust' that Odysseus has passed through. Her dangerous power is most explicit in 'To a Travelling Friend' (1957, *CP* 182—cf. 'To One Travelling by Sea', N19.16): 'think how Circe / Tempts, with song, then with eyes of rock. / We die with the birth-cord round the throat.' Baxter alludes more flippantly to Circe as temptress when, in 'Education', *MH* 135, he calls the girl at primary school who used to give him pies 'a large, square-built Circe'.

A different strain of imagery relates Circe's transformation of men into beasts to issues of perception, the ways in which men and women create idealised or degraded images of each other. In the early poem 'Me Also' (1944, *Spark* 334) it is Odysseus/Ulysses' disillusionment which transforms Circe: 'Circe was not to blame. Ulysses' brain changed her / From the elusive beauty, daughter-of-Sun divine; / Saw from the eyes of the beast, no, not beast but swine, / Tears running down the snout for the irretrievable vista.' Similarly in 'Beatrice' (1961, *CP* 228—earlier titled 'For a Sexual Idealist'), the lover who seeks a perfect and pure woman finds that the idealised 'image he has made' transforms him into a beast and 'Sees the swinish bristle sprout / On his rough jowl in Circe's cage.'

The Homeric story of Circe and Odysseus is also drawn upon in 'The Journey' (1952, *CP* 127), which describes the hero's journey from Circe's island to the land of the dead, and in two versions of Odysseus's encounter with ELPENOR (see that entry for details).

Clytemnestra The adulterous wife of Agamemnon, who murdered him on his return from the Trojan War (see ATREUS). Despite these murderous associations, Baxter's one reference in the poems is surprisingly sympathetic; her name is applied to the wife in a frigid marriage in 'Soliloquy of a New Zealand Husband on Holiday in Rotorua' (1961, N22.18): 'How do you bear, Clytemnestra, the nights / Of our convivial travelling zoo? / [. . .] My girl, I see you fretting, / But cannot forge the right key to unlock / Our celibate menage.' Her ghost also appears in Baxter's fragmentary play on the ORESTES story, *The Gentle Ones* (MS-0975/051).

Creon Brother of Jocasta and uncle/brother-in-law of OEDIPUS, regent of Thebes after his fall. A major character in all three plays of Sophocles' Theban trilogy. In *The Temptations of Oedipus* Baxter keeps him offstage, giving part of his dramatic role to POLYNEICES. Oedipus characterises him as a cautious politician, 'the man who walks very carefully in the middle of the road' (*CPlays* 253). Other reference: 'Choice of Belief in Modern Society', on Creon in *Antigone*.

Cressida A Trojan lady who became the lover of the young prince Troilus; they were separated when she was forced to leave Troy for the Greek camp (to which her father, the prophet Calchas, had defected), and she subsequently betrayed Troilus by becoming the lover of the Greek Diomedes, making 'as false as Cressida' a byword for women's fickleness. Cressida is in fact a figure of medieval romance rather than classical mythology, though she borrows her name from a minor but pivotal character in Homer: Chryseis, daughter of a priest of Apollo whose anger at her capture and enslavement by the Greeks sets in motion the whole action of the *Iliad*. The Troilus/Cressida story was the invention of the twelfth-century French romancer Benoît de Sainte-Maure, later taken up by Chaucer in *Troilus and Criseyde* and Shakespeare in *Troilus and Cressida*. Baxter uses the story as the framework for his lyric sequence 'Cressida' (1951, *CP* 101–11), which reflects his unhappy first love affair with Jane Aylward (see also PYRRHA). Other reference: 'Threnos' (N18.31).

Creusa Daughter of the king of Corinth; when JASON deserted MEDEA in order to marry her, the vengeful Medea sent her a poisoned wedding dress which burned her to death (along with her father, who tried to save her). Her death is floridly described in 'I Jason' (1944, N10.627): 'O in hell-gyre / Creusa, created pure (drake-seed) is shrill / I'the anguish-pyre, death-robe.' The description of Creusa as 'drake-seed'—i.e. 'offspring of dragons'—is mysterious. Baxter may be confusing the royal house of Corinth with that of Thebes, which was partly descended from the 'Sown Men' who arose out of dragons' teeth planted in the ground by Cadmus; the appearance of the same motif in the Jason story would make this an easy muddle.

Cybele An Asiatic mother-goddess, often identified by the Greeks and Romans with Rhea (wife of Kronos/Saturn and mother of the gods), and hence a figure of mother earth. She was depicted riding in a chariot drawn by lions, attended by ecstatic cymbal-clashing worshippers. The most famous story about her concerns her young lover ATTIS who castrated himself with a flint knife (for reasons variously explained)—a story memorably told by Catullus in his poem 63. Her priests followed the precedent in ecstatic rituals of self-castration.

In 'The Man on the Horse' (*MH* 116) Baxter lists Cybele among the prime representatives of 'the *anima*, that mysterious archetype'. In 'Letter to Australia' (1955, *CP* 151–52) she seems to be primarily an earth mother and embodiment of the natural world: '[I] rest / My head upon the cancered breast / Of Cybele who is the dream's mother.' In the poems of the 1960s Cybele becomes associated more with the tyrannical power of obsessive sexual love. Adapting Catullus in 'The Wound' ('Words to Lay a Strong Ghost' 8, *CP* 360; cf. 'The Friend', poem 10, *CP* 361), Baxter uses the Cybele/Attis story to convey the traumatic effect of his old affair with Jane Aylward; in 'Epithalamium' (1965–66, N26.48) he reminds her of 'The day you handed me / The altar knife by which my sex was torn / And thrown to Cybele.' The final lines of 'Reflections at Khandallah Baths' (1963, *CP* 288–89) refer to 'the shade of the multiple Cybele / Whose gate of love is an open grave'. Other references: 'A Little Letter to Auckland Students' (1964, *CP* 291–93); 'The Eccentrics' (1968, *CP* 434).

Cynthia see DIANA

Daedalus The great craftsman and inventor who, among other things, built the LABYRINTH for King Minos of Crete. When Minos imprisoned him there Daedalus built wings out of feathers fastened with wax for himself and his young son ICARUS, and flew back to Greece—though Icarus fell to his death. Daedalus is the archetypal scientist, and may also be seen as a figure of the artist (most famously by Joyce, whose fictional stand-in was 'Stephen Dedalus'). Baxter's view of him is less sympathetic. In the early 'Song of the Sea-Nymphs at the Death of Icarus' (1942, *CP* 5–6) he is briefly dismissed as 'gross Daedalus' and 'stolid Daedalus', a dull survivor beside his gloriously doomed son. In 'The Labyrinth' (1970, *CP* 488–89) the Labyrinth is 'the uneven filthy floor / Daedalus made and then forgot'; since for Baxter the Labyrinth often symbolises the fallen world, there may be a hint here of the responsibility of science and technology for creating the unhappy world we live in.

Danaids The fifty daughters of King Danaus, who (all but one) murdered their husbands; as a result they were condemned in HADES to spend eternity trying to draw water from a well, using leaky vessels. Along with other famous sinners of the underworld (SISYPHUS and TANTALUS), they appear (unnamed) in 'The Descent of Orpheus' (*Landfall* 1957), where Baxter describes the effect of ORPHEUS's music on them: 'The drugged daughters of the well / Prodded by your singing, / Let their dribbling sieve spill, / In frilly skirts and sashes / Jive, rock'n'roll.'

Delphic Oracle The Oracle at APOLLO's temple at Delphi, on the slopes of Mount Parnassus, was the most important site of prophecy in ancient Greece. Apollo's priestess, the Pythia (sometimes rendered into English as 'Pythoness'), gave oracles seated on a tripod (three-footed stool) in a cave, in a prophetic trance brought on (it was said) by vapours arising from a subterranean chasm; her unintelligible words were translated into riddling verse by the priests of the shrine. Delphi was considered by the Greeks to be the centre or 'navel' of the earth, and it was belived to have been originally the holy place of an earth goddess (as the Pythia says in the opening speech of Aeschylus's tragedy *Eumenides*) before being taken over by Apollo.

Despite his lukewarm attitude to APOLLO, Baxter treats the Delphic Oracle with respect, associating it with wisdom and poetry, and with the chthonic powers of the earth rather than with Apollonian sunlight and air. In 'Further Notes on New Zealand Poetry' he says of the 'burrow' above the sea in which he had his first poetic experience, 'I did not realise it was the Delphic cave'. In his admiring talk on Edith Sitwell, 'The Pythoness' (*Listener* 1965), he associates her with the oracle: 'An old woman has the right to give her thoughts to others—a speaking part of the earth itself—like the Delphic oracle—from outside the cycle of generation.' In other contexts he associates Delphi with water, and thus with the mystery of death. In 'The Creek' (1951–52, N16.45) the sound of the creek flowing creates the 'voice of a Delphic mourning / For woman, man and child'; in 'Beach Poem' (c.1963, N23.91—an earlier version of 'Shingle Beach Poem', *CP* 270–71) the ocean makes a 'more-than-Delphic murmur' unheard by the drowned woman lying on the beach. 'The Sea Lion' (c.1952, N16.62) is portrayed as 'priest of the Delphic mystery' who 'has seen Earth's secret fountains and the chambers of the Sea'.

Baxter also uses the image satirically. In 'The Old Earth Closet' (1954–65, *CP* 322–23) the outdoor lavatory becomes a parody of the cave of poetry, where the young poet would sit and meditate 'In the cave of the Delphic oracle, / Till my backside was numb.' In 'Kiwi Habits' (*Otago University Review*, 1967) he imagines a hostile philistine reader addressing him 'from her Delphic tripod erected in front of the kitchen range, in a cave where the windows are fogged with drizzle and the oven is always full of salty scones'. This is the oracle of the 'kitchen god', Apollo's enemy (cf. *MH* 74), usurping his tripod.

Other references: 'In Numeris' (1942, *Spark* 152–56 (153)); 'The Creative Mask' (*FA* 43)—half-seriously asserts that McGonagall has 'the true Delphic utterance'; 'An Attitude to Pine-Cones' (1966, *CP* 348–49)—the 'Delphic pines' surrounding the shrine.

Demeter Greek goddess of agriculture and fertility, personification of corn; known to the Romans as Ceres (a name Baxter never uses). Her most famous myth concerns her year-long search for her daughter PERSEPHONE (Proserpina) who was abducted to the underworld by HADES. Demeter's search and the fall and return of Persephone were re-enacted in the famous Mysteries of Eleusis, rituals which communicated to their initiates the secrets of life, death and rebirth.

Demeter is for Baxter a version of the great earth mother goddess who presides over the cycles of life and death, and who also appears as GEA, CYBELE, or Persephone. In 'The Matriarch' (1960, *CP* 217) she is fearsome, invoked as an image of the title figure's oppressive power over her family: 'Vesuvius, the Snow Queen's cauldron, / She lay above her children's lives; / Some elemental, ancient power . . . / Say Demeter, uprooted pines / In either hand . . .' In 'Skull Hill' (1963, *CP* 275) she is a more benevolent figure, as Baxter praises his wife's care for her dying mother: 'you commodious obey / The laws of Demeter, through earth and water / Finding that cradle whose flames will purify, / Teaching me neighbourly how to die.' In 'The Red-Haired Girl' (1962–63, N23.45) Persephone is called 'Demeter's child'.

Diana [Latin] or **Artemis** [Greek] The virgin huntress, a goddess of the wild and of women, chastity and (paradoxically) childbirth; depicted as a fierce and beautiful young huntress with bow and arrows. In later times she becomes identified with the moon, as her twin brother APOLLO is with the sun, and is sometimes imagined as a triple goddess: Artemis/Diana on earth, Selene (the moon) in the heavens, and HEKATE in the underworld. Other names for her are Phoebe or Cynthia. Baxter identifies her in 'The Man on the Horse', along with Hekate, CYBELE and VENUS, as a figure of the anima (*MH* 116). In Baxter's juvenilia she appears as Arcadian huntress in 'The Gods of Greece' (1941, N3.157), and as 'proud and chaste' moon goddess in 'Ode: Where nets of time encircle and destroy' (1943, *Spark* 282–88 (285)); in 'Bracchiae', in a more grotesque Modernist vision, 'glancing upward you may see / in starry woods of Arcady / Diana's crotch and knee / lucid with perspiration' (1944, *Spark* 473–74). In 'Epithalamium' (c.1951, N16.18) 'Cynthia's stag and Aphrodite's dove' are summoned to bless a marriage bed.

In Baxter's mature poetry, Diana is almost always associated with the moon and seen as a fearsome figure: 'No, not the virgin huntress' grace / Of glimmering limbs; rather the Gorgon's eye, / Whose loveless brow must burn and petrify / Washed by the sterile winds of outer space' ('To the Moon', c.1949, N15.74). The moon as a female symbol is characteristically sinister in Baxter, the 'skull moon' as 'summer gorgon' ('At Rotorua', 1961, *CP* 228–29). (He attributes a similar view to the English poet Roy Fuller in 'The World of the Creative Artist', *Salient* 1955.) In 'Tarras Moon' (1947–51, *CP* 112–13) two 'moonstruck' drunks have a vision of Diana as 'Queen Death': '"Ripe archaic" her feature / From a Sicilian metope, / Two snakes for a knotted rope / About her middle: the creature / That eats our carrion hope: / Glass of malignant Nature, / *Diana chastely fair*' (the conventional poetic tag turned cruelly ironic). In a group of unpublished poems of 1961–62 Baxter creates a sinister parody of the myth of Diana and Endymion, as Diana, 'her cheeks bone-white, / Wearing her serpent girdle', rides the body of a drowned suicide ('Black Water', N22.74, see ENDYMION for details). In *Horse* a 'wild moon [. . .] inhuman among the hurrying clouds' is seen as 'the horned Diana of sex and death' (30). In 'The Party' ('Words to Lay a Strong Ghost' 1, 1966, *CP* 356) PYRRHA is described as 'smiling / Like a stone Diana' at her clownish lover—a description which suggests the enigmatic smile of archaic Greek statues, but may also echo Baxter's image elsewhere of the moon's 'boneyard smile' ('My Love Late Walking', *CP* 164–65).

In the late poems a more positive treatment of the moon goes along with a shift in its mythological associations from Diana to a very different Virgin. 'Mary at Ephesus' (1967, *CP* 383) links the two, drawing on that city's associations both as a cult centre of Artemis ('Diana of the Ephesians' in Acts 19) and as the legendary home of the Virgin Mary, to proclaim Mary 'a greater than Diana'. In 'The Moon and the Chestnut Tree' (1971, *CP* 496–98) 'the clear moon in a clear sky' is associated with Te Whaea, the Maori version of the Virgin; the moon as sinister death-goddess is transformed into a positive aspect of 'the darkness that is God, / The darkness that is Te Whaea' ('The Ikons', *CP* 499).

Dido Queen of Carthage, who, in Virgil's *Aeneid*, fell in love with the shipwrecked AENEAS; they consummated their love while trapped together in a cave during a storm; when he deserted her to pursue his destiny in Italy, she burned herself to death on a pyre. 'Aeneas' (1943, *CS* 3) describes how Aeneas 'once with Dido in the storm-hid cave / Found himself, unclothed by destiny'. In the same year she appears in a fragmentary lyric, 'Queen Dido sang' (N12, after poem 742), where the little birds echo her lament—'Di-do. Poor Di-do. / Di-di-di-do.'

Dionysus [Greek] or **Bacchus** [Latin] One of the more complex of the Greco-Roman gods. His Roman form, Bacchus, can be fairly simply described as the god of wine, intoxication and 'Bacchanalian' revelry; Baxter associates Bacchus and his followers with Kiwi 'pub culture'. His older Greek form, Dionysus, is a more complex, dangerous and sometimes sinister figure. Dionysus presides over not only alcoholic intoxication but all states in which one is lifted out of one's normal self—religious ecstasy, poetic inspiration, acting (he is also god of the theatre), or madness. He has power over wild nature and vegetation, causing vines and ivy to spring up and transforming his enemies into beasts. He leads a train of nymphs and satyrs (including the wise old drunkard SILENUS), and human, mostly female worshippers known as BACCHANTES or Maenads, who in their Dionysian frenzy were reputed to tear animals and even human beings to pieces—as they do ORPHEUS, or King Pentheus of Thebes in Euripides'

Bacchae. As 'Dionysus-Hades' (a compound form used by Baxter in 'Christchurch 1948' and in *Horse*) Dionysus becomes a god of death. Baxter ignores the various myths surrounding Dionysus/Bacchus's birth and early life, but does allude to his relationship with ARIADNE, whom he rescued fom her abandonment on the island of Naxos and afterwards married.

Dionysus/Bacchus is one of Baxter's more important and deeply ambiguous mythic figures, associated both with his own suffering from alcoholism and with the eruption of joy and poetic inspiration from the subconscious mind—he several times describes his own poetry as 'Dionysiac'. His treatment of the god is discussed in detail in chapter 7. The relevant texts are as follows (references to 'Bacchus' are asterisked): [POEMS] *'The Gods of Greece' (c.1941, N3.157); 'The Bell' (c.1951, N5.267—'the lord of the flowering vine'); 'Songs of the Desert' 4 (1947, *CP* 56); *'Bar Room Elegy' (1951, *CP* 119—'no Bacchic rite'); 'Spring Song' (1953, *SP* 50–51); 'Inscription for Dylan Thomas' (*Listener* 1954—misnamed as 'Dionysius'); 'Crossing Cook Strait' (1947–56, *CP* 159–60); 'Christchurch 1948' (1960, *CP* 215–16—'Dionysus-Hades'); *'An Appreciation of Fried Squid' (1961, N22.6—'a bacchanalian fish'); 'Thoughts of a Headmistress in Spring' (c.1961, N22.40); 'At Rakiura' (1966, N27.34); 'Fitz Drives Home the Spigot' (1966, *CP* 375); 'The Jar' (1967, *CP* 392–93); 'The Bluegums (for Patric Carey)' (1967, *CP* 410); 'Ballade in Love's Defence' (undated, FM 8/27); [PLAY] *The Temptations of Oedipus*, *CPlays* 244; [PROSE] *Horse* 52 ('Dionysus-Hades'); 'Symbolism', *FA* 63, 68, 77; 'Creative Mask', *FA* 48–49; 'Virgin', *MH* 74; 'Man', *MH* 110; 'Essay on the Higher Learning' (*Spike* 1961); 'Further Notes on New Zealand Poetry'; *'When is a Book Pornographic?', *FC* 113 ('Bacchanalian orgies'); Weir 'Interview' 244; [LETTER] to Fleur Adcock, 30 Oct. 1961 (FM 27/1/13).

Dis see HADES

Electra Daughter of Agamemnon and CLYTEMNESTRA, who helped her brother ORESTES avenge their father's murder by killing their mother. Hence the term 'Electra complex', coined by Jung as a female counterpart to Freud's 'Oedipus complex', for a daughter's excessive love of the father and jealousy of the mother. In a letter of 20 Oct. 1961 (FM 27/1/13), apropos of the father-fixated speaker in 'Thoughts of a Headmistress in Spring' (N22.40), Baxter suggests that 'An unchanged Electra complex is, I think, much commoner than an unchanged Oedipus one'.

Elpenor In Homer's *Odyssey*, a young member of ODYSSEUS's crew who died by drunkenly falling off the roof of CIRCE's house (he was sleeping there, as Greeks often did in hot weather). His ghost appears to Odysseus in HADES and begs for proper burial (*Odyssey*, book 11). Baxter adapts Elpenor's plea in 'Traveller's Litany' (1954, *CP* 139–45 (144–45)): 'At table when the cup stands empty / Remember Elpenor.' His note explains: 'For me [Elpenor] symbolizes the old drinking-companion,—"when the cup stands empty"—in one aspect, at a party; in another aspect, the "remembering" is a prayer of intercession at the Communion table.' He reworks the passage in 'The Watch' (1963, *CP* 273–74), where the words of Elpenor (here unnamed) come back to the poet when he is at sea and in a state of physical and spiritual malaise.

Elysium (Elysian Fields) The paradisal place reserved for the souls of the blessed dead (originally, those related to or specially favoured by the gods; later, those of exceptional virtue or merit). It may be imagined as a part of HADES or as a separate place, the Islands of the Blessed at the edge of the world. There are several conventional references to Elysium in Baxter's juvenilia: 'The Garden' (age 14, N2.89); 'I will go into the fields' (age 15–16, N6.369); 'Transparent Mural' (age 17, N10.626). In his mature poetry it occurs only in a reference to 'rare and Elysian' flowers in 'September Walk' (*NZPY* 1952).

Endymion The lover of the moon goddess, Selene (or in later versions DIANA or Cynthia); so that he should always remain young and beautiful, she cast him into an enchanted sleep in a cave on Mount Latmos, where she would visit him every night. In three successive drafts of an unpublished poem in N22 ('Moonlight on Water', 67; 'Black Water', 74, 'Moonlight on the Sea', 78), Baxter macabrely applies the image to the moonlight falling on the drowned body of a suicidal businessman or lawyer who has jumped from the Kapiti ferry: 'Diana crosses the dark sea to ride / One who welters in the waves' cradle [. . .] She mounts that old Endymion like a horse / In the astride position. / His two dead eyes like discs of paua glisten' ('Black Water').

Eros The Greek word for (sexual) love and desire, and also the personified god of love; his Roman counterpart is Cupid (Latin *cupido*, desire), a name Baxter never uses. In Hesiod's *Theogony*, Eros, 'most beautiful of all the deathless gods', is also one of the oldest, emerging after primal Chaos along with Earth (GEA) at the beginning of creation. In later myth he becomes the son of Aphrodite or VENUS, envisaged first as a beautiful winged youth but later as the familiar mischievous child; he carries a bow and arrows, which he shoots at random to inflame desire. His most famous myth concerns his relationship with PSYCHE.

'Eros' occurs very frequently in Baxter, but seldom with explicit mythological reference; it is hard to to draw clear lines between his use of Eros as classical god, as personification, and as mere abstract noun. (He consistently writes the word with a capital letter and no italics.) In his prose essays and letters, especially from the 1960s on, the nature of Eros (erotic love) and its relationship to Agape (Christian charity) is a recurring concern. He insists on the necessary connection between them, several times using the metaphor of 'Eros as the horse and Agape as the rider. Shall Agape go always on foot for fear of ever taming a difficult horse? I hope not' ('A Postscript to a Postscript to "Letter to a Catholic Poet"'). At the same time he expresses his wariness of the overmastering power of sexuality by personifying Eros as 'a dangerous god' ('The Pythoness', *Listener* 1965), speaking of the 'the power of the god Eros' and 'the religion of Eros' (in a set of 'Additional Notes for Teachers'). Similarly in an unpublished 'Elegy' he refers to 'the god Eros / Who turns us always into animals and madmen' (c.1966, N28.36).

In other contexts the contrast is not between Eros and Agape but between Eros and PRIAPUS: deeply felt passion versus pure physical lust. In a letter of 3 Nov. 1965 (FM 27/1/6), Baxter speaks of 'that twanging of wires in the chest, the wind-harp, which belongs to Eros rather than Priapus'; but for that very reason Eros, 'the green-slimed Eros of the fountains', may be 'a more dangerous god than Priapus, because he disguises himself more and claims to be the lord of heaven and earth' ('Virgin', *MH* 84).

Some of Baxter's poems play more explicitly with the iconography of the classical love-god. In 'The Coffeehouses' (1961, N21.103) these teen hangouts are depicted as 'the garden of the lame-winged Eros'. 'To Mack and Maureen' (c.1962, N23.56) contrasts 'sun-bright Eros' with 'Priapus, the Freudian god' who 'rummages ashcans'. 'The Death of Eros' (c.1959, N20.11) allegorises the transition from Eros to Agape: 'Young Eros in his raging dies, / A vain wave beating on the sand; / And in his death the soul may rise / And enter to another land / Where hangs the everlasting Vine / Where fruits like blood of ruby shine.' This unexpected, unclassical association of Eros with the beach and the sea (Baxter's perennial symbol of death and transformation) recurs more strikingly in 'Jottings (for Mike Doyle)' (c.1963, *Tuatara* 1972): 'At Scorching Bay, I saw that proud / Eros the seagod walk / The ancient beach, dripping black fire, in a cloud / Of sandflies—in whose unploughed / Kingdom of waves I have no part.' Baxter's most bizarrely personal vision of Eros is the reference in 'The Caryatids' (1967, *CP* 410–11) to 'The mad boathouse-keeper with his box of photographs / Whom poets have called Eros'—a memory of the Brighton fisherman-hermit Mackenzie who terrorised Baxter and his brother as children (see *Spark* 52–54), transformed into an image of love as madness and obsession.

In a late poem, 'Desert Psalm' (1970, *CP* 488), Baxter applies the classical imagery of Eros to the Christian God: 'our King is great; / He has pulled back the bowstring / And sent his arrows flying through the world— // Arrows of love! Wherever one of them strikes / That man is set on fire with love for him.' This Christianising of the image is fairly traditional; compare Blake's 'arrows of desire' in 'Jerusalem', and the statue conventionally known as 'Eros' in London's Piccadilly Circus, which is officially 'The Angel of Christian Charity'.

Other references: [POEMS] 'Annales' (age 17, *CS* 28–30);

'Metamorphosis' (c.1951, N16.36); 'Rapunzel' (c.1952, N17.13); 'Traveller's Litany' (1954, *CP* 139–45 (139)); 'Christ and Eros (for E.A.)' (c.1960, N21.7); 'Looking at Women' (c.1966, N26.81); 'The Gale' (1968, *CP* 418); [PROSE] 'Literature and Belief', *MH* 48; 'Virgin', *MH* 74, 84; *Aspects* 35.

Eumenides see FURIES

Eurydice The wife of ORPHEUS, who descended into HADES in an attempt to reclaim her after she died of snakebite. 'Eurydice' (N6.345) is the fifteen-year-old Baxter's rather conventional (and ungrammatical) version of Orpheus's lament: 'Whither art thou Eurydice?' *The Runaway Wife* puts a more radical spin on the story: this Eurydice deliberately escapes her unhappy marriage by taking refuge in 'the Hades coffee bar' and the mask of a GORGON, and resents the measures Orpheus takes to bring her back. 'Seances (for Colin Durning)' (1968, *CP* 426) echoes the play's imagery, with its underground café where one can see 'the stone-white face of Eurydice / Carrying in scorn her great gold helm of hair'. For further discussion see ORPHEUS.

Fates The three goddesses (Clotho, Lachesis, Atropos) who preside over human destinies, respectively spinning, measuring and cutting the thread of life. Baxter has only a single casual reference to them, in a Greek context, when Oedipus in *The Temptations of Oedipus* (1968, *CPlays* 236) refers to humans and gods being 'under the rule of the Fates'. Norah in *The Wide Open Cage* (1959, *CPlays* 22) may also be evoking the image when she describes 'Hunger, dark, and cold: the three ugly sisters. They stand above the cradle; they go to bed with every human soul; they hammer down the coffin lid.' But this threefold pattern is not one of the archetypal images that Baxter often returns to.

Furies Demonic goddesses who pursue and torment evildoers, especially those who have killed their parents or other blood kin. They appear most memorably in Aeschylus's tragedy *Eumenides*, where they pursue ORESTES for the killing of his mother CLYTEMNESTRA; they are portrayed as hideous and repulsive creatures, snake-haired, pursuing their victims on all fours like hounds sniffing blood. At the end of the play they are pacified by

ATHENE and agree to exchange the name of Furies (*Erinyes*) for the flattering title of **Eumenides** ('Gentle Ones'), and to take up residence in the soil of Athens, becoming largely benign (if still terrifying) chthonic guardians of the city. According to Hesiod's *Theogony*, the Furies were born of the drops of blood that fell from the sky god URANUS when he was castrated by his son—an image that links them oddly (and appropriately for Baxter) with the origins of VENUS. In later texts they are often charged with punishing evildoers in the underworld (see HADES), and are sometimes named as Alecto, Megaera and TISIPHONE.

The Furies/Eumenides are among the most fearsome of Baxter's negative female images. Punishing 'the crime of being born' ('The Furies'), they embody the fear and guilt which he sees as an inextricable part of the human condition, and which can be read as a pagan analogue for the Christian concept of original sin; as such they have, just as in Greek myth, an ambiguously positive role, and Baxter in a late letter to Weir identifies them as 'the image of the love of God—the devourers of the relics of sin in the soul'. They appear particularly in Baxter's drama, playing prominent roles in *The Gentle Ones* (an abortive adaptation of the *Eumenides*), *The Runaway Wife*, and *The Temptations of Oedipus* (where they may or may not appear physically on stage). In the first two plays Baxter gives them the repetitive chant *Epi de toi*; these are the opening words of a repeated line in the *Eumenides* (328, 341) in which the Furies curse Orestes: *Epi de toi tethumenoi tode melos* ('Against the consecrated [victim] this is our song').

Baxter's use of the Furies is discussed in more detail in chapter 4. The relevant texts are: [POEMS] 'A Rented Room' (1950, *CP* 93–94); 'The Worlds Press on Me' (c.1943, N10.620—'Eumenides hell-spawned'); 'Letter to Noel Ginn II' (earlier version, 1946, *Spark* 118); 'The Furies' (prose poem, *Canta* 1948); 'The Eumenides' (c.1963, N23.67); 'Ancestors (I)' (1963, N24.7); 'Prayer for a Duck-Shooting Uncle' (1961–64, *CP* 304–05); 'The Need for Public Brothels' (c.1963, N25.25—both title and text hard to decipher); 'The Newcastle Disease' (c.1966, N26.75); [PLAYS] *The Gentle Ones*; *The Runaway Wife*; *The Spots of the Leopard* 3–4; *The Temptations of Oedipus*; [PROSE] *Horse* 86; 'Notes on the Making of "The Martian"'; 'Essay on the Higher Learning' (*Spike* 1961) 62; [LETTERS] to Fleur Adcock, 12 Dec. 1961 (FM 27/1/15); to John Weir, 4 March 1967 (FM 20/4/7).

Galatea The name of two different mythological women: the sea nymph who was unwillingly wooed by the Cyclops Polyphemus (Ovid, *Metamorphoses*, book 13); and the statue-bride of the sculptor Pygmalion (*Metamorphoses*, book 10—though the statue's name is a post-classical invention). Baxter perhaps has both in mind in 'Galatea' (1955, N18.26), a rather cryptic love poem addressed to his wife, which draws on imagery both of statues ('donor in marble at love's tomb') and the sea ('the seadeep jewel [. . .] of a woman's heart and body'). The address to Jacquie as 'darkest Galatea' is a playful allusion to the meaning of the Greek name: 'milk-white'.

Gea Primordial earth goddess and personification of the earth as universal mother. (More commonly spelt Gaea or Gaia, but 'Gea' is Baxter's consistent form.) She is one of the feminine and maternal figures whom Baxter treats most positively, an embodiment of the natural world as a support and a refuge from modern society. In 'At Day's Bay' (1965, *CP* 308–09) he pictures himself lying 'on Gea's breast, the broad nurse / who bears with me' (a neat twist on the expected 'bears me'). In 'At Aramoana' (1966, *CP* 336–37) he sees the beach as a place 'where Gea / speaks in parables of rock'; 'There is no other / rest for the heart, but these drab / mats of cutty-grass, no truth // outside her changing and austere / testament of sand.' 'Conversation' (*MH* 25) explicates the passage, describing how in despair at the acedia of modern life the poet turns for support 'to the least demanding and most supporting reality, Gea, the earth herself, the oldest of the tribe of gods', who is 'the symbolic ground of existence—away from her I feel lost; yet because all men die, she can only comfort, never save', and so he must move on past her to the sea, associated with God the Father, death and transfiguration. In 'Education' (*MH* 153) Baxter similarly imagines the beach as a place where people might dance 'honouring the Earth Mother', and laments that in modern society there is no such ritual connection with the earth. In 'Air Flight

North' (1967, *CP* 391–92), air travel is seen as a violation of her privacy: 'My mother Gea below me is undressed / Showing her stretchmarks got by long childbearing. // One should not look.' A rare negative use of the earth mother image is the unpublished 'A Different Kind of Nothing' (two versions, N25.74 and 75), where a woman with 'doll-like' eyes and a 'broad square arse' is at first seen as having 'Something of the Earth Mother', but is then denounced as a walking corpse and a sexual threat.

In 'Husband' (1965, *CP* 327–28) Baxter compares Jacquie to 'the earth itself, the long-haired / Daughter of Zeus who likes whatever happens / Because it happens to her.' Gea is the grandmother, not the daughter of Zeus; if Baxter has a classical referent for his earth goddess here, it may be PERSEPHONE, but he may be thinking in more general terms of the earth as God's daughter.

Golden Fleece The fleece of the miraculous flying ram which carried the children Phrixus and Helle from Greece to Colchis, on the Black Sea. JASON and the Argonauts sailed to Colchis in quest of this priceless relic, and achieved it with the help of the enchantress MEDEA. Baxter uses the image, romantically or satirically, in five poems: 'Husband to Wife' (N18.45); 'Husband to Wife (modern version)' (N19.46); 'The Phoenix' Nest' (N19.30); 'To My Wife' (N19.91); 'The Fleece' (N23.54). For discussion see JASON.

Gorgon A snake-haired female monster whose face was so hideous that the mere sight of it would turn one to stone. In Greek art a Gorgon is depicted as a squat, winged creature, her eyes glaring and mouth gaping wide with boar's tusks and lolling tongue; post-classical depictions are often more human (apart from the snaky hair) and sometimes weirdly beautiful. There were three sister Gorgons, of whom two, Stheno and Euryale, were immortal; the third and most famous, **Medusa**, was originally a beautiful mortal woman, transformed into a monster as punishment by ATHENE. The hero PERSEUS was given the task of killing Medusa, and accomplished this with the help of Athene, who advised him to look at the monster's reflection in his shield rather than confronting her directly; he later used the petrifying power of

Medusa's severed head against his enemies.

The Gorgon has offered a feast for interpreters: for Freudians she represents the female genitals (an interpretation Baxter alludes to in 'The Advantages of Analysis'); for Jungians she embodies the dark side of the anima; feminists, such as Hélène Cixous (*The Laugh of the Medusa*), sometimes read her against the grain as a positive symbol of female empowerment. Baxter repeatedly alludes either to Medusa or less specifically to 'the Gorgon' as a symbol of terror, despair and social paralysis, and as an archetype of the destructive feminine—but also, in the paradoxical form of 'the snake-haired MUSE', as one of the driving creative forces of his poetry. Baxter's use of the Gorgon is discussed in detail in chapter 4. The relevant texts are as follows (Medusa references are asterisked): [POEMS] *'Resurrection' (1944, *CS* 32–35); 'Poems to a Glass Woman' 9; 'Songs of the Desert' 2 (1947, *CP* 54–55); 'To the Moon' (c.1947, N15.74); 'The Fallen House' (1950, *CP* 97); 'The Surfman's Story' (1950–52, *CP* 124–25); 'The Bankrupts' (c.1951, N16.54); 'A Country Idyll' (c.1952, N16.73); *'Perseus' (1952, *CP* 129–30); *'Discussion of the Heart's Infirmity' (c.1955, N17.101); 'Song' (1956, N18.66), revised in 'Tuatara Poem' (N20.77); 'Mandrakes for Supper' (1959, *CP* 200–01); 'The Advantages of Analysis' (c.1960, N20.68), revised in 'The Sponge of Vinegar' (N21.59); 'Poem on a Clay Tile' (c.1960, N20.76); 'At Rotorua' (1961, *CP* 228–29); 'The Storm' (1961, *CP* 243); 'Inscription' (1965, *CP* 329); 'The Instruments' (1967, *CP* 401); 'Rotorua' (1961, N21.67); *'Letter to Robert Burns' (1963, *CP* 289–91); 'Design for a Mural' (c.1965, N25.66); *'Kelp' (1966, *CP* 343); *'Autumn Testament' 33 (1972, *CP* 557); *'Letter to Peter Olds' (1972, *CP* 578–81 (578)); *Notes on the Country that I Live In*; [PLAY] *Jack Winter's Dream*, *CPlays* 9; [PROSE] 'The Phoenix and the Crow' (*Spike* 1954), 57); 'The World of the Creative Artist' (*Salient* 1955), 24; 'Literature and Belief', *MH* 44; 'Further Notes on New Zealand Poetry' 21; *Autumn Testament* p.9; [LETTER] to Fleur Adcock, 11 Sept. 1961 (FM 27/1/4).

Hades A name which refers both to (1) the god of death, and (2) the realm he rules over—the underworld.

(1) The god, known variously as **Hades** (Greek), **Pluto** (Latin/Greek) or **Dis** (Latin), is a fairly minor figure in Baxter's pantheon, less often and less significantly invoked than his queen PERSEPHONE. 'Stern Pluto' appears in 'The Gods of Greece' (c.1941, N3.157). 'Webs of Circumstance' (c.1941, N2.92) associates him with 'worldly gain', drawing on an ancient identification or confusion of Pluto with Plutus, the god of wealth. In 'Thoughts of a Remuera Housewife' (1962–65, *CP* 314–15) the speaker identifies herself as Persephone, married to 'Pluto, that rough king', and making her home on 'Pluto's / iron-black star, the quiet / planet furthest from the sun'. In *The Runaway Wife* 'Mr Pluto' is the manager of the Hades Coffee Bar, a comically harrassed, brandy-tippling figure, subordinate to the enigmatic Mr RHADAMANTHUS. In 'Education' Baxter pairs VENUS and Hades as representations of EROS and THANATOS: 'When Venus leaves us to ourselves, her uncle Hades enters the door of the heart' (*MH* 154). The composite figure of 'Dionysus-Hades', invoked in 'Christchurch 1948' (1959, *CP* 215–16) and in *Horse* (52), is perhaps best considered as an aspect of DIONYSUS. In 'The Eyes of Dis' (1962, *CP* 259–60), the eyes may be those of the god but more probably of the underworld collectively.

(2) The underworld, the kingdom of the dead, ruled over by the god Hades/Pluto and his queen, and also known as **Hades** or occasionally as **Dis**. Baxter's frequent allusions to the mythology of the classical underworld are discussed in chapter 8; explicit references to Hades include 'The Journey' (1952, *CP* 127); 'The Sirens' (1952, *CP* 130–33 (133)); 'Obiter Dicta' (1959, N20.75—'a grip in Hades on the springs of joy'); 'Morning Train' (1959, *CP* 272–73); 'The Eyes of Dis' (1962, *CP* 259–60); 'Some Possibilities for New Zealand Drama' (comparing the 'myth' created in a play by Henry Livings to that of 'the Greek Hades'). For places in and around the underworld, see also ACHERON, CIMMERIA, ELYSIUM, LETHE, PHLEGETHON, STYX, TARTARUS; for its inhabitants (staff and prisoners), see also CERBERUS, CHARON, FURIES, HERMES, IXION, RHADAMANTHUS, SISYPHUS, TANTALUS, THANATOS, TISIPHONE.

Hector The greatest warrior of Troy in the Trojan War. Like his adversary and slayer ACHILLES, almost completely ignored by Baxter, except for a gibe at his expense by ODYSSEUS in *The Sore-Footed Man*: 'frankly, Hector is also a bore' (*CPlays* 151).

Hekate An underworld goddess associated with witchcraft and sorcery. Often seen as an aspect of DIANA or Artemis; her common title 'triple Hekate' is sometimes understood as reflecting her triple role as Artemis on earth, Selene (the moon) in the heavens, and Hekate in the underworld. Though she is usually a sinister figure in classical and post-classical texts, Hesiod's *Theogony* suggests she was originally a benevolent fertility goddess. Something of this ambiguity is reflected in Baxter, who refers to Hekate in several poems of the early 1960s as one of his images of simultaneously nurturing and terrifying chthonic female power. In 'Waipatiki Beach' (1963, *CP* 263–65) he sees 'Her lion face, the skull-brown Hekate, / Ruling my blood since I was born', and associates her with 'the oldest Venus [. . .] The manifold mother to whom my poems go / Like ladders down'. In 'The Goddess' (1966, *CP* 351–52) he describes being once looked after as a child by a reportedly 'wicked', violent and promiscuous neighbour woman and having an epiphany of 'Earth, great trees, a nature saying "Yes" / Beyond all bargains [. . .] / I'd say, Hekate taught / Me to act, fight, groan, give'; in an unpublished poem ('Blue Notes for Mack', 1963–64, N25.31) he sums this episode up with the epitaph 'Hekate taught him love.' In 'A Girl's Invocation' (1963, *CP* 271–72) a young girl prays to Hekate to save and guard her from various threats, and to give her a lover 'like the hot sun' yet 'gentle as the moon'.

In two unpublished poems Baxter describes how he carved out of seashore pumice a fertility-goddess figure with 'hanging dugs, great belly and panther head'. In the first, 'The Strong One' (1963, N23.98), he associates this figure with his lover or wife (and perhaps by implication with all women): 'Though your back is straight, my girl, and your body slim, / Not like hers, and you wear no grim beast-mask [. . .] / Yet my dreams have told me I am Hekate's lover—// Praise be!' In the other, 'The Rostrum: a memorial ode on hearing the news of my appointment as a Robert Burns Fellow' (1965, N26.13), he implies that 'Blind Hekate, /

Mother of drunks and fools' is his MUSE: 'Have mercy! [. . .] Don't take it hard— / This joke of being paid to service you.'

In 'The Man on the Horse', discussing Burns' 'Tam o' Shanter', Baxter names Hekate as one of the most important images of the anima—'that mysterious archetype who has been called variously Venus, Cybele, Artemis—but in Burns' case, one could say definitely, Hekate, patroness of witches, the goddess of the underworld' (*MH* 116). As often, his comment on Burns applies to himself as well.

Other reference: 'Poetry and Education'—on educated and uneducated responses to a poem to Hekate (cited in ch. 1).

Helen Queen of Sparta, the most beautiful woman in the world, who became the cause of the Trojan War (see TROY) when she was seduced or abducted by Paris of Troy from her husband Menelaus. In 'Viaticum' (age 17, N13.768) she is simply an image of supernatural, life-enhancing beauty: 'One has one's moments of expansion: / when Helen walks clothed in the flower-sky petal [. . .]'. More often she is associated with the destructive power of female beauty and sexuality. 'At Balclutha' (1944, *Spark* 358–59) calls her 'the dame / Whose eyebrow-curve set Ilion's roofs on flame,' recalling Marlowe's famous image of 'the face that [. . .] burnt the topless towers of Ilium' (*Doctor Faustus* (A-text), 5.1.91). Similarly, an untitled fragment begins 'When Troy was burned for Helen' (N13, after poem 844); and in 'The Soldiers' (1963, N24.1), 'In a pub at Puhoi / I saw the small grim face of Helen look / Back like a ghost at the ashes of Troy.' In 'The Party', poem 1 of the sequence 'Words to Lay a Strong Ghost' (1966, *CP* 356), Helen (unnamed) is linked to Baxter's old obsessive love for Jane Aylward: 'Two breasts like towers—the same face / That brought Troy crashing / Down like a chicken-coop—black wood and flames!'

Helicon A mountain frequented by the Muses (see MUSE), on which rose the sacred spring of Hippocrene which granted poetic inspiration. A cliché of poetic diction, used only in Baxter's juvenilia, e.g. 'To My Father' (N4.183): 'had I known thee not I could not be / A fount where Heliconian waters flow, / Partaker of the joys of Poesy!' Other references: 'The Kiln' (N8.479); 'The Swan' (N9.509).

Hera [Greek] or **Juno** [Latin] Queen of the gods, wife of ZEUS or Jupiter, patroness of women and marriage. Not a goddess figure who was significant to Baxter. As Hera, she is named only in the very early poem 'The Gods of Greece' (N3.157): 'now deserted woman-kind / Olympian Hera shall not find / By temple altar'. As Juno, a story about her is mentioned in 'Mask'; see under IXION.

Hercules [Latin] or **Herakles** [Greek] The greatest of the Greek heroes, a demigod of gigantic size and strength; he is depicted dressed in a lion-skin and armed with bow and arrows and a huge club. The son of ZEUS by a mortal woman, Alcmena, he was cheated of a kingdom by his jealous stepmother HERA, and instead became subject to his cowardly cousin King Eurystheus, who sent him on twelve increasingly dangerous quests, the 'Twelve Labours'. Baxter refers to six of these: to kill the Nemean Lion (from which he took his lion-skin); to kill the Erymanthian Boar; to kill the multi-headed HYDRA (from which he took the poison for his arrows); to capture the magical belt of the AMAZON queen Hippolyta; to clean out the dung-encrusted Augean Stables (which he did by diverting a river through them); and to steal the Golden Apples of the HESPERIDES (which he did with the help of ATLAS)—the deed which most fascinates Baxter. His other deeds include killing the earth-giant ANTAEUS and wrestling with Death (THANATOS) for the soul of Queen Alcestis. Hercules killed his first wife Megara and their childen in a fit of madness inflicted on him by Hera (a story Baxter never alludes to). His death was brought about inadvertently by his second wife Deianeira, who sent him a tunic dyed in the blood of the CENTAUR Nessus, whom Hercules had killed. The dying Nessus had assured her that the blood was a love potion which would restore Hercules' waning affection; in fact it was poisoned from Hercules' Hydra-arrows, and burned his flesh agonisingly. To end the pain he had his friends (among them PHILOCTETES, to whom he gave his bow and arrows) burn him on a funeral pyre. After death he was received onto Olympus as a full god.

For a full discussion of Baxter's treatment of Hercules/Herakles, see chapter 5. The texts in which he is mentioned are: [POEMS] 'Letter to Noel Ginn' (1944, *CP* 27–29—the lion-skin); 'City of Desolation' (1946, N14.957); 'As we have sown' (1947, N15.7); 'Threnos' (1956, N18.31); 'The Dream' (1961, N22.3); 'The Betrayal' (1962, *CP* 254–55); 'The Tiredness of Me and Herakles' (1972, *CP* 595); [PLAYS] *The Sore-footed Man, CPlays* 127–59, esp. 139–40, 158; [PROSE] *Horse* (as a patterning myth though never explicitly mentioned); 'Conversation', *MH* 17; *Aspects* 31; 'The Body and Blood of Christ', *FC* 179.

Hermes [Greek] or **Mercury** [Latin] Messenger of the gods, recognisable by his winged hat and sandals and his serpent-entwined rod; god of travel and communication, trade and thievery, rhetoric and eloquence; also the psychopomp, the communicator between life and death who conducts the souls of the dead to HADES. In a Keatsian ode 'To Hermes' (N4.175) the fifteen-year-old Baxter, declaring 'I hail thee high above all deities', alludes to a number of the god's roles: he prays to Hermes as 'god of dreams' to protect him from demonic nightmares, as 'Patron of music, art, and eloquence' to foster his inspiration and save him from lapsing into 'pedantry', and as 'Conductor of all souls' to preserve his soul from Hades. Despite this early declaration of allegiance, the mature Baxter turns to less rational and reassuring versions of his MUSE, and Hermes/Mercury is largely absent from the published poems, apart from a passing mention of 'benignant Hermes' in 'Perseus' (*CP* 129–30).

In *The Bureaucrat* the character of Tom Harness formally corresponds to Hermes in Aeschylus's *Prometheus Bound*, though the resemblance is tenuous due to Baxter's ironic reversal of roles: here Fireman/PROMETHEUS is the conformist servant of authority, while Harness/Hermes becomes the rebel. However, there is a nod to Hermes in Io Gould's description of Harness: 'He's a kind of messenger. Both ways. Up and down. Between the dark inside and the cold outside' (*CPlays* 170).

Other references: 'The City Wakes (Dunedin)' (N2.119)—breezes 'Fleet-footed as the moon-shod Mercury'; 'The Postman' (N15.112)—an implicit comic comparison with Mercury in 'Swift on feathered feet I come'; see also ARGUS.

Hero and Leander Young lovers who lived on opposite sides of the Hellespont (the Dardanelles). Hero, a priestess of Aphrodite, lived in a tower in Sestos, and Leander would swim across the strait from Abydos to visit her each night. One stormy night the lamp in Hero's tower was blown out, and Leander lost his way and drowned; Hero threw herself to her death from the tower. The story was told by the late classical poet Musaeus, and retold in Christopher Marlowe's unfinished *Hero and Leander* (1598); Baxter several times quotes Marlowe's poem (e.g. *Aspects* 31) and once proposed to write a continuation of it, 'which would be very much Baxter and very little Marlowe' (letter to Perce Rae Munro, 26 June 1950, FM 11/6/9). He cites the story in 'A Small Ode on Mixed Flatting' (1967, *CP* 396–99): 'Leander, that Greek lad, was bold / To swim the Hellespont raging cold / To visit Hero in her tower / Just for an amorous half-hour, / And lay his wet brine-tangled head / Upon her pillow.' Other reference: 'Ode: Where nets of time encircle and destroy' (*Spark* 282–88 (286)).

Hesperides Nymphs, daughters of the evening, who live in a paradisal garden in the far west (Greek *hespera* means both 'evening' and 'west') where they dance around a dragon-guarded tree bearing golden apples. Baxter's use of the image of the Hesperidean garden and HERCULES' quest for the apples, mainly in his unpublished poems to Jane Aylward in 1946–47, is discussed in chapter 5. The texts in which the myth is explicitly invoked are: [POEMS] 'Ode to the New Zealand Summer' (N14.916); 'Night Song' (N14.923); 'Aubade' (N14.948); 'O do not strip' (N14.987); 'Hesperides was growing' (N14.1004); 'Threnos' (1956, N18.31), revised as 'Landfall at the Hesperides (circa 1820)' (1959, N20.2); 'The Tiredness of Me and Herakles' (1972, *CP* 595); [PROSE] letter to Keith Sinclair, 13 Nov. 1951 (FM 14/4/9—'the good Hesperides, the live place'); *Aspects* 31.

Hesperus The evening star (that is, the planet Venus, when it appears in the western sky in the evening), in classical myth identified as the son or brother of ATLAS. In an unpublished poem 'To My Wife' (FM 14/4/18) Baxter addresses Jacquie as 'Star, Hesperus; yet tired flesh'. The reference to 'Hesperus [. . .] where charmed rivers nightlong fill the night' in 'Loved face my own and not my own' (1946, N14.953) seems to be Baxter's confusion of Hesperus with the garden of the HESPERIDES, frequently referred to in the poems of that period. 'Lament for Barney Flanagan, Licensee of the Hesperus Hotel' (1953, *CP* 136–37) may also carry an ironic allusion to the Hesperides.

Hippolyta A queen of the Amazons; one of the Twelve Labours of HERCULES was to capture her belt. For Baxter's references to her, see under AMAZONS.

Hydra A monster faced by HERCULES as one of his Twelve Labours. A multi-headed serpent infesting the swamp of Lerna, it grew two new heads whenever one was cut off; Hercules finally killed it with the assistance of his nephew Iolaus, who cauterised the stumps with a firebrand. He used its blood thereafter as poison for his arrows (see *The Sore-Footed Man*, *CPlays* 140). In 'The Tiredness of Me and Herakles' (1972, *CP* 595–97), stanza 7, the Hydra represents the multiplying demands made on Baxter by his (especially female) followers, who threaten to devour him: 'To kill the heads of the Hydra / You need a clever branding iron.'

In 'In Numeris' (*Spark* 152–56 (155)) the 'Hydra' which 'can sway below the sullen river' is probably the real creature (a primitive freshwater polyp) rather than the mythological one.

Icarus Son of the great inventor DAEDALUS, who made wings for them to escape captivity in the LABYRINTH; but Icarus flew too near the sun, melted the wax holding his wings, and fell to his death in the sea. Though traditionally used as an example of reckless pride or over-ambition (Brumble 177–79, Rudd), Icarus is usually a positive figure of aspiration in Baxter. In the early 'Song of the Sea-Nymphs at the Death of Icarus' (1942, *CP* 5–6) he embodies 'youth immortal', beauty and grace, contrasted favourably with adult dullness and compromise: 'Lament ye for young Icarus, / Lament again! / For he is youth / Forever living and forever slain.' In 'This Indian Morning' (1959, *CP* 198), the morning 'brown as Icarus / Flows guiltless to the vault of noon,' and rises above the mundane world's 'Cretan labyrinth / Of money, conscience, work, glum dreams'. More gloomily, in the first version of 'Letter to Noel Ginn II' (1945, *Spark* 118–20) Baxter repesents himself returning to New Zealand as 'one drowned Icarian'. In *Aspects* (7) he suggests Icarus (along with PHAETON) as an archetype for New Zealand poets: 'These images signify the minor talent determined to be major; and I do not find the ambition in any way unsuitable or singular.' The more traditional moral view surfaces (slightly tongue-in-cheek) in 'Air Flight North' (1967, *CP* 391–92), where Baxter's sense of the 'Faustian' hubris of modern air travel causes him to 'meditate the doom / Of Icarus' over the airline coffee. Other references: 'Go down, go down in flames' (1947, N14.1017); 'The Drones (on the new magazine, *Encounter*)' (1956, N18.15)– 'their high Icarean flight'.

Ida, Mount The scene of ATTIS's self-castration in 'The Wound', poem 8 of 'Words to Lay a Strong Ghost' (1966, *CP* 360).

Io A river-god's daughter who became the target of ZEUS's lust. Either Zeus or his jealous wife HERA transformed her into a cow; Hera placed her under the care of the many-eyed ARGUS, and tormented her with a stinging gadfly which drove her helplessly from place to place across Europe and Asia. Finally she came to Egypt, where she recovered her human form; in some contexts she became identified with the goddess ISIS. Her story is told in Aeschylus's *Prometheus Bound* and, rather differently, in Ovid's *Metamorphoses*, book 1. In Aeschylus she visits Prometheus as a fellow-victim of the unjust power of Zeus; in Baxter's adaptation *The Bureaucrat* she becomes Io Gould, tormented by a psychological 'gadfly' of restlessness and sexual compulsion. In *Horse* the hero's girlfriend Fern is associated with Io, both explicitly (58; see ARGUS) and indirectly through the game of 'bulls and cows' (96) and Horse's final dream of her transformation into a heifer (119).

Isis The great Egyptian mother-goddess, a figure of fertility and benevolence, wife of Osiris (whom she restored to life after he was killed and dismembered) and mother of Horus. She was widely worshipped in the Greco-Roman world, and sometimes identified with the Greek heroine IO. Baxter associates her with the Virgin Mary. In 'Ode: Where nets of time encircle and destroy' (1943, *Spark* 282–88 (288)), 'Mother and child we worship, Isis and /

God Horus, Christ and Mary: for all guess / That from birth-pangs, from pain and swaddling-band / Hath sprung the vision marvellous'; and in 'Traveller's Litany' (1954, *CP* 139–45 (143)) he prays to the Virgin as '*Dei Genetrix* / goddess prefigured by / Isis and Semele'. Other references: 'Here is the Tomb of Time' (N4.225); 'Phantasmagoria of Silence' (N9.561).

Ismene Daughter of OEDIPUS (by his incestuous union with his mother Jocasta) and sister of ANTIGONE. She appears in Sophocles' *Oedipus at Colonus* and *Antigone*, where she is a more timid and conventional foil to her heroic sister. In *The Temptations of Oedipus* Baxter radically reconceives her as a compulsively promiscuous woman driven by incestuous love for her brother Eteocles, and gives her an outspoken defence of incest: 'The people we love best—with sex and soul and everything—are our own relatives. We're not peculiar. The savage hatred people have towards father [. . .] it comes from *their* knowledge that *they* love *their* relatives' (*CPlays* 248). In his Introduction Baxter suggests that Ismene is 'the heroine of many modern novels of female emancipation' (*CPlays* 336).

Ixion One of the famous criminals punished in the underworld, along with SISYPHUS and TANTALUS. Ixion, a king of Thessaly, planned to rape HERA (Juno), but was tricked into having intercourse with a duplicate of her made of clouds, a union which produced the first CENTAURS. ZEUS condemned him to be fastened on a perpetually turning wheel of fire. Most of Baxter's references are to this torment, sometimes used as an image of human bondage in the body or in the temporal world: 'Ixion wheel of time and memory' ('Ode: Where nets of time encircle and destroy', 1943, *Spark* 282–88 (283)); 'Adam's sons / On wheel of flesh or heaven, each one an Ixion' ('Janus Unheard', *Spark* 457–67 (463)); 'When will the body cease to turn / Like Ixion on a wheel of dreams?' ('The Body', 1966–67, N27.65); see also 'Mandrakes for Supper (1959, *CP* 200).

In 'Mask' (*FA* 35) Baxter uses another aspect of the story as a metaphor for the way 'a poet may, without the impetus of a unique and real experience, so arrange his verbal symbols as to produce the appearance of a poem, as Ixion embraced a cloud mistaking it for Juno and so fathered the race of centaurs.'

Janus Roman god of doorways, and hence of beginnings and transitions; the month January is named after him. He was depicted with two faces, one looking backwards and one forwards. The most literally two-faced of Baxter's many ambivalent mythological figures, Janus briefly becomes prominent in his adolescent poetry, associated with his sense of being in a liminal state between childhood illusion and harsher adulthood. In 'Of Future Serenity' (1942, N9.537), 'The sallow Janus of my manhood year / will not sing of crisp leaves, thrushes' nests, / nor sleep on the floor of a snow-line hut.' This rejection of the pastoral is elaborated in the long poem 'Janus Unheard' (1944, *Spark* 457–67): 'And I must raise again / My Janus-head out of a country coma / Of pastoral falsity, of rain on leaves; / Hear history's abstract music thunder' (457). Janus makes his last appearance in 'Crossing Cook Strait' (1947–56, *CP* 159–60), where the 'ambiguous' figure of 'the socialist father' who wears the 'mask of Dionysus' is described as 'the Janus made formidable by loveless years'. For further discussion see chapter 2.

Jason Adventurer and tragic hero, quester for the Golden Fleece. He was the dispossessed heir to the kingdom of Iolcos; when he turned up to reclaim the throne from his usurping uncle Pelias, the king dispatched him on a quest to reclaim a lost treasure, the Golden Fleece, from the barbarian kingdom of Colchis on the Black Sea. Jason assembled a crew of other heroes, the Argonauts (including HERCULES and ORPHEUS), and set out on a perilous voyage in the ship *Argo*. In Colchis, King Aeetes was hostile but his daughter MEDEA, a powerful enchantress, fell in love with Jason. She used her magic to help him carry out the impossible tasks imposed by her father (to yoke fire-breathing oxen and plough a field, sow the field with dragons' teeth, and then defeat the armed warriors who would sprout up from the teeth). When Aeetes then broke his word, Medea helped Jason to steal the Fleece and escape from Colchis; in the escape she killed her brother ABSYRTUS to distract pursuit. On their return to Iolcos Medea treacherously killed King Pelias to restore Jason to his throne; instead, the people drove them out. They went to Corinth, where Jason tried to desert his barbarian sorceress and marry a local princess, CREUSA; Medea murdered Creusa on her wedding day, and then, to complete her revenge on Jason, killed her own children by him, before escaping in a dragon-drawn chariot. Jason died when a piece of the rotting hulk of the *Argo* fell on his head. The story of the Argonauts is told in Apollonius's short epic *Argonautica*; the tragic conclusion is most familiar from Euripides' tragedy *Medea*.

Jason almost never appears in Baxter's published work, but is a recurring presence in the unpublished poems. 'I Jason' (1944, N10.627), a sonnet in the style of Hopkins written when Baxter was seventeen, shows the old Jason looking back in grief and guilt over the sorcerous trickery by which he won the Fleece and the calamitous end of his relationship with Medea: 'ill-made, heart-mauled, in racking dire / I'll curse sure-fruits of God-forgetting, spill / Remorse to acid-eat.'

'Husband to Wife' (1956, N18.45) and 'Husband to Wife (modern version)' (1957, N19.46) satirically apply the names of Jason and Medea to a modern-day suburban couple and their tidy birth-controlled sex life: 'My sweet Medea, let us sing / Below the dragon-guarded star: / We have two kids, hey-ding-a-ding, / A flat, a fridge, a motor car' ('Husband to Wife'). Here the Golden Fleece is satirically reduced to a symbol of the female genitalia: 'The Golden Fleece that Jason found / And held and guarded with his sword, / Your fanny in its flannel gown / Has left me feeling slightly bored' ('Husband to Wife (modern version)'). But in 'The Phoenix' Nest' (1957, N19.30), Baxter applies the image more romantically to his wife's hair: 'Let it hang below your shoulders, / The gold Jason stole: / A gaol to ease the body's pain, /A cloister for my soul'—an image he recalls and partly retracts in 'To My Wife' (1959, N19.91): 'Once I wrote of Jason's fleece / Because your hair was long, / But now I am a Catholic / I sing a different song.'

In two versions of a poem written in 1961–62, looking back on his year in Christchurch in 1948, Baxter associates Jason with his friend and mentor Denis Glover: 'You were the Jason of our times, / The one who had the courage of his crimes; // You taught me how to think' ('A View from the Port Hills', N22.35); 'You seemed / The impossible Jason I had dreamed / About: a man who'd grabbed and baled the Golden Fleece // Simply by being tough' ('The Fleece', N23.54). The allusion, appropriate to Glover's nautical background and buccaneering air, also hints at Baxter's ambivalence towards his youthful hero.[1]

'To M.A.B.' (1943, *CP* 18), an early poem addressed to his mother, uses the image of Jason's Sown Men as contrast to our evolutionary relationship with the natural world: 'No mind and body / Unique and sudden birth / Like dragon-tooth sprang sprightly / New-clothed from earth.'

Jove see ZEUS

Juno see HERA

Jupiter see ZEUS

Labyrinth The maze-like structure, made up of impossibly complex winding corridors, constructed by the craftsman DAEDALUS for King Minos of Crete, as a prison for the MINOTAUR; THESEUS, with the help of ARIADNE's thread, found his way through it and killed the Minotaur. A favourite image of Baxter's, associated both with the complexities of the fallen world and with the unconscious mind; for discussion, see chapter 5. The references which seem to have clear mythological associations are: [POEMS] 'Reverie of a Prisoner' (c.1943, N10.588); 'Poem in Naseby Graveyard' (1946, *CP* 48); 'Lost in the labyrinth no Ariadne' (c.1947, N14.1013); 'Virginia Lake' (1947–48, *CP* 74); 'Wellington' (1949, *CP* 76–77); 'Spring Song' (1953, *SP* 50–51); 'Letter to the World' (1955, *CP* 149–50); 'How through that labyrinth' (1956, N18.58); 'For Kevin Ireland' (1957, *CP* 186); 'The Carvers' (1958, *CP* 195–96); 'This Indian Morning' (1959, *CP* 198); 'Christchurch 1948' (1960, *CP* 215–16); 'The Ballad of One Tree Hill' (1963–64, *CP* 293–96); 'The Rock' (1966, *CP*

1 These poems and Baxter's other references to Jason and Medea are discussed in more detail in Miles, 'Baling the Golden Fleece'.

362); 'The Labyrinth' (1970, *CP* 488–89); 'Autumn Testament' 17 (1972, *CP* 549); [PLAY] *The Temptations of Oedipus*, *CPlays* 244; [LETTER] to Frank McKay, 3 Dec. 1969 (FM 22/4/11).

Laertes ODYSSEUS's father, who had handed over the kingship of Ithaca to his son. When Odysseus returned home after twenty years he found the old man, broken by despair of his son's return, dirty and ragged, working as a labourer in his orchard (*Odyssey*, book 24). Baxter draws a more romanticised contrast between Laertes' contentedness at home and Odysseus's lonely wandering. In 'The Sirens' (1952, *CP* 130–33) the Sirens describe to Odysseus how 'pious Laertes labours / Within his garden plot, where pollen-heavy / Bees dart beside him, homing to their hive.' In 'To My Father' (1954, *SP* 54–56) Baxter compares his father to Laertes—'Yours are Laertes' garden-walls / Green and abiding, where fruit swells / For earth's good reasons'—whereas 'My own Ulysses' heart recalls / With grief, gone seasons.'

Lares and Penates Two varieties of Roman household gods, the *Lares* (singular *Lar*) associated with ancestral spirits and the *Penates* with the store cupboards; collectively they embody the welfare of the house and family. Sometimes Baxter treats these figures neutrally, as in 'Prelude N.Z.' (1943, *CP* 16–17), where Maori bring their *penates* with them to Aotearoa. But he tends to see them more critically, as classical versions of 'the kitchen god', the false idol of domestic respectability and propriety ('Virgin', *MH* 73–74). As early as 'Who hath not heard' (N2.85), written when Baxter was fourteen, 'the ancient Lars' [*sic*] are associated with the 'bars' which hold us back from union with nature and the 'laws of love'. In 'In Praise and Blame of Marriage' (c.1959, N20.52) the stultifying effect of a dull marriage is blamed on them: 'It seems our gods require it—those grim Lars / We feed with pieces of ourselves. / They make the plates ride firm upon the shelves. / Households obey the order of the stars.' There are similar implications of confinement in the traveller's return to his 'Lares et penates' in 'Return to Exile' (*SP* 82). In 'To a House Spider Building above the Lavatory Door' (N17.54) the spider is hailed with nervous jocularity as the 'Lars' [*sic*] of the place: 'I would have chosen a less candid Lars.'

Latona In Greek, Leto; mother (by Zeus) of APOLLO and DIANA. In 'Bracchiae' (1944, *Spark* 473–74) Baxter calls them 'Latona's children'. 'There was an altar' (*Spark* 333) draws on Ovid's story (*Metamorphoses*, book 6) of how she turned a group of peasants into frogs when they churlishly prevented her from drinking at their spring.

Leander see HERO AND LEANDER

Leda Queen of Sparta who was seduced by ZEUS in the form of a swan, and gave birth to an egg (or several) containing HELEN of Troy, her sister CLYTEMNESTRA, and her brothers Castor and Pollux. Baxter's only reference to the story is in the early 'Bird-Envocation [*sic*]' (c.1943, N12.729), invoking the 'silver swan / Whom Zeus divine / Didst put as raiment on / For rape of Leda.'

Lethe One of the rivers of the underworld (see HADES); when the souls of the dead drank its water they forgot their past lives. Baxter has several references to its power to erase memory and hence pain. Early poems allude to our yearning for 'cold Lethaean seas' ('The Earth No Mother', N10.629) and to the 'Lethe-draft' of Buddhist Nirvana ('Bhudda' [*sic*], N4.224). In 'Night in Tarras (1947–49, *CP* 81–82) the oblivion comes from alcohol—a country pub is 'Lethaean night's abode'. An unpublished longer draft of 'At Rakiura' (1966, N27.34, cf. *CP* 376–77) presents Stewart Island as a place of abnegation and void—'A good place to die in!'—which 'taught / Us that the waters of Lethe were real'. In 'Bar Room Elegy' (1951, *CP* 119) 'the Oblivious' is one of the 'twelve great rivers' flowing out of Eden. Other reference: 'Symbolism', *FA* 62.

The Leith Stream in Dunedin—though Baxter never explicitly makes the connection—is often mentioned in contexts of memory of past pain which may be seen as evoking the Lethe: for instance, in 'The Weirs' (1960–62, *CP* 262–63), which recalls a lovers' quarrel and 'acrid tears' beside 'the muscled Leith water' ('I think of them after fourteen years / As a kind of awkward benediction'); or 'Henley Pub' (1961–65, *CP* 324–25), whose speaker remembers with guilt and self-loathing making love to his mistress, her 'window open to the Leith Stream's roar'.

Maenads *see* BACCHANTES

Mars [Latin] or **Ares** [Greek] God of war and lover of Aphrodite/ VENUS. Revered by the Romans but regarded more equivocally by the Greeks, Ares/Mars is an entirely negative figure for the pacifist Baxter. His adolescent anti-war poetry contains several references to the destructive power of 'Mars, red Mars' ('The Gods of Greece', N3.157); see also 'The Sacred Fire', (N1.77), 'Ode MCMXLIV' (N12.727), 'Leap-Year' (N12.728). The most vivid and degrading image is in 'The Return' (1956, *CP* 179), where 'Rigid Mars, / Demon of the middle earth, leprous / Chewer of continents' is reduced to 'a boy tumbling / In a ditch with a bloody nose'. In 'Education' Baxter describes the dehumanising effect of military cadet training on his schoolmates: 'They were entering the borders of the collective fantasy generated by Ares, dealer in souls. My own fantasies were Venusian, perhaps less harmful' (*MH* 137).

Marsyas A satyr (half-man, half-goat). As Baxter summarises the story (*CP* 628), 'Marsyas the goatman [. . .] competed with Apollo in playing the ukelele and was flayed alive when he lost' (more traditionally, he played the flute in competition with Apollo's lyre; see Ovid, *Metamorphoses*, book 6). Baxter calls him 'a likely emblem of the [. . .] modern poet, a member of a dying species, flayed by his neuroses'. He is explicating 'Pig Island Letters' 10 (*CP* 283), on the ways in which poets end their lives: 'For the mystery requires / A victim—Marsyas the manbeast / Hung up and flayed on a fir tree, / Or a death by inches, catheter and wife / Troubling an old man's vanity' (which in turn spells out the allusion to the poet's friends as 'Companions to the manbeast [. . .] touching the flayed hide gently' in section 9).

Medea The witch-princess of Colchis who fell in love with JASON and helped him win the Golden Fleece, then took a terrible revenge when he betrayed her; for the story, see under JASON. Though some writers (such as Euripides in his tragedy *Medea*) have treated Medea sympathetically, for Baxter she is unequivocally evil. 'I Jason' (1944, N10.627) avoids naming her but alludes to her sinister magic and her hideous murder of CREUSA. In 'For those who lie with crooked limbs in the straight grave' (1944,

Spark 368–70) Medea becomes, as Baxter explained to Ginn (letter 16 July 1944, *Spark* 366) a 'symbol of that which survives by craft and coldness'; the passage conflates her dragon-flight from Corinth after the murder of her children ('Medea rides / The black and marble midnight: twin dragons / Before her chariot flaming') and her dismemberment of her brother ABSYRTUS ('Young Absyrtus dead / In the blue seaway, drowned and floating head'), making her the archetypal child-killer and destroyer of the hopes of the future. In 'Husband to Wife' (1956, N18.45) the modern bourgeois wife is 'My sweet Medea'; her efficient use of modern contraceptive techniques ('diaphragm and Koromex') to limit her family ('More kids would strain our bank account / And spoil your lovely figure, dear') is implicitly equated with the ancient Medea's child-murder. (In 'Husband to Wife (modern version)', N19.46, the wife becomes 'My dearest Psyche', though the allusions to Jason and the Golden Fleece remain; see PSYCHE.)

Medusa *see* GORGONS

Meleager Hero, prince of Calydon, leader of the hunt for the Calydonian Boar. At his birth it was prophesied that he would live until a certain log burning on the fire was consumed. His mother Althaea retrieved and carefully preserved the log, until she learned that Meleager had killed her brothers in a hunting quarrel; then she thrust it back into the fire, destroying it and her son. Baxter's only allusion to the story is in a semi-legible passage about 'Meleager's twig' in 'Oration for Unaccepted Death' (N25.22).

Memnon An Ethopian king, son of Aurora the dawn goddess, killed by Achilles in the TROJAN WAR. According to Ovid (*Metamorphoses* book 10), Jupiter transformed the ashes of his funeral pyre into a flock of birds, which fought to the death and fell back onto the pyre. This association of Memnon with ashes may explain a cryptic allusion in 'Transparent Mural' (N10.626), which links sunset, dying embers and human mortality: 'for night they wait not, no deep-blooded night / But Memnon's grey, even life's frail jade-green / in their Elysium. Like coals, like men.'

Mercury see HERMES

Midas A foolish king whose ineptitude in judging a music contest caused APOLLO to give him ass's ears. In Ovid's version of the story (*Metamorphoses*, book 11), Midas's barber, unable to keep this secret to himself, whispered it into a hole in the ground, but a bed of reeds that grew up on the spot betrayed it by whispering 'Midas has ass's ears!' Baxter alludes to this story in *Jerusalem Journal* (MS 0975/82.15).

Minerva see ATHENE

Minotaur A monster with a human body and a bull's head, product of the Cretan Queen Pasiphae's unnatural intercourse with a bull; King Minos kept in hidden in the heart of the LABYRINTH and fed it on human victims, until it was killed by THESEUS. For a discussion of Baxter's often sympathetic treatment of the Minotaur, see chapter 5. The key references are: 'Reverie of a Prisoner' (c.1943, N10.588); 'Lost in the Labyrinth no Ariadne' (1947, N14.1013); 'Letter to the World' (1955, *CP* 149–50); 'The Labyrinth' (1970, *CP* 488); *The Temptations of Oedipus* (*CPlays* 231).

Muse The Nine Muses, daughters of ZEUS and companions of APOLLO, lived on Mount HELICON and were the patron goddesses of the arts and literature. Poets from Homer onwards have invoked them as the source or symbol of poetic inspiration. Late classical and post-classical writers name the Muses (Calliope, Clio, Erato, Euterpe, Melpomene, Polyhymnia, Terpsichore, Thalia, and Urania), and assign them individually to particular art forms or literary genres (Calliope to epic, Clio to history, and so on), but Baxter ignores these details; his 'Muse' is anonymous and (usually) singular. His changing conception of her, and in particular his startling conflation of her with the GORGON Medusa in the figure of 'the snake-haired Muse', is discussed in chapter 1. The relevant texts are: [POEMS] 'At School I have no time to Dream' (1939, *NSP* 170); 'Apollo But Sleeps' (c.1940, N4.203); 'Horatian Ode on the Banishment of Beer', 1944, *NSP* 173); 'Poetry in New Zealand' (*NZ Listener*, 4 June 1954); 'To My Father' (1954, *SP* 54–56); 'The Muse' (1961, *CP* 234–35); 'Letter to Robert Burns' (1963, *CP* 289–891); 'The Clock Tower' (c.1966, N26.74); 'A French Letter to Louis Johnson' (1966, N26.62); 'The Muse (to Louis Johnson)' (1966, *CP* 352); [PROSE] 'Mask', *FA* 42; 'Portrait of the Artist as a New Zealander' (*ODT* 1960); 'Essay on the Higher Learning' (*Spike* 1961), 61; *Aspects* 7; 'Man', *MH* 116–17; 'Education', *MH* 135; 'Virgin', *MH* 65–66; 'Kiwi Habits' (*Otago University Review* 1969); 'On the Burns Fellowship' (*Landfall* 1968); [LETTER] to Fleur Adcock, 11 Sept. 1961 (FM 27/1/4).

Naiads A class of NYMPHS associated with water, especially rivers and springs. Baxter's only references are in three early unpublished poems: a tourist's 'dreams of naiads' in 'Soliloquy on a Train' (N11.669); 'Naiads are dead' in 'Sea-Elegy' (N13.781); and a comparison of a woman to 'a naiad yearning / To her own shape' reflected in the water, in 'The Creek' (N16.45).

Narcissus The handsome and vain youth who fell in love with his own reflection in a pool, pined away, and was transformed into the flower that bears his name (Ovid, *Metamorphoses*, book 3). Freud coined the term 'narcissism' for a pathological degree of self-love.

Baxter associates him—both at the time and in retrospect—with the solipsistic self-enclosure of adolescence. In 'Autobiographical' (N10.634) the seventeen-year-old Baxter looks back on his fifteen-year-old self: 'girded about / With a world-embracing solitude there stood / Narcissus, master of the iron wood.' 'Narcissus' (N11.678), written in the same year, shows him gazing at 'The face most strangely known and beautiful' and seeing it turn into an image of the external world—'Perhaps he saw a God before he died.' Several later poems associate Narcissus with his younger self (e.g. 'Youth', N27.52, or 'An Old Photograph', originally titled 'Narcissus', N20.29). The most famous is 'At Day's Bay' (written New Year 1965, *CP* 308–09): 'I think of / adolescence: that sad boy / I was, thoughts crusted with ice / on the treadmill of self-love, // Narcissus damned, who yet brought / like a coal in a hollow / stalk, the seed of fire that runs / through my veins now.'

The fusion in these lines of Narcissus with PROMETHEUS suggests how Narcissus can also, more positively, become a figure of the artist. In 'Symbolism' Baxter quotes Auden's view of Narcissus as the archetype of 'the poet who loses his soul for poetry', but adds that 'it does not seem that a man can be an artist without also being a narcissist—that is, without creating a fictitious self more powerful, knowledgeable, than, in fact, he is' (*FA* 70). 'The Doctrine' (1967, *CP* 413–14), a defence of poetry and the imagination, immortalises Narcissus: 'The boy who went out and gazed at his face in the river / Was changed, they say, into a marvellous flower / Perpetually renewed in each Greek summer / Long after his tough companions had become old bones'—a neat twist on the cliché.

Two 1966 poems play darkly with images of reflection and selfhood. In 'Daughter' (*CP* 354–55) the poet, looking down at his daughter in bed, is 'Narcissus bending over / The water face! [. . .] My own eye looks back.' And in 'At the Fox Glacier Hotel' (*CP* 368), a tourist photo of the Southern Alps reflected in a lake becomes 'a lovely mirror / For any middle-aged Narcissus to drown in'; here Baxter contrasts a narcissistic 'kind of love', which sees the beloved merely as a mirror of the self, with 'some other / Kind of love' which acknowledges the terrifying otherness of the beloved.

Neoptolemus Greek warrior, son of ACHILLES, who came to TROY after his father's death and played a major role in the sack of the city. Also known as **Pyrrhus**, a name Baxter does not use. In Sophocles' *Philoctetes* he reluctantly accompanies ODYSSEUS on his mission to trick PHILOCTETES back to Troy, but after a conflict of conscience shifts his allegiance to Philoctetes. For Sophocles, Neoptolemus is the moral centre of the play; Baxter's adaptation *The Sore-footed Man*, elevating Odysseus to hero, greatly diminishes Neoptolemus's dramatic importance and moral stature, reducing him to (in Baxter's terse description) 'a necessary fence post' (Introduction, *CPlays* 335).

Neptune see POSEIDON

Niobe Queen of Thebes, whose rash boast that her numerous sons and daughters (seven of each, according to Ovid) made her superior to the goddess LATONA (who had only two) was punished by the killing of all her children; the bereft Niobe wept until she turned to stone (Ovid, *Metamorphoses*, book 6). In 'The Eyes of Dis' (1962, *CP* 259–60), Baxter compares CIMMERIA (Wellington) to 'A square black stone, an armless Niobe / Whose surface sweats [. . .] An inconsolable weeping stone.' In the surreal dream-poem 'Nocturnal on a Friday' (c.1959, N20.65), 'Tears, tears of a giant Niobe / Flood the red aisle and float me out the door.'

Nymphs Nature spirits in the form of beautiful women, who frequented and personified features of the landscape—dryads in the trees, oreads in the mountains, NAIADS in the rivers, and so on. Baxter's scattered references show no consistent pattern of symbolism. 'Song of the Sea-Nymphs at the Death of Icarus' (1942, *CP* 5–6) and 'There was an altar' (1944, *Spark* 333–34) draw on Ovidian stories (see ICARUS and LATONA); the 'wild nymph of water' embodied in the underwater spring at Waimarama ('Pig Island Letters' 13, 1963, *CP* 284–85) alludes to the story of ARETHUSA but gives it a Christian significance as an allegory of divine grace. The 'woman with a bone-white face' who inspires a longing 'to die in the arms of the nymph' in 'Hog-Fat' (1967, *CP* 413) is one of Baxter's sinisterly alluring anima figures, evoking CIRCE (though Circe is not a nymph). In 'The Bohemians' (1968, *CP* 428) the 'companions / Who rose like off-white marble nymphs / From blankets and tree-roots' are presumably human art-groupies ('nymph' as slang for prostitute goes back at least to the sixteenth century), but also carry a touch of mythical glamour. In 'Mining Town' (1968, *CP* 433–34) 'the rusted iron cradle / In which the great nymph screamed and died' suggests the violation of the river by human greed. In 'Autumn Testament' 30 (1972, *CP* 555) Baxter recalls talking to the trees in the Auckland Domain, described as 'The tree nymphs—their great beauty made me tremble'—the personification of trees as women hinting again at Ovidian myths of transformation. See also NAIADS.

Odysseus [Greek] or **Ulysses** [Latin] King of Ithaca, warrior, voyager, trickster, the hero of Homer's *Odyssey*, and by far Baxter's favourite classical hero. Odysseus was reluctant to leave his home, his wife PENELOPE, his newborn son TELEMACHUS, and his old father LAERTES, to fight in the Trojan War (see TROY). But he proved a great tactician and secret agent, recovering PHILOCTETES from the island of Lemnos (an incident Baxter dramatises in *The Sore-footed Man*), and devising the stratagem of the Wooden Horse to capture Troy after ten years of war. His homeward voyage took another ten years, as he was delayed by the hostility of POSEIDON but repeatedly helped by his patroness ATHENE (neither of whom Baxter makes significant reference to). Of his many adventures on the voyage, Baxter focuses on his stays with the the nymph CALYPSO (*Odyssey*, book 5) and the sorceress CIRCE (book 10), his visit to the underworld (book 11; see HADES), his passage of SCYLLA AND CHARYBDIS and his temptation by the SIRENS (book 12). Episodes ignored by Baxter include his encounter with the man-eating Cyclops Polyphemus (book 9) and his stay with the Phaeacians, who (after all his companions have been lost at sea) help him to return alone and disguised to Ithaca (books 6 and 13). There the faithful Penelope is beset with suitors who have occupied his palace, trying to force her to marry one of them; helped by Telemachus and a few loyal servants, Odysseus kills the suitors and is reunited with Penelope. In Homer's account he lives out his old age in peace; but some classical sources, and post-classical writers such as Dante, Tennyson, and Nikos Kazantzakis, send him out on further wanderings, establishing the image (important to Baxter) of Odysseus as a man driven by insatiable wanderlust.

Baxter's treatment of Odysseus is discussed at length in chapter 6. The texts in which he appears are: 'Me Also' (1944, *Spark* 334); 'At Balclutha' (1944, *Spark* 358–59); 'Letter to Noel Ginn' (1944, *CP* 27–29); 'Odysseus'-1 (1945–47, *CP* 42); 'What the Sirens Sang' (1951, N16.15); 'The Homecoming' (1945–47, *CP* 121); 'The Journey' (1945–47, *CP* 127); 'Greek Interlude' (1945–47, N16.59); 'The Sirens' (1952–55, *CP* 130–33); 'Traveller's Litany' (1954, *CP* 139–45); 'To My Father' (1954, *SP* 54–56); 'Threnos' (1956, N18.31); 'Letter to Bob Lowry' (1956, N18.39); 'To One Travelling by Sea' (1956, N19.16); 'To a Travelling Friend' (1957, *CP* 182–83); 'Odysseus'-2 (1957, N19.22); 'Green Figs at Table' (1957, *CP* 183); 'Odysseus'-3 (1957, N19.33); 'The Old Age of

Odysseus' (1958–59, N19.89); 'The Tempter' (1959–60, *CP* 205); 'Footnote to *Antony and Cleopatra*' (1959–60, *CP* 212); 'The Strait' (1962, *CP* 253; see ELPENOR); 'The Watch' (1963, *CP* 273–74); 'The Horse's Grave' (1963–65, N25.43); 'Back to Ithaca' (1966–67, *CP* 384–85); 'Autumn Testament' 10 (1972, *CP* 541); [PLAY] *The Sore-footed Man* (*CPlays* 127–59).

Oedipus King of Thebes, whose tragic story is familiar from Sophocles' plays *Oedipus the King* and *Oedipus at Colonus*, and also from Freud's use of it in defining the 'Oedipus complex'. As the result of an oracle that he would grow up to kill his father (King Laius) and marry his mother (Jocasta), the newborn Oedipus was lamed (his name means 'swollen-foot') and cast out on a mountainside to die; but he was rescued by a shepherd and brought up, in ignorance of his parentage, by the king and queen of Corinth. Coming of age, and learning of the prophecy, he fled Corinth and headed for Thebes. On the road he unwittingly killed Laius; arriving in Thebes, he solved the riddle of the SPHINX and won the hand of the widowed Jocasta. They had four children together: Eteocles, POLYNEICES, ANTIGONE, and ISMENE. *Oedipus the King* dramatises how the truth came to light, Jocasta killed herself, and Oedipus blinded himself. In *Oedipus at Colonus* the old, blind king, in exile accompanied by his daughter Antigone, comes to Colonus (outside Athens), is received and protected by King THESEUS, and dies in mysterious circumstances.

In an article headlined 'The human being is object and subject' (*Critic* 1967), Baxter names the classical Oedipus along with the biblical Adam and Eve, Job and Christ as an archetype of the human. His earliest reference to Oedipus ('Letter to Noel Ginn II', 1946, *Spark* 118–20) is a rather dark Freudian joke, implying that his youthful libido is a displacement of the Oedipal desire to return to the womb: 'Time's natural Oedipus, I find a token / Of God in girls and mountain scenery— / The girls to ——, the hills for climbing on' (119). Later, more grimly, he offers Oedipus as a tragic image of 'man's condition', as the Sphinx sees him in 'Canticle of the Desert' (c.1955, N17.98): 'Here came the limping Oedipus / To answer me in terms of man's condition / With incest and a hated crown.' 'A Sermon for All Fools Day' (c.1960, N20.74) broods over our enslavement to 'the axe and rope of sex, / The fatal crown of Oedipus'. Oedipus embodies the fatal connections between human birth, sexuality and death. In Baxter's words, 'Whether or not Freud was in the right of it, the Oedipus tragedy is fundamental to all men, since we marry our mother when we descend into the grave' (Introduction to *The Temptations of Oedipus*, *CPlays* 335).

In 1968 Baxter adapted Sophocles' *Oedipus at Colonus* as *The Temptations of Oedipus* (*CPlays* 230–60). He had earlier parodied his own self-identification with Oedipus in the character of the drunken poet Grummet in *Horse*, declaiming to the shocked Literary Club, 'I am Oedipus the King of many-gated Thebes' (85). Baxter's adaptation of Sophocles intensifies the sense of sexual doom by doubling Oedipus's incest, giving him a child begotten on his daughter/half-sister Antigone. He reconfigures the Oedipus/Theseus relationship into a conflict between the ascetic 'yogi' Oedipus and the ruthlessly worldly 'commissar' Theseus (see chapter 6), and focuses the play on Oedipus's struggle to overcome the 'temptations' of life and embrace death (see chapter 8) .

Other references: passing references to the Oedipus complex in Baxter's letters (to Noel Ginn, 4 May 1943, *Spark* 215; to Fleur Adcock, 30 Oct. 1961, FM 27/1/13), and in 'Virgin' (*MH* 81); a parodic Modernist poem on 'Oedipus in his tower' in 'Mask' (*FA* 38); Oedipus's blinding as a castration symbol in 'Symbolism' (*FA* 75).

Orestes Son of Agamemnon and CLYTEMNESTRA; with the help of his sister ELECTRA, he avenged the murder of his father by killing his mother and her lover Aegisthus, and was afterwards pursued by the FURIES for the crime. The story is told in Aeschylus's *Oresteia* trilogy: *The Libation-Bearers* deals with the revenge, and *Eumenides (The Kindly Ones)* with Orestes' trial before an Athenian court, in which he is cleared and the Furies pacified. Baxter began but soon abandoned a dramatic adaptation of the story, *The Gentle Ones* (MS 0975/051); parts of it were reworked in *The Runaway Wife*, which also features the pursuit of the hero (ORPHEUS) by the Furies. 'Recollection' (N16.35) pairs Orestes with PROMETHEUS as images of himself in adolescence: 'That green Orestes, groaning in a gyre / Of unremarkable booze, sweated out / In farm or factory the blood's mire; / Sucked milk of metaphor at a woman's tit [. . .] These alter egoes [*sic*] haunt me as I go.'

Orion A great hunter who after his death (from the sting of a scorpion) was transformed into the constellation of that name. The reference in 'The Phoenix' Nest' (N19.30) to 'King Orion / Fettered by a hair' is primarily to the constellation.

Orpheus The archetypal poet and musician of Greek mythology, who played on the lyre and sang with such beauty that not only human beings but birds and animals, trees and rivers and rocks came to listen to him. When his wife EURYDICE died from a snakebite, Orpheus descended into the underworld and sang for HADES and PERSEPHONE, pleading for her return. The gods granted his prayer, on condition that he should go on ahead and not look behind to see whether she was following him. Near the exit to the upper world, Orpheus's resolve broke, he looked back, and lost Eurydice for ever. In his grief he retreated to the wilderness where he played to wild nature, until a band of BACCHANTES in their Dionysiac frenzy tore him to pieces. According to Virgil (*Georgics* book 4) and Ovid (*Metamorphoses* books 10–11), his severed head continued to sing a lament as it floated down the river Hebrus. His legend has repeatedly been invoked by poets, artists and musicians as a self-reflexive image of their art, its powers and tragic limitations.

Perhaps surprisingly, Orpheus is not one of Baxter's major 'figures of self', but he is a significant secondary figure. He first appears as the speaker of 'Eurydice' (c.1941, N6.345), mourning his wife's loss and concluding that 'Beauty has no place upon the cold earth-face'. In subsequent poems Orpheus himself comes to stand for the combined power of art (poetry) and love which may be able to restore and regenerate this fallen winter world. In 'Ode: Where nets of time encircle and destroy' (1943, *Spark* 282–88), 'grief-torn Orpheus' embodies the 'language of love' and teaches us that 'love immortal in time's sphere is found' (286). In 'Songs of the Desert' 5 (1947, *CP* 56), 'The dull nerve strung upon the harp of love / Resounds, and earth achieves her unborn spring—/ For this is Orpheus' music and his grove. / See how the bitter field is blossoming!' The appropriately titled 'Descent of Orpheus' (*Landfall* 1957) transposes this life-giving power into a more unromantic and bawdy vein, apostrophising Orpheus as 'Sallow, small, with broken teeth, [. . .] no hero'; his underworld journey, encountering and transforming CERBERUS, TANTALUS, SISYPHUS and the DANAIDS, culminates in a reunion with Eurydice 'Like any boy under a railway arch / Hot under frogskin [i.e. condom], coming to the clinch.'

In the 1960s Baxter's regenerative vision of Orpheus the poet takes on a darker tone. In 'Reflection at Khandallah Baths' (1963, *CP* 288) the poet's 'dry mind' cannot 'renew or find / The Orphic light in what is mortal'; and the reference to 'Orphic harmony' in 'Ballad to the Dunedin City Mothers' (1964, N24.76) is bitterly ironic. Kendrick Smithyman is associated in 'The Whale's Paunch' (1963, *CP* 274) with 'The head of Orpheus bloody and smiling, / In a land of rivers the dry man singing.' In 'Doppelganger' [*sic*] (1964, N25.63) the poet encounters his alter ego in a bleak underworld landscape where 'snakes of grey water hiss / in praise of Orpheus'. The verse dialogue *Requiem for Sebastian* (*CPlays* 87–92) recalls the earlier Romantic celebrations of Orpheus as the renewer of life, as the titular musician is hailed as 'an Orpheus underground' who renewed for his listeners the possibility of joy, so that 'Zombies turned into people' (91); but Sebastian himself is an artist *maudit*, drunken, promiscuous and ultimately suicidal. There is a similarly unflattering self-portrait of the artist in Baxter's most extended treatment of Orpheus, the unpublished Aristophanic tragicomedy *The Runaway Wife* (discussed in chapter 8). Here Orpheus's recklessly Bohemian behaviour drives Eurydice to retreat to 'the Hades coffee bar', and he is only able to recover her at the cost of castration by the FURIES. Orphic power does not necessarily make the poet either good or happy.

Orpheus's most significant appearance in Baxter's prose is the fable in 'Criticism' (*FA* 28–29), where Orpheus the poet must resist exploitation by the politician and technocrat PROMETHEUS. Other references: 'Symbolism', *FA* 62; *Aspects* 7.

Pan The horned and goat-legged god of wild nature, who haunts woods and mountains, playing his pan-pipes and inspiring 'panic' terror in those who encounter him. A figure beloved of the Romantics and of Edwardian writers, Pan appears only in Baxter's juvenilia. He takes for instance the central role in the Keatsian 'The Gods of Greece' (c.1941, N3.157): 'most beauteous of the gods [. . .] he who was once the voice / Of nature and the woodland solitude [. . .]. Chant now his requiem who was the light / That shines beneath the husk of mortal things.' See also 'Enchanted Night' (N1.66); 'The Old Gods' (N2.112); 'I have beheld' (N6.347). After the age of sixteen, however, Baxter turns to less conventionally Romantic images of nature.

Pandora The first woman, whose name means 'all gifts', and who was created—according to the misogynistic myth told by Hesiod in *Works and Days* (and, with some variation, in *Theogony*)—as a trap for mankind. She brought a sealed jar ('Pandora's box', in post-classical versions) as her dowry; when the foolish Epimetheus opened it, out flew all the evils which afflict human life, leaving only Hope caught on the lip. Baxter's only reference to the story is in the unpublished 'Words to a Country Friend' (1960, N21.47): 'A secret knowledge is the last illusion. / When we unlock the black Pandora box / Out fly a hundred dubious assignations, / A bushel of humiliations / To float like blown-up condoms.'

Parnassus A mountain regarded as the home of APOLLO and the Muses (see MUSE). A cliché of poetic diction, used only ironically by Baxter, for instance in his account of Percival, the drunken poet and ex-convict whose priggish fellow-poets had 'agreed to shove him off the brink of Mount Parnassus' for his unrespectability.

Pegasus The winged horse which sprang from the blood of the GORGON Medusa when she was beheaded by PERSEUS, and whose hoofbeat on Mount HELICON caused the Hippocrene fountain to spring up. Hence Pegasus has become a now clichéd symbol for the poetic imagination. Baxter comments on Burns' fondness for the image ('the myth of Pegasus has great vigour in his thought [. . .] a magical beast signifying the imagination itself'—'Man', *MH* 107–8), and used it with reference to him in a juvenile poem, 'Burns'

(N5.315). For his own part, however, in his frequent returns to the Perseus/Gorgon myth, he avoids mention of Pegasus.

Pelion and Ossa Two mountains in Thessaly; the rebellious giants Otus and Ephialtes piled Mount Pelion on top of Mount Ossa in an attempt to invade heaven and overthrow ZEUS. Addressing Glover in 'A View from the Port Hills' (1961, N22.35), Baxter recalls that 'That year we piled / Pelion on Ossa'—an image suggesting both wild excess and rebellion against authority.

Penelope Wife of ODYSSEUS, famous for her chaste fidelity. During her husband's absence she fended off the suitors occupying his palace with the plea that she must first finish weaving the shroud of her father-in-law LAERTES—but carefully unravelled each night what she had woven during the day. Homer emphasises the deep bond between Odysseus and Penelope, and her canny intelligence which matches his. Baxter's lifelong identification with Odysseus, however, is balanced by a deep distaste for Penelope, whom he calls 'one of the most unattractive characters in fiction' (letter 20 Oct. 1961, FM 27/1/11). There is a fairly sympathetic vision in "The Sirens' (1952, *CP* 130–33 (132)) of 'sad Penelope, her tired fingers / Plucking at tapestry'—though even here it is qualified by the Sirens' reminder that Odysseus's desire to return home to her is only an illusion. More often Baxter emphasises her failure to understand her husband ('blind Penelope' in 'Odysseus'-1, 1945–47, *CP* 42), her unimportance in his life ('Pride was his polestar, never Penelope'—'What the Sirens Sang', 1951, N16.15), her drab domesticity and lack of sexual allure ('Burying your salt sperm / In the cupboards of a bony wife'—'Odysseus'-3, 1957, N19.33). The Odysseus of *The Sore-footed Man* (1967) cynically speculates that Penelope will 'very likely' have betrayed him in his absence—'If she hasn't then she's a fool' (*CPlays* 133). Most memorably, 'The Homecoming' (1952, *CP* 121) reconceives her as the mother rather than wife of the Odysseus figure—'his mother, grief's Penelope'—and her loyalty as a suffocating maternal possessiveness. This poem, and Baxter's view of Penelope in general, is illuminated in his discussion of Burns' 'Tam o' Shanter' in 'Man', *MH* 100–01: Tam's shrewish wife is seen as a 'domestic Penelope', demonstrating 'the melancholy dimension of distance between the independent male and his wife, who is also very much a mother figure, from whom his actual mode of being isolates him'.

Persephone [Greek] or **Proserpina** or **Proserpine** [Latin] Goddess of spring and queen of the underworld. The virgin daughter of DEMETER, she was gathering flowers with her nymph companions when HADES/Pluto rose up in his black chariot and carried her down to the underworld to be his consort. Demeter searched for her for a year, while the world grew barren, and when she discovered the truth demanded her daughter's return. But Hades had tricked Persephone into eating some seeds of a promegranate and, having eaten the food of the underworld, she could not return permanently to the world of the living. ZEUS arranged a compromise whereby she would spend six months of the year above ground and six months below, thus accounting for the cycle of the seasons. Baxter's references to Persephone/Proserpina (he uses both names, with a preference for the Greek) are discussed in chapter 8. The relevant texts are: [POEMS] 'Returning after many months' (1944, N13.785); 'Time lost in Winter' (c.1944, N13, unnumbered fragment after poem 806); 'Resurrection' (1944, *CS* 35); 'Persephone' (1946, N14.932); 'The Cave' (1948, *CP* 69); 'The Journey' (1952, *CP* 127); 'The Red-Haired Girl' (1962–63, N23.49); 'Thoughts of a Remuera Housewife' (1962–5, *CP* 314–15); [PLAY] *The Temptations of Oedipus* (*CPlays* 232, 233, 246, 247, 254, 259); [PROSE] 'The Pythoness' (*Listener* 1965); [LETTER] to Frank McKay, 22 April 1964 (FM 22/4/4).

Perseus A major hero of Greek mythology. Baxter ignores the stories of his birth and childhood (how his mother Danaë, locked inside a brazen tower, was impregnated by ZEUS in the form of a shower of gold; how mother and child were set adrift in a chest and came to the island of Seriphos), to focus on the central story of Perseus and the Gorgon. Perseus made a rash promise to the tyrant Polydectes to bring him the head of MEDUSA, one of the three GORGONS. He was helped by the gods ATHENE and HERMES, who lent him winged sandals and a cap of invisibility, and showed him how to avoid being petrified by the Gorgon by looking only at her reflection in his polished shield. With these aids Perseus killed Medusa; the winged horse PEGASUS sprang from her headless body. Flying back home, Perseus saw the princess ANDROMEDA about to be sacrificed to a sea monster; he rescued and married her. The rest of his story (which, unusually for a Greek hero, ends happily) is ignored by Baxter.

Given the importance of the Gorgon figure in Baxter's work, Perseus appears surprisingly rarely; but when he does, it is always with a strong sense of self-identification (even if disclaimed) on Baxter's part. In 'To the Moon' (N15.74) the poet advises the Gorgon-moon to turn from his window: 'I am no Perseus, gentle to destroy / Ending your vigil.' His fullest treatment of the myth is in 'Perseus' (1952, *CP* 129–30), in which he has, as he wrote to Brasch, 'adapted it to my own purposes as allegory' (31 March 1953, FM 20/2/3). Medusa here is an 'image of the soul's despair [. . .] child of derisive Chaos / And hateful Night'; Perseus is the artist, who on humanity's behalf confronts this chaos and overcomes it. Having done so, however, he must surrender to the gods who lent them 'the borrowed / Sandals of courage and the shield of art', descend to earth and trudge back to ordinary human life and domesticity with Andromeda.

In two later (unpublished) prose passages Baxter similarly allegorises aspects of the myth. In 'Further Notes on New Zealand Poetry', the young 'endeavour from time to hold up a mirror to the inhuman pattern of public events, as Perseus held up a shield to the Gorgon'. And in 'Jerusalem Journal' 3: 'In the Greek story a girl was left chained to a rock, to be eaten by the dragon that came out of the sea. I think the soul of my country is in the same predicament—and in particular, the Maori soul, te wairua Maori. The dragon is the dragon of materialism. I am a most unlikely hero. Yet I am prepared to die for that girl, even if I have no magical sword or winged sandals.'

Phaeton (More correctly 'Phaethon'.) Son of the sun god (Helios or APOLLO), who insisted on driving his father's sun-chariot, lost control, and was killed by a blast of ZEUS's lightning lest his erratic course should destroy the earth. Baxter has two brief allusions to him: in 'Ode: Where nets of time encircle and destroy' (1943, *Spark* 282–88), clouds are described as fleeing to earth, 'Phaeton-wise' (285); and in *Aspects* (7) he is taken (along with ICARUS) as an archetype for the New Zealand poet, signifying 'the minor talent determined to be major'.

Philoctetes Greek warrior of the TROJAN WAR, bearer of the bow of HERCULES. On the way to Troy he was marooned by his companions on the island of Lemnos, after a snakebite caused an incurable and festering wound; later, when it was prophesied that Troy could not be taken without his bow, ODYSSEUS and NEOPTOLEMUS (according to the best-known version in Sophocles' tragedy *Philoctetes*) came to persuade or trick him into rejoining them. Sophocles' play is adapted by Baxter in *The Sore-footed Man* (1967, *CPlays* 127–59). For a discussion of the play and of Baxter's rather ironic and reductive treatment of Philoctetes, see chapter 6.

Phlegethon One of the four rivers of the underworld (see HADES), known as the river of fire. Baxter associates it with the pains of alcoholism in 'Portrait of a Fellow-Alcoholic' (N23.36): 'Mother, have mercy on / Two idiot burnt brothers walking by / That cindered Phlegethon / Whose waves of fire and blackness I / Know better than the Mass.' It is alluded to but not named in 'Bar Room Elegy' (1951, *CP* 119): 'Out of Eden flow the the twelve great rivers / (The Flaming and the Oblivious are best known)'—again associating the power of alcohol with pain and oblivion (the Oblivious river is LETHE).

Phoebus see APOLLO

Pluto see HADES

Polyneices Son (and half-brother) of OEDIPUS by his incestuous marriage with Jocasta; after Oedipus's exile, he fought a civil war against his brother Eteocles for the throne of Thebes. In Baxter's *Temptations of Oedipus*, as in Sophocles' *Oedipus at Colonus*, Polyneices comes to beg Oedipus for his support against Eteocles, without success; but where Sophocles' Oedipus angrily rejects and curses his son, Baxter's Oedipus more gently tries to argue him out of the pursuit of worldly power, and offers him the 'blessing' of death. Baxter also assigns to Polyneices the attempted kidnapping of ANTIGONE and ISMENE which is carried out in Sophocles by his uncle CREON. Baxter describes the confrontation between Oedipus and Polyneices as 'the interior crux' of the play (Introduction, *CPlays* 336).

Poseidon [Greek] or **Neptune** [Latin] God of the sea and of earthquakes ('Earthshaker'). As the personification of the sea, he takes on the sea's symbolic associations for Baxter, as an image of the harsh and inimical aspects of the natural world, of death and of transformation or regeneration. In 'Napier' (1955, N18.6) he is shown punishing the complacent townspeople, who 'deplore the natural graces', by unleashing the 1931 earthquake: 'Truculent, in a gust of humour / Poseidon the Earth Shaker / altered the harbour, substituting / a mile of mudflats, pasture too salt to plow / for slateblue, rolling, savage sea' (perhaps an echo of Poseidon's punishment of the Phaeacians by damming up their harbour in *Odyssey* 13). The same harsh ironic humour is suggested in 'Summer 1967' (1967, *CP* 408–09): watching the young surfing and swimming, 'One can begin to shake with laughter, / Becoming oneself a metal Neptune.'

Poseidon becomes a recurring figure in Baxter's poetry in the 1960s, consistently associated with death. 'Poseidon's Acre' (1961, N21.110) and 'The Bronze Gate' (c.1963, N23.26) figure the poet-lover as a bee hopelessly searching for clover at sea and finding only 'death's pollen on Poseidon's acre'. 'Guy Fawkes Night' (1962, *CP* 259) sees the sea beating on the graves of the Calvinist settlers as 'Poseidon hammers on their house of clay'; in 'Shingle Beach Poem' (1963, *CP* 270–71), with similar violence, 'Poseidon banged on the kelp-beds' the body of the drowned girl. Other references give him a more ambiguously paternal function: 'The Waves' (1962–63, *CP* 265) are 'Daughters of Poseidon, you who dandle / Us in your thundering cradle,' and who 'have not heard / Of any God born in a stable.' In 'The Rock' ('Words to Lay a Strong Ghost' 8, 1966, *CP* 362), the image of 'arms of Promethean rock' thrust out to sea leads to the poet's vision of himself as 'a child torn from the breast // Who remembers—who cannot forget / The shielding arms of a father, / Maybe Poseidon.'

In a letter (23 July 1948, FM 27/2/4) Baxter describes 'Poseidon the Earthshaker' as a pagan symbol of 'God in his might'; Baxter's Poseidon could be read as an image of the harsher aspect of God, which ultimately leads through death to reunion with the Father. (Compare the characterisation of the sea in 'At Aramoana', *CP* 336–37, and in Baxter's discussion of that poem, *MH* 25–26.)

Other references: 'The Gods of Greece' (N3.157); 'The Sirens' (1952, *CP* 130); *The Temptations of Oedipus, passim.*

Priapus A minor rustic god of sexuality and fertility, depicted in garden statues as a kind of gnome with a huge erect phallus, and celebrated in comically obscene epigrams called *Priapeia.* Priapus never appears in Baxter's published poetry, but makes some significant appearances in the prose and in unpublished poems, in a range of tones that reflect Baxter's ambivalent view of physical sexuality. In some contexts his frank bawdy energy is treated sympathetically. 'Priapus, the god of masculine sex and fertility' is an enemy of the 'kitchen god' ('Virgin', *MH* 74); men's bawdy pub stories are 'a kind of funeral ceremony for the great god Priapus', reminding us that 'obscene meant also sacred to the Greeks' (letter 22 April 1963, FM 11/6/36); the Puritans 'forget or ignore what is a hinge of the imagination: that Eros, or even Priapus, are gods of dreams and doorways' (*Aspects* 35). Baxter celebrates these 'dreams' in a Priapean epigram 'For a Beatnik Friend' (1961, N21.136): 'To Priapus the virgins come / Forsaking book and candlewick / And hang the garlands of their dreams / On that gigantic wooden prick.'

But another unpublished poem of the same year invokes Priapus with disgust and a hint of the satanic: the host of 'New Year's Party' (N21.43) is 'a broken bar room Priapus [. . .] a stagnant boy / With greasy hair and bloodshot eye, / In his black orbit like a dwarf star burning, / *Ipsissimus*, the lord of nanny-goats.'[2] And in other contexts Eros and Priapus are not paired but contrasted, Eros's full erotic passion versus Priapus's merely physical itch (see EROS for examples). The contrast is most memorably drawn in

2 *Ipsissimus* is a comic superlative of Latin *ipse* 'himself'; it was also (as Baxter may have known) the supreme title in the magical order founded by the occultist and self-styled 'Great Beast' Aleister Crowley.

another unpublished poem, 'To Mack and Maureen' (c.1962, N23.56): 'Old biddies have / Handed over sun-bright Eros to the grave / And only Priapus, the Freudian god, / Rummages ashcans with his dragon-rod / That breeds despair.'

Other references: 'Literature and Belief', *MH* 48; 'Additional Notes for Teachers'; and see EROS.

Procrustes A bandit who forced travellers to lie on his notorious bed, and either cut or stretched them to fit its length exactly; THESEUS killed him using the same method. Procrustes' bed has become a conventional image for the enforcement of a cruelly rigid system. In Baxter's 1944 anti-war poem 'In July' (N13.783) 'the child Hope lies naked / On a Procrustes bed.' In a 1961 letter (FM 20/2/11) he applied the image to the editorial policy of Curnow's 1960 *Penguin Book of New Zealand Verse.*

Prometheus The TITAN Prometheus (whose name means 'forethought') enraged ZEUS by stealing fire from Olympus in a hollow fennel stalk and giving it to humans. The punishment for his transgression was to be chained eternally to a pillar (in Hesiod's *Theogony*, the earliest surviving account), or to a rock in the Caucasus mountains, where every day an eagle or a vulture (or in some versions a crow) claws his side and consumes his liver, which then grows back during the night. The blood splashing from his side onto the snow, according to Apollonius (*Argonautica* 3.846), grows into the magical iceflower. He is eventually freed by the hero HERCULES. The tragedy *Prometheus Bound* (traditionally but probably wrongly attributed to Aeschylus) dramatises the Titan's punishment, enlarging his culpability (or heroism) by letting him claim to have taught humans all the civilised arts and sciences. Baxter never explicitly refers to the (late) story that Prometheus himself created human beings out of clay, nor to Hesiod's connection of his story with that of PANDORA, nor to his tricking of Zeus over the custom of animal sacrifice—or indeed to the 'trickster' aspect of his character in general.

Prometheus is one of Baxter's central mythic figures from a very early age, and appears in several distinct versions. In the early poetry he is a figure of the poet's adolescent self, suffering for his poetry; later he becomes a figure of the poet as culture hero, breaker and remaker of social order. But parallel with this develops a deeply negative reading of him as an embodiment of dehumanising rationalism and the futile attempt to better the world through technological advancement. For a detailed discussion of Baxter's Prometheus see chapter 2. The relevant texts are: [POETRY] 'Prometheus' (1943, *Spark* 183–84); 'I Jason' (1943, N10.627—the iceflower); 'Prometheus' (1945, *Spark* 416; shorter version, *CP* 35); 'Autumn Waking' (1948, *CP* 69–70); 'For those who lie with crooked limbs in the straight grave' (1944, *Spark* 368–70—the iceflower); 'Byron' (1944, N13.820), 'Seascape' (1944, N13.826); 'Poem to Hoelderlin' (c.1947; N14.1014); 'Recollection' (c.1951, N16.35); 'An Undelivered Address to a Catholic Reading Group' (c.1962, N23.33)—a comic use of 'the black Promethean vulture; 'Ballad of the Runaway Mother' (c.1964, N24.63); 'At Day's Bay' (1965, *CP* 308–09); 'Letter to Papua I' (c.1966, N26.65); 'The Rock' ('Words to Lay a Strong Ghost' 12, 1966, *CP* 362); 'The Titan' (1963–66, *CP* 372–73); [PLAYS] *The Bureaucrat* (an adaptation/parody of *Prometheus Bound*); *The Temptations of Oedipus, CPlays* 234–35; [PROSE] 'Symbolism', *FA* 62, 75; 'Criticism', *FA* 28; 'Education', *MH* 125–26, 154; *Aspects* 27; 'Some Notes on Drama' (*The Spots of the Leopard* as Promethean myth); 'The Church and the Alcoholic', *FC* 31; 'Choice of Belief in Modern Society'; [LETTERS] to Noel Ginn, 16 Jan. 1943 (*Spark* 180) and 11 Dec. 1945 (*Spark* 416).

Proserpine see PERSEPHONE

Proteus A shape-shifting sea god who had the power of prophecy; however, those who wished to learn his knowledge—like Homer's Menelaus (*Odyssey*, book 4) or Virgil's Aristaeus (*Georgics*, book 4)—had to wrestle him into submission despite his successive 'protean' changes of shape. In 'The Creative Mask (*FA* 35) Baxter uses the image for the difficulty of grasping 'the *significance* of a poem': 'Like the seagod Proteus, it takes a thousand shapes—a forest fire, a bull, a serpent, a waterspout, a running river—and one has to grasp it through every change till it delivers up its identity.'

Psyche The Greek word for 'soul', and the heroine of a myth first recorded by Apuleius in his *Metamorphoses (The Golden Ass)*; it tells how Psyche wins, loses, and regains the love of the love god Cupid (or EROS), and has often been read as an allegory of the relationship between the human soul and God. Baxter's use of 'Psyche' in three unpublished satiric poems of the late 1950s seems to draw on the Greek meaning of the word more than on the myth. In 'Theme for the Middle Years' (c.1955, N17.108) 'She whom I hated worse than death, / The Psyche of suburban homes, / Beckons with arch, maternal breath / And lawns ornate with plaster gnomes.' In 'Husband to Wife (modern version)' (c.1957, N19.46) the 'Medea' of the original poem becomes 'My dearest Psyche' (see MEDEA). And 'A Rough Approval' (c.1959, N19.98), praising 'roughness' over 'smoothness', declares that 'The rounded globe of the Platonic wish, // The wheel of karma, Psyche's under-vest, / Are creatures of the uncreated void.' In each case 'Psyche' suggests a Puritan priggishness, hostile to the body and sexuality, which Baxter strongly associates with women and especially with suburban bourgeois womanhood.

Pyrrha The mythological Pyrrha was the wife of Deucalion (the Greek Noah), who with him survived the great Flood and repopulated the world. However, Baxter's use of the name for his early love Jane Aylward, in the sequence 'Words to Lay a Strong Ghost' (*CP* 356–64) and elsewhere, has a different, non-mythological source. Though the poems themselves are based on Catullus's sequence to Lesbia, the name 'Pyrrha' comes from an ode by Horace (*Odes* 1.5) in which the poet congratulates himself on surviving a love affair with the tempestuous Pyrrha (see Harrison 305–07). Her name, from the Greek word for 'fire', implies red or golden hair.

Rhadamanthus A Cretan king, son of ZEUS, renowned for his justice, who after death became one of the judges of the underworld (see HADES)—presiding either in ELYSIUM (according to Pindar) or in TARTARUS (according to Virgil). He makes some striking appearances in Baxter's later work. In 'Rhadamanthus' (1966–67, *CP* 407–08) the poet returns to Tunnel Beach where he once made love (to Pyrrha/Jane Aylward), to find that 'Above the place of love / The cliff was a high stone Rhadamanthus / Washed by the black froth of the sea.' A longer draft version ('The Tunnel', N26.71) spells out the symbolism: 'one vast face / Like Rhadamanthus crowned with / Toppling rocks, who is the myth / Of judgement when love dies.'

In 'Firetrap Castle Song' ('Ballad of Firetrap Castle' 7, 1971, *CP* 530–32) Rhadamanthus embodies the cruelty of society's 'justice': 'Number One Police Court / Where Skully sits like Rhadamanthus / Weighing the guts of the poor in his scales'. But 'Autumn Testament' 27 (1972, *CP* 554) reverses the image as the drunks of Firetrap Castle pass judgement on society: 'Sober as Rhadamanthus / They judged the town and found it had already been judged.' This ambiguity is most strikingly captured in *The Runaway Wife*, in which 'Mr Rhadamanthus' is the bureaucratic master of Hades (a much more formidable figure than the comic Mr Pluto), but also appears in disguise as the drunken derelict Calico Jack. This enigmatic figure, alternately anarchic, implacable and benign, may be read as an image of the incomprehensibility of God.

Scylla and Charybdis A narrow strait (traditionally identified with the Straits of Messina, between Sicily and the toe of Italy) was guarded on the one side by a huge whirlpool, Charybdis, and on the other by a cliff in which lurked Scylla, a monster with six barking heads on long prehensile necks which would snake down to pluck victims from passing ships. Ships passing through the strait had to choose between these two dangers. In *Odyssey* 12 ODYSSEUS steers close to the cliff face, losing six crewmen to Scylla but saving his ship from Charybdis.

'Between Scylla and Charybdis' has become proverbial for being caught between unpalatable alternatives. Like many writers, Baxter exploits the image's allegorical possibilities. In the early ode 'Where nets of time encircle and destroy' (1943, *Spark* 286) the poet–helmsman must steer between 'Scylla of cynic wit' and 'Charybdis of sweet sentiment'. In 'Traveller's Litany' (1954, *CP* 139–45 (142)) 'It is the time of turning [. . .] / From Scylla's yelping pride / Charybdis' cave of ruin / equally from the betraying joy / As from the malice of self-loathing.' In 'The Strait' (1962, *CP* 253), Odysseus's passage through the strait is similarly allegorised as a choice between 'the rock of Pride, the whirlpool of Despair'; Baxter implies that Odysseus's pride is the less ruinous of the two sins.

Scylla appears alone in 'Odysseus'-2 (1957, N19.22), where the old Odysseus is not haunted by 'the doggy bark of Scylla', and is alluded to in 'The Rival' ('Words to Lay a Strong Ghost' 9, *CP* 360), where PYRRHA has 'the eight-headed / Sea-rock-monster barking between [her] thighs'. In 'Clutha' (1961, *CP* 229) the river is 'older than Charybdis'.

Semele A Theban princess, lover of ZEUS and mother of DIONYSUS. She unwisely asked Zeus to appear to her in his full divine glory, and was blasted to ashes; but Zeus rescued the unborn child and implanted it in his thigh, from which Dionysus was subsequently born. In 'Traveller's Litany' (*CP* 139–45) Baxter links her with Isis as an analogue to the Virgin Mary, mother of a divine child: '*Dei Genetrix* / goddess prefigured by / Isis and Semele' (143).

Silenus A follower of DIONYSUS, an old, fat, drunken satyr who rides unsteadily on the back of a donkey, playing a pipe. In classical literature he is often a figure of fun (he was a regular hero of the farcical 'satyr plays'), but could be treated more seriously: in Plato's *Symposium* (215) Alcibiades compares Socrates to a Russian doll-type statuette of Silenus, grotesquely ugly on the outside but concealing the figure of a god inside. Baxter's references reflect this ambiguity and his ambivalent view of his own alcoholism. In 'The Shepherd's Reply' (1966, *CP* 344–45) Silenus simply represents Kiwi male pub culture: Damon rejects his marriage-hungry girlfriend to 'go to old Silenus and learn / A couple of drinking songs'. In other contexts he is a more potent figure, embodying the poetic wisdom and insight of the drunken outcast. In the unpublished 'Drinking Bout' (c.1967, N27.59), which seems to recall Baxter's Christchurch days with Glover, the poet wakes from a debauch feeling that, in 'a country that has no gods', he has 'stepped over [. . .] the doorstep of Silenus'. Elsewhere he compares Shakespeare's Falstaff to 'the wise and drunken Silenus'

('Some Possibilities for New Zealand Drama' 14—an association earlier made by Auden), and calls his own character Concrete Grady 'a Fool or Silenus' (letter to Fleur Adcock, 12 Dec. 1961, FM 27/1/15). Calico Jack in *The Runaway Wife*, who is really RHADAMANTHUS in disguise, is described in a manuscript castlist as a 'drunk Silenus'.

Sirens Depicted in Greek art as creatures with the bodies of birds and the faces of beautiful women, the Sirens lurked on a small island and sang so sweetly that they enticed sailors onto the rocks to be devoured. ODYSSEUS, in *Odyssey* 12, contrives to hear the song but escape death by having himself tied to the mast, while his rowers' ears are blocked with wax. The Sirens' song has become an almost proverbial image for irresistible temptation.

Two early poems, 'What the Sirens Sang' (1951, N16.15) and 'The Sirens' (1952, *CP* 130–33), deal with Odysseus's encounter with the Sirens, and suggest that their most powerful temptation for him was the offer of death, his 'longed-for bourne of oblivion' (see chapter 6 for further discussion). They have a similar appeal in 'Letter to Australia' (1956, *CP* 151–52): 'And in the cave of memory / Ring always the salt siren voices / Proclaiming to the flesh that dies / Original breath and enmity.' In 'Kiwi Habits (II)' Baxter compares Fairburn to Odysseus, 'the man who had heard the song of the Sirens, strapped to the mast and sweating, and remembered some of the words of that terrible song, while others had their ears stopped with wax'.

In Baxter's later poetry the Sirens become a less important image, and their temptations more conventional: militarism in 'The Killers (1959, N20.15: 'Generals and executioners [. . .] Enchant our blood as once the sirens did'); domesticity in 'Words to a Country Friend' (1960, N21.47: 'the worst siren sings of peace'); sex (comically) in 'The Consolation of Remembered Immorality' (1965, N26.94: 'My sagging prick won't stand up straight / For any song that the Sirens sung'). In the 1966 radio play *The First Wife* the alluring 'sea woman' Lilith is called 'that damned siren' (*CPlays* 62).

Sisyphus One of the great sinners punished in the underworld (HADES). A king of Corinth and a famous trickster, Sisphyus defied the gods by trying to outwit death. He was sentenced to perpetually roll a great rock up a hill, only for it to roll back down just as he reaches the top. Baxter's uses of the figure of Sisyphus are discussed in chapter 8. The relevant texts are: [POEMS] 'Ode: Where nets of time encircle and destroy' (1943, *Spark* 285); 'Orpheus' (*Landfall* 1957); 'Air Flight to Delhi' (1958, *CP* 193); 'Sisyphus' (1959, *CP* 202); 'Dunedin Revisited' (1961, *CP* 235); 'Pigeon Park' (c.1965, N25.45; earlier versions at 24.44 and 25.8); 'Stephanie' (1968, *SP* 181–82); [PROSE] 'Writers in New Zealand: A Questionnaire' (*Landfall* 1960), 41–42; 'Some Possibilities for New Zealand Drama'; [LETTERS] to Ginn, 16 March 1960 (FM 15/7/18—writer's block compared to Sisyphus's boulder); to Bill Oliver, 21 Feb. 1961 (FM 27/2/11); to Margaret Still, 11 March 1966—being without a boss as 'Sisyphus feeling lost without his boulder'.

Sphinx A female monster with a woman's head, a lion's body, and wings. Common in Greek art, Sphinxes originally derive from Egypt, where the most famous is the monumental statue of the Great Sphinx of Giza (which however has a man's head). In Greek myth the Sphinx was the monster that terrorised Thebes, devouring all those who could not answer its riddle: what walks on four legs in the morning, two in the afternoon, and three in the evening? OEDIPUS solved the riddle (a man, who crawls as a baby, walks as an adult, and leans on a stick in old age), and the Sphinx killed itself in chagrin. It has become a commonplace image for something which poses an impenetrable, and perhaps threatening, enigma.

The Sphinx makes a number of appearances in Baxter's juvenilia, but always with reference to the Egyptian monument, seen in conventionally Romantic terms as a figure of ancient and inaccessible wisdom: 'The Sphinx' (N2.117); 'Truth' (N2.128); 'Ode: Where nets of time encircle and destroy' (*Spark* 287); 'Ode MCMXLIV' (*Spark* 336); 'Than Stone' (N12.747). In some unpublished poems of the 1950s Baxter uses the Sphinx as a more personal symbol, a fearsomely challenging force of negation which calls into question personal and social identity. In 'Canticle of the Desert' (1954, N17.98), for instance, it appears (unnamed but identified by explicit reference to Oedipus) as 'That face behind the manifold delusion, / That monster sibylline with lion's paws / Courted and feared, the Questioner', which describes itself as 'the Wind / Between the stars, the night of history', and demands of the poet: 'Are you indeed yourself? / What choices are meaningful?' Similarly in 'The Sphinx's Eye' (N19.25), the poet endures a cold scrutiny 'under the Sphinx's eye' which leads him to the conclusion, 'Who I am I cannot say, / Who you are I do not know' (the phrase recurs in 'The Picasso', N19.60). The 'lion-headed incubus' of 'For Kevin Ireland' (*CP* 186) is perhaps a related figure.

The references to the Sphinx in Baxter's published verse are more tongue-in-cheek: the Charles Brasch parody 'Colloquy with a Breadboard' (1956, *CP* 171) turns the fearsome Questioner into a figure with the face of 'an old tabby going to sleep in the window' who mildly asks, 'What do you want with a breadboard?'; and the drunk 'Mr Gallonguts' (1959, *CP* 204–05) boasts that he has 'solved the Sphinx's problem / Of fate against freewill' (a reference to the theme of Sophocles' *Oedipus the King* rather than specifically to the Sphinx's riddle).

Oedipus's encounter with the Sphinx is mentioned only once in *The Temptations of Oedipus*, in a joke which nevertheless reflects the play's association of the feminine with chaos and death. Talking to his estranged son Polyneices, Oedipus mentions the Theban hills 'where I met the Sphinx and had the misfortune to beget you':

POLYNEICES My mother was not the Sphinx.
OEDIPUS I was never wholly able to distinguish between the two of them. (*CPlays* 251)

Other reference: 'Galatea' (1955, N18.26).

Styx One of the four rivers of HADES, the underworld, by whose black waters the gods swore their most unbreakable oath. It is never explicitly named in Baxter's published verse, but the Taieri River with its 'serpent waves' in 'Henley Pub' (1961–65, *CP*

324–25) is identified with Styx, 'the river of death', in Baxter's commentary in 'Virgin', *MH* 77. More lightheartedly, in 'Ballade for a PEN Soirée' (letter 19 Oct. 1961, FM 27/1/8) he mocks artistic 'party-givers' who 'wear the fiddlebow to slivers / Playing beside the Stygian stream'.

Symplegades The 'Clashing Rocks' at the entrance to the Black Sea which would come together to crush ships which tried to pass between them. JASON succeeded in passing them in the *Argo* by sending a dove ahead to trigger them prematurely (Apollonius, *Argonautica*, book 2). Baxter uses the Symplegades in the last stanza of 'Letter to Noel Ginn' (1944, *CP* 27–29) as an image for 'the thundering gates of war' beyond which he hopes his (potential) son will find peace. He also uses 'these Clashing Rocks' to describe the pitfalls of religious poetry in a response to Owen Leeming in *Landfall* 98 (1971), 209.

Tantalus One of the great sinners tormented in the underworld (see HADES, TARTARUS). According to the best-known version of the story, Tantalus tried to trick the gods into eating human flesh, and was punished with eternal hunger and thirst, standing in a pool which drains away when he tries to drink, and surrounded by fruit trees just outside his reach—hence the English word 'tantalise'. Though less important than his fellow-sufferer SISYPHUS, Tantalus makes several appearances in Baxter, and sometimes with an effect of painful self-caricature: as a self-pitying alcoholic in 'Tantalus' (1951–2, N16.41); as a suicidal tycoon in 'Orpheus' (*Landfall* 1957); as a long-winded and ineffectual protest poet writing about 'the experience of the void in modern life' in *The Runaway Wife*. See chapter 8 for further discussion. Other references: 'The Gods of Greece' (age 15, N3.157); 'Ode: Where nets of time encircle and destroy' (1943, *Spark* 285); 'Some Possibilities for New Zealand Drama'.

Tartarus The deepest part of HADES, the underworld, where the greatest sinners (such as IXION, SISYPHUS, TANTALUS) were tormented; often conflated with the Christian Hell, as in 'The Last Judgement' (1962, *CP* 257–58), where Baxter mocks the idea that hell and heaven are merely creations of the unconscious mind:

'the smoke of Tartarus / Was never hard to find'. An enigmatic reference in 'Traveller's Litany' (1954, *CP* 139–45) to 'the savage spears / of Tartarus' (142) seems to draw on its traditional confusion or conflation with Tartary, the Central Asian realm of the Tatars or Tartars (fierce mounted warriors whom medieval Europe saw as the hordes of hell).

Telemachus The son of ODYSSEUS; a major character in Homer's *Odyssey*, where he goes in quest of his father, and later helps him defeat the suitors. Baxter, with little sympathy for Odysseus's family ties, has only two brief dry references to Telemachus in his Odysseus poems: the Sirens mockingly hold out to Odysseus the possibility of returning home to instruct his son 'from the fruit of long experience' in 'The Sirens' (1952, N17.6); and in 'Odysseus'-2 (N19.22) one of the retired hero's pastimes is to 'quarrel with Telemachus'. Telemachus is also cited in an ironic passage in *The Sore-Footed Man* (*CPlays* 131–32), where Odysseus, blandly manipulating Neoptolemus into helping him carry out his deception, praises his honest scruples as just what he would expect from 'my own son Telemachus'.

Tellus Latin for 'earth', and hence the Roman goddess and personification of the earth, equivalent to the Greek GEA. 'To Be Written on Asbestos' (c.1953, N17.73), an ironic epitaph for the human race following a nuclear holocaust, declares of its subject: 'Here lived in shade of Tellus' laws / Her sweetheart and annihilator.'

Thanatos Greek for 'death', sometimes a mythological personification (as in Euripides' *Alcestis*, where Herakles wrestles with him—see HERCULES). But in Baxter's lines 'Eros and Thanatos / the bitter stars combine' in 'Traveller's Litany' (1954, *CP* 139–45 (143)) it is not clear that he is thinking of them as mythological figures rather than as the abstract forces Love and Death, and embodiments of the Freudian opposition between the love-instinct and the death-instinct. See also EROS.

Theseus King of Athens, one of the major heroes of Greek myth, and the Athenian counterpart of the Dorian hero HERCULES. Brought up by his mother Aethra, on discovering his true parentage he left her to seek out his father King Aegeus in Athens; on the journey he heroically slew a number of monsters and evildoers, including PROCRUSTES. Having been acknowledged by Aegeus as his son and heir, he embarked on his most famous adventure, accompanying the Athenian prisoners who were sent as tribute to King Minos of Crete, there to be sacrificed to the MINOTAUR in the Cretan LABYRINTH. Minos's daughter ARIADNE fell in love with him and secretly gave him a ball of thread, with which he was able to find his way to the heart of the Labyrinth, kill the Minotaur, and escape with Ariadne. He subsequently abandoned her (an action variously explained or excused) on the island of Naxos. Sailing back to Athens, he forgot his father's instruction to change his black sail to white to indicate that he was safe; Aegeus, thinking his son dead, threw himself from a cliff in grief, and Theseus returned to find himself king.

Theseus's reign was remembered in Athens as a golden age: he united the land of Attica, established law and justice, and protected the weak—including the exiled OEDIPUS (a story dramatised in Sophocles' *Oedipus at Colonus* and, from a very different point of view, in Baxter's *The Temptations of Oedipus*). Baxter does not explicitly refer to the tragic events of Theseus's later life, though they may colour his treatment: his marriage to Phaedra (Ariadne's sister) and her fatal passion for her stepson Hippolytus (Theseus's child by the AMAZON queen Hippolyta); his expedition to HADES with Peirithous in an attempt to abduct PERSEPHONE; and his final exile from Athens and ignominious death on the island of Scyros. In historical times, Theseus's gigantic bones were allegedly found on Scyros and brought back to be entombed in Athens (a story recalled with a difference in 'At the Tomb of Theseus').

For a full discussion of Baxter's generally hostile treatment of Theseus, see chapter 5. The texts in which he is mentioned or alluded to are: 'The Gods of Greece' (c.1941, N3.157); 'Reverie of a Prisoner' (c.1943, N10.588); 'Lost in the labyrinth no Ariadne' (c.1947, N14.1013); 'Spring Song' (c.1953, *SP* 50–51); 'Letter to the World' (1955, *CP* 149–50); 'At the Tomb of Theseus' (1959, *CP* 199); 'The Labyrinth' (1970, *CP* 488–89); [PLAY] *The Temptations of Oedipus*; [LETTER] to Frank McKay, 3 Dec. 1969 (FM 22/4/11).

Thetis A sea nymph, mother of the hero ACHILLES. She is invoked in *Horse* as Fern is making love to Horse: 'Like Thetis on a dolphin, or a child riding a log across a lagoon, she rode her prostrate Horse to final victory' (64).

Tiresias The blind prophet of Thebes, who appears in a number of Greek tragedies, and as a ghost in Homer's *Odyssey*. According to Ovid (*Metamorphoses*, book 3), he once struck two copulating snakes with his stick, and was transformed into a woman; seeing them again seven years later, he struck them again, and was transformed back to a man. As a result of his unique experience, ZEUS (Jupiter) and HERA (Juno) called on him to arbitrate an argument about whether men or women got more pleasure from sex; when he said 'women' he was struck blind by Hera but given the compensating gift of prophetic foresight by Zeus. The myth is famously recalled in Eliot's *The Waste Land*, where Tiresias is an omniscient and disillusioned spectator of modern sexuality: 'And I Tiresias have foresuffered all [. . .]'. Baxter is clearly recalling Eliot in the unpublished poem 'Love', formerly titled 'I Tiresias' (1962, N22.98), which expresses the speaker's longing to withdraw from 'love' to 'a tent beside a lake': 'From that hermitage/ Like Tiresias at the boundary stone / I could watch more calmly, till the bunfight ends, / Those melancholy copulating snakes / Who are my nearest, dearest friends.'[3]

Tisiphone One of the FURIES. In 'Annales' (*CS* 29) 'Trees with chafing burn / When strong south winds flail the italian sky / Tisiphone scourging the lost.' In a letter to Ginn (13 Aug. 1944, *Spark* 373) Baxter notes that the image was 'annexed with improvements from Lucretius and Virgil'. He is combining Lucretius's description of a storm with Virgil's image of the Fury tormenting sinners in TARTARUS (*Aeneid* 6.570–72): 'the avenger girdled with her whip, / Tisiphone, leaps down to lash the guilty, / Vile writhing snakes held out on her left hand'.

Titans The generation of pre-Olympian gods, Kronos (or Saturn) and his siblings. In a series of 'titanic' battles, they were

3 Transcription is speculative; Baxter's heavy revision of these lines leaves it hard to see what his intended final version was.

overthrown and replaced by Kronos's son ZEUS and his Olympian family. Two of Baxter's major mythological figures, ATLAS and PROMETHEUS, were sons of the Titan Iapetus, and Baxter extends the title to them: Atlas is 'benignant Titan' in 'The Giant's Grave' (1951–55, *CP* 153) and Prometheus is 'The Titan' (and 'the dark Titan') in the poem of that title (1963–66, *CP* 372–73).

Tithonus Young lover of the dawn goddess Eos/Aurora, who granted him immortality but forgot to also ask for agelessness; he shrivelled away with old age (and in some versions was transformed into a cicada). The story is told by APHRODITE to ANCHISES in the Homeric *Hymn to Aphrodite*; Baxter never refers to Tithonus but applies his fate to Anchises himself in 'Education' *(MH* 144).

Triton A minor sea god, attendant and herald of POSEIDON/ Neptune, depicted as a fish-tailed merman blowing on a conch-shell horn. Originally a single character, in later usage 'triton' is often the name for a whole class of merpeople. He is most famous in English literature from Wordsworth's sonnet 'The world is too much with us', whose speaker longs to 'have sight of Proteus rising from the waves, / Or hear old Triton blow his wreathèd horn' (Wordsworth 237). Wordsworth's use of Triton as a quintessentially mythic figure, embodying the wonder and joy missing in our everyday world, seems to colour Baxter's references, as in the very Yeatsian 'To My Father, Forbidding Grief' (c.1955, N17.112) with its 'undead blessed' crying joy from the 'triton saddled sea', or 'Ballad of the Runaway Mother' (1963, N24.63), where 'Sun triton and sea unicorn' are called on to protect the heroine. In 'Autumn Testament' 27 (1972, *CP* 554) he suggests a massive dignity, as the drunks of Macdonald Crescent sit in judgement, 'like Tritons their faces'; in 'Letter from the Mountains' (1968, *CP* 415–16) he has a tragic quality, as the poem's addressee (Bob Lowry?) 'rise[s] like a Triton, / A great reddish gourd of flesh, / From the sofa' to 'shout as if drowning' to his lover. A rather different response to the Wordsworth poem is the bawdy 'Ballade of the Sailor's Dong' (c.1961, N22.69), with its cheerfully phallic refrain, 'He blows old Triton's wreathèd horn.' Other reference: 'Who hath not heard?' (N2.85).

Troy and the Trojan War The story of the ten-year war between the Greeks and the city of Troy (or Ilium) in Asia Minor—a war which began with the abduction of HELEN by the Trojan prince Paris, and ended, thanks to ODYSSEUS's strategem of the Wooden Horse, with the capture, sack, and burning of Troy—is the most important of the Greek mythic sagas. It is the subject of what the Greeks regarded as the first and greatest work of their literature, Homer's *Iliad* (and to a lesser degree of Homer's *Odyssey*, which deals with Odysseus's homecoming from the war), which has made this the Western world's archetypal war story. The central concerns of the *Iliad*—the celebration of heroic valour, and the tension between human mortality and the quest for fame and glory—have little interest for Baxter. His references to Troy focus on three related aspects of the story:

(1) The Trojan war as part of the life history of ODYSSEUS, Baxter's favourite mythological character (see chapter 8). In early poems including 'Letter to Noel Ginn' (*CP* 27–29), 'Odysseus'-1 (*CP* 42), 'The Homecoming' (*CP* 121), and 'The Sirens' (*CP* 130–33), Baxter presents Odysseus's war as an opportunity to exercise his natural talents, but as ultimately traumatic and futile (like the Second World War). In *The Sore-footed Man*, which takes place late during the war, Odysseus sums up: 'Do you think I care who wins the Trojan war? [. . .] Iron clashing on iron. Blood and corpses every day of the week—ten years of it. And at the end of it, a small trading town burnt to the ground' (*CPlays* 156).

(2) The figure of HELEN of Troy, the incarnation of dangerous female beauty and sexuality, whose face 'brought Troy crashing / Down like a chicken-coop—black wood and flames!' ('The Party', 1966, *CP* 356). Other examples are given in the entry for HELEN.

(3) The fall of Troy as an archetypal image of human suffering and human destructiveness. This image, which draws less on Homer than on Virgil's tragic account of the city's fall in *Aeneid*, book 2, appears mainly (and at times with some unconscious bathos) in Baxter's unpublished early poetry. 'Me Also' (1944, *Spark* 334) speaks of the 'tragedy world-shaking' of the decay of love: 'It is more than the burning walls of hell / Or Ilion . . . It ends when life ends.' In 'What wonder men go mad?' (1946, N14.912) Baxter recalls a childhood epiphany of the cruelty of life: 'More loud with tragedy than Troy burning / Or the drunk run over in the street / My three-year-old memory of a ewer / A cold room and the cold night coming: / First recognition of the eyes of night / And since familiar canker in the flower.' (The same experience in his grandmother's house is evoked in 'Winter Sea', *CP* 389–90.) The nineteenth-century English burning of Scottish Highland farms is compared to that of Troy in 'On the Highland Evictions' (c.1947, N14.990). Baxter's most famous and powerful deployment of the image is in 'Wild Bees' (1941–49, *CP* 82–83), where it gives a tragic dimension to children's wanton destruction of a beehive: 'O it was Carthage under the Roman torches, / Or loud with flames and falling timber, Troy!'

Two humorous references fall outside these categories. 'The Old Earth Closet' begins mock-heroically (with an echo of 'The British Grenadiers'): 'Oh some will sing of Dannevirke / And some will sing of Troy' (1954–65, *CP* 322–23). And in 'Letter to Robert Lowry' (c.1952, N16.69) 'Homunculus must steer a course / Right slap between / The Greek fire and the Trojan whores / For pastures green'—between THANATOS and EROS, perhaps, with a sly pun on 'Trojan horse' hinting at the treacheries of sexuality.

Ulysses see ODYSSEUS

Underworld see HADES

Uranus (Greek Ouranos.) Primordial god of the sky (his name means 'heavenly'), husband of GEA; his castration by his son Kronos or Saturn led to the creation of VENUS (Aphrodite) and of the FURIES. Baxter does not refer directly to him as a mythological figure, but Professor Lucas in *The Day Flanagan Died* has a long speech about the astrological significance of the planet Uranus: 'It's not easy to be a Uranian, Captain Stone—it means you die without ever living [. . .]. Uranus—not gold, not silver—it's the grey metal—it's the colour of light when the world has come to an end [. . .]. It's the star of peace born out of trouble' (*CPlays* 300). Baxter is probably covertly alluding to the late Victorian and Edwardian use of 'Uranian' to mean 'homosexual'.

Venus [Latin] or **Aphrodite** [Greek] Goddess of erotic love and sexuality, embodiment of beauty and of the feminine; a major divinity and perhaps Baxter's most important and most frequently invoked mythological figure. (Except in early poems, he almost always uses her Latin name.) According to Homer, Aphrodite is the child of ZEUS and Dione, but the grotesque and beautiful account of her birth in Hesiod's *Theogony* is far better known. When the sky god URANUS was castrated by his rebellious son Kronos (Saturn), his severed genitals fell into the sea; Aphrodite arose from the foam (Greek *aphros*) which gathered round them, and came ashore on the island of Cythera (hence the title 'the Cytherean' used in 'Traveller's Litany', *CP* 139–45 (139)). This story, famous from Botticelli's painting of *The Birth of Venus*, is reflected in Baxter's repeated images of Venus rising from the sea and his constant association of her with the beach, the meeting-place of sea and land.[4]

She is married to VULCAN (Hephaestus), less than faithfully; her great love is the war god MARS (Ares), who represents masculinity as she represents femininity. She also has numerous mortal lovers, among whom Baxter makes reference to ADONIS and ANCHISES; the Homeric *Hymn to Aphrodite*, which tells the story of her encounter with Anchises, clearly had a major imaginative influence on him. However, Baxter is less interested in the specific legends of Venus than he is in her as a symbol: she represents the irresistible power of sexual desire (in all its forms from the cheerfully bawdy to the tormented), and serves as one of his most powerful embodiments of the female archetype he thought of as the anima.

Baxter's Venus is discussed in detail in chapter 3. The relevant texts are as follows (references to Aphrodite are asterisked): [POEMS] *'The Birth of Beauty' (c.1941, N3.137); *'The Gods of Greece' (c.1941, N3.157); *'I from high windows' (c.1941, N5.304); *'The Unicorn' (1943, *CP* 10); 'Aeneas' (1943, N10.613; revised *CS* 3); 'Ode MCMXLIV' (1944, *Spark* 335–38); 'Psyche' (1944, N13.770); 'Flower-Venus' (1944, *Spark* 475–76); 'Ex Nihilo' (c.1947, N15.19); *'Epithalamium' (1951, N16.18); 'Bar

4 The Greek phrase conventionally used to describe this image is *Aphrodite anadyomene* ('rising'), misspelt 'Anadyamone' by Baxter in 'The Unicorn'.

Room Elegy' (1951, *CP* 119); ⋆'On His Mistress Dressing' (1952, N17.14); 'Lugete, O Veneres' (1952, N17.34); 'Cras Amet Qui Numquam Amavit' (c.1952?, MS 682.22); ⋆'Elegy at the Year's End' (1953, *CP* 135); 'Litany of the Sea' (N17.97), revised as 'Traveller's Litany' (1954, *CP* 139–45); 'To My Father' (1954, *SP* 54–55); 'Crossing Cook Strait' (1947–56, *CP* 159–60); 'Husband to Wife' (1956, N18.45); 'In fires of no return' (1956, *CP* 165–66); 'At the Vernal Equinox' (1956, N18.67; primarily referring to the planet); 'The Rock-Born Stream' (1956, *CP* 167; the planet); 'The Return' (1956, *CP* 179); 'Song of the Years' (1958, *CP* 188–89); 'The pain of others dissuasion from lechery' (1961, N21.58); 'Ballad of the Fortunate Guest' (1961, N21.84); 'Coffee Bar Ballade' (c.1961, N21.94); 'Ballad of the Venus Man-o'-War' (c.1962, N22.59); 'The Matriarchs' (c.1962, N22.97); 'Waipatiki Beach' (1963, *CP* 263–65); 'A Solemn Event' (1963, N24.3); 'The Land-Crab and the Goddess Venus' (c.1964, N24.68); 'Near Kapiti' (1964, *CP* 302–03); 'The Need for Public Brothels' (c.1963, N25.25); 'Encounter with Venus' (c.1964, *Landfall* 1965); 'Gun-Pits' (c.1964, N25.70); 'The Kraken' (1966, *CP* 335–36); 'A Ballad for the Men of Holy Cross' (1966, *CP* 337–39); 'At Brighton Bay' (1966, *CP* 371); 'Winter River' (1966, *CP* 377–78); 'Apparition of the Goddess Venus to a Sleepy Man' (1967, *CP* 384); 'At Pompolona Hut (Easter Sunday)' (1966, N26.38); 'The Tunnel' (1967, N26.71); 'A Small Ode on Mixed Flatting' (1967, *CP* 396–99); 'Spring' (1967, *CP* 404); 'The Climber' (1967, N28.9); 'Rhadamanthus' (1966–67, *CP* 407–08); 'Summer 1967' (1967, *CP* 408–09); 'Letter to Sam Hunt' (1968, *CP* 429–31); 'The Bohemians' (c.1968?, MS 975/16.10); 'Ballade in Love's Defence' (undated, FM 8/27); 'Ballade of Malediction' (undated, FM 8/28); [PLAYS] *The Spots of the Leopard*, 22; ⋆*The Temptations of Oedipus*, *CPlays* 249; [PROSE] 'Conversation', *MH* 20, 25; 'Virgin', *MH* 74; 'Man', *MH* 116; 'Education', *MH* 137, 138, 144, 153, 154); *Horse*, 62; 'Essay on the Higher Learning'; 'Notes on the Making of "The Martian"'; 'Kiwi Habits (II)'; 'The Pythoness'; 'The Idea of Progress'; 'Additional Notes for Teachers'; [LETTERS] to Noel Ginn, 25 Feb. 1944 (*Spark* 331–33); to Charles Brasch, 31 March 1953 (FM 20/2/3).

Vulcan The lame blacksmith god, Roman equivalent of the Greek Hephaestus, who has his forge under the volcano of Mt Etna. He is mentioned only in Baxter's juvenilia, which contains several images of Vulcan's 'fiery hammer-stroke' and 'subterranean flame': 'Pompeii' (N1.83); 'The Gods of Greece' (N3.157); 'I from high windows' (N5.304).

Zeus [Greek], **Jupiter** or **Jove** [Latin] King of the gods, 'father of gods and men', god of sky and storm, power and justice. Given his central importance in Greco-Roman mythology and religion, he is a surprisingly faint presence in Baxter's work. He makes some conventional appearances in the juvenilia: 'The Gods of Greece' (N3.157); 'Thunder and Lightning (N3.156); 'I from high windows' (N5.304). 'In Numeris' (*Spark* 152–56 (153)) lists 'Zeus the All-Mover' as one of the names of God, and this syncretism is sometimes echoed later, as in a letter of 23 July 1958 (FM 27/2/4): 'God in His might—perhaps the pagans tell us in the glimmering of symbols something of this—Zeus the Thunderer, Poseidon the Earthshaker [. . .]'. But Baxter has little interest in Zeus/Jupiter as a specifically mythological character, and almost ignores the huge repertoire of stories (most familiar from Ovid's *Metamorphoses*) about the god's erotic relationships, apart from a mention of LEDA and the swan in the early 'Bird-Envocation [*sic*]' (N12.729), and a joke in *The Runaway Wife* about the begetting of HERCULES: 'the son of Zeus by a mortal woman—with his father's energy and his mother's stupidity—a fatal combination!' (*RW* 24). The imagery of Ovidian transformation in 'To Mate With' (1967, *CP* 399) perhaps prompts the use of 'Zeus' there as a synonym for God.

Baxter refers to 'the fire of Zeus' in 'The Titan' (1963–66, *CP* 372–73), but the power struggle between Zeus and PROMETHEUS is not central to his understanding of that myth; in *The Bureaucrat* 'the Director' is a remote paper-shuffler issuing memos about semicolons (*CPlays* 164), not the threatening tyrant of *Prometheus Bound*. In 'At the Grave of a War Hero' ('Words to Lay a Strong Ghost' 14, *CP* 363–64) the hubris of secular authority is embodied in 'Caesar's mad black eye / That imitates Zeus'.

In general Zeus is rarely mentioned in Baxter's classical plays, though ODYSSEUS in *The Sore-Footed Man* has a characteristically unorthodox creation myth: 'A man is a lie that Zeus created to amuse himself on a hot, stagnant afternoon' (*CPlays* 134). 'Jupiter' in 'Noises from Jupiter' and 'Pigeon Park' (N24.44, 25.8, 25.45) refers to the planet rather than the god.

BIBLIOGRAPHY

Primary

(a) books

Baxter, James K. *Aspects of Poetry in New Zealand.* Christchurch: Caxton Press, 1967.

———. *Autumn Testament.* 1972. Ed. Paul Millar. Oxford: Oxford University Press, 1997.

———. *Cold Spring: Baxter's Unpublished Early Collection.* Ed. Paul Millar. Auckland: Oxford University Press, 1996.

———. *Collected Plays.* Ed. Howard McNaughton. Auckland: Oxford University Press, 1982.

———. *Collected Poems.* Ed. John Weir. Reissue with additions. Melbourne: Oxford University Press, 2004.

———. *The Fire and the Anvil: Notes on Modern Poetry.* Wellington: New Zealand University Press, 1960.

———. *The Flowering Cross.* Dunedin: New Zealand Tablet, 1969.

———. *Horse.* Auckland: Oxford University Press, 1985.

———. *Jerusalem Daybook.* Wellington: Price Milburn, 1971.

———. *The Man on the Horse.* Dunedin: University of Otago Press, 1967.

———. *New Selected Poems.* Ed. Paul Millar. Auckland: Oxford University Press, 2001.

———. *Recent Trends in New Zealand Poetry.* Christchurch: Caxton Press, 1951.

———. *Selected Poems.* Ed. Paul Millar. Auckland: Auckland University Press, 2010.

McKay, Frank, ed. *James K. Baxter as Critic: A Selection from His Literary Criticism.* Auckland: Heinemann Educational Books, 1978.

Millar, Paul, ed. *Spark to a Waiting Fuse: James K. Baxter's Correspondence with Noel Ginn 1942–1946.* Wellington: Victoria University Press, 2001.

Westra, Ans. *Notes on the Country I Live In.* [Text by James K. Baxter and Tim Shadbolt. Wellington: Alister Taylor, 1972.]

(b) shorter published texts

'The Advantages of Not Being Educated'. Poem. *NZ Listener* 24 Dec. 1959: 8.
'The Burns Fellowship'. *Landfall* 87 (1968): 237–48. (Essays by various holders of the fellowship; Baxter's contribution, 243–47.)
'Choice of Belief in Modern Society'. *Critic* 28.1, 6 March 1952: 1, 7.
'Conversation About Writing'. *NZ Monthly Review* 60 (Sept. 1965): 28.
'The Descent of Orpheus'. Poem. *Landfall* 43 (1957): 189–90.
'Encounter with Venus'. Poem. *Landfall* 75 (1965): 243.
'Essay on the Higher Learning'. *The Spike* 1961: 61–64.
'The Furies'. Prose-poem. *Canta* 19.8, 7 July 1948: 4.
'The Idea of Progress'. *NZ Monthly Review* 63 (Dec. 1965–Jan. 1966): 13–14.
Introduction. *The Memoirs of John Macmillan Brown.* Christchurch: University of Canterbury, 1974.
'I remember, I remember'. Poem. *NZ Listener* 4 June 1954: 5.
'Jottings (for Mike Doyle)'. Poem. *Tuatara* 8/9 (Fall 1972): 120.
'Kiwi Habits'. *Otago University Review*, 1967. *Review: 1888–1971.* Ed. Kevin Jones and Brent Southgate. Dunedin: University of Otago Bibliography Room, 1972: 84–86.
'The Lady and the Boatman'. *Meanjin* 14 (1955): 154.
[Letter in reply to Owen Leeming's review of *The Rock Woman.*] *Landfall* 98 (1971): 209–12.
'The Maori Motif'. Letter. *Here and Now* 3 (1952): 51.
'On Dylan Thomas'. Poem. *NZ Listener* 2 April 1954: 13.
'Outlook for Poetry'. *NZ Poetry Yearbook* 5 (1955): 8.
'The Phoenix and the Crow: A Parable'. *[The] Spike* 1954: 57–59.
'Portrait of the Artist as a New Zealander'. *Otago Daily Times* 28 Jan. 1960: 4.
'A Postscript to a Postscript to "Letter to a Catholic Poet"'. *Dialectic* 7 (Oct. 1970): 30.
'The Pythoness'. *NZ Listener* 19 Feb. 1965: 8.
Review of *Man Alone* by John Mulgan. *Landfall* 3 (1949): 374–76.
'September Walk'. Poem. *NZ Poetry Yearbook* 11 (1952): 11.
'Some Notes on Drama'. *Act* 1.3 (July/Sept. 1967): 20–22.
'The World of the Creative Artist'. *Salient* literary issue, Sept. 1955: 20–26.
'Writers in New Zealand: A Questionnaire'. *Landfall* 53 (1960): 36–70 (Baxter's contribution, 41–43).

(c) unpublished material

(Note: Letters among the Frank McKay papers are not separately listed here.)

'Additional Notes for Teachers: Fifth Series (Forms V and VI): Love'. FM 13/11.
'The Adventures of Harry Glass' [working notes for *Horse*]. Hocken MS-0975/109.

'Further Notes on New Zealand Poetry'. Hocken MS-0975/115.
'Jerusalem Journal 3'. Hocken MS-0975/080.
'Kiwi Habits (II)'. Hocken MS-0975/127.
'Notes on Being a New Zealander'. Hocken MS-0975/124.
'Notes on the Making of "The Martian"'. FM 20/4/19.
'Poems to a Glass Woman: 1944–1945'. Collection of early poems. Hocken Misc-MS-0682, item 9.
'Poetry and Education'. FM 19/1/16.
Poetry notebooks, N1–N28. Hocken MS-704/1 to MS-704/28.
The Runaway Wife. Play (typescript). Hocken MS-0975/069. (Earlier manuscript, together with *The Gentle Ones,* Hocken MS-0975/051.)
'Some Comments on Women's Liberation'. Hocken MS-0975/120.
'Some Possibilities for New Zealand Drama'. Hocken MS-0975/114.
The Spots of the Leopard. Play. Hocken MS-0975/071.
'Things and Idols'. Hocken MS-0975/160.
'Thoughts of an Old Alligator'. Hocken MS-0975/131.
Tiger Rock. Play. Hocken MS-0975/073.

Secondary

Adams, Michael Vannoy. *The Mythological Unconscious.* London: Other Press/Karnac, 2001.
Alpers, Anthony. *Maori Myths and Tribal Legends.* Auckland: Longman Paul, 1964.
Apollonios Rhodios [Apollonius]. *The Argonautika.* Trans. Peter Green. Berkeley: University of California Press, 2007.
Aristotle. *Historia Animalium.* Trans. A. L. Peck. Loeb Classical Library. Vol. 2. London; Heinemann, 1970.
Auden, W. H. *Another Time: Poems.* New York: Random House, 1940.
———. *The Enchafèd Flood, or The Romantic Iconography of the Sea.* London: Faber, 1951.
Baxter, Millicent. *The Memoirs of Millicent Baxter.* Whatamongo Bay: Cape Catley, 1981.
Blake, William. *William Blake's Writings.* Ed. G. E. Bentley, Jr. Vol. 1. Oxford: Clarendon Press, 1978.
Brasch, Charles. 'Phrases and Poems'. Review of *Pig Island Letters,* by James K. Baxter. *NZ Monthly Review* 74 (Dec 1966): 22–23.
Browne, Sir Thomas. *The Major Works.* Ed. C. A. Patrides. Harmondsworth: Penguin, 1977.
Brumble, H. David. *Classical Myths and Legends in the Middle Ages and Renaissance: A Dictionary of Allegorical Meanings.* London: Fitzroy Dearborn, 1998.

Burkert, Walter. *Greek Religion: Archaic and Classical.* Trans. John Raffan. Oxford: Blackwell, 1984.

Buxton, Richard. *The Complete World of Greek Mythology.* London: Thames and Hudson, 2004.

———. *Imaginary Greece: The Contexts of Mythology.* Cambridge: Cambridge University Press, 1994.

Caldwell, Richard. *The Origin of the Gods: A Psychoanalytic Study of Greek Theogonic Myth.* New York and Oxford: Oxford University Press, 1989.

Campbell, Alistair. *Mine Eyes Dazzle.* Christchurch: Pegasus, 1950.

Camus, Albert. 'The Myth of Sisyphus'. 1942. *The Myth of Sisyphus and Other Essays.* Trans. Justin O'Brien. New York: Vintage, 1991: 1–138.

Chaucer, Geoffrey. *The Riverside Chaucer.* Ed. Larry D. Benson. 3rd edition. Oxford: Oxford University Press, 1988.

Cleary, Farrell. 'Baxter's Plays: The Search for Life Before Death'. *Journal of NZ Literature* 13 (1995): 121–132.

Coleridge, Samuel Taylor. *Biographia Literaria.* Ed. James Engell and W. Jackson Bate. Collected Works of Samuel Taylor Coleridge, vols. 7.1–2. London: Routledge & Kegan Paul, 1983.

Curnow, Allen, ed. *A Book of New Zealand Verse, 1923–45.* Christchurch: Caxton Press, 1945.

———. *Early Days Yet: New and Collected Poems 1941–1997.* London: Carcanet, 1997.

———, ed. *Penguin Book of New Zealand Verse.* Harmondsworth: Penguin, 1960.

Dante Alighieri. *The Comedy of Dante Alighieri the Florentine: Cantica I, Hell.* Trans. Dorothy L. Sayers. Harmondworth: Penguin, 1949.

Davidson, John. 'Euripides' *Bacchae* in New Zealand Dress'. *Antichthon* 41 (2007): 97–108.

———. 'Greek Tragedy and a New Zealand Poet'. *The Play of Texts and Fragments: Essays in Honour of Martin Cropp.* Ed. J. R. C. Cousland and James R. Hume. Leiden: Brill, 2009: 445–57.

———. 'James K. Baxter and the Classics'. *Islands* 4 (1975): 451–64.

———. 'James K. Baxter at Colonus'. *AUMLA* 83 (1995): 43–54.

———. 'Odysseus, Baxter and New Zealand Poetry'. *Landfall* 134 (1980): 107–119.

———. 'Philoctetes Down Under'. *AUMLA* 47 (1978): 49–56.

———. 'Some New Zealand Poetic Faces of Dionysus'. *Theatres of Action: Papers for Chris Dearden.* Ed. John Davidson and Arthur Pomeroy. Supplement to *Prudentia.* Auckland: Polygraphia, 2003: 224–37.

———. 'Venus/Aphrodite and James K. Baxter'. *Refashioning Myth: Poetic Transformations and Metamorphoses.* Newcastle: Cambridge Scholars, 2011: 203–18.

———. 'Venus Is Rising: The Goddess in New Zealand Poetry'. *Journal of Commonwealth Literature* 25 (1980): 97–106.

Donne, John. *John Donne*. Ed. John Carey. The Oxford Authors. Oxford: Oxford University Press, 1990.

Doob, Penelope Reed. *The Idea of the Labyrinth from Classical Antiquity through the Middle Ages*. Ithaca: Cornell University Press, 1990.

Dowden, Ken. *The Uses of Greek Mythology*. London: Routledge, 1992.

Doyle, Charles. *James K. Baxter*. Boston: Twayne, 1976.

Durrell, Lawrence. *Collected Poems*. London: Faber, 1960.

Eliot, T. S. *Collected Poems 1909–1962*. London: Faber, 1963.

———. *Selected Prose of T. S. Eliot*. Ed. Frank Kermode. London: Faber, 1975.

Fairburn, A. R. D. *Collected Poems*. Christchurch: Pegasus, 1966.

Feder, Lillian. *Ancient Myth in Modern Poetry*. Princeton: Princeton University Press, 1971.

Freeman, Kathleen. *Ancilla to the Pre-Socratic Philosophers*. Oxford: Blackwell, 1947.

Galinsky, G. Karl. *The Herakles Theme: The Adaptations of the Hero in Literature from Homer to the Twentieth Century*. Oxford: Blackwell, 1972.

Gantz, Timothy. *Early Greek Myth*. 2 vols. Baltimore: Johns Hopkins University Press, 1996.

Garber, Marjorie, and Nancy J. Vickers. *The Medusa Reader*. New York: Routledge, 2003.

Garland, Robert. *The Greek Way of Death*. London: Duckworth, 1985.

Gide, André. *Philoctetes, or The Treatise on Three Ethics*. [In] *My Theater: Five Plays and an Essay*. Trans. Jackson Matthews. New York: Knopf, 1954: 129–60.

Goethe, Johann Wolfgang von. *Faust*. Trans. Barker Fairley. *The Sorrows of Young Werther; Elective Affinities; Italian Journey; Faust; Novella; Selected Poems and Letters*. London: Everyman, 1999: 747–1049.

Goulter, John. 'A Guide to the Use of Classical Mythology in the Poetry of James K. Baxter'. MA thesis. University of Canterbury, 1980.

Graves, Robert. *Collected Poems (1914–1947)*. London: Cassell, 1948.

———. *The White Goddess: A Historical Grammar of Poetic Myth*. 1948. Rev. Ed. London: Faber, 1961.

Grimal, Pierre. *The Penguin Dictionary of Classical Mythology*. 1986. London: Penguin, 1991.

Harcourt, Peter. *A Dramatic Appearance: New Zealand Theatre 1920–1970*. Wellington: Methuen, 1978.

Harkiman. 'The Poetry of Death: A Thematic Study of the Verse of James K. Baxter and Chairil Anwar'. MA thesis. Victoria University of Wellington, 1993.

Harrison, Stephen. 'Catullus in New Zealand: Baxter and Stead'. *Living Classics: Greece and Rome in Contemporary Poetry in English*. Ed. S. J. Harrison. Oxford: Oxford University Press, 2009: 295–323.

Heaney, Seamus. *Selected Poems 1965–1975*. London: Faber, 1980.

Homer. *The Iliad*. Trans. Robert Fitzgerald. 1974. London: Everyman, 1992.

———. *The Odyssey*. Trans. Robert Fitzgerald. 1961. London: Everyman, 1992.

———. *The Odyssey*. With a trans. by A. T. Murray, rev. George E. Dimock. Loeb Classical Library. 2 vols. 2nd edition. Cambridge, Mass.: 1995.

The Homeric Hymns. Trans. Apostolos N. Athanassakis. Baltimore: Johns Hopkins University Press, 1976.

Hunt, Sam. Introduction. *Poems* by James K. Baxter. Auckland: Auckland University Press, 2009: 1–10.

Jackaman, Rob. 'Ways of Failing (James K. Baxter)'. *Landfall* 37 (1983): 335–47.

James, Trevor. 'Poetry in the Labyrinth: The Poetry of James K. Baxter'. *World Literature Written in English* 22 (1983): 342–351.

———. 'Toward A Primal Vision: A Study of the Writings of James K. Baxter [1926–1972]'. PhD thesis. University of London, 1978.

Jensen, Kai. 'The Drunkard and the Hag: James K. Baxter's Use of Jung'. *JNZL* 13 (1995): 211–34.

———. 'The Woman Inside a Man'. *Whole Men: The Masculine Tradition in New Zealand Literature*. Auckland: Auckland University Press, 1996: 127–48.

Jones, Lawrence. 'The Mythology of Place: James K. Baxter's Otago Worlds'. *JNZL* 13 (1995): 65–96.

———. Review of *Spark to a Waiting Fuse* by Paul Millar. *Kite* 22 (July 2002): 24–28.

Jung, C. G. *The Collected Works of C. G. Jung*. Ed. Herbert Read, Michael Fordham, Gerhard Adler. 20 volumes. London: Routledge; Princeton: Princeton University Press, 1953–79.

Jung, C. G., and Carl Kérenyi. *Science of Mythology: Essays on the Myth of the Divine Child and the Mysteries of Eleusis*. 1941. Trans. R. F. C. Hull. London: Routledge, 2002.

Juvenal. *The Sixteen Satires*. Trans. Peter Green. Harmondsworth: Penguin, 1970.

Kaske, Carol. *Spenser and Biblical Poetics*. Ithaca: Cornell University Press, 1999.

Keats, John. *John Keats*. Ed. Elizabeth Cook. The Oxford Authors. Oxford: Oxford University Press, 1990.

Kerényi, Carl. *The Gods of the Greeks*. Trans. Norman Cameron. London: Thames and Hudson, 1951.

———. *The Heroes of the Greeks*. Trans. H. J. Rose. London: Thames and Hudson, 1974.

Kirk, G. S. *The Nature of Greek Myths*. London: Penguin, 1974.

Koestler, Arthur. 'The Yogi and the Commissar'. *The Yogi and the Commissar and Other Essays*. London: Jonathan Cape, 1945: 9–20.

Kruz, Jane. 'Baxter's "Tragic Moment": James K. Baxter's Adaptations of Sophocles' *Philoctetes* and *Oedipus at Colonus*'. MA thesis. Victoria

University of Wellington, 2008.

Lang, Andrew. *Poetical Works.* Vol. 2. London: Longman, 1923.

Lawlor, Pat. *The Two Baxters: Diary Notes.* With an essay by Vincent O'Sullivan. Wellington: Millwood, 1979.

Lawrence, D. H. *The Complete Poems of D. H. Lawrence.* Ed. Vivian de Sola Pinto and Warren Roberts. 3 vols. London: Heinemann, 1964.

Lawson, Donald W. 'Greek Myth in Four Plays by James K. Baxter'. MA thesis. University of Otago, 1974.

The Layman's Missal and Prayer Book [. . .] with the text to be used in the Mass as approved by the hierarchy of New Zealand. London: Burns and Oates, 1962.

Leeming, Owen. 'And the Clay Man? Reflections on *The Rock Woman*, selected poems by James K. Baxter'. *Landfall* 97 (1971): 9–19.

Lighter, J. G. *Random House Historical Dictionary of American Slang.* Vol. 1. New York: Random House, 1994.

Macmillan Brown, John. *The Memoirs of John Macmillan Brown.* Christchurch: University of Canterbury, 1974.

———. *The Riddle of the Pacific.* London: Unwin, 1924.

———. *Student Life and the Fallacies that Oftenest Beset It.* Christchurch: Canterbury College Dialectic Society, 1881.

McKay, Frank. *The Life of James K. Baxter.* Auckland: Oxford University Press, 1990.

McNaughton, Howard. 'Baxter as Dramatist'. *Islands* 2 (1973): 184–92.

———. 'Baxter's Strong Ghost'. *Landfall* 137 (1981): 62–66.

McNeill, Dougal. 'Being a Bard'. Review of *Selected Poems* by James K. Baxter, ed. Paul Millar. *New Zealand Books* 91 (Spring 2010): 3–4.

Mailer, Norman. 'The White Negro: Superficial Reflections on the Hipster'. 1957. *Advertisements for Myself.* London: Panther, 1968: 269–89.

Manhire, Bill. 'Stranger at the Ranchslider'. *JNZL* 13 (1995): 11–22.

March, Jenny. *Cassell Dictionary of Classical Mythology.* London: Cassell, 1998.

Marlowe, Christopher. *The Complete Poems and Translations.* Ed. Stephen Orgel. Harmondsworth: Penguin, 1971.

———. *Doctor Faustus and Other Plays.* Ed. David Bevington and Eric Rasmussen. Oxford: Oxford University Press, 1995.

Mikalson, Jon D. *Athenian Popular Religion.* Chapel Hill: University of North Carolina Press, 1983.

Miles, Geoffrey. 'Baling the Golden Fleece: Baxter's Jason'. *Kotare: New Zealand Notes and Queries.* 2008. <http://www.nzetc.org/tm/scholarly/tei-MilBali.html>.

———. 'Baxter as Icon'. *In View: Works from the VUW Art Collection.* Wellington: Adam Art Gallery, 2006: 6–7.

———. *Classical Mythology in English Literature: A Critical Anthology.* London: Routledge, 1999.

———. 'Three Calypsos: Baxter's Variations on a Mythic Theme'. *Still Shines When You Think of It: A Festschrift for Vincent O'Sullivan.* Ed. Bill Manhire and Peter Whiteford. Wellington: Victoria University Press, 2007: 234–48.

Millar, Paul. 'Hemi te Tutua/Jim the Nobody: The Gap and the Void in the Poetry of James K Baxter'. *Stimulus* 11 (2003): 9–16.

———. 'He Who Would Be a Poet: James K. Baxter's Early Poetry Manuscript Books'. *Kotare* 2.1 (May 1999): 28–43.

———. *No Fretful Sleeper: A Life of Bill Pearson*. Auckland: Auckland University Press, 2010.

———. 'The Tension of Belief: Some Remarks on the Criticism of James K. Baxter's Poetry'. *Span* 45 (Oct 1997): 103–08.

Milton, John. *Complete Shorter Poems*. Ed. John Carey. London: Longman, 1971.

Minnis, A. J. *Chaucer and Pagan Antiquity*. Cambridge: Brewer, 1982.

New Catholic Encyclopedia. 2nd edition. Farmington Hills, MI: 2003.

Newton, John. *The Double Rainbow: James K. Baxter, Ngati Hau and the Jerusalem Commune*. Wellington: Victoria University Press, 2009.

———. Review of *Cold Spring* by James K. Baxter, edited by Paul Millar. *Landfall* 193 (1997): 149–51.

Nietzsche, Friedrich. *Beyond Good and Evil: Prelude to a Philosophy of the Future*. Trans. Walter Kaufmann. New York: Vintage, 1966.

——. *The Birth of Tragedy and The Genealogy of Morals*. Trans. Francis Golffing. New York: Doubleday, 1956.

O'Brien, Greg. 'After Bathing at Baxter's'. *Sport 11* (Spring 1993): 122–57.

———. 'No Dream But Life: James K. Baxter's *Spark to a Waiting Fuse* and Peter Jackson's *Lord of the Rings*'. *Sport* 28 (Autumn 2002): 95–108.

Olds, Peter. 'Two Personal Memories of James K. Baxter'. *Islands* 3 (1973): 2–7.

Oliver, W. H. *James K. Baxter: A Portrait*. Wellington: Port Nicholson Press, 1983.

O'Sullivan, Vincent. *James K. Baxter*. New Zealand Writers and Their Work. Auckland: Oxford University Press, 1976, rpt. 1982.

———. 'The Sore Thumb of the Tribe'. Review of *Collected Poems* by James K. Baxter. *NZ Listener* 25 Oct 1980: 84.

Ovid. *Metamorphoses*. Trans. Charles Martin. New York: Norton, 2004.

Pausanias. *Description of Greece*. With an English trans. by W. H. S. Jones and H. A. Ormerod. Loeb Classical Library. Vol. 2. Cambridge, Mass., 1926.

Pharand, Michel. 'Greek Myths, White Goddess: Robert Graves Cleans Up a "Dreadful Mess"'. *Graves and the Goddess: Essays on Robert Graves's 'The White Goddess'*. Ed. Ian Firla and Grevel Lindop. Selinsgrove: Susquehanna University Press, 2003.

Pearson, Bill. 'A Confessional Letter'. *Kotare* 2.2 (Nov. 1999): 46–47.

Plato. *The Collected Dialogues of Plato*. Ed. Edith Hamilton and Huntingdon Cairns. Princeton: Princeton University Press, 1961.

Plutarch. 'Life of Theseus'. *Plutarch's Lives*. Trans. Bernadotte Perrin. Loeb

Classical Library. Vol. 1. London: Heinemann, 1914.

Pound, Ezra. *The Cantos*. London: Faber, 1987.

Rudd, Niall. 'Daedalus and Icarus (i) From Rome to the End of the Middle Ages' and 'Daedalus and Icarus (ii) From the Renaissance to the Present Day'. *Ovid Renewed: Ovidian Influences on Literature and Art from the Middle Ages to the Twentieth Century*. Ed. Charles Martindale. Cambridge: Cambridge University Press, 1988: 21–53.

Russell, Keith. 'Kenosis in Baxter's "Pig Island Letters"'. *JNZL* 13 (1995): 109–120.

Schouten, Erica. 'The "Encyclopaedic God-Professor": John Macmillan Brown and the Discipline of English in Colonial New Zealand'. *JNZL* 23:1 (special issue, 2005): 109–23.

Segal, Robert A., ed. *Jung on Mythology*. Princeton: Princeton University Press, 1998.

Shakespeare, William. *The Norton Shakespeare: Based on the Oxford Edition*. Ed. Stephen Greenblatt et al. New York: Norton, 1997.

Sharp, Iain. 'Interview: Les Murray'. *Landfall* 166 (1988): 150–68.

———. 'My Grudge Against Baxter'. *Quote Unquote* 14 Aug. 1994: 12–14.

Sitwell, Edith. *Collected Poems*. London: Macmillan, 1958.

Smith, Harold W. 'James K. Baxter: The Poet as Playwright'. *Landfall* 85 (1968): 56–62.

——— [as Hal Smith]. 'Baxter's Theatre: A Critical Appraisal'. *James K. Baxter Festival 1973: Four Plays*. Theatre programme. Wellington: Manaaki Society, 1973.

Sophocles. *Antigone, The Women of Trachis, Philoctetes, Oedipus at Colonus*. Ed. and trans. Hugh Lloyd-Jones. Loeb Classical Library. Cambridge, Mass.: Harvard University Press, 1994.

———. *Electra and Other Plays. (Philoctetes, Women of Trachis, Electra, Ajax.)* Trans. E. F. Watling. Harmondsworth: Penguin, 1953.

———. *The Theban Plays.* (*King Oedipus, Oedipus at Colonus, Antigone.*) Trans. E. F. Watling. Harmondsworth: Penguin, 1947.

Spender, Stephen. *Poems*. London: Faber, 1933.

Stanford, W. B. *The Ulysses Theme: A Study in the Adaptability of a Traditional Hero*. 1954; Dallas: Spring Books, 1992.

Sullivan, Robert. 'The Chrysalis Stage'. Review of *Cold Spring*, by James K. Baxter. *NZ Listener* 25 Jan. 1997: 50–51.

[Taylor, Alister.] *James K. Baxter 1926–1972: A Memorial Volume*. Wellington: Alister Taylor Publishing, 1972.

Tennyson, Alfred. *Tennyson: A Selected Edition*. Ed. Christopher Ricks. Berkeley: University of California Press, 1989.

Toynbee, J. M. C. *Death and Burial in the Roman World*. London: Thames and Hudson, 1971.

Trzaskoma, Stephen M., et al. *Anthology of Classical Myth: Primary Sources in Translation*. Indianapolis: Hackett, 2004.

Viereck, George Sylvester. *Glimpses of the Great.* London: Duckworth, 1930.

Virgil. *The Aeneid.* Trans. Robert Fitzgerald. 1984. London: Everyman, 1992.

———. *The Georgics of Virgil.* Trans. C. Day Lewis. London: Jonathan Cape, 1940.

Ward, Anne G., et al. *The Quest for Theseus.* New York: Praeger, 1970.

Weir, J[ohn] E[dward]. 'An Interview with James K. Baxter'. *Landfall* 28 (1974): 241–50.

———. 'Man Without a Mask: A Study of the Poetry of James K. Baxter'. MA thesis. University of Canterbury, 1968.

———. *The Poetry of James K. Baxter.* Wellington: Oxford University Press, 1970.

Wilson, Edmund. 'Philoctetes: The Wound and the Bow'. *The Wound and the Bow: Seven Studies in Literature.* 1941. London: Methuen, 1961: 244–64.

Witheford, Hubert. 'The Silver Tongue. (A note on the poetry of James K. Baxter.)' *New Zealand Poetry Yearbook* 3 (1953): 52.

Wordsworth, William. *William Wordsworth.* Ed. Stephen Gill. 21st-Century Oxford Authors. Oxford: Oxford University Press, 2010.

Yarnall, Judith. *Transformations of Circe: The History of an Enchantress.* Urbana: University of Illinois Press, 1994.

Zeitlin, Froma. 'Dionysus in 69'. *Dionysus Since 69.* Ed. Edith Hall, Fiona Macintosh, and Amanda Wrigley. Oxford: Oxford University Press, 2004: 49–75.

INDEX OF BAXTER'S WORKS

GENERAL INDEX